NATIONAL POST

Smart Funds 1999

A Fund Family Approach to Mutual Funds

**JONATHAN CHEVREAU AND STEPHEN KANGAS
WITH SUSAN HEINRICH**

KEY PORTER BOOKS

Canadian Cataloguing in Publication Data

Chevreau, Jonathan, 1953-
    National Post smart funds 1999 : a fund family approach to mutual funds

Includes index.

ISBN 1-55263-014-5

1. Mutual funds—Canada—Handbooks, manuals, etc. I. Kangas, Stephen.
II. Heinrich, Susan. III. Title.

HG5154.5.C46   1998   332.63'27   C97-931423-5

THE CANADA COUNCIL | LE CONSEIL DES ARTS
FOR THE ARTS | DU CANADA
SINCE 1957 | DEPUIS 1957

The publisher gratefully acknowledges
the support of the Canada Council for the
Arts and the Ontario Arts Council for its
publishing program.

"Smart Funds" is a trademark of the National Post.

Key Porter Books Limited
70 The Esplanade
Toronto, Ontario
Canada M5E 1R2

www.keyporter.com

Electronic formatting: Alissa Lee

Printed and bound in Canada

98 99 00 01 6 5 4 3 2 1

Acknowledgements

The authors wish to acknowledge the members of the Smart Fund Selection Committee: Patrick McKeough, Warren Baldwin, Harland Hendrickson, and John Platt; Mary Ann McCutcheon, of Key Porter Books, for pushing everyone and keeping the project on track; and all the talented people in the Canadian mutual fund industry, who were both prompt and patient in providing the detailed information that makes *Smart Funds* possible.

Stephen Kangas would like to thank his mother and father, for their encouragement throughout the years, and Catherine and Taylor, for their love and their unlimited patience with this project. Susan Heinrich would like to thank her family and Sean for their encouragement.

Contents

Preface to the Fifth Edition

This fifth edition of the annual *National Post* mutual fund guide—*Smart Funds 1999: A Fund Family Approach to Mutual Funds*—is a completely revised version of the *Financial Post's Smart Funds 1998*. We again profile the 50 top fund families but have focused our selection criteria more tightly with this edition, and have therefore reduced the number of Smart Funds by 20 per cent—from the previous edition's 125 to the current 100.

Our eight new fund manager profiles feature, among others, Mark Holowesko, manager of Canada's largest fund, the $11-billion Templeton Growth Fund; Phil Fortuna at Scudder Canada's far newer Scudder Canadian Equity; and Lyle Stein, manager of Sceptre Investment Counsel Ltd.'s Sceptre Balanced Growth Fund.

On these profiles we have come full circle on some key money managers. The first edition in 1995 featured profiles of Trimark chairman Robert Krembil and Altamira Investment Services Inc.'s Frank Mersch. Four years later, both firms have come through their trials, despite Trimark being dubbed "the brokers' choice" and Altamira at one time characterizing itself as "the people's choice." For this edition, we have reinterviewed and updated Krembil's profile, while we have interviewed Ian Ainsworth and the other Altamira managers replacing Mersch. Mersch and Susan Coleman, one of the three managers replacing Mersch, were both interviewed in the first edition of this book. All told, the five *Smart Funds* books have profiled 42 fund managers.

While our format remains similar to the two most recent editions, the big difference this year is the addition of several major life insurance "segregated fund" families, which provide investors who are nervous about a possible stock-market correction with some guarantees against loss. New fund families include Investors Group sister company Great-West Life, the Manulife Guaranteed Investment Funds (GIFs), and, of course, those fund companies that now offer seg funds directly, such as BPI, C.I. Mutual Funds and Trimark Investment Management Inc. We have also added a few fund company start-ups, such as Synergy Asset Management, and made way for the low-MER CentrePost Funds. A handful of smaller fund families have been dropped to make way for the newcomers.

Readers of earlier editions will note that many Smart Funds return this year, albeit with revised performance data generally current to September 30, 1998. When possible, we prefer to maintain as many Smart Funds as possible: our objective is to identify funds that investors will feel comfortable owning for years or decades. The last thing we wish to do is to encourage wholesale portfolio shifts every year by highlighting a crop of unproven hot new concept funds. A single bad year is unlikely to result in a Smart Fund demotion, nor will one good year necessarily result in a promotion of a fund still unproven over the longer haul. We hope that such perennial Smart Funds as Trimark Fund and Templeton Growth continue to perform well into the next century.

Despite this, dozens of funds have been dropped from the Smart Funds list, replaced by a combination of new and old funds. One major reason is manager changes: manager departures is why Investors U.S. Growth Fund, Scotia Excelsior Latin America, and First Canadian Special Growth do not return as Smart Funds in this edition, to name just a few examples.

Those readers who look to *Smart Funds* to identify promising new "young" funds years before rival guides will also not be disappointed. We were the first Canadian mutual fund guide to identify, for example, Clarington Global Telecommunications, Global Strategy World Companies, and Green Line Science & Technology. That tradition continues: debuting as a Smart Fund this year, for example, is Synergy Canadian Style Management Class.

Equity funds always play a major role in the *Smart Funds* books, for we maintain our long-term stance that ownership in companies provides the best growth potential and protection from those twin ravages of taxation and inflation. However, our fund selection has further emphasized funds and families that provide a conservative, consistent approach to investing, with fund managers who have proven they can conserve capital in a down market as well as make money on the upside.

Regular readers of the *Financial Post*—and now the *National Post*—will have perceived a growing concern about high management expense ratios (MERs), a subject that has become a greater concern for Canadian fund investors in the past few years. Generally, load funds carry higher MERs than no-load companies that sell their funds directly to investors. The reason is that load fund companies must pay the costs associated with distributing their product through investment advisers. Most load funds today are sold with a deferred sales charge, where the investor pays nothing initially, but the broker receives a commission from the fund company, typically about five per cent. Those commissions, coupled with ongoing service or trailer fees paid annually to advisers, are a huge expense to fund companies. Much of that expense is passed on to unitholders in the form of an MER, which is higher than in no-load funds. We suggest that investors who buy load funds through full-service advisers ensure that they receive adequate service to justify the cost.

That said, MERs have always been a major criterion in our fund selection, and they play a still greater role in *Smart Funds 1999*. *Smart Funds* was the first fund guide to give prominence to newer, low-MER strong-performing fund groups such as Bissett and Scudder, and that type of fund family is well represented in this year's edition.

At the same time, our co-authors and selection committee have tried not to throw the baby out with the bath water: fund families and individual funds that justify their fees are still well represented, as in previous years. Keep in mind that the publicly available performance numbers are always net of expense ratios.

The fund matrix introduced in *Smart Funds 1997* and refined in *Smart Funds 1998* has been retained in the new edition, but we have added an entry for RESP availability: the 1998 federal budget greatly improved incentives for families to invest in Registered Education Savings Plans (RESPs). As we went to press, almost 20 fund families already had RESPs up and running or ready for announcement.

As in previous editions, Smart Funds are indicated with a blue star. Noteworthy funds are indicated with a black pyramid. All other funds that are offered in a family are in black. Look then for a sea of blue stars and black pyramids in the matrices as an indicator of the relative strength of fund families.

If the fund you're interested in is shown with a blue star, you'll find a full one-page analysis of that fund in the second half of the book.

Use the index at the end of the book to locate the particular fund. If the fund you're considering is shown with a black triangle, then a short comment on the fund is contained in the pages immediately following the matrix.

Generally, a "Noteworthy" fund is either potentially a future candidate for Smart Fund status, a former Smart Fund whose circumstances have changed or a specialty fund such as a country or sector-specific portfolio. We have de-emphasized these in this edition as they are more volatile than broader-based funds. Generally, there are other strong funds in a family we'd consider using to round out a portfolio. If you have selected a particular fund family and three of its Smart Funds as core funds, for example, the Noteworthy funds allow you to stay within that fund family and fill in niches such as small-cap, precious metals, and so on.

The co-authors and Smart Fund Selection Committee are virtually the same as last year but this year we added *Financial Post* mutual funds reporter Susan Heinrich to the writing team. Jonathan Chevreau returns for his fifth year on the project. Stephen Kangas returns for his fourth year as co-author, but has moved from First International Asset Management Inc. to vice president of third-party mutual funds for Canada Trust.

As in previous years, the co-authors submitted a short list of possible Smart Funds to a selection committee. Most of the previous members of the selection committee have kindly stayed in place, with the addition of Warren Baldwin, vice president of fee-only planner T. E. Financial Consultants Ltd. this year to beef up our no-load coverage, which was previously handled by Roger Cann. Returning to the committee are Patrick McKeough, editor of the *Successful Investor* newsletter, co-author of *Surviving Canada's Separation Anxiety*, and a contributing editor to the *MoneyLetter*; Harland Hendrickson, editor of the *Market Trend Follower*; and John Platt, vice president of fund research at Nesbitt Burns Inc. The authors made the final cut to identify the 100 Smart Funds, however, so we cannot say that all the committee members necessarily endorse all the choices.

There are no guarantees in mutual fund investing. Those who want guarantees should stay with GICs or investigate index-linked GICs, life insurance industry segregated funds or Manulife Financial's new Guaranteed Investment Funds.

Anyone contemplating the purchase of a Smart Fund, or any other mutual fund, should be fully acquainted with the nature of risk. That's why we have retained the introductory material on asset allocation. Many Smart Funds are load funds sold through brokers, dealers, or financial planners: obtain the advice and service that you are already paying for from these individuals. Discuss with them how some of these funds or fund families may meet your investment objectives; be clear about what volatility and risk mean and how any particular fund selection can lead to losing money.

If you're not sure what a mutual fund is, buy the primers written by Gordon Pape or Ranga Chand. This book does not explain the basics for beginning mutual fund investors.

Above all, understand that any given fund is unlikely to be a panacea for all that ails you financially. Some funds should not take up more than five or 10 per cent of a total investment portfolio, although conservative balanced or dividend growth funds can account for a far larger portion of your wealth. That's why it's critical that the choice of any fund be placed in a broader context of asset allocation, preferably conducted with a professional financial adviser.

In the section on asset allocation, we've retained the authors' philosophy of choosing two or three core fund families. We continue to emphasize our belief that diversification across asset classes, geographical areas, and management styles is the best protection against market volatility. To repeat: equity mutual funds—and even bond funds—can diminish in value and should be made with an understanding of the associated risks. Accordingly, the full page devoted to each Smart Fund includes important measures of associated risks. If you do not feel comfortable with the risk level of a particular fund, do not invest in it. Find a more conservative fund that is better suited to your investment personality.

Mutual fund investors who are worried about the many contradictory predictions and advice that abound today will again find plenty of new material here. But the underlying premise still holds true: own equities or equity funds for the long term, diversify your holdings, and choose your holdings from the best fund companies and managers available.

Many Smart Funds readers who have been with us from the outset may find that they did so well in the bull market that they now have a significant amount of money in mutual funds. Consequently, this year, as part of the fund family overviews, we have tried to identify so-called "High Net Worth" products and services that complement the group's mutual fund products. A glance at the revised section on CIBC Securities Inc. reveals how more and more fund companies or their sister firms (CIBC Trust in the above case) are targeting affluent baby boomers who are just on the cusp of achieving real wealth (defined as $200,000 in investable financial assets).

Many of these products are mutual fund-like products, such as pooled funds ($150,000 minimum, sold without a prospectus), or "wrap programs" that include portfolios of mutual funds, with investors paying a flat annual fee for money management services. While open-end retail mutual funds are appropriate for many investors, young and old, they are not necessarily the only investment alternative available. Fee-conscious high-net-worth investors and those who are prepared to do more legwork may wish to investigate a new companion volume also published by the *National Post* and Key Porter Books in the fall of 1998: *The Wealthy Boomer: Life After Mutual Funds* (by Jonathan Chevreau, Michael Ellis, and Kelly Rodgers, CFA).

How to Use This Book

Smart Funds 1999 is organized into four parts.

The first part shows how to assemble a portfolio of mutual funds tailored specifically to your own situation. It starts with the central philosophy of this book—that the most important first step for fund investors is to select two or three major fund families, then draw individual fund selections from those families. That way, you'll minimize fees, paperwork, and confusion, while avoiding the over-diversification that may actually reduce your returns. This section explains the key attributes of the better fund families, such as having a full complement of fund types and management styles and an experienced money management team. In addition, this section contains a large section on various asset-allocation strategies and how to use them to develop a portfolio that's just right for you.

The second part profiles eight top money managers—the smart managers behind the Smart Funds. Through the five editions of this book, we have now profiled 42 top managers. Don't skip this section—after all of the numbers are crunched and charts consulted, the manager or team of managers is still the most important factor in identifying a top-notch fund.

The largest part of this book is devoted to the major mutual fund families in Canada and the best individual funds, which we call Smart Funds, most of them sold by the families profiled in Part 3. In this part, you'll find profiles of the top 50 fund families, arranged alphabetically. A fund matrix at the beginning of each fund family shows at a glance which core and specialty funds it offers. It's arranged so all Canadian funds are in the top half of the matrix; all international funds are in the bottom half.

BLUE STAR ★ = Smart Fund. Refer to index at the end of the book to find the page the Smart Fund is on. Think of it as a Buy recommendation.

BLACK TRIANGLE ▲ = Noteworthy Fund. This indicates a fund that may eventually become a Smart Fund but we have certain reservations about it. Depending on your other fund selections, it may still be an appropriate investment. A short comment on the fund follows immediately after the matrix. Think of it as a Hold recommendation.

BLACK SQUARE ■ = Available. This indicates only that the fund family has a fund in a particular category, such as Far East or Precious Metals. It may be an average or below-average fund, and occasionally even above-average in performance, but the authors did not believe that the fund possesses the investment characteristics to merit a Smart Fund or Noteworthy designation.

Finally, we list the 100 Smart Funds in the fourth part of the book. These are mutual funds selected by the authors and the six-member selection committee from the more than 1,800 funds available in Canada. Each listing contains comments on the fund and its manager, measures of the fund's risk, the portfolio's asset allocation, and cumulative and year-over-year performance data for the past 10 years. The graph illustrates the growth of a $1,000 investment in the fund, the appropriate benchmark, and Canada Savings Bonds. You will also find the fund's quartile ranking, which shows how well the fund has performed relative to other funds in the same category.

Clearly, choosing fund families with several Smart Funds should increase the odds of creating a high-performance portfolio. We expect that readers, using this guide as a reference, will flip back and forth between the fund families and the Smart Funds, narrowing down first their choice of major fund families and then choosing the most appropriate Smart Funds within each.

Foreword

After several consecutive years of double-digit returns, the much-feared correction brought the late-1990s bull market to an apparent close in 1998. At press time, the U.S. market was down almost 20 per cent and the Canadian stock market was down 25 per cent—effectively bear markets.

Smart Funds readers in particular need to be particularly cautious in the next few years, since Smart Funds are primarily equity, or stock-owning, mutual funds. This was the asset class to be in through most of the past decade and, since the first 1995 edition was published, any Smart Funds owner should be well above water, even after the market took back some gains in 1998.

Now however, more than ever, the principles of diversification and asset allocation are crucial. Readers who may have skipped over our introductory section on market timing and asset allocation may want to reacquaint themselves with these principles.

Normally, we minimize bond funds because we believe many investors may get better exposure to this asset class through a ladder of bonds. Money-market funds are not normally designated Smart Funds, since we regard them as a place to park money in the short term, normally using the money-market fund of whatever fund family you happen to be invested in.

While the authors still do not believe in market timing, observant readers will have noticed a rising degree of caution in the last two editions of this book. Last year, we made special note of the families we regarded as being especially defensive in volatile or bearish markets: Guardian Group of Funds, Trimark Investment Management Inc., Dynamic Mutual Funds, Investors Group Inc., Templeton Management Ltd. and the Mackenzie Universal funds managed by former Trimark managers.

Investors seeking prudent growth may want to emphasize Smart Funds and Noteworthy Funds that are large cap, dividend funds, balanced, or value in orientation.

Investors who have no appetite for any risk at all can, as always, retreat to GICs, CSBs, bonds, money-market funds or other products. As we said in previous editions, there are no guarantees with equity mutual fund investing. The price of long-term probable larger gains is short-term risk and, sometimes, losing money. Investors who experienced only the upside of this equation have now learned the hard way about the flip side. If you were balanced across asset classes, and properly diversified, your losses should have been mitigated. If you did not work with a financial adviser and were overweight in equities or, worse, highly leveraged, then you now have a better idea of what your risk tolerance is.

Normally, investors should take only the amount of risk needed to meet their long-term investment objectives. If you are 25 years from retirement and need only 10 or 12 per cent a year to reach that target, and if a balanced fund can get you there, then there is no need to reach for the moon with aggressive special equity or regional funds, only to fall short when subjected to unforeseeable events such as the Asian crisis and soon, the Millennium Bomb or Y2K (Year 2000) problem.

For this reason, the authors have further retrenched on the regional or special equity fund front, and chosen instead more broadly based diversified funds.

It was clear to us that the fund companies themselves anticipated the market volatility of mid- to late 1998. The proof is in the newfound alliances they are making with the life insurance segregated fund industry. With this edition of *Smart Funds*, we include several select Seg Fund groups, such as Great West Life and the Manulife Guaranteed Investment Funds.

Now that stock markets have corrected and equity mutual funds have fallen in value, the impact of high management expense ratios (MERs) will play a more noticeable role in performance. *Smart Funds* has led the charge among all fund guides to emphasize lower MERs. This year's edition has demoted many funds whose MERs we felt no longer justified the performance that was generated when the market's direction was decidedly up. Remember that mutual fund management fees are deducted from your investment even in bear markets. You may not notice a 2 per cent fee when what would have been a 22 per cent return becomes a 20 per cent return net of fees. But if a 4 per cent return becomes 2 per cent, the MER's impact is all too apparent. And if the fund loses money, then a 10 per cent loss becomes a 12 per cent loss after the MER.

At the same time, we note that the higher-MER load funds are usually sold by seasoned investment advisers and that it is in volatile investing climates that the true worth of a competent adviser reveals itself. If the adviser does nothing other than keep an investor committed to a long-term plan, he or she has probably justified the fees.

Unless the current situation degenerates into a 1930s-style depression and grinding bear market, the worst thing an investor can do now is to abandon the faith and crystallize losses. We have already seen one-day rallies of as much as 5 per cent—more than most money-market funds will return in a year.

In this environment, and following years of heady returns and media enthusiasm about mutual funds, critics have started to take a second look at the pluses and minuses of mutual funds. This includes *Smart Funds* creator and co-author Jonathan Chevreau, who has also written a new *National Post* book targeted at high-net-worth investors. It's called *The Wealthy Boomer: Life After Mutual Funds* (written with Michael Ellis and Kelly Rodgers).

Other new books on the market have attacked mutual fund returns and MERs, counselling a return to direct stock picking or indexing. *The Wealthy Boomer* examines such alternatives but also concludes that "mutual fund investors have been on the right track all along."

The authors agree that in a bull market it may seem easy to pick your own stocks and watch them go up. It's in a bear market, however, that things become difficult, and it appears that is precisely the sort of market we are now in. Bear markets normally last 18 months to two or three years, far less than the duration of the typical bull market.

As *The Wealthy Boomer* describes in detail, mutual funds are the mass market or entry level of a series of products and services called "managed money." Whether you choose mutual funds or more sophisticated variants called "pooled funds" or "mutual fund wrap programs," you are still engaging a professional to navigate the complex waters of the capital markets on your behalf.

No, mutual funds are not perfect. Yes, stocks are down and investors with equity mutual funds have experienced losses. Nevertheless, the authors still believe that a greater risk than short-term market panics is the risk of outliving your money. You may not want to commit 100 per cent of your portfolio to stocks and mutual funds, but a 25 to 50 per cent exposure is probably prudent at all times, given the ravages of taxation and inflation.

Patrick McKeough, one of several respected investment professionals on our Smart Funds Selection Committee, has long argued that three factors argue in favor of a resumption in the upward trend of stock markets: the trend to technology, economic globalization and the demographic trend wherein the massive baby-boom generation has embraced stocks and equity mutual funds to secure themselves a comfortable retirement.

The authors cannot categorically state that any of this year's 100 Smart Fund selections will not go down in value over the next year or two. But we do know that if you are a long way from retirement, you may as well buy these financial assets while they are "on sale."

While the bull market was roaring it must have been frustrating indeed for younger investors to feel priced out of the market. Just as baby boomers put real estate out of reach for younger home buyers in the late 1980s, the boomers' insatiable appetite for stocks and equity funds had driven up the price of financial assets. Now, Generation X can afford to buy in again, just as they were able to finally afford Toronto real estate when prices tumbled a comparable 25 per cent in the early 1990s.

To us, provided you have a competent adviser and adhere to the asset-allocation and diversification principles outlined in our annual introduction, then the smart thing to do is to buy our Smart Funds while they are on sale. If you're squeamish about the Y2K problem's impact on the stock market, hold off purchasing new Smart Fund equity funds until it's clear the market has bottomed. This may not occur until after the year 2000. An alternative to pure equity funds will be Canadian and global balanced funds, domestic and global bond funds, mortgage funds and money market funds.

Yes, there is danger in the capital markets as the century closes. The Clinton drama and the Y2K problem could indeed make things worse before they get better. But as the old Chinese saying goes, in danger there is opportunity.

Clearly, the exigencies of book publishing preclude up-to-the-minute market updates and revised recommendations. There is no substitute for having an excellent newspaper to keep abreast of the latest political and economic developments.

Two of *Smart Funds'* three co-authors are employed on Canada's new national newspaper, *National Post*, which incorporates the former *Financial Post*. Both *Smart Funds* and *The Wealthy Boomer* proudly bear the new name *National Post*. We are confident that the reader who buys both *Smart Funds* and *The Wealthy Boomer*, and subscribes to and reads the *National Post* six days a week, will be well equipped to handle the investment challenges of the 21st century. Feel free also to check our related web sites: http://www.nationalpost.com and http://www.wealthyboomer.com.

Jonathan Chevreau, Stephen Kangas and Susan Heinrich

The Fund Family Approach to Building a Fund Portfolio

The proliferation of mutual funds in Canada continued into 1998. The latest tally is over 1,800 mutual and segregated funds as of June 30, 1998, more than the 1,250 companies listed on the Toronto Stock Exchange. In the United States, by the end of 1997, there were 5,020 equity mutual funds alone, more than 40 per cent of them launched since 1995, according to the March 1998 edition of *Consumer Reports.*

The number of choices is daunting, not only for the casual mutual fund investor but also for financial planners and other investment professionals, some of whom employ full-time staff dedicated solely to mutual fund research. The 1990s boom in fund investing resulted in a proliferation of exciting new funds. Unfortunately, it also led to many investors buying too many funds from too many fund companies.

But the task of sorting the wheat from the chaff is not as overwhelming as it appears. Armed with this book and, if you wish, a trusted financial adviser, you can rapidly whittle down the selection to a reasonable number. But first you must shift your focus from the merits and demerits of individual mutual funds and concentrate instead on fund families and, especially, the managers of those funds.

Too many investors start their fund search with the question "What fund(s) should I buy?" In fact, that should be your third question. Start, instead, with "Should I be in mutual funds at all?" If you can't answer that question objectively, find someone who can help you—and whose fortunes aren't tied to the mutual fund industry.

For most Canadians, the answer is "yes," as more and more of us are being forced to take responsibility for our financial future. Surveys have shown that most Canadians in their twenties and thirties do not expect the federal or provincial governments to assume even partial financial responsibility for their retirement. At the same time, employers are getting out of the defined benefit pension business and putting the investment onus on employees through defined contribution plans or group RRSPs—vehicles that frequently use mutual funds as their main form of investing.

Many Canadians have realized that, in order to meet their financial goals, they must transform themselves from savers to investors. That means holding less money in bank accounts, Guaranteed Investment Certificates (GICs), Canada Savings Bonds, and money market accounts, and more in domestic and foreign equity investments.

Although investing in equities can increase your return over time, it does mean taking on more risk. The 25 per cent drop in Canada's TSE 300 index and almost 19 per cent drop in the Dow Jones Industrial Average in 1998 (as of the end of August) vividly demonstrated the reality of risk. But, while most people still define investment risk as losing principal, many are beginning to recognize a bigger risk: not having enough money in the future to support themselves as their capital is eroded by inflation and taxes. The stark reality is that the biggest risk facing most Canadians is outliving their income.

Over the long run, equity—or common stocks—is the only asset that will keep up with inflation and provide the kind of returns necessary to meet your goals. Mutual funds should be at least part of any properly diversified investment portfolio and they may even be your entire portfolio.

So, if you answered "Yes" to the question "Should I be in mutual funds at all?", you're ready to tackle the second question: "What core fund family or fund families should I choose?" This is the kick-off point of your overall investment strategy, and the first half of this buyer's guide is devoted to this essential question.

Some years ago, the accounting firm KPMG Peat Marwick reported that affluent Americans consider the reputation of a fund family to be the single most important factor in choosing a mutual fund. It cited a survey by U.S. Trust, a bank that serves affluent investors, that showed that 65 per cent of wealthy investors consider the status of a fund's family the primary factor in their decision of whether to invest. Only then do they consider a fund's future prospects, its past performance, and its expenses.

KPMG also found that despite higher costs, funds sold through sales forces are most favored: 84 per cent of the investors surveyed purchased funds that way. Of course, many do not restrict themselves to just one fund family: the typical investor used more than one distribution channel to assemble a portfolio.

That appears to be true in Canada as well: even fund families that have built up a loyal clientele find that their clients typically hold at least three fund families. With more than 30 categories of mutual funds available in Canada, a single fund family may not provide enough variety. In fact, Dr. Jon Kanitz, contributing editor of *The FundLetter*, sees nothing wrong with a portfolio as large as 20 funds— as long as their individual investment styles and objectives vary.

Since many of the fund families outlined in this book offer more than 20 funds, it's quite possible to construct an entire fund portfolio from any one of these families. But, for most investors, owning funds from two or three fund families, with perhaps a specialty boutique family and the odd special situation thrown in, makes the most sense. Sir John Templeton, founder of Templeton International and a pioneer of global investing, recommends that most people diversify among eight or more funds spread among three fund families.

It's worth noting that if you ask a broker or financial planner to select your fund portfolio, he or she will usually choose your funds from, at most, six or seven fund families. Most investment advisers have two or three favorite fund groups, and there are a few families, such as Mackenzie, Trimark, and Templeton, that crop up on many professionals' short lists.

Clearly then, the most important decision is settling on one or two fund families. They will provide your core funds, as well as the base within which you will make any switches—from one fund to another, for instance, or from funds into cash (or a money market fund).

Most advisers agree that the best way to pick your core fund family is to choose a reliable manager, or team of managers, with a solid track record of performance and an investment philosophy compatible with your own. You must also consider the number of fund types offered by each family; how many of these funds are highly rated (that is, Smart Funds); whether there are charges for switching from one fund to another in the same family; whether the family offers enough fund types to enable you to diversify by asset class, geography and management style; and whether management expenses and other fees are reasonable.

Use the following five steps to decide on your core fund families:

1. Determine your optimum asset allocation

Although you're probably anxious to jump right in and start assessing fund families, a critical first step is much closer to home. You must decide what percentage of your portfolio should be in each of the major asset classes—equity (funds invested in the stock market, both domestic and foreign), fixed income (bond and mortgage funds), and cash (money market funds.)

If your goal is long-term growth, for instance, and you can tolerate a little volatility along the way, then equity funds should comprise the largest portion of your portfolio. If, on the other hand, you're nearing retirement age and/or want your investments to generate income, you should put most of your portfolio into fixed-income funds. The traditional range for the equity portion of a portfolio is 25 to 75 per cent, as established by Benjamin Graham, author of the classic investment text *The Intelligent Investor* (Harper & Row, New York, 1973, 4th ed.) To decide where you fall within that range, you can use a general rule suggested by many advisers, which is to make the fixed-income allotment equal to your age. That is, a typical 40-year-old would have 40 per cent fixed income and 60 per cent equities. If you are a little more aggressive, equities might rise to 65 or 70 per cent; if you are on the cautious side, fixed income might rise to 45 or 50 per cent. You may also have a small cash component, either because you need some money in the short term for another purpose or because you haven't yet committed it to a specific investment. It's usually more convenient if you use a money market fund or funds from your core families to hold any cash.

If you're uncertain how to divide your portfolio, you can use balanced funds, asset-allocation funds, or asset-allocation services—in which case one or more fund managers will make this decision for you. Asset-allocation services such as Mackenzie's STAR, Merrill Lynch Canada's COMPASS, Bank of Montreal's MatchMaker, Canada Trust's Investment Planner Plus, and many others provide questionnaires that assess your personal financial situation and suggest the best asset mix. Or you can rely on a professional investment adviser to make this recommendation.

Asset-allocation strategies are discussed in more detail at the end of this section.

2. Choose a core Canadian fund family

Once you've sorted out your asset allocation, you're ready to choose your first core fund family—your core Canadian-content fund family.

Why? About half of all mutual fund dollars are invested j RRSPs. Since equity funds offer the best chance of growth and protection against inflation, and the federal government requires pensions and RRSPs to be 80 per cent Canadian content, Canadian equity funds are naturally more popular than foreign equity funds. The top half of the fund matrices that begin each fund family profile shows at a glance the Canadian funds available in each family.

Your core Canadian family should also be strong in fixed-income products since they'll also be an important part of your overall portfolio (and are subject to the same Canadian-content rules).

Note: If you have significant investments outside your RRSP, consider arranging your holdings so fixed-income funds—which are 100 per cent taxable—are held inside your RRSP, and equity funds—which generate capital gains that are taxed at a more favorable rate—are held outside your RRSP to make use of the dividend tax credit, which reduces the tax payable on dividends from Canadian companies. Be aware of any tax implications of making switches.

3. Choose a core international fund family

As the fund matrices show, many fund families are strong domestically, many are strong internationally, but only a handful are strong in both areas.

If your core Canadian fund family is not also a strong international player, ensure that your second core family has a strong global emphasis. That way, you can select funds for the 20 per cent foreign-content portion of your RRSP, as well as for your taxable (open or outside RRSP) portfolio. The bottom half of the fund matrices lists the international funds offered by a family. Note that if you own labor-sponsored venture capital funds, you may be able to take your foreign content up to 40 per cent.

Outside your RRSP, of course, you can invest as much as you want in global equities or bonds. Inside your RRSP, you or your adviser must decide whether maximizing foreign content is your main goal. If 20 per cent is enough, almost any fund family will do, provided it qualifies on other criteria. But you can have as much as 36 per cent of your RRSP in foreign content if you include Canadian funds that invest the permitted 20 per cent of their portfolios in foreign equity.

And, finally, if your belief in Canada is so shaky that you want to fill your RRSP with 100 per cent non-Canadian product, look for internationally oriented fund families that offer 100 per cent RRSP-eligible bond funds, equity funds, or balanced funds that are invested in foreign products through derivative-based strategies.

In the fund matrices, under the heading "RRSP/Foreign," "RRSP" indicates that a fund can be held in an RRSP without using any of the 20 per cent foreign-content limit, even if it appears to be a foreign fund. The entry "Foreign" indicates that a fund must be counted as part of that valuable foreign-content portion. Many of these use futures contracts to invest in the index of foreign markets.

4. Diversify your management styles with complementary families or funds

Step 1 diversified your portfolio among asset classes. Steps 2 and 3 diversify your holdings by geographical area. The next step is to diversify by management style.

No single fund family is perfect. One may have most fund types, for instance, but perhaps not all those funds are winners. But there's no point choosing similar funds from more than one family—for instance, more than one Canadian equity fund—unless they're complementary, or, to use the fund industry's jargon, "non-correlated"; that is, their performance fluctuates in different directions at the same time. The idea is to find pairs of funds in which one zigs when the other zags, so that overall performance is less volatile.

For this reason, it may make sense to choose a third fund family to supplement your core Canadian and core international families. Then, from these three families, choose at least two funds for each of your Canadian and international allotment: one a value investment style, the other a more aggressive growth style. Generally, growth funds are invested companies growing market share and sales, while value funds tend to emphasize out-of-favor blue chips that will outperform at the end of a recession and during an economic recovery. Some fund groups provide multiple investment styles. For example, Mackenzie Financial has three different fund families: the value-oriented Ivy Family, the growth-oriented Industrial Group, and the globally oriented Universal Group, which has subadvisers with various styles under contract.

Some international specialists, such as Templeton and Fidelity, maintain a very consistent investment approach through in-house managers. Others, such as C.I. Mutual Funds, Global Strategy Financial Inc., and Spectrum United Mutual Funds, diversify styles by contracting outside advisers.

5. Round out your portfolio with some specialty funds

Once you've chosen your core fund families, consider specialty funds. These higher-risk, higher-reward funds are usually volatile and should be restricted to no more than five or 10 per cent of your portfolio. They include precious metals, commodity futures funds, technology, and other sector funds and real estate funds. You can choose top-ranked funds that belong to the families you have already selected or funds from boutique-like firms that offer only one or two excellent funds, such as Saxon Funds.

HOW TO USE THE FUND FAMILY SECTION AND THE FUND MATRICES

Applying the fund family approach will be easier once you've studied the fund families. Representing more than half of the content of this book, it presents 50 major Canadian fund families, arranged alphabetically. We again downplay the distinction between load and no-load. The distinctions continue to blur, as seen in the "low-load" pricing schemes used by companies such as O'Donnell Funds. Many load funds are also sold by discounters at zero commission, as even large financial institutions such as Canada Trust opt to be compensated only through annual trailer fees.

Once you have selected, say, three core fund families, the next step is choosing individual funds from these families. Leading off each fund family profile entry is a "fund matrix," which shows at a glance all the Canadian and international funds available from any given fund group.

If one of the matrix entries shows a Smart Fund (indicated by a blue star), you'll find an analysis of that fund in the Smart Funds section in the second half of the book, and an index at the very end of the book to direct you to the appropriate page. It presents 100 funds ranked as the best in their class by the experts involved with this book.

A second category is Noteworthy Funds, indicated with a black triangle, which are commented upon in the text immediately following the fund family overview. Because there are so few Smart Funds compared with the more than 1,800 funds that are available, and because some fund families have relatively few Smart Funds, we've decided to include a few hundred other funds worthy of investor consideration. We call this secondary list the "B Team." We believe that if you have narrowed your choice to two fund families, each having several Smart Funds, this "B team" provides other good funds, many of them first quartile (that is, among the top 25 per cent in investment performance), that weren't selected as Smart Funds but can nevertheless be used to round out a fund portfolio.

BUY-AND-HOLD VERSUS FREQUENT SWITCHING

There are those who believe that mutual funds should be bought and held for the long term, relying on the manager for all day-to-day tactical shifts. Theoretically, a single global balanced fund or asset-allocation fund could be bought and held for decades, without the investor ever giving a thought to shifting stock and bond markets.

In practice, however, many investors want to participate in adjusting their fund portfolios. Given the bombardment of information through media, newsletters, books, seminars, and now even the Internet, it's little wonder such adjustments may seem necessary from time to time.

These two approaches illustrate the two main competing philosophies of mutual fund investing: market timing versus buy-and-hold. Both approaches can be executed in various combinations with load and no-load funds.

The mutual fund industry is sometimes accused of favoring the buy-and-hold approach for its own convenience. Money managers don't like frequent redemptions because they may be forced to liquidate positions at inopportune times. The switches also impose administrative costs, which, they say, are borne by the buy-and-hold investors.

On the other hand, several fund dealers and newsletters advocate frequent switching, both inside and between fund families.

It's not for us to judge the pros and cons of switching. But if you're unsure of what you're doing, an argument can be made for staying put and letting the manager do his or her job—particularly if you have a competent adviser who helped you buy the right funds in the first place.

Investors who attempt to second-guess fund managers may end up being "whipsawed"; that is, buying and selling at the wrong times. The odds are against you.

Consider, for instance, the performance of the Standard & Poor's 500 Composite Stock Index from 1980 to 1989, a period that included 2,528 trading days. An investor in the market for the entire period (in other words, a buy-and-hold approach) received a total return of 17.5 per cent, including dividends reinvested. If she missed the 10 biggest gaining days, her return dropped to 12.6 per cent. If she missed the 20 best trading days, her return would have been only 9.3 per cent. If she missed the 30 best trading days, her return would have declined to 6.5 per cent. And, if her market timing had her sitting in 30-day T-bills or a money market fund while missing the 40 best days (just 1.33 per cent of the total trading days in that period), her return would have been an abysmal 3.9 per cent.

If you're willing to put in the time and energy required to track the frequent oscillations in mutual funds' net asset values, then by all means engage in the switching game. The same energy could be exerted directly in the stock and bond markets, without paying managers the two per cent annual management fees. Wasn't the whole idea of mutual funds to sit back and let someone else make these decisions?

There is, of course, a comfortable middle ground here. Some investors will want the diversification and convenience of funds and still want to switch funds occasionally, perhaps because current macroeconomic trends favor certain fund types over others, or perhaps simply to rebalance their asset mix. Fund managers do change jobs, after all, which is one reason certain Smart Funds are replaced by others as subsequent editions of this book are released.

For those who believe in market-timing strategies—and even for those who want to make only occasional adjustments to their portfolio—there are some compelling arguments for sticking with just one fund family. This is particularly the case since many fund groups have now broadened their lineup of funds to cover different management styles, fund types, and geographic areas. In addition, the growing trend to asset-allocation services—such as AGF's service or Mackenzie's STAR—greatly expands the number of choices available for investors who prefer to stay within one family. But, most importantly, owning too many fund families can reduce your return. Each time you sell a fund from one family and replace it with a fund from another, you may have to pay redemption charges—which will reduce your net performance.

About 80 per cent of load funds are still sold with rear loads; that is, redemption fees payable on a declining schedule. These funds are commission-free when purchased but, if you sell them within a few years, you'll have to pay a redemption fee of as much as six per cent; the rate shrinks to zero over several years. Usually, though, you can switch from one fund to another within the same family, or to and from the family's equity or fixed-income funds to money market funds, without charge. (Some brokers or dealers may still impose a sales commission of up to two per cent to switch, although this fee is typically negotiable.)

There are no redemption charges if you sell a no-load fund and, if you have an account directly with a no-load fund company, you won't have to pay sales commissions on purchases or sales. However, some no-load companies, such as Altamira, limit the number of annual switches, and others charge a fee for more than a certain number of switches per year.

The simplest course, then, would be to buy funds within a single fund family that offers 30 or more funds and stick with them. And many investors have done so, generally through the no-load funds of Altamira, Royal Mutual Funds, or TD Greenline, or with the three fund families of load firm Mackenzie Financial.

Still, it is unlikely that any one fund company can have winners across the gamut of a 30-fund portfolio. By choosing two or three core families, and owning a money market fund in each group to minimize redemption charges, it's possible to select excellent individual funds within all major fund types.

GLOBAL TACTICS

When choosing your core international fund family, it helps to know what kind of global investor you are. Here are the major types:

1. Regional

You have a strong interest in geography, politics, and economics. Perhaps you subscribe to the *Economist* as well as the *National Post*. When you think of the investment world, you can't help having a strong opinion that, for example, the United States is overvalued and Asia is the economy of the future and ready for a big rebound. You will likely gravitate to strong international fund families that let you invest in individual regions, either through single-country funds invested in countries such as India (AGF), Israel (Dynamic), or Germany (AGF), or funds invested in broader geographic regions (such as Asia, Europe, and Latin America). The bottom half of each fund matrix is devoted to international funds, so you can see at a glance which approach a particular family takes. Some regional investors include Altamira, Fidelity, C.I., Mackenzie, Spectrum United, Global Strategy, AGF, and many of the bank groups.

2. All-global

To you the world is a black box. You're all for maximizing foreign content but want to leave the specifics up to the fund managers. You prefer to let them decide how much, if any, to allocate to Latin America, Japan, and so on. If you're this type of investor, then Templeton is the classic family for you. Or you might consider BPI, Trimark, and Phillips, Hager & North. In the fund matrices, these types of funds are shown as "all-global." Some families, such as AGF, C.I., Investors Group, and Mackenzie, provide both global and regional options.

3. Sectoral

You have strong opinions about how to invest your money. However, you don't divide the investment world into geographic areas, but into industries or sectors—such as technology, resources, or manufacturing. If you believe in sector funds, the classic family is AIM GT Canada, which lets you invest in telecommunications, infrastructure, natural resources, and health sciences around the world. C.I. Mutual Funds and Fidelity Canada now offer similar funds.

4. Non-domestic ("Quebec-averse")

You may fall into some or all of the above groups, but your overall concern is that Quebec will send Canada's stock and bond markets plunging. You want every penny of your RRSP outside Canada. If so, you need the 100 per cent RRSP-eligible foreign funds provided by families such as Global Strategy, Mackenzie's Universal Family, C.I. Mutual Funds, BPI, Canada Trust, and Scotia Excelsior. Look for the notation "RRSP" under the RRSP eligibility entry in the international half of the fund matrices.

5. Tax-averse

You have a large taxable portfolio. You don't mind having lots of Canadian content in your RRSP, but globally you want to move in and out of Asia, Europe and so on as you see fit—without triggering capital gains. You should investigate the "umbrella" programs of AGF, AIM GT, and C.I.'s Sector Funds, which allow you to defer capital gains.

MARKET TIMING VERSUS STRATEGIC ASSET ALLOCATION

Many of our Smart Funds are equity funds, because we believe they offer the best prospects for long-term growth. But that doesn't mean we think an investor should be invested in equities only, particularly in these turbulent times of record high North American stock markets, volatile gold prices, and crashing stocks such as Bre-X Minerals Ltd. As the Trimark television commercials graphically illustrate, equities go up and down. And while nobody complains about the ups, the downs sometimes test even the most dedicated investor.

The answer is to diversify your fund portfolio among the major asset classes: stocks, bonds, and cash and, in some portfolios, gold or precious metals, real estate, and perhaps even futures, through a strategy called asset allocation—which is simply the process of choosing a combination of investments that will achieve your financial goals with an acceptable level of risk.

The power of asset allocation is that it establishes a framework within which all your investments are made. An appropriate mix of cash, bonds, and equities in an investment portfolio will increase your return and decrease risk. This simple strategy can be enhanced by adding international bonds and stocks to the portfolio and by seeking out alternative money management styles—options made available through mutual funds to even the most modest investor.

Not only can you diversify into different asset classes, but now there are asset-allocation services available that try to identify the most optimal or efficient (in terms of risk versus reward) combination for each investor.

Asset allocation protects investors from their two worst enemies: themselves and media hype. It's not the same as market timing, which so many investors think is a "magic bullet" against risk and loss. The plaintive cry of those naive individuals typically goes like this: "I need to find somebody or something to tell me which funds will go up, which ones will go down and when it's best to simply be in cash!"

For some professionals, market timing is a practised science but most are lazy about it. Without bothering to learn or practise a disciplined approach to investing, they try to convince themselves that they can "make the perfect calls."

The authors of this book are skeptical about market timing. The reality is that, for most people, investing and following the markets are immensely challenging chores. It's difficult and time consuming to learn and to keep up with the professionals. Finding the time to plan an investment strategy, to achieve short-, medium-, and long-term goals, determine the best way to execute a plan, and regularly monitor its success is a daunting task. Most people are just too busy—trying to work a double load at the office, grab a workout, spend some time with the kids, and enjoy a little peace and quiet with the significant other. As a result, too many put off the need to plan, execute, and maintain an appropriate investment strategy.

Asset allocation, on the other hand, is not a fad. There is a strong foundation for the principles of asset allocation. The most often-cited research in this area is "Determinants of Portfolio Performance" (*Financial Analysts Journal*, July-August 1986, pp. 39-44), a study conducted in 1986 by three investment practitioners, Gary P. Brinson, L. Randolph Hood, and Gilbert Beebower. The authors examined the returns of 91 large U.S. pension plans for the period 1974-1983. They examined the variation in quarterly returns over that 10-year period and determined the following:

- On average, 93.6 per cent of the total variation in the actual plans' return was explained by the investment policy (asset mix) alone.
- Market timing, when combined with investment policy, "added modestly to the explained variance." It raised it to 95.3 per cent. Adding the selection of individual stocks accounted for 97.8 per cent of the variance.

This study, which was updated in 1991, shows that the emphasis must be on selecting the right asset mix and sticking with it. Clearly, asset allocation is important; in fact it's more important than choosing the right stocks.

MODERN PORTFOLIO THEORY AND THE NOBEL PRIZE

Behind the concept of asset allocation is years of work by two prominent professors: Harry Markowitz and William Sharpe. Beginning in the mid-1950s, they developed the hypothesis that became known as Modern Portfolio Theory, which examines the correlation of assets. Their work was recognized with the Nobel Memorial Prize for Economics in 1990.

When the values of two assets fluctuate in the same direction at the same time, they are said to be "correlated." The degree to which they are "correlated" can be measured mathematically. If two assets have a correlation measure equal to one, the values will fluctuate by exactly the same amount at exactly the same time. If you own these two assets, you have not helped your portfolio. You would do just as well or poorly by owning either one.

If you combine assets that are non-correlated (those that have a correlation measure of less than one), you have diversified your portfolio. More importantly, by using this approach, you can add riskier (and potentially more rewarding) assets to your portfolio and still lower the overall risk of your combined assets. In theory you can do this until your portfolio is "optimized"—that is, it combines the highest potential reward with the lowest potential risk.

Computer programs analyze past returns of asset classes (using benchmarks, such as the TSE 300 composite index for Canadian equities) and calculate correlation measures in order to combine assets into an "optimal" or "efficient" portfolio. Given the almost infinite number of possible combinations of risk and return preferences, an almost infinite number of portfolios can be generated. Plotting all these portfolios on a graph of risk and return produces a line known as the efficient frontier.

An Efficient Frontier

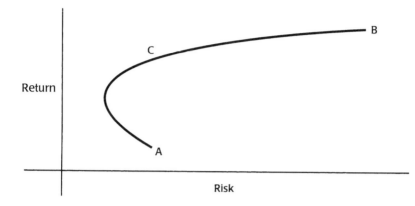

On this graph, point A is usually representative of a portfolio consisting entirely of T-Bills, and point B, a portfolio entirely of equities. People who have never seen this graph are often surprised by its shape. It clearly shows that if their portfolio is at point A, they can move all the way up to point C (increase their return) without taking any more risk. This movement would be accomplished by the addition of a combination of bonds and stocks. Even more significant is the fact they can move to any point on the frontier between A and C and both increase their return and decrease their risk.

While the concept of the efficient frontier is appealing, the question remains, "How do I get on the curve?" And, more importantly, "Where on the curve is the best place for me?"

Determining the exact answers to these questions is a difficult task. The efficient frontier is, after all, a theory. Computers generate efficient frontiers using historical data (that is, past performance). and expected returns based on forecast data. In practice, the efficient frontier is a moving target wholly dependent on the data fed into a computer. Indeed: "The sensitivity analysis we performed with optimizations...should convince anyone that the output is indeed very sensitive to minor changes in the input variables," wrote Roger C. Gibson in *Asset Allocation—Balancing Financial Risk*, (Irwin Professional Publishing, 1990, p. 176).

The more appropriate task for individual investors should be to try to get as close to the optimal portfolio. There are two ways to do that: strategic and tactical asset allocation. Strategic asset allocation defines the appropriate limits of each asset class for a type of portfolio and sticks with those limits regardless of market conditions. Tactical asset allocation focuses more on market conditions and varies the proportions of each asset class in an effort to have more of the portfolio in any class that appears ready to outperform the others. In other words, TAA is a form of market timing.

STRATEGIC ASSET ALLOCATION (SAA)

The simplest form of strategic asset allocation is a fixed balanced fund. Such funds have restricted limits on how much can be invested in equities and fixed income. A neutral stance is 50 per cent of each asset class, with limits for each typically 40 to 60 per cent That means that even if a fund manager believes that equities will outperform bonds, she could never invest more than 60 per cent of the portfolio in equities or, vice versa, less than 40 per cent even if she believes the market is due for a correction. (A variation of this is a "fund of funds" in which a fund company pools two or more of its funds, say one equity fund and one bond fund, to create a balanced portfolio with stringent allocation allowances.)

Examples of fixed balanced funds are:

- Altamira Balanced
- Royal Balanced
- Saxon Balanced
- Trimark Income Growth
- Universal Balanced Fund

Recently, the mutual fund industry began recommending personalized portfolios of mutual funds with different investment objectives, with the mix of funds based on investor responses to questionnaires. The idea behind these questionnaire-driven services is that personal asset allocation depends on four factors: objectives, time horizon, ability to tolerate risk, and financial situation.

A number of SAA services exist, based on a similar process. A questionnaire is given to assess these factors, and the resulting score identifies the investor as a particular type (income, balanced, growth, and so on). An investor with a maximum income profile will be matched with a portfolio that is heavily, if not entirely, invested in fixed income. The maximum growth investor, on the other hand, will be shown a portfolio with a substantial equity portion. And there are any number of variations in between—for example, emerging market funds have a place in a growth portfolio, but not in a maximum-income portfolio.

The mix, once allocated, does not change unless the investor's profile changes (for example, through job loss, approaching retirement, or inheritance). The portfolio is rebalanced periodically, however, to maintain the initial allocation if one asset group does particularly well relative to the rest.

TACTICAL ASSET ALLOCATION

Tactical asset allocation (TAA) is a form of market timing. These types of services or mutual funds offer the small investor a one-stop investment vehicle that:

1. Tries to overweight whichever asset class is deemed by the manager to be undervalued and likely to outperform over the near term, and;

2. Avoids market downturns by moving to safer assets before one occurs.

The following are the more prominent TAA funds available in Canada:

- Dynamic Partners Fund
- Fidelity Canadian Asset Allocation Fund
- First Canadian Asset Allocation Fund
- Canada Trust Global Asset Allocation Fund
- Investors Asset Allocation Fund
- Universal World Asset Allocation Fund

The performance of most of these funds is, so far, somewhat below the high expectations that the industry has had for fund category. That's because even the most sophisticated models, coupled with highly experienced managers, are up against big odds of not getting it right. And, as we saw earlier, missed opportunities can have a significant effect on portfolio return.

The other problem with tactical-asset-allocation funds is they are not tailored to the individual investor. The manager's market calls might be too aggressive for some investors, or at other times not aggressive enough. For most investors, the alternative—strategic asset allocation—is more appropriate.

Money Manager Profiles

ALTAMIRA'S IAN AINSWORTH, SUSAN COLEMAN, AND SHAUNA SEXSMITH

The sudden departure of Frank Mersch from Altamira Investment Services Inc. last May, brought together three very different money managers to form a new team at Altamira. Ian Ainsworth, Susan Coleman, and Shauna Sexsmith are all highly regarded, but have different areas of expertise. What they share is a common investment philosophy.

In an interview only weeks after Mersch's departure, it is obvious that the members of the trio are very different people. Coleman is relaxed and casual, Ainsworth outgoing, and Sexsmith precise and no-nonsense. Together they manage the giant 1.4 billion Altamira Equity Fund.

Before their arrival, the fund had been managed by Mersch since its inception in 1987. Mersch was known for his flashy sector-rotation style, moving quickly in and out of industries based on his calls on the market. When he was right, the fund's investors did well. In recent years, however, he was not always right.

Without a doubt, Mersch gave the fund a personality. Ainsworth, age 47, believes the new Altamira Equity is just as aggressive, but better than ever. "It is not going to be a run-of-the-mill kind of fund. It takes big positions in really targeted companies that meet our criteria. We're not taking market weight, plus or minus 10 per cent on Bell Canada, for example. We'll be either all or none in most of these situations."

They feel that their distinctive approach to stock selection is analyzing major sectoral themes they believe are changing business in Canada. Currently, the team is investing in companies positioned to take advantage of four particular trends.

The first theme is increasing globalization of industries. Ainsworth points to Canada's banking and telecommunications sectors as examples of the impact of this trend. They like a company that is globally positioned in that it either has "the ability to take a franchise international or protect itself domestically."

The second trend, toward government deregulation, is connected to globalization. "The whole drive to become low-cost competitors globally is forcing governments to deregulate and allow their telephone companies, banks, or utilities to become global competitors," Ainsworth explains.

The third trend is a greater emphasis on shareholders. Companies that recognize the importance of this will "buy back their shares or change management if it doesn't work. They have to be focused on increasing return on assets," he says.

And the final trend involves the growth of technology, which Ainsworth says has an impact on every industry.

To get into the portfolio, a company must be positioned to benefit from one of these trends and pass Altamira's quantitative tests. The individual picks determine the allocation to each industry.

Ainsworth, Altamira's vice president, equities, believes these themes are "driving global markets to highs that don't make sense unless you really believe in them." And he does. He used the same method to screen stocks when he was head of Altamira's international investing. He notes that investors understand the approach: "When we go out and talk about it, people really get excited."

It's a markedly different strategy than that of Mersch, who emphasized small-cap and resource stocks with high growth potential. Sexsmith, age 39, says the different approach has caused some observers to mistakenly label the fund as more conservative. "That's just not the case. We are very growth oriented and very performance oriented. We're just looking at the world in a different way." She uses a similar approach in managing the Altamira Growth & Income and Altamira Balanced Funds. Altamira Equity's size restricts it from buying the smaller stocks in the Canadian universe.

While Ainsworth and Sexsmith divide up the larger stock universe by sharing their expertise in different sectors, Coleman's focus is on the small-cap picks. Each of the managers has his or her favorite industries. Ainsworth knows technology stocks inside out, following his stint on the Altamira Science & Technology Fund, while Sexsmith is more familiar with the mining and resource sectors.

Ainsworth has been with Altamira the longest, since 1992. Coleman joined the firm in 1993, moving from the Canadian Imperial Bank of Commerce (CIBC). Sexsmith joined in 1997, moving from the Workers' Compensation Board of Ontario. She also worked for CIBC between 1992 and 1994. All three individuals are Chartered Financial Analysts.

Although the trio shares a philosophy, there are definite differences in their individual styles. Sexsmith is diligent about her sell strategy, notes Ainsworth. "Shauna has very strict sell criteria. [She] is very much concentrated on catching her catalyst on the stock."

"I'm a bit of a computer nerd," Sexsmith admits. "I always have my portfolios up in models and I have a lot of quantitative [analysis] that I look at."

She always buys a stock with a specific target price. If it gets close, she re-evaluates her position. "Either earnings have got to go up or I have to justify a reason for multiples to go up. Otherwise I will start turning back no matter what, even if there's strong momentum."

"I'm not as disciplined as Shauna," says Ainsworth. "I like to ride with the wave of some companies...I buy big, quality strong companies that have exposure to the themes in a major way and then track the issues related to sentiment and relative value rather than an absolute number."

Coleman, age 42, specializes in small-cap investing. She also manages the Altamira Special Growth and Triax labor-sponsored funds using the same theme approach. Altamira Equity has 10 to 20 per cent invested in small caps, which are used "to fill in the corners," says Coleman. "You have such a vast array of opportunities at small cap and they're so good at coming in and filling in the holes that get created," by bigger companies in the same industry. Because Altamira Equity is a large fund, she usually picks stocks that fit into the higher end of the market capitalization range—from $300 to $800 million, to keep the investments concentrated.

Coleman says they do not buy small cap unless there is legitimate opportunity. "If we can't find an appropriate smaller-cap play to develop a story, then we won't be there."

Another difference in the old and new Altamira Equity is that Mersch kept the portfolio almost completely Canadian whereas the new team maximizes its allowable 20 per cent foreign content. Those picks are also concentrated. "We might have two to three per cent in one stock," Ainsworth says. "So it will be highly concentrated on some of the best names that we see internationally."

Sexsmith believes that a team approach offers definite advantages in money management. "It's human frailty that you get hooked on an idea and you say 'the market is wrong and I am going to turn out to be right.' When you have three people on the fund, watching what is going on, we can eliminate some of the personal biases."

LYLE STEIN—SCEPTRE INVESTMENT COUNSEL LTD.

Balanced funds may be perceived as conservative, defensive investments but Sceptre Investment Counsel Ltd.'s Lyle Stein knows they can also be used to play offence.

The 41-year-old manager of the Sceptre Balanced Growth Fund seeks strong returns with low volatility. Stein calls himself a contrarian and strives to make decisions that will keep him several moves ahead of the competition. He has done that successfully for the last five years. Not only is the fund perched at the top of the balanced category, but it has also kept pace with the average performance of pure Canadian equity funds over the same period. That is a noteworthy feat for a portfolio that maintained a sizable bond weighting during a bull market.

Most balanced funds have not performed as well as a combination of straight equity and bond funds. Stein attributes the lag to the affinity of many balanced fund managers for "blue-chip, garden-variety type equities." In Canada, those stocks have historically underperformed, although that trend changed more recently.

Stein takes a bottom-up approach, viewing every investment as a security first and foremost. Stock or bond, every investment has three characteristics: a risk, a return opportunity, and a time frame. Even investing in a treasury bill carries risk because it can represent a lost opportunity to buy something else. His mandate: "To get the best rate-of-return opportunity for a given level of risk." A former soccer player, Stein uses a sports analogy to explain his strategy: generally, stocks are like offence and that is where he is willing to take more risk if the growth potential justifies it. "To me, low-risk stocks mean low-return opportunity stocks. If you are not buying a growth company, you should buy a bond." Bonds, for the most part, represent defence.

The balanced mandate allows him to move freely among the asset classes, seeking the best risk/reward tradeoff. For example, the fund owned stock in Calgary-based Hurricane Hydrocarbons, an oil servicing company with significant operations in Kazakhstan. It had appreciated substantially since he bought it. When the company came out with a debt issue yielding 10.75 per cent with warrants attached, Stein sold some of the stock to buy the bonds.

"I looked at the debt issue and it had all the upside associated with the common stock, plus I got a coupon yield that is probably as good as an equity rate of return over the next five years." Most equity funds would not have that flexibility, while traditional bond funds would not have touched the debt because it was not rated. "To me it was just another security. I assessed the balance between risk and return and it was justified."

Stein is originally from Wisconsin, but has lived in Canada for 10 years. After graduating with a bachelor's degree in economics and finance from the University of Wisconsin, he landed a job as a consultant with Foster Associates in Washington, D.C. There he provided financial market analysis to utilities companies. While so engaged, he frequently liaised with economics professors from the University of Toronto. Consequently, in 1981, when he decided to return to school for a master's degree in economics, he chose the University of Toronto for his studies.

After graduating, he returned to Washington and married a woman from Virginia shortly thereafter. But he continued to be drawn to Toronto. Consequently, when Nesbitt Thomson Bonguard (now Nesbitt Burns Inc.) offered him a job as a utilities analyst in 1988, he grabbed the opportunity to return to Canada. Two weeks into the job, he was offered a position as portfolio strategist.

During his six years at Nesbitt, Stein earned a Chartered Financial Analyst designation and a top ranking from the prestigious Brendan Wood International institutional equity survey. When he left Nesbitt in 1992 for Sceptre, he had risen to the position of chief portfolio strategist, but the "buy side" of the street beckoned.

Although Stein enjoyed working on the "sell side," he found it to be a hectic life. Managing money at Sceptre gives him the flexibility to devote time to being dad, soccer coach, and a part-time teacher. His three children, aged twelve, nine, and seven, are schooled at home—part of a network of neighborhood families that have chosen this alternative over the public school system. Stein teaches math, science, and geology, and throws in some supply-and-demand economics for good measure. The students are also having fun with a stock-picking contest. Stein recognizes it is a lifestyle choice with tremendous rewards. "I know my kids well," he says.

If home and family are his inspiration, money management is clearly a passion. Stein tries to schedule as many face-to-face meetings with company management as possible—about 100 companies a year. Because Sceptre is a highly regarded pension and private manager with more than $17 billion in assets, Stein has "access to top management at every company in Canada." He explains, "To me, there is nothing more exciting than to watch a CEO or CFO talk about their vision for their company. I ask myself, 'Does that vision make sense?'"

Furthermore, company visits reveal aspects of the businesses that financial statements cannot. "I like to see smiling employees," he says. His pet peeve: "The president's name on a parking spot— that bugs me." Stein believes the employee who arrives at work at 6:15 a.m. should get the best spot, regardless of job title. (Sceptre does not offer reserved parking.)

Personal meetings also foster an in-depth understanding of a company's long-term strategy, which he believes provides him with a competitive edge. While investors with a short-term view are driving down a stock price on the news of today's disappointment, Stein is quietly buying with a view that may extend 36 to 48 months out.

Stein covers golds, utilities, technology, transportation, and chemical stocks, and works closely with the rest of Sceptre's Canadian equity team, all of whom share their ideas freely. The balanced fund portfolio has many small-cap names, thanks to the expertise of Allan Jacobs, manager of Sceptre's Growth Equity fund. The largest international holding in the balanced fund is Sceptre's International Fund.

Stein believes that a good balanced fund could be the core holding for most investors. Depending on the investor, smaller commitments to other fund types would provide more exposure to growth or protection of capital.

Although asset allocation is critical to success, Stein insists he is not a market timer. He notes it is extremely difficult in the short term to call markets but over time one can make correct asset decisions. He avoids market timing by limiting any change in asset mix to five per cent per quarter. At the time of this interview in the spring of 1998, the portfolio was about 50 per cent in equities, which is lower than some competitors. Although that will drag on performance when markets rise, he's not concerned about following the crowd.

"Everybody else is sitting in what I like to call the pub sector, enjoying pipelines, utilities, and banks. I tend to be more concentrated on long bonds and I have a bit more of a resource and industrial bet." But Stein is proud to be different. Who but a contrarian would scour the stock pages in search of companies hitting new lows?

FRED PYNN—BISSETT & ASSOCIATES INVESTMENT MANAGEMENT LTD.

Little more than a year ago Calgary-based no-load firm Bissett & Associates Investment Management Ltd. celebrated what seemed to be a major milestone. Fred Pynn's Bissett Canadian Equity Fund had just reached $100 million in assets. At the party that Pynn hosted in the summer of 1997, his colleagues had no inkling that by the following spring the fund would quadruple to more than $400 billion in assets.

Bissett's other 10 funds have also enjoyed strong growth. "It's been wild," says Pynn, vice president of equities and one of four partners at the no-load firm. "Obviously the profile of Bissett has increased."

In fact, the *1998 Smart Funds* guide designated Pynn the Smart Fund Manager of the year. Furthermore, four of the funds that he manages received "Smart Fund" status in the same edition. Bissett's rapid ascent could be compared to a better-known no-load group whose early strong performance brought rapid growth earlier this decade: Altamira Investment Services Inc. And that kind of success is not without growing pains.

A case in point: the money was pouring into Bissett so quickly in the 1998 RRSP season that a significant cash position developed in Pynn's funds—not an ideal situation. In addition to the Canadian fund, he manages Bissett's Dividend Income and Multinational Growth funds and is subadviser to Atlas Canadian Large-Cap Growth Fund. He also manages pension assets.

"In the past we could buy stocks from any capitalization range but I can no longer buy true small caps. I can probably buy stocks down to about $500 million market capitalization. Below that, I can't get enough to put in all the portfolios."

For that reason, he says that investors who want to "to get the full range of opportunity" represented by Bissett Canadian Equity in the past, would do well to consider investing a portion in Bissett's Small Cap Fund, which is managed by David Bissett.

Pynn believes "there is a correlation between performance and size," which is a hotly debated issue. "The bigger you get, the harder and harder it gets to beat the market."

A $10,000 minimum investment per fund does not seem to be a deterrent to unitholders, nor has the fact that the firm does not pay trailers or service fees dampened the enthusiasm of some dealers and financial planners who sell the group's funds.

Pynn, age 39, believes the firm's consistent strategy has been the key to its growing acceptance in the marketplace. This strategy was created by founder David Bissett and shaped by the team of four partners. The objective is to be consistently in the northwest quadrant of the risk/return universe—to attain above-average returns with below-average volatility. "We want to outperform the market and the peer group of mutual funds, but not at the sake of volatility."

Pynn joined Bissett in 1987, five years after it was founded. He began as Bissett's controller, putting his expertise as a chartered accountant to good use. But Pynn's career switch from Price Waterhouse to Bissett had been a deliberate one. He chose to work in the money management business. In a small entrepreneurial firm such as Bissett, he was able to grab every opportunity to do investment research and help with money management. As the firm grew, so did his opportunities. By 1993, the firm had hired a new controller and Pynn was a full-time money manager.

Pynn spent his childhood in Montreal. During his high school years, the family moved to Calgary after his father, who was also an accountant, was transferred there. Pynn Senior was an avid investor who introduced Fred to the stock market and would announce an impromptu family trip when one of his stocks did particularly well. Pynn's interest was piqued further by an unusual English teacher who also had a penchant for the markets. She taught an optional course on investing. While studying commerce at the University of Calgary, Pynn was a member of the stock club for four years. He tasted his first successes investing in penny stocks. "I was an amateur investor and in Calgary in the late '70s, that was like shooting fish in a barrel. It was a good market, the end of the inflationary era."

After completing his bachelor of commerce degree, Pynn earned his chartered accountant designation and worked at Price Waterhouse in Calgary for five years. With his eyes set on the investment world, Pynn next tackled the Chartered Financial Analyst designation, which he achieved in 1989.

While he works from 7:30 a.m. to about 6 p.m. and takes home lots of reading material, he tries to spend evenings with his wife and three children, aged nine, seven, and six. On weekends, family ski trips and outdoor fun are a perk of living near the Rockies.

Like the rest of the Bissett team, Pynn is a bottom-up stock picker, looking for growth companies. He does not try to time the market or change directions on a whim. "We don't change our investment style depending on what stage we are at in the economic cycle. We're buying companies that we think offer above-average growth prospects and good value." Over the long term, those should do well no matter what, he says.

An aversion to excess volatility keeps him away from some otherwise good opportunities, such as Newbridge Networks Corp.

It is "a good company but the stock is all over the place." Rather, he seeks companies with growing earnings and dividends. "We are looking for a demonstrated growth record, reasonable return on equity, and companies that generate positive cash flow."

Valuations are considered next. From a pool of prospects, the most expensive stocks are eliminated. Also cut are the cyclical stocks that may still be in their growth phase but are considered too volatile. "We're left with two-thirds of the stocks in the middle that we'll do further work on." The last overlay is the economic outlook for various sectors.

It's a formula that has worked for the Bissett group for a long time. What has changed is investors in all parts of the country have now discovered Bissett.

TRIMARK CHAIRMAN ROBERT KREMBIL

Dressed in an elegant suit, Robert Krembil is speaking in his relaxed manner to a group of journalists who have assembled in the Toronto office of Trimark Investment Management Inc. to meet the company's two newest portfolio managers. The Trimark chairman's style is conservative, not flashy, just like the firm he co-founded in 1981. At the end of the presentation, the observer is left with one overriding impression: these two managers already seem so much a part of Trimark that it's hard to believe they haven't worked with Krembil their whole lives.

Krembil was first profiled by the *Smart Funds* books in 1995. In the four years since then, much has changed. Trimark has been one of the most successful beneficiaries of Canadians' widespread acceptance of mutual funds. In the spring of 1998, the company had more than $28 billion in assets, although it had slipped from second to third place in the asset rankings of Canadian fund companies.

The portfolio management team has grown and the fund line-up expanded. Trimark Trust is now an important part of parent Trimark Financial Corp. And in preparing for the next evolution of the industry, Trimark launched the Trimark Seg Funds in June 1998. In partnership with insurance company AIG Life Canada, 13 Trimark funds have been repackaged as seg funds, giving the company access to the distribution power of thousands of life insurance agents who are not licensed to sell mutual funds.

Along the way, Krembil and president Arthur Labatt have been dealt a few curve balls. Highly regarded money managers have left the firm, including Dina DeGeer, Bill Kanko, and Dennis Starritt, all whom are now managing funds for rival Mackenzie Financial ⌐⌐ p. More recently, the company has been hit hard by redemptions in its Canadian equity funds, due to a lag in performance. But through this period of explosive growth and change, much at the Toronto-based company has stayed the same, most notably the investment strategy. Since Trimark Investment Management Inc. was founded in 1981 by Krembil, Labatt, and Mike Axford—the three representing the "Tri" in Trimark—the company has maintained the same approach to investing. That continuity has been led by Krembil, head of Trimark's investing team as well as chairman of the publicly traded Trimark Financial Corp. And Krembil has created a portfolio management team that shares his belief in bottom-up, value investing.

Through market cycles, some of Trimark's competitors have become fickle, changing investment strategies with fluctuating markets. Others have introduced a new brand of funds when an existing brand faltered. Trimark has chosen a more focused approach. All funds are managed the same way: by investing in a small number of good businesses for the long term and buying them when they are trading at reasonable prices.

Diligent adherence to that philosophy, however, has led Trimark to this troublesome period. Its three Canadian equity funds—its core product with over $10 billion in assets—have stumbled, in some cases significantly underperforming similar rival funds. Despite concerns expressed by some brokers about the lead Canadian equities manager, Vito Maida, Krembil's faith in him has not visibly wavered. Maida remains in charge of two Canadian equity funds. The RSP Equity Fund is now managed by newcomers Keith Graham and Geoff MacDonald. Looking back on 1997—a great year for the stock market but a disappointing one for Trimark's Canadian funds—the 56-year-old Krembil explains, "In hindsight, we've been too cautious on the market and we've had more cash than we should have. We didn't make a bet on the market, but our concern about valuations made us cautious." A few months later, as North American stocks "corrected" 20 per cent or more, Krembil's caution seemed fully justified.

An overzealous stock market meant fewer stocks passed Trimark's valuation methodology. The Canadian team avoided the high-flying bank stocks, for example, which had been top performers. Krembil says it is a case of its investment strategy being out of line with the market. "It's just the way it goes and we suffer the consequences of that [performance]. But I believe it's short term." Some critics wonder whether the Canadian funds have become too big, particularly for the "Growth at a Reasonable Price" style Trimark supposedly espouses. The "value" part of this equation is why Trimark passed on the banks and made an uncharacteristic investment in gold bullion as an alternative to cash. Krembil downplays the difference between the terms "value" and "growth," and says size of the Canadian funds is not a problem. For now, there are no plans to "cap" (stop accepting new investments in) any of the Canadian equity funds. At the same time, unitholders have been provided with an alternative: new Canadian resource and small-cap funds, managed by Keith Graham and Geoff MacDonald.

While the redemptions are disappointing, Krembil tries to stay focused on the longer term. "We'd like everyone to love us every day but life is not that way. We have to make sure we are doing the right thing for investors over the long haul."

Trimark's success has made Krembil a wealthy man. The stock of the publicly traded company has climbed steadily over recent years, although it is down 70 per cent from its peak. Krembil and Labatt each continue to own 14.8 per cent of the shares outstanding.

Krembil says he is asked frequently about his plans for retirement. His answer: he is still having too much fun to retire. He remains directly involved in portfolio management on the international side and still loves coming to work.

"Most of my time is still spent looking at companies. That's where I get my jollies and I'll do that as long as I can function. And I would prefer to do that here at Trimark than anywhere else." He still travels regularly for business but tries to keep that separate from vacation time spent with his family. He rarely takes a vacation for more than one week at a time but tries to take about five weeks each year. An annual ski holiday is usually taken with his wife and his son's family, which includes his two grandchildren—twins, a boy and a girl.

He particularly enjoys ski holidays because it is difficult to combine them with work since not many ski resorts are located in major financial centres. He also enjoys spending time at his farm north of Toronto and boating on Georgian Bay.

While Krembil gets his kicks from money management, he admits that managing people is not his strength and tries to limit his involvement on the business side. "From the beginning we divided it so that Arthur [Labatt] was responsible for the business side and I was responsible for the investment side and we just communicate like mad with each other so we know what is going on."

That's still the way it is. Much of the daily running of the business now falls to president Brad Badeau. "He knows the culture, he's part of the culture and he's got a good team under him so I don't worry much."

Staying out of day-to-day business issues gives Krembil more time for impromptu debates around the trading desk where analysts and portfolio managers meet informally. "Having the right people and exchanging ideas and debating possibilities for investments is exciting and I like that." He is not a fan of structured meetings.

Trimark will continue to try and separate itself from an ever-growing pack of mutual fund companies by being different. "The objective here is to win, to have a better performance than others," Krembil concludes. "If you want to do better than others, in my judgment, you have to do things differently. That's the underlying belief or principle in what we do. We consciously try to do things that are different from the crowd."

TEMPLETON'S MARK HOLOWESKO

When Mark Holowesko decided to enrol in the Chartered Financial Analyst program in 1984, he was informed that he needed sponsorship by another CFA. He lived in Nassau and it turned out there was only one other CFA on the Bahamian island, a man well known to him. So he wrote to the man requesting his assistance. The man agreed. It was another year before Holowesko met his sponsor. He wrote a second letter thanking him—he had passed the first of three CFA exams. Holowesko was invited for a meeting and a job interview with his sponsor, Sir John Templeton, the world's pre-eminent global investor.

In fact, it was Holowesko's second interview with Templeton Global Advisors Ltd. He had been turned down by the company the first time he applied. This time, however, he got the job. That was 1985. Thirteen years later, Holowesko, age 39, now manages US$80 billion for Templeton. As director and chief investment officer of Templeton Worldwide, Inc., he also oversees 42 analysts and several portfolio management groups. He is also president of Templeton Global Advisors Ltd. in Nassau.

Holowesko is best known to Canadians as manager of the giant Templeton Growth Fund, Ltd. It broke through $10 billion dollars in assets in March 1998 and is the largest mutual fund in Canada by a couple of billion dollars.

Like all managers at Templeton, Holowesko invests based on the value philosophy embraced by Sir John, who founded the predecessor company in 1940 that evolved into Templeton. Managers scour the globe in search of hidden gems: cheap stocks they believe will come to life. Today Templeton is part of one of the largest money management firms in the world. Its parent, Franklin Templeton Worldwide, manages more than US$240 billion.

Much has changed in the 13 years since Holowesko first met with Sir John. "When I started working at Templeton, Sir John was the premiere global investor and he had investments in [only] nine countries. Today we have investments in 40 countries." The adoption of a capital market system by so many countries has allowed Templeton to grow to what it is today and to create so much opportunity for investors.

Holowesko grew up in the Bahamas. His parents sent him to a high school in Rhode Island run by Benedectine monks. "I thought my parents had disowned me, sending me to a school run by monks but actually it was a phenomenal school and great experience." He went on to Holy Cross College in Massachusetts, where he earned a bachelor of arts in economics. Because Holowesko wanted to study business, he stayed in Massachusetts, earning a master's of business administration degree with a concentration in finance at Babson College.

After graduation, he considered remaining on the East Coast and applied to investment firms in New York City but had no luck. He returned to the Bahamas and, after being turned down by Templeton, resumed a job with Roy West Trust Corp. (Bahamas) Ltd., where he had worked during eight summer breaks. There he managed trust and individual accounts and researched international equity markets for a year. He devoted his spare time to studying for the CFA.

Holowesko's first love remains learning about companies and finding great investments. Management responsibilities are onerous, but he spends half his time doing research. "We're stock pickers and our accounts are driven by stock ideas rather than portfolio management decisions. The day I get out of research, I should also get out of running money."

His research takes him on the road 100 days a year. "I prefer to go and see corporate facilities rather than sit in a boardroom. Boardrooms are boring and most treasurers will tell you what you could read in an annual report. I prefer to go to a factory floor and walk from the door where the raw materials come in to the door where the product goes out."

He also notes that it's an effective way to learn about the company's competition: "You go to the Volvo factory and you ask them questions about BMW and they're going to tell you everything you need to know."

Often an analyst who covers the company will come along. "It is somebody else to ask questions while you think, and you can bounce ideas around when the meeting is over. I say 'What did you think about this or how did this compare to what you see at other factories?' That's fun. That's really the most exciting part of our business."

The downside of being on the road is the actual travel and time spent away from his wife and four children. In his free time, he shares his passion for sailing with his two boys and two girls, aged five through 13. In fact, he was a competitor for the Bahamas in the 1996 Summer Olympic Games in Atlanta. His wife prefers horseback riding.

When in the Nassau office, he is busy with administrative duties and more research. To become part of a Templeton portfolio, a company must pass stringent tests. Holowesko uses three methods to qualify value stocks.

The first is determining future earnings. Rather than forecast the next quarter or year, he will forecast the full business cycle. "We think the market is fairly efficient in the short term but it is inefficient in the longer term. So we concentrate on the typical business cycle, which is three to five years."

Much of his time is spent forecasting all the elements of growth. He asks how a company will grow its revenues and how it will finance that growth. "Are they going to sell more of what they make? Is the price going to change? And do they have the money to do those things, or do they have to raise money?" Based on that, research earnings growth is forecast and compared to the current stock price to determine whether the stock is undervalued.

The second measure is the stock price relative to the company's assets. "We try to find stocks that are selling at a discount to their assets. There are a lot of stocks that are cheap relative to assets, but many deserve to be cheap." The difference is they will buy where they think there is some catalyst for change.

Stocks that generate free cash flow—cash they don't have to put back into their business—are also prized. "To us those are very interesting companies because they can either buy back their stock or make acquisitions."

Unlike some global managers who use the country weightings within an index as a guideline for where to invest, Holowesko ignores world indexes in allocating the portfolio. He explains, "It's ludicrous to me that you would buy a stock that you don't think is cheap, just because it is in an index that you're compared to." He only concerns himself with country or industry allocations if concentrations get very large. He notes, "I like to be diversified."

Holowesko believes that North America, and to some extent Europe, have entered a new era in terms of stock valuations, but notes, "You have to ask how long it will last." Interviewed shortly before stocks entered a major "correction," Holowesko expressed concern that investors' expectations had become unrealistic in the bull market. "Investors could never be too cautious. People have thrown caution to the wind and are willing to pay ridiculous prices for securities."

FIDELITY'S RICHARD HABERMANN

Richard Habermann feels fortunate to still be working in a business he has enjoyed for more than 30 years. He joined Fidelity Management & Research Co. in 1968, immediately after graduating from Harvard Business School. Today he still gets the same kick out of investing. "I really liked the market when I came into this business and I still like it because it's always changing. I've been very lucky to be able to do this for so many years."

Habermann, age 58, is senior vice president and managing director at Fidelity in Boston. He oversees billions of dollars and hundreds of analysts around the world. He is well known to Canadian investors as the portfolio manager of the Fidelity International Portfolio Fund, which has enjoyed a solid performance record since its introduction in November 1987. He also oversees the asset-allocation and foreign portion of Fidelity's Canadian and Global Asset Allocation Funds.

Fidelity International Portfolio (a Smart Fund) sets the standard for bottom-up stock picking. "This is probably the most research-intensive global fund there is," he explains. "We have more than 350 analysts and fund managers around the world that every day are seeing hundreds of companies. They are in fact creating the buy list." More than 4,000 companies are actively followed, which means that analysts have written a review or seen the company within the last 90 days. "We probably follow 7,000 companies in total, but 4,000 on a very tight schedule. Out of those, we might have 1,000 buys that are available at any time. That's quite a nice menu."

From that buy list, four regional portfolio managers in the United States, Europe, Japan, and Hong Kong choose the stocks that they believe offer the best growth potential at a reasonable price. Those recommendations are made to Habermann, who is the final filter in the process and determines the asset allocation of the fund. Continuing the restaurant analogy, Habermann says, "I determine the menu, but they are the chefs." He laughs when he admits he hates to cook.

The allocations within the fund are not based on macro forecasts. "Fidelity's core discipline is to build these portfolios stock by stock. And then ideally you end up with country weights that reflect the most opportunity." He also uses some of Fidelity's estimates and ratings, which give him some insight into which regions or sectors might be improving or declining.

This research-intensive process sets Fidelity apart from its competitors. "What differentiates us from a lot of people is they don't have this infrastructure on the ground, so they're forced to make high-level strategic decisions on industries or countries."

Habermann describes his style of management as conservative. "In any steps I make, I tend to be cautious because I want to make sure we don't take anything away from that research success." But he will overweight the fund in regions based on a proliferation of good opportunities. Sometimes he takes the heat for it. For example, the team has received criticism about the fund's heavy weighting in the United States in recent years. "And yet this is where we have found the most opportunity over the last five years: companies that were growing faster than their global peers," he explains. The decision was evidently a good one given the performance of U.S. stocks.

Habermann travels to London, England four or five times each year, spending a total of about one month in Europe and at least another month in the Far East. "It really gives me insight into what's happening out there. It's the only way I can build conviction on these regional weights." Typically he'll visit companies that represent the key sectors in the economy of the region.

It was a trip to Southeast Asia in November 1996 that led him to begin reducing the Asian stocks in the fund, a timely decision given the subsequent fall-out in the region. "Being there really helped me to actually see what was developing to be a major problem."

He still enjoys the travel and no matter how much time he spends visiting companies, would like to do more. The downside to travel, of course, is time spent away from his family and his favorite activities—sailing and skiing with his four children. The less time he has to ski, the better his family members seem to become. He notes, "My whole family skis better than I do. I'm always trying to get better."

Prior to attending Harvard, Habermann earned a bachelor of arts degree from Yale University. He also served as a lieutenant in the U.S. Navy for four years between undergraduate and graduate school. He says there is a parallel between the discipline required in the navy and the job of the money manager. "When you're on a ship, there is a lot of discipline involved. You have to be persistent, you have to keep going over the same routines." The same is true in money management: "There really aren't any shortcuts."

When he joined Fidelity, it was still a small company but already emerging as a leader in the mutual fund business. He was intrigued by what seemed like such an exciting, creative place and so began his career there as an analyst. He has held many positions in the ensuing 30 years. His current job evolved out of his position as chief investment officer for sister company Fidelity International, Ltd. in London in the early 1990s. "In our U.K. pension business, we had multi-regional, multi-currency funds. As I worked in a management role, I also started managing money and really tried to implement a lot of [strategy] into the sub-portfolio management. That's really the role I have evolved into; I asset allocate and try and work closely with my fund managers."

Habermann faces a hectic schedule and recognizes that prioritization is crucial. "Otherwise you just get swamped. There's so much information from Fidelity alone, it's just staggering. In the morning when I come in there are probably 50 internal phone messages, from offices around the world."

Habermann believes the key to success in selecting stocks is consistency. "We're not trying to have that exceptional year and then run the risk that we'll have a dreadful year. We're trying to string together a series of good to very good years and then you end up with an excellent long-term record." To illustrate the point, he quotes a famous football coach who said, "'three yards and a cloud of dust,' that's essentially what we do."

Despite the obvious importance of his role as gatekeeper, Habermann is quick to give credit to the Fidelity analysts and portfolio managers around the globe. "There are some very talented analysts and subportfolio managers and this fund has really been built on their success."

SCUDDER CANADA'S PHIL FORTUNA

Phil Fortuna's investment philosophy was born out of his study of finance and psychology. In 1984 he was working toward a master of business administration in finance at the University of Chicago and a degree in cognitive psychology. In studying finance and psychology side by side, something became very clear. "I saw the investment industry was paying no attention whatsoever to the cognitive biases that might be driving investing." That intrigued him.

Today, as Director of Quantitative Services at Scudder Kemper Investments, Inc. in San Francisco, he oversees computer programs that aim to benefit from those human biases in investing. Using a computer, Fortuna and his team have been more successful at picking Canadian stocks over the last two and a half years than most Canadian managers taking the old-fashioned approach.

The Scudder Canadian Equity Fund was launched in October 1995, when Boston-based Scudder came to Canada. Performance has flown far above the TSE 300 index since then. Over one year to June 30, 1998, the fund returned 26.2 per cent, compared with an average 10.3 per cent for Canadian equity funds.

Boston-based Scudder, one of the oldest fund companies in the United States, is not strictly a quantitative manager—most of its funds are actively managed. Before coming to Canada, the Scudder team did some research to determine how it could manage a Canadian equity fund differently than Canadians. "We looked at about 40 different factors in the Canadian market, ranging from valuation criteria to fundamentals to see if the stocks that had done well recently would continue to do well. We found there are some very consistent factors at work in the Canadian marketplace." A Canadian equity fund, it turned out, would lend itself very well to quantitative investing.

Based on that research, Fortuna and Mac Eysenbach, his co-manager on the Canadian Equity Fund, developed a computer model that would select stocks to achieve the goal of the fund: to outperform the TSE 300 over a market cycle of about three to five years, and do so with less risk.

The computer model may sound mysterious but it isn't, says Fortuna. "We don't run black boxes here. We develop an underlying logic and then try to find real world markers that correlate to that logic."

The computer is programmed to use historical statistics and current data to identify bargains: stocks with current assets and earnings trading at low multiples, which also have improving growth prospects.

Fortuna likes to think of these as low-expectation stocks rather than value stocks, as they are commonly called. Historically, he says, value stocks have benefited more from earnings surprises than growth stocks and have been hurt less. That's where the psychology comes in. When analysts get a negative earnings surprise on a high expectation or "growth" stock, it shakes the entire foundation on which they made the estimate. He notes, "There is a revision of the entire way the [analyst] is thinking about the company and this can lead to a large downward price move." With low expectation or "value" stocks, however, disappointment is less dramatic because expectations were lower. On the flip side, a positive earnings surprise has a more dramatic impact on the value stock. Since there are approximately an equal number of positive and negative earnings surprises, "you don't have to be a math major to see what the net effect is going to be. All of the risk lies with the high expectation stocks."

Fortuna calls himself "a techno-weenie," and admits to being a voracious reader, especially of books on statistics and hypothesis testing. He is also a classical music nut and has a collection of about 2,000 compact discs. His favorite pastime, however, is spending time with his wife of 17 years and two children, aged nine and seven, whom he calls "the joy of my life." Together they enjoy bike rides around the San Francisco hills.

Before attending the University of Chicago, Fortuna received a bachelor of science degree in economics from Carnegie Mellon University in 1978. After graduating with his MBA in 1984, he took a job as a strategic planning officer and later investment officer for Crocker National Corp., a financial institution in San Francisco. Serendipity provided an opportunity with Scudder soon after. Fortuna was attending an investing conference and during a discussion session made some comments about the future of computers in investing. An executive from Scudder, who was also in attendance, was impressed enough to offer him a job on the spot.

He began with Scudder as an institutional portfolio manager but shortly after founded the quantitative group in 1987. He has designed and developed the products along with Eysenbach.

The computer model that runs Scudder Canadian Equity relies on widely used ratios such as price to earnings and price to cash flow. They do not use the price-to-book-value ratio, which Fortuna's research found was not consistently reliable. "We find that price to book does not work consistently in Canada and for us consistency is very important."

The fund is also managed with an eye to tax implications and it paid out zero in distributions in the last year. So far, stocks have been held for two years on average.

Unlike many funds that maximize the permitted 20 per cent foreign content, the only non-Canadian asset of this fund is Fortuna. He believes that when investors buy a Canadian equity fund, they should get just that.

True to the quantitative stereotype, Fortuna and Eysenbach never talk to company management. Fortuna tells the following joke about "quant" managers: "'The portfolio management team of the future will consist of an investor and a dog. The investor's job is to run the model and trading and the dog's job is to guard the door and make sure that's all the manager does.' No company visits. Mac's the investor, I'm the dog." On a more serious note, he says although the portfolio is run based on the model, it is critically important for someone to be looking at it every day.

As convinced as he is in the inability of humans to be completely objective and the merits of "quant" investing, Fortuna believes there is a place for traditional qualitative management. "Quant isn't always right and qualitative isn't always right. You can draw from both disciplines and you'll do better. We try and do that here at Scudder."

TD GREEN LINE'S CHARLES (CHIP) MORRIS

Managing the biggest science and technology fund in the United States is a high-stress job. Charles "Chip" Morris jokes that he loses weight in step with the declines of the U.S.'s Nasdaq stock index. Jokes aside, Morris, a managing director of T. Rowe Price Associates Inc. in Baltimore, wouldn't have it any other way. In his view, technology investing is so much fun, he figures he's got one of the best jobs around.

Morris, now 35, was only 28 when he became manager of the T. Rowe Price Science and Technology Fund. He had been working as an analyst with the fund's former portfolio manager and was given the opportunity to run the money himself when the manager left the firm. It was 1991 and the fund had about US$150 million in assets. Today it is US$3.88 billion, the biggest of its kind.

For Canadians, the opportunity to invest in a similar fund came a couple of years later, in 1993, when TD Green Line hired T. Rowe Price to manage its Science and Technology Fund. Today, the Canadian version (and a perennial Smart Fund), with about $216 million in assets in the spring of 1998, continues to be managed as a clone of its larger U.S. cousin, with some minor differences.

Early in 1998, Morris adopted a slightly new strategy for the Green Line fund. Because of the difference in size of the two funds, an analyst has been assigned to concentrate entirely on technology stocks with a market capitalization of less than US$1 billion. Those stocks often get past the radar screen of the U.S. fund because they are too small to make an impact on the portfolio. Broadening the scope of the fund has increased the number of stocks in the portfolio from 60 to 100.

In the fast-paced technology industry, choosing tomorrow's winning companies may seem a formidable task. But the many independent technology experts and consultants in the United States provide a tremendous flow of information and analysis to Morris. "The role of the technologist has been assisted over the last five years because of a proliferation of sources that actually do the technical work for you." He is not referring to Wall Street analysts, however, who he says tend to be overly optimistic. "They can downgrade a stock five times before it is actually called a sell." He also attends many conferences to understand new innovations and get ideas. "I also go to see whose booth is really busy and whose isn't." He points out that his position requires more than technology expertise. "Part of you has to be a technologist, part of you an accountant, part a strategic planner, and part of you a spy." For Morris, that's what makes his job fun.

Morris joined T. Rowe Price in 1987. He began as a technology analyst, fresh out of Stanford University in California, where he had earned a master of business administration degree, with honors in finance. He knew he wanted to get into the money management business, so after graduating from Indiana University with a bachelor in science degree, he went straight to graduate school.

Morris, who grew up in Maryland, figures he was first bitten by the investment bug when he made some money on an investment in Wendy's Restaurants at the ripe age of 14. His father, a colonel in the U.S. Air Force, had suggested he learn about investing. Morris picked Wendy's the way many people pick stocks—because he liked the product. The stock went up and that was enough to endear him to the market. "I got charged about how you could do a bit of research up front and could pull more money out than you put in."

Morris had worked at T. Rowe Price for the summer between his two years of the MBA program and enjoyed the people from the start. "It was a fantastic group of people to work with and I fit in... When they offered me a job, I took it."

All of the team members at T. Rowe Price are bottom-up stock pickers, and pay little attention to macroeconomic factors. Morris works with six others on the technology team, which includes analysts and portfolio managers. To narrow down the universe of stocks, they look for trends in the technology business. "We start out by identifying secular waves that are impacting the technology arena. It could be the shift to network computing, for example, the big thing that's happening in electronic technology today. After we identify a tidal wave of change, we then try and find the small currents."

He says the tidal waves sweeping over the technology sector today are the continued growth of the Internet, specifically the development of electronic commerce and broadband networking that allows for the efficient movement of information electronically. On a global scale, the rapid growth of wireless communications is creating great opportunities for equipment suppliers.

Once they identify possible companies, the team members consider several factors, including the level of intellectual property a company has and whether it has a business model that is sustainable over time. Companies embarking on strong product cycles are attractive. "They create the opportunity for positive earnings surprises because the sector is momentum driven." And strong management is essential. "They have to have a vision and they have to have shown evidence they know how to execute the business plan."

Company visits are crucial. Morris travels to the West Coast of the United States eight to 10 times each year. Those trips don't allow for much free time. His schedule is jam-packed and he usually sees 20 companies in a four-day trip. "The typical day away from the office consists of two meetings in the morning, two meetings in the afternoon and either a breakfast or dinner." And he doesn't like to be away from home for too long with a wife and one-year-old baby daughter at home.

Speaking before the correction in the U.S. market, Morris said that even with the gyrations of the Nasdaq index, we still had record absolute valuations of technology stocks, although he believed they were still attractive compared with the broader Standard & Poor's 500 index. For him, the bottom line is no matter how great the growth prospects of a company if he thinks it is overpriced, he won't invest. "It doesn't matter how great anything is, if it costs too much, you should be a seller not a buyer."

The 50 Major Fund Families

1. AGF FUNDS INC.

Strengths: Canadian bonds
Some strong single country funds
Weaknesses: High MERs
Confusing mix of bond and A.A. funds
RESPs?: Yes
Web Site: www.agf.com   **Toll Free:** 1-800-268-8583

CANADIAN	Category	Rating	Fund Name	M.E.R.%	RRSP/Foreign
Money Market:		■	AGF Money Market Account	1.42	RRSP
Fixed Income:	Long-term	▲	AGF Canadian Bond Fund	1.93	RRSP
	Short-term	■	AGF High Income Fund	1.68	RRSP
Equity:	Mid-Large Cap	■	AGF Canadian Equity Fund	2.95	RRSP
		■	AGF Canadian Growth Fund	2.46	RRSP
		■	AGF Canada Class	2.63	RRSP
	Small Cap	▲	AGF Growth Equity Fund Ltd.	2.80	RRSP
		■	20/20 RSP Aggressive Equity Fund	2.47	RRSP
		■	20/20 RSP Aggressive Smaller Companies	2.73	RRSP
	Resource	▲	20/20 Canadian Resources Fund Ltd.	2.88	RRSP
	Other	▲	20/20 Managed Futures Value Fund	3.69	RRSP
Tax Advantaged	Dividend	★	**AGF Dividend Fund**	1.87	RRSP
Multi-Asset	Balanced	▲	AGF Growth & Income Fund	2.50	RRSP
	Asset Allocation	■	AGF Asset Allocation Service		RRSP
		■	AGF U.S. Asset Allocation Service		Foreign
		■	AGF Canadian Tactical Asset Allocation Fund	2.42	RRSP

FOREIGN	Category	Rating	Fund Name	M.E.R.%	RRSP/Foreign
Money Market		■	AGF U.S. Dollar Money Market Account	0.84	Foreign

Fixed Income:		■ AGF U.S. Income Fund	2.46	Foreign
		▲ AGF High Income Fund	1.68	RRSP
		▲ AGF Global Government Bond Fund	1.86	Foreign
		■ AGF RSP Global Bond Fund	1.97	RRSP
		■ AGF U.S. Short-term High Yield Income	2.48	Foreign
		■ AGF International Short-Term Income Class	2.69	Foreign
Global Equity:	All-global	■ AGF World Equity Class	3.07	Foreign
		★ **AGF International Value Fund**	2.77	Foreign
		▲ AGF International Stock	2.98	Foreign
		■ 20/20 Aggressive Global Stock Fund	3.64	Foreign
		■ AGF Global Real Estate Equity Fund	new	foreign
Regional Equity:				
	U.S. Large-cap	★ **AGF American Growth Class**	2.78	Foreign
		■ 20/20 Aggressive Growth Fund	2.55	Foreign
	U.S. Small-cap	■ AGF Special U.S. Class	2.86	Foreign
	Latin American	▲ 20/20 Latin America Fund	3.24	Foreign
	Emerging Market	■ 20/20 Emerging Markets Value Fund	3.57	Foreign
	Far East	▲ AGF Asian Growth Class	3.03	Foreign
	Japan	▲ AGF Japan Class	3.07	Foreign
	Europe	■ AGF European Growth Class	3.03	Foreign
	Other	▲ AGF China Focus Class	3.49	Foreign
		▲ AGF Germany Class	2.99	Foreign
		■ 20/20 India Fund	3.74	Foreign
Global Balanced:		■ AGF World Balanced Fund	2.46	Foreign
		■ AGF RSP International Equity Allocation Fund	2.45	RRSP
		■ AGF American Tactical Asset Allocation Fund	2.56	Foreign
		■ AGF European Asset Allocation Fund	2.56	Foreign

AGF Management Ltd. seems to have hit a comfortable stride. With the integration of the 20/20 Funds now well behind them, the group seems satisfied with its fund line-up and management roster.

What makes AGF both a desirable and challenging fund family is the variety of product it offers. Although most investors can find something they like from among the now 40 funds offered by the company, that number also makes construction of a coherent portfolio a complex task. This is further complicated by nine income funds, five asset-allocation funds, a couple of asset-allocation services, and the assignment of "Class" status to 10 funds under the AGF International umbrella.

AGF continues to offer two brands of funds—a result of its acquisition of 20/20 Funds Inc. in late 1995. The riskier growth equity funds are prefixed "20/20" to signal to unitholders their aggressive growth characteristics. More conservative funds carry the AGF prefix.

Only one fund was added in the last year—the AGF Global Real Estate Equity Fund, which was launched in June 1998. It invests in public real estate companies and still-popular Real Estate Investment Trusts (REITs). Portfolio management changes include AGF Japan Class, now being managed by Mitsuuo Saegusa of Nomura Asset Management, the fund's ongoing subadviser. More recently Laura Wallace was replaced by Martin Hubbes on the AGF Canadian Equity Fund.

AGF possesses some formidable strengths and, by sheer virtue of quantity of offerings, always manages to have a dozen or so top-quartile performers. A continuing strength is bonds, particularly the domestic bond funds overseen by chairman Warren Goldring, who is ably assisted by Clive Coombs.

AGF funds give investors access to management by an impressive collection of subadvisers. They cover different regions and, unlike fund families that use a single style, AGF offers investors a variety of investment strategies. On the global equity side, for example, Charles Brandes is a classic value investor available through the renamed AGF International Value Fund and AGF International Stock Class, launched in June 1997. If you want access to aggressive, growth-oriented global equity funds and don't mind volatility, AGF also offers those. Highly regarded Richard Driehaus uses his momentum style to manage the 20/20 Aggressive Growth Fund. Momentum investing is widely used by U.S. money managers and is becoming more popular in Canada. The 20/20 RSP Aggressive Equity and 20/20 RSP Aggressive Smaller Companies Fund use the same Driehaus style and are fully RRSP-eligible.

The down side of subadvisers, however, is that the funds usually carry higher management expenses than in-house funds, and AGF is no exception. Some of the country-specific funds are particularly expensive. AGF China Focus has an MER of 3.49 per cent, while 20/20 India Fund is the most expensive of the group at 3.74 per cent.

Closer to home, the experience at AGF's Toronto office matches that of its subadvisers. In addition to Goldring and Coombs, there are veterans such as Bob Farquharson and Steve Rogers.

AGF has always been a forward-thinking company. Several of its single-country funds, as mentioned above, are not found at most rival firms. Goldring has always believed that fund products depend on strong markets. Thus, AGF was early in the American market (hence the original acronym, American Growth Fund) back when cutting-edge technology consisted of color television, new wonder drugs, and jet airplanes.

For international equity investors with taxable (non-RRSP) portfolios, AGF, like C.I. and AIM GT Global, is an especially attractive fund family. There are now 10 funds in the AGF International Group, which allows investors to switch among these funds without triggering a capital disposition. This also maximizes foreign-content capacity in an RRSP or RRIF, because the book value of the investments doesn't increase unless you leave the group.

Asset allocation has always been a strong suit of AGF. For help putting this myriad of product together in a sensible way there is the

MAP personal computer-based asset-allocation program. It is a questionnaire-based service that uses modern portfolio theory to combine a group of AGF funds in order to maximize return and minimize risk.

Smart Funds 1999:

AGF Dividend Fund, AGF International Value Fund, AGF American Growth Class.

Noteworthy Funds:

20/20 Canadian Resources Fund. Demoted because it's a high-MER sector fund and we believe that Canadians should let their Canadian equity manager choose resource stocks within a diversified portfolio.

20/20 Latin America. The reputation of portfolio manager Peter Gruber, in Latin America investing, is comparable to Templeton's Mark Mobius' reputation in emerging markets. Unfortunately, recent performance of the fund has been disappointing, which has pulled down its three-year CAGR to 5.2 per cent versus a category median of –0.77 per cent at June 30, 1998. We have demoted all Latin funds in favor of more diversified emerging-markets funds.

AGF Canadian Bond. This continues to be a consistent performer, benefiting from the experience of Warren Goldring and Clive Coombs. At June 30, 1998, it is in the second quartile over one, three, five, and 10 years. A 1996 Smart Fund, but we have become tougher on bond funds and this one's 1.93 per cent expense ratio is just too high.

AGF International Stock. New Fund based on Charles Brandes as manager and his success with the International Value Fund. Because this fund is part of the "Class" group, investors can move between it and the other nine funds in the class. It invests globally, with the exception of the United States. So far it's in the second quartile as at June 30, 1998. On the down side, the MER is high at 2.98 per cent.

AGF Global Government Bond Fund. Also managed by Coombs with Scott Colbourne of AGF, this fund sticks to global bonds with a minimum A credit rating. It has achieved above-average performance over one, two, three, five, and 10 years ended June 30, 1998.

AGF Growth & Income. The performance of this balanced fund has fallen off recently, but it has a solid track record over the longer term. This fund will have a high cash position at times. At the end of March 1998, for example, it had 24.1 per cent in cash.

AGF High Income. This 1998 Smart Fund has been demoted based on several years of underperformance: below average over one, two, and three years at June 30, 1998.

AGF Growth Equity Fund. Bob Farquharson's small- to mid-cap equity fund had below-average performance over one, two, three, and five years to June 30, 1998.

20/20 Managed Futures Value Fund. This highly volatile fund deflated, a casualty of falling prices of many of the commodities it buys. Under the management of John Di Tomasso, it could be a good bet for an aggressive investor with a long-term horizon.

AGF Germany. Formerly a closed-end fund, this is one of the few pure Germany plays available in Canada. Its 43.1 per cent return for the year ended June 30, 1998 put it firmly in the top quartile versus competitors.

AGF Asian Growth Glass. This former Smart Fund has been demoted, based on underperformance versus comparable funds; it is a fourth-quartile performer over one, two, and three years, and it carries a high MER of 3.03 per cent.

AGF China Focus. Another demotion, following fourth-quartile performance for the year ended June 30, 1998. Its high MER of 3.49 per cent and single-country focus make this appropriate only for aggressive investors.

AGF Japan Class. If you want exposure to the Japanese market, this is worth consideration. It is the top performer in the category over 10 years and continues to be advised by Nomura Asset, now under a new lead manager. The fund is in the top quartile, and ranked fourth of 71 funds over one year—still, that was a negative 13.7 per cent. The only other drawback is its 3.07 per cent MER.

Availability:

Through brokers and discount brokers, dealers, and financial planners.

2. AIC LTD.   FRONT OR REAR

Strengths:	Investing in the wealth industry		
	Warren Buffett–style equity investing		
Weaknesses:	Potential for high volatility in Advantage funds		
RESPs?:	Yes		
Web Site:	www.aicfunds.com	**Toll Free:**	1-800-263-2144

CANADIAN	Category	Rating	Fund Name	M.E.R.%	RRSP/Foreign
Money Market:		■	AIC Money Market Fund	1.00	RRSP
		■	AIC Income Equity*	2.46	RRSP

Equity:	Mid-Large Cap	★	**AIC Advantage Fund**	2.31	RRSP
	Mid-Large Cap	★	**AIC Advantage Fund II**	2.63	RRSP
	Mid-Large Cap	★	**AIC Diversified Canada Fund**	2.39	RRSP

FOREIGN	Category	Rating	Fund Name	M.E.R.%	RRSP/Foreign
Global Equity:	All-global	★	**AIC World Equity Fund**	2.7	Foreign
	All-global	▲	AIC World Advantage	new	Foreign
Regional Equity:	U.S.	★	**AIC Value Fund**	2.44	Foreign
	U.S.	■	AIC American Advantage Fund*	2.72	Foreign
Mult-Asset:	U.S.	■	AIC American Income Equity Fund	new	Foreign

* The MERs have been annualized since the funds' inception in August, 1997.

AIC continues its reign as one of Canada's fastest-growing fund companies. Much of its success is due to the eye-popping returns of its two original Advantage funds, which target investments in Canada's explosive wealth-management industry.

But AIC has been trying to downplay its emphasis on the wealth-management business and broaden its horizons instead. Until recently, the family consisted entirely of equity funds and one money-market fund for short-term cash parking. But in an attempt to position itself as a more diversified core fund group, it has introduced the new AIC Income Series funds. The fully RRSP-eligible AIC Income Equity was launched in March 1998 and the AIC American Income Equity Fund was added in August 1998. Both are balanced funds with the equity portions managed in the same way as AIC's three Diversified funds. The managers continue to buy the best companies they can find in what they believe are fast-growing industries.

But AIC is in no way walking away from the strategy that has made it the sweetheart of many fund investors. AIC has launched two new "Advantage" funds in the past year. Like the Canadian Advantage Funds, AIC American Advantage and AIC World Advantage invest most of their portfolios in wealth-management companies.

That affinity for financial companies has been a licence to print money for investors in the last few years. The demographic trends driving baby-boom retirement savings have played nicely into the Advantage funds, a credit to founder Michael Lee-Chin and president Jonathan Wellum, profiled in the 1995 edition of this book.

The potential problem with the Advantage funds is that investing in these relatively illiquid Canadian wealth stocks becomes an increasingly dicey strategy as more and more latecomers crowd into the party. Should this virtuous cycle ever reverse itself in a market setback, which appeared to happen by August 1998, wealth stocks and these funds would take it harder on the chin than broader funds.

Management seems aware of this risk and the funds have become more diversified as markets become pricier. In the spring of 1998, both Advantage and Advantage II had about 65 per cent of their portfolios in financial services stocks.

For investors who believe that buying the Advantage funds now is more risky than they are comfortable with, AIC offers three diversified equity funds that are broader in focus. The funds are invested using the Warren Buffett "buy good companies for the long term and hold them" approach. Names such as Adidas, Nestlé, and Novartis are recent holdings in AIC's World Equity Fund, for example. The two other diversified portfolios in the family are AIC Diversified Canada and AIC Value, a U.S. equity fund.

Because of the lower turnover that comes with the buy-and-hold strategy, AIC funds make good holdings for outside an RRSP.

AIC no longer distributes an emerging-markets fund. In August 1997, the tiny AIC Emerging Markets was absorbed by AIC World Equity Fund and those assets reinvested under the mandate of the larger fund.

Smart Funds 1999:

AIC Advantage and Advantage Fund II, AIC Diversified Canada, AIC Value, AIC World Equity.

Noteworthy Funds:

AIC World Advantage. Launched in August 1998, this new global version of the Advantage Fund may prove to be less risky than the original Canada-based Advantage Fund or the U.S.-based AIC Value.

Availability:

Through full-service or discount brokerages across Canada, financial planners and insurance companies.

3. AIM GT INVESTMENTS   FRONT OR REAR

Strengths:	Some global funds, style investing	
Weaknesses:	Temporarily, no free switching between the two fund groups	
	High M.E.R.s on some funds	
RESPs?:	No	
Web Site:	www.aimgt.ca	**Toll Free:** 1-800-588-5684

CANADIAN	Category	Rating	Fund Name	M.E.R.%	RRSP/Foreign
Money Market:		■	AIM GT Global Canada Money Market Fund	0.75	RRSP
Money Market:		■	AIM Cash Performance Fund	1.03	RRSP
Fixed Income:		■	AIM Global RSP Income Fund	2.39	RRSP
Equity:	Mid-Large Cap	★	**AIM GT Canada Growth Class**	2.47	RRSP
Equity:	Mid-Large Cap	■	AIM Canadian Premier Fund	2.80	RRSP
Equity:	Mid-Large Cap	■	AIM GT Canada Value Class	2.87	RRSP
Tax-Advantaged:	Dividend	★	**AIM GT Canada Income Class**	2.10	RRSP
Mult-Asset:	Balanced	■	AIM Canadian Balanced Fund	2.71	RRSP

FOREIGN	Category	Rating	Fund Name	M.E.R.%	RRSP/Foreign
Money Market:		■	AIM GT Short-Term Income Class	1.64-2.15*	Foreign
Fixed Income:		■	AIM GT World Bond Fund	2.45	Foreign
Global Equity:	Global Index	▲	AIM Global RSP Index Fund	2.39	RRSP
	All-Global	■	AIM International Fund	2.97	Foreign
		▲	AIM GT Global Theme Class	2.89	Foreign
	Specialty	■	AIM GT Global Infrastructure Class	2.76	Foreign
		■	AIM GT Global Natural Resources Class	2.95	Foreign
		★	**AIM GT Global Telecommunications Class**	2.82	Foreign
		★	**AIM Global Technology Fund**	2.94	Foreign
		▲	AIM GT Global Health Care Class	2.78	Foreign
		★	**AIM Global Health Sciences Fund**	2.94	Foreign
Regional Equity:	U.S.	■	AIM GT America Growth Class	2.86	Foreign
	U.S. Large Cap	■	AIM American Premier Fund	2.78	Foreign
	U.S. Small Cap	■	AIM American Aggressive Growth Fund	2.74	Foreign
	Europe	■	AIM Europa Fund	2.91	Foreign
	Latin American	▲	AIM GT Latin America Growth Class	2.86	Foreign
	Far East	■	AIM GT Global Pacific Growth Class	2.95	Foreign
	Pacific Rim	■	AIM Tiger Fund	3.36	Foreign
	Japan	■	AIM Nippon Fund	3.26	Foreign
	South Korea	■	AIM Korea Fund	3.25	Foreign
Global Balanced:		■	AIM GT Global Growth & Income Fund	2.87	Foreign

The April 1998 merger between AIM Funds Group Canada Inc. and the larger GT Global has resulted in a comprehensive fund group with a good selection of specialty and regional funds. The resulting AIM GT Investments is the Canadian result of a global acquisition. AIM's parent, British-based Amvescap PLC, bought LGT Asset Management, parent to GT Global in Canada.

For now, the two fund groups have been maintained as they were before the merger. As no funds have been merged, the new family consists of a total of 29 funds. The former GT funds have kept their names but an "AIM" prefix has been added. The 14 AIM funds are unchanged.

The two companies are similar in several ways. Both were subsidiaries of global money management businesses. Most funds were run by portfolio managers based outside Canada, particularly in the United States. And both companies offered funds with a variety of styles, as well as more narrowly focused regional and sector funds. In fact, G.T. Global was the first of the Canadian fund companies to make theme investing accessible to small investors, a strategy imitated by C.I. Mutual Funds and Fidelity Investments Canada. Both companies are also similar in having high MERs on some products.

Investors should expect to see some changes. There are duplications in the line-ups, and acting president Gary Littlepage has stated that some portfolios will be merged to streamline the family. Both companies have a Global Health Care fund, for example. And both offer a Canadian equity fund managed with a momentum growth style. GT's version is now called AIM GT Canada Growth, and is managed by Derek Webb out of the company's San Francisco office. It returns as a Smart Fund after being dropped in 1998. The AIM Canadian Premier fund has a similar mandate. It has a smaller portfolio that has underperformed the average over three and five years. Which funds will be left standing at the end of the integration is unclear. At the time of writing, the company had not made any decisions on this.

The merger also filled various gaps. AIM had no value-style Canadian equity fund, a popular choice as a core holding. AIM brings several regional funds to the family, including a Europe fund.

In the short term, one disadvantage to investors is the inability to do low-cost "switches" between the two fund groups. That option is coming—expected for the spring of 1999. But for now, these are treated as two separate fund companies in that respect, meaning the usual redemption and sales fees would apply when moving between an AIM fund and an AIM GT fund.

When the merger is complete, the combined fund group and global research that backs it up should be a strong contender. AIM GT is part of one of the world's biggest money management operations, with assets under management of $360 billion. Its parent, Amvescap, has 27 offices in 20 countries and is the fifth-largest money-management firm worldwide.

AIM GT continues to provide an interesting option for more active investors who like to move between funds and are concerned about triggering capital gains. The AIM GT Global Fund Inc. is an umbrella fund with nine share classes: the five theme classes; three regional classes: America Growth, Latin America Growth and Pacific Growth; and Short-Term Income Class. Switching between these classes does not trigger a deemed disposition. Capital gains are realized only upon redemption from GT Global Fund Inc. A similar structure is used for the domestic funds: Canada Growth Class and Canada Income Class exist under the umbrella of GT Global Canada Fund Inc.

For investors who find the idea of one sector fund too risky, the AIM GT Global Theme Class continues, as in the past, to be a compilation of the best ideas from seven sectors.

Smart Funds 1999:

AIM GT Canada Income Class, AIM Global Health Sciences, AIM Global Technology Fund, AIM GT Canada Growth Class, AIM GT Global Telecommunications Class.

Noteworthy Funds:

AIM GT Global Theme Class. This fund spares investors the anguish of trying to market-time and switch various key sectors of the economy by holding a selection of stocks from seven global sectors. Two of the seven themes it invests in—consumer products and financial services—are not available separately from the AIM GT group. The strategy worked well in the last year. The fund gained 29.57 per cent to June 30, 1998.

AIM GT Global Health Care. Solid performance thus far although it does not have the five-year history of its AIM-brand sister fund.

AIM GT Latin America Growth Class. This fund is the top performer of the Latin American fund group, based on its three-year CAGR of 13.1 per cent to June 30, 1998. But buying a regional emerging market fund is aggressive investing no matter how good past performance looks.

AIM Global RSP Index Fund. This fund was closed to new purchases in November 1997. It may still be a good choice for existing unitholders, although it has a 2.39 per cent MER.

Availability:

Only through brokers and discount brokers and dealers.

4. ALTAMIRA INVESTMENT SERVICES INC.   NO LOAD

Strengths:	Fixed income MERs below average	
	Service & unitholder education	
Weaknesses:	Loss of Frank Mersch and Will Sutherland	
	Instability of ongoing redemptions	
RESPs?:	Yes	
Web Site:	www.altamira.com	**Toll Free:** 1-800-263-2824

CANADIAN	Category	Rating	Fund Name	M.E.R.%	RRSP/Foreign
Money Market:		▲	Altamira T-Bill Fund	0.24	RRSP
Fixed Income:	Long-term	★	**Altamira Bond Fund**	1.3	RRSP
	Medium-term	▲	Altamira Income Fund	1	RRSP
	Short-term	■	Altamira Short Term Government Bond	1.3	RRSP
		▲	Altamira Short Term Canadian Income Fund	0.35	RRSP
Equity:	Mid-Large Cap	■	Altamira Capital Growth Fund Limited	2	RRSP
		■	Altamira Equity Fund	2.28	RRSP
	Small Cap	▲	Altamira Special Growth Fund	1.8	RRSP
	Gold/precious metal	■	Altamira Precious & Strategic Metal Fund	2.3	RRSP
	Resource	■	Altamira Resource Fund	2.35	RRSP
		■	AltaFund Investment Corp.	2.32	RRSP
Tax Advantaged:	Dividend	★	**Altamira Dividend**	1.56	RRSP
	Labor-sponsored	■	Triax Growth Fund	3.6	RRSP
Mult-Asset:					
	Tactical asset allocation	■	Altamira Balanced Fund	2	RRSP
		■	Altamira Growth & Income Fund	1.4	RRSP

FOREIGN	Category	Rating	Fund Name	M.E.R.%	RRSP/Foreign
Fixed Income:		■	Altamira Short Term Global Income Fund	1.22	RRSP
		■	Altamira Global Bond Fund	1.81	RRSP
		★	**Altamira High Yield Bond Fund**	1.95	Foreign
Global Equity:	Small-cap	▲	Altamira Global Small Company	2.95	Foreign
	Specialty	★	**Altamira Science & Technology Fund**	2.31	Foreign
Regional Equity:					
	U.S. Large-cap	■	Altamira U.S. Larger Company Fund	2.3	Foreign
	U.S. Small-Med	■	Altamira Select American Fund	2.28	Foreign
	NAFTA/N.Am.	■	Altamira North American Recovery Fund	2.3	RRSP
	Emerging Market	■	Altamira Global Discovery Fund	2.95	Foreign
	Far East	■	Altamira Asia Pacific Fund	2.34	Foreign
	Japan	■	Altamira Japanese Opportunity Fund	2.37	Foreign
	Europe	▲	Altamira European Equity Fund	2.32	Foreign
Global Balanced:		■	Altamira Global Diversified Fund	2	Foreign

For many frustrated Altamira unitholders, the May 1998 departure of ace manager Frank Mersch must have been the final straw. In a June settlement with the Ontario Securities Commission concerning personal trading, Mersch agreed to withdraw from the investment-management field for six months. But even before that telling event, so-so performance and the apparent distractions of a bitter ownership battle had already led many Altamira unitholders to redeem out of the family.

Altamira is a classic case of the "live by the sword, die by the sword" philosophy. When Mersch was at the top of his game, he virtually was Altamira, and his superior early performance made him a thorn in the sides of the broker-sold funds. But Altamira's lack of redemption fees meant that unitholders could leave without penalty once they decided the jig was up.

This overview is not addressed to those who have already left this fund family. They're long gone and are unlikely to return. Our Smart Funds analysis is therefore addressed to two camps: those unitholders who are still wholly or partially invested in Altamira, and newcomers to the concept of no-load mutual fund investing in general, and Altamira in particular.

It's hard to sugar-coat the Altamira situation. We had already stripped Mersch's flagship Canadian equity fund, Altamira Equity, of Smart Fund status in last year's edition. With his departure, and the unwieldy $1.4 billion still invested in it, we now remove its Noteworthy designation.

But Mersch was not the only departure in the past year. In June, lead bond manager Will Sutherland, profiled in our 1997 edition, also left Altamira. Less heralded was the earlier loss of veteran manager Cedric Rabin, who managed the Altamira Growth and Income Fund. Rabin was replaced by Shauna Sexsmith, who was also appointed vice president, Canadian Equities in 1997.

The picture is not all bleak, however. Altamira had already entered a new era months before the Mersch departure, when it appointed Gordon Cheesbrough as president and CEO. Cheesbrough had been chairman and CEO of ScotiaMcLeod and Scotia Capital Markets and evidently will not tolerate substandard performance for long. The popular Philip Armstrong was named managing director, with a focus on strategy, partnering, acquisitions, and regulation.

Altamira's management expense ratios on its fixed-income funds are below the category averages, though no screaming bargain relative to competitors like PH&N or Scudder. Altamira Bond and Altamira High Yield Bond return as Smart Funds. Many of Altamira's global equity funds have MERs slightly below average, although the performance of the funds is literally all over the map. Altamira is gradually moving from externally managed global funds to internal management, which should cut costs. It moved Altamira Global Discovery Fund in-house, removing State Street Bank. For now, that fund loses its Noteworthy status.

Altamira's global investment management team now has seven members, including Mark Grammer, formerly an international equities vice-president at HSBC James Capel Canada. He manages the Altamira Japanese Opportunity Fund, which booted out Regent's Peter Everington some time ago.

The Global Small Company's MER has come down and becomes noteworthy. Altamira European Equity shared in the gains of most European funds over the last few years and is therefore Noteworthy. Altamira Science & Technology had a good year and moves up to Smart

Fund status this year. Its manager, Ian Ainsworth, has been promoted and must fill the large shoes of the departed Mersch on Altamira Equity.

Although we have great respect for Ainsworth, the sheer size and problems of Altamira Equity will present an immense challenge. Despite its size, the MER of 2.28 per cent remains higher than the category average of 2.22 per cent; that's a high price to pay for a fund that will be lucky to beat the indexes.

For those who want to stick with Altamira for Canadian equities, we suggest a reinstated Smart Fund, Altamira Dividend Fund, or Susan Coleman's small-cap Special Growth Fund, which has been elevated to Noteworthy status in this edition.

It's clear that under Cheesbrough, the high-net-worth market will receive greater attention. For example, in Altamira's March 1998 unitholder letter, Cheesbrough hinted of new products specifically for the wealthy. In June, he appointed Chris Hodgson as managing director, wealth management.

It goes without saying that Altamira is a good corporate citizen, has excellent service, an interesting web site, and top-notch unitholder communications. But just as the religious think faith without work is nothing, all the goodwill in the world will count for naught if Altamira doesn't return to the consistent high performance that it used to be famous for.

Smart Funds 1999:

Altamira Bond, Altamira Dividend, Altamira High-Yield Bond Fund, Altamira Science & Technology Fund.

Noteworthy Funds:

Altamira Special Growth Fund. A possible harbor for Altamira Equity investors. In some respects, the small-cap focus of Susan Coleman and the smaller amount of money in the fund makes this similar to the early days of Altamira Equity under Mersch. Its MER of 1.8 per cent is half a per cent point lower than the category average. But the one-, two-, three-, and five-year CAGR numbers are below the median as of June 30, 1998.

Altamira Global Small Company Fund. Decent though not spectacular 11 per cent return for year ended June 30, 1998 for this former Smart Fund. Last year we called its 3.02 per cent MER "punitive" but that's now down to 2.36 per cent, which is about average for the category.

Altamira European Equity Fund. Shared in the strong rise of European stocks last year and would have made up for losses in the ailing Altamira Asia Pacific Fund. In the spring, *The Economist* declared that Europe's economies were approaching "bubble-like" proportions. Chasing this fund late in the cycle could result in buying high and selling lower later if things reverse.

Altamira Income. Lower MER than Altamira Bond, but this fund's one-year return of 9.5 per cent to June 30, 1998 was less than half of Altamira Bond's 22.9 per cent.

Altamira T-Bill Fund and **Altamira Short Term Canadian Income.** As money-market yields decline, management expense ratios become a serious performance issue. These two new funds have competitive low MERs that are almost one-third the average for money-market funds and short-term bond funds respectively.

Availability:

Directly from Altamira or some brokers and discount brokers and dealers on request. Minimum investment of $1,000 or $50 through Automatic Investment Plan.

5. ATLAS CAPITAL GROUP NO LOAD OR FRONT OR DEFERRED LOAD

Strengths:	Style diversification (value and growth)
	Access to many external advisors
Weaknesses:	Complexity of fund types
	Some higher than average MERs
RESPs?:	No
Web Site:	www.atlasfunds.ca **Toll Free:** 1-800-463-2857

CANADIAN	Category	Rating	Fund Name	M.E.R.%	RRSP/Foreign
Money Market:		■	Atlas Canadian Money Market Fund	1.11	RRSP
		■	Atlas Canadian T-Bill Fund	1.30	RRSP
Fixed Income:	Long-term	■	Atlas Canadian Bond Fund	1.99	RRSP
	Short-med	▲	Atlas Canadian High Yield Bond Fund	1.90	RRSP
Equity:	Mid-Large Cap	★	**Atlas Canadian Large Cap Growth Fund**	2.46	RRSP
		■	Atlas Canadian Large Cap Value Fund	2.61	RRSP
	Small Cap	■	Atlas Canadian Emerging Growth Fund	2.47	RRSP
		■	Atlas Canadian Small Cap Value Fund	2.59	RRSP
		■	Atlas Canadian Small Cap Growth Fund	2.77	RRSP
Tax Advantaged:	Dividend	■	Atlas Canadian Dividend Growth Fund	2.31	RRSP
	Income	■	Atlas Canadian Income Trust Fund	1.86	RRSP
Mult-Asset:	Balanced	★	**Atlas Canadian Balanced Fund**	2.28	RRSP

FOREIGN	Category	Rating	Fund Name	M.E.R.%	RRSP/Foreign
Money Market:		■	Atlas American Money Market Fund	1.14	Foreign
Fixed Income:		▲	Atlas World Bond Fund Fund	2.15	RRSP

Global Equity:	All-global	■	Atlas Global Value Fund	2.75	Foreign
		■	Atlas International Large Cap Growth Fund	2.99	Foreign
	Index	■	Atlas International RSP Index Fund	2.06	RRSP
Regional Equity:	U.S.	▲	Atlas American Large Cap Growth Fund	2.70	Foreign
		▲	Atlas American Advantage Value Fund	2.65	Foreign
	U.S. index	■	Atlas American RSP Index Fund	1.58	RRSP
	Latin American	▲	Atlas Latin American Value Fund	2.95	Foreign
	Emerging Market	■	Atlas International Emerging Markets Growth	3.5	Foreign
	Far East	■	Atlas Pacific Basin Value Fund	2.90	Foreign
	Europe	■	Atlas European Value Fund	2.75	Foreign

The Atlas Mutual Funds are available through a growing number of brokerage and investment sales firms, making it more convenient for investors to include them in a diverse portfolio. Originally the 24 funds were Midland's in-house product and were sold under the Atlas and Hercules name.

Further expanding distribution continues to be the mandate of new president Victor Dodig. He replaced Sue Dabarno when she moved to Atlas' parent, Midland Walwyn Capital Inc., in the fall of 1997, to head up its retail brokerage division.

It remains to be seen, however, how this fund group will be affected by its parent's decision to be absorbed by U.S. brokerage giant Merrill Lynch, as announced in June 1998. Merrill Lynch is the second-largest mutual fund company in the United States.

The Atlas funds are managed externally by a variety of advisers around the world. Most of the Canadian funds have established track records and some feature well-known Canadian managers such as Calgary's Bissett Associates and Vancouver's Deans Knight.

Atlas offers a style-based approach, with both value and growth versions in many fund categories and, in some cases, small- and large-cap versions too. They are available under four sales options: no-load with a one-year clawback; no-load with no clawback; deferred load with a six-year declining-redemption schedule; or front load with commission negotiable between zero and five per cent. (In fact, in the case of almost all funds, the commission is negotiable on the front-load option.) The clawback refers to the commission paid by the fund company to the dealer.

One new fund was launched in the last year—Atlas Canadian Income Trust Fund—also managed by Bissett. The Canadian Emerging Growth Fund, managed by Wayne Deans of Deans Knight Capital, was reopened for investment in November 1997. The small-cap fund was closed when it reached $125 million, about a year earlier.

Atlas has changed the manager of its two Canadian Value Funds: Large-Cap and Small-Cap. They are now managed by BonaVista Asset Management Ltd., which replaced RT Capital Management.

The global funds are also noteworthy. They feature such prominent advisers as Bankers Trust, Salomon Brothers, and Oppenheimer Capital Advisors.

Smart Funds 1999:

Atlas Canadian Balanced Fund, Atlas Canadian Large Cap Growth.

Noteworthy Funds:

Atlas Canadian High Yield Bond Fund. Demoted because of high MERs.

Atlas World Bond. Demoted because of high MERs.

Atlas American Large Cap Growth. High MER and tough category.

Atlas American Advantage Value Fund. Managed by Oppenheimer Capital Advisors, this fund is in line with the CAGR of the group over three years to June 30, 1998, but falls short in the last year, a strong one for the U.S. market. Still, a three-year return in excess of 20 per cent is not bad.

Atlas Latin American Value. This is a solid fund within this specialized category. It far outperformed competitors in the last year and is better over three years as well.

Availability:

Most major full-service brokerages and major financial planners and discount brokers.

6. BANK OF MONTREAL FIRST CANADIAN FUNDS   NO LOAD

Strengths: Declining fees for large volume of assets
MatchMaker asset allocation service
Weaknesses: Lack of 100% RRSP eligible global funds
RESPs?: Yes
Web Site: www.bmo.com/fcfunds or   **Toll Free:** 1-800-665-7700 or
www.bmo.com/fondsm (French)(in Quebec)   1-888-636-6376

CANADIAN	Category	Rating	Fund Name	M.E.R.%	RRSP/Foreign
Money Market:		■	First Canadian Money Market	1.05	RRSP
		■	First Canadian T-Bill	1.06	RRSP
		■	First Canadian Premium Money Market*	new	RRSP
Fixed Income:	Long-term	■	First Canadian Bond	1.49	RRSP
	Mortgage	■	First Canadian Mortgage	1.36	RRSP
Equity:	Mid-Large Cap	▲	First Canadian Growth	2.20	RRSP

				M.E.R.%	RRSP
Small Cap	▲	First Canadian Special Growth		2.16	RRSP
Index	▲	First Canadian Equity Index		1.28	RRSP
Gold/precious metal	■	First Canadian Precious Metals		1.95	RRSP
Resource	■	First Canadian Resource		2.22	RRSP
Tax Advantaged: Dividend	★	**First Canadian Dividend Income**		1.64	RRSP
Mult-Asset: Asset Allocation	■	First Canadian Asset Allocation		1.93	RRSP

FOREIGN	Category	Rating	Fund Name	M.E.R.%	RRSP/Foreign
Fixed Income:		■	First Canadian International Bond	1.98	Foreign
Global Equity:	EAFE	■	First Canadian International Growth	2.00	Foreign
	Specialty	■	First Canadian Global Science & Technology	1.90	Foreign
Regional Equity:					
	U.S. Large cap	■	First Canadian U.S. Growth	2.20	Foreign
	U.S. Small cap	■	First Canadian U.S. Special Growth	1.64	Foreign
	U.S. Value	▲	First Canadian U.S. Value Fund	1.77	Foreign
	U.S. Index	■	First Canadian U.S. Equity RSP Index	1.19	RRSP
	NAFTA/N.Am.	■	First Canadian NAFTA Advantage	1.97	Foreign
	Latin American	■	First Canadian Latin American Growth	1.81	Foreign
	Emerging Market	■	First Canadian Emerging Markets	2.16	Foreign
	Far East	▲	First Canadian Far East Growth	2.25	Foreign
	Japan	■	First Canadian Japanese Growth	2.08	Foreign
	Europe	■	First Canadian European Growth	2.13	Foreign

After adding a number of new funds in 1996 and early 1997, Bank of Montreal is concentrating on its existing product and its portfolio management. It added just one new fund, following the lead of several other banks, with the First Canadian Premium Money Market Fund in October 1997. This short-term parking spot is for investors with a minimum $150,000 investment. The MER is much lower as a result; it has been capped at a maximum 0.40 per cent.

BMO also implemented a few portfolio management changes in the last year. First Canadian hired two more external managers: J.P. Morgan Investment Management Inc. to manage the First Canadian Japanese Growth Fund and Sanford C. Bernstein & Co., Inc. to advise the First Canadian European Growth Fund.

The firm's four U.S. equity funds continue to be managed by BMO subsidiary Harris Investment Management Inc. of Chicago, with good results in its first full year. Three of the four beat the group average; only one, First Canadian U.S. Equity Index Fund, performed below the group average over the year ended June 30, 1998.

The MatchMaker Strategic Investment Service, announced early in 1996, has proven to be successful. It had attracted more than $3 billion in net fund assets as of the spring of 1998, surpassing even Mackenzie's well-established STAR program. It is accessible to most investors with a minimum $1,000 investment.

New this year is First Canadian's "In-tuition," a registered education savings plan launched in May 1998. It offers portfolios of

First Canadian funds along with rebalancing designed for investors saving for their children's education.

First Canadian continues to be almost alone among mutual fund companies in giving a price break to large investors. BMO's declining management-fee schedule kicks in with a $50,000 investment in a fund. The two per cent fee that investors pay on First Canadian Growth would, for example, fall to 1.6 per cent, then 1.4 per cent, 1.2 per cent, 1.1 per cent, and finally, 1 per cent on amounts greater than $1 million. If performance in funds falls to single digits, as it inevitably will, this feature may strengthen returns for large portfolios.

Smart Funds 1999:

First Canadian Dividend Income.

Noteworthy Funds:

First Canadian Special Growth. When manager James Lawson jumped ship to Guardian, it meant automatic demotion for the fund.

First Canadian Equity Index. This well-established index fund has continued to show up many of its actively managed counterparts. It had better performance than the average Canadian equity fund for the one-, two-, three-, and five-year periods ended June 30, 1998, and with an MER that has dropped again this year to 1.2 per cent.

First Canadian Growth. This fund has been in either the first or second quartile for the last three years under Michael Stanley of Jones Heward Investment Management. The MER is 2.2 per cent, which is average for the category but higher than average for the no-load set.

First Canadian Far East Growth. In a difficult year for these regional funds whacked by the Asian flu, this fund performed better than the group average once again and holds a better-than-average track record for three years. Still, these region-specific funds are not for the faint of heart nor should they comprise more than a small slice of most portfolios.

First Canadian U.S. Value Fund. On the heels of the strong U.S. bull market, there is a certain appeal to value-style equity funds that shun high-priced stocks. This fund fits the bill with a low MER and a better-than-average 36.1 per cent return in the year ended June 30, 1998. Value funds often underperform growth-style funds in strong markets.

Availability:

Any Bank of Montreal branch across Canada, First Canadian Funds Call Centre, Nesbitt Burns, and InvestorLine Discount Brokerage Service.

7. BISSETT & ASSOCIATES

Strengths:	Low MERs, No-Load	
	Small-cap equities	
Weaknesses:	Minimum investment of $10,000 per fund	
RESPs?:	No	
Web Site:	www.bissett.com	**Toll Free:** (888)-247-7388

CANADIAN	Category	Rating	Fund Name	M.E.R.%	RRSP/Foreign
Money Market:		■	**Bissett Money Market Fund**	0.5	RRSP
Fixed Income:	Mixed-term	★	**Bissett Bond Fund**	0.75	RRSP
Equity:	Mid-Large Cap	★	**Bissett Canadian Equity Fund**	1.29	RRSP
	Small Cap	★	**Bissett Small Cap Fund**	1.82	RRSP
	Micro Cap	▲	Bissett Microcap Fund	2.5	RRSP
Tax Advantaged:	Dividend	★	**Bissett Dividend Income Fund**	1.4	Foreign
	Income Trust	▲	Bissett Income Trust Fund	1.25	RRSP
Mult-Asset:	Portfolio of Funds	★	**Bissett Retirement Fund**	0.37	

FOREIGN	Category	Rating	Fund Name	M.E.R.%	RRSP/Foreign
Global Equity:	All-global	★	**Bissett Multinational Growth Fund**	1.44	Foreign
	EAFE	■	Bissett International Equity Fund	2	Foreign
Regional Equity:	U.S.	■	Bissett American Equity Fund	1.48	Foreign

Bissett & Associates Investment Management Ltd., a low-MER no-load family with several strong-performing funds, was one of the big success stories of 1998—so much so, in fact, that the company went public in June 1998 in an oversubscribed issue of its stock. Ownership continues to be concentrated among top management, who held 70 per cent of shares when the stock began trading.

Alberta's largest pension and private investment manager is now available across Canada, with the exception of Quebec, and word about this low-key shop has spread quickly.

Calgary-based Bissett now manages more than $4 billion for various institutional pension plans and wealthy individuals. Assets in some of its retail funds tripled in one year. It's also the adviser for several external funds, such as Atlas Canadian Growth, and is one of three subadvisers to Canada Trust Special Equity Fund.

Like other low-MER no-load groups, Bissett rarely advertises, although founder David Bissett is frequently quoted in the business press. As a result, minimal marketing expenditures translate into reasonable MERs: 1.5 per cent for most of the equity funds (1.9 per cent for the small-cap and 2 per cent for the international equity fund), 0.75 per cent for the bond fund, and just 0.5 per cent for the money-market fund. There are no switching fees.

Bissett's emphasis remains on North American equities. Its Canadian content tends to centre on western Canada and, to some extent, the oil sector. That emphasis makes the group attractive to investors wishing to "Quebec-proof" their portfolios.

Several Bissett funds return as Smart Funds this year, based on the best possible combination: top performance and low MERs. Fred Pynn, portfolio manager of the Canadian Equity Fund, is profiled on page 27.

An EAFE (Europe, Australia and Far East) fund, Bissett International Equity Fund, which is advised by Jardine Fleming Investment Management of Hong Kong, is not for general distribution.

No manager changes have occurred in the past year, although a microcap fund was added in August 1997.

Smart Funds 1999:

Bissett Bond, Bissett Canadian Equity Fund, Bissett Small Cap Fund, Bissett Dividend Income Fund, Bissett Multi-National Growth Fund, Bissett Retirement Fund.

Noteworthy Funds:

Bissett Income Trust Fund. Created in June 1996, this fund provides an income stream by investing in royalty trust units. The income is taxed more efficiently than interest income.

Bissett Microcap Fund. Launched in August 1997, this fund is designed for aggressive investors looking for opportunities among small Canadian companies. It targets investments in companies with market capitalization of less than $75 million, and as low as $10 million. Bissett has said that it will cap the fund when it reaches $50 million in assets. Because the stock of smaller companies is less liquid, redemptions of the fund could be limited during a volatile market.

Availability:

Directly from the company at no load for investors in every province except Quebec. Also available through all brokerage firms and most planners. Brokers and discount brokers may charge a two per cent front load. Minimum investment remains $10,000 per fund.

8. BPI CAPITAL MANAGEMENT CORP. FRONT OR REAR

Strengths: Small-caps; income funds
New Legacy Seg Funds
Weaknesses: Load structure tends to be high
Equity fund MERs still high
RESPs?: No
Web Site: BPIFUNDS.COM **Toll Free:** 1-800-937-5146

CANADIAN	Category	Rating	Fund Name	M.E.R.%	RRSP/Foreign
Money Market:		■	BPI T-Bill Fund	0.65	RRSP
		■	BPI Legacy T-Bill Segregated	0.7	RRSP
Fixed Income:	Long-term	■	BPI Canadian Bond Fund	1.5	RRSP
		■	BPI Legacy Canadian Bond Seg	1.65	RRSP
	Corporate Bond	■	BPI Corporate Bond Fund	1.5	RRSP
Equity:	Mid-Large Cap	■	BPI Canadian Equity Value Fund	2.46	RRSP
		■	BPI Legacy Canadian Equity Value Seg	2.71	RRSP
	Mid-cap	▲	BPI Canadian Mid-Cap Fund	2.76	RRSP
		■	BPI Legacy Canadian Mid Cap Seg3.16	3.16	RRSP
	Small Cap	■	BPI Canadian Small Companies Fund	2.78	RRSP
	Resource	■	BPI Canadian Resource Fund Inc.	2.99	RRSP
	Other	■	BPI Canadian Opportunities RSP Fund	2.47	RRSP
		■	BPI Canadian Opportunities II Fund	1.94	RRSP
Tax Advantaged:	Dividend	★	**BPI Dividend Income Fund**	1	RRSP
		■	BPI Legacy Dividend Income Seg	1.15	RRSP
	Div/High yield	★	**BPI High Income Fund**	1.25	RRSP
		■	BPI Legacy High Income Seg	1.45	RRSP
	Labor-sponsored	■	VenGrowth	3.9	RRSP
	Labor/Manitoba	■	ENSIS Growth Fund	new	RRSP
Mult-Asset:	Balanced	■	BPI Canadian Balanced Fund	2.2	RRSP
	Div/Bal'd	▲	BPI Income & Growth Fund	2.5	RRSP
		■	BPI Legacy Income & Growth Seg	2.65	RRSP

FOREIGN	Category	Rating	Fund Name	M.E.R.%	RRSP/Foreign
Money Market:		■	BPI U.S. Money Market Fund	0.65	Foreign
Fixed Income:		■	BPI Global RSP Bond Fund	1.5	RRSP
Global Equity:	All-global	■	BPI Global Equity Value Fund	2.43	Foreign
		■	BPI Legacy Global Equity Value Seg	2.78	Foreign
	Small-cap	■	BPI Global Small Companies Fund	2.61	Foreign
	Specialty	■	BPI Global Opportunities Fund	2.56	Foreign
	EAFE	■	BPI International Equity Value Fund	2.47	Foreign
		■	BPI Legacy International Equity Value Seg	2.82	Foreign
Regional Equity:					
	U.S. Mid-large	■	BPI American Equity Value Fund	2.37	Foreign
		■	BPI Legacy Amer. Equity Value Seg	2.77	Foreign
	U.S. Small-cap	■	BPI American Small Companies Fund	2.63	Foreign
	Emerging Market	■	BPI Emerging Markets Fund	2.82	Foreign
	Far East	■	BPI Asia Pacific Fund	3.25	Foreign
Global Balanced:		■	BPI Global Balanced RSP Fund**	2.24	RRSP
		■	BPI Legacy Global Balanced RSP Seg	2.59	RRSP

BPI is something of an enigma. On the one hand it has super-aggressive small- and mid-cap equity funds, and runs two labor-sponsored venture capital funds and high-risk "shooter" hedge funds for high-net-worth investors; on the other it has a growing presence in conservative balanced and income-oriented funds and its new ultra-cautious BPI Legacy Segregated Funds. Investors who gravitate to the one camp are likely to be far different from those in the other.

BPI's strength used to be small-cap equity funds, both domestically and globally. For a long time, these carried hefty MERs, but were worth it.

Former Smart Funds, previously managed by New York-based Lazard Freres Asset Management, return after we watched them after the removal of Lazard; the reopened Canadian Small Companies Fund run internally by Steven Misener lost 23.98 per cent in the year ended June 30, 1998 even while the Nesbitt Burns Small Cap Index lost just 2.16 per cent.

BPI's varied global equity and American equity funds are now run in-house by the new subsidiary, BPI Global Asset Management LLP of Orlando, Florida.

BPI's two Canadian high-net-worth hedge funds, known as the Opportunities Funds, lost money in the year ended June 30, 1998, although the global Opportunities Fund had a strong 49.2 per cent return over the same period. The original—and now closed—BPI Canadian Opportunities RSP Fund had a spectacular debut and press to match, but its two-year compounded performance to June 30, 1998 is just negative 8.53 per cent. BPI Canadian Opportunities II was launched early in 1997 as a closed-end fund trading on the Toronto and Montreal stock exchanges (as BOI.UN). Managed by Misener, it uses aggressive techniques such as short-selling and options.

Still, there are places where BPI shines. Ironically, given BPI's aggressive tendencies, its strength appears increasingly to be in its more conservative domestic income and balanced funds.

In addition to launching five new funds in 1997, BPI also made a major initiative with its BPI Legacy Funds, launched in February 1998 with Transamerica Life Insurance Co. of Canada. These new Segregated Funds give squeamish investors the same maturity and death benefits of the life insurance industry's traditional seg funds. Eleven of the Legacy Funds invest in units of the underlying BPI Mutual Funds, as shown in the fund matrix. Seg funds can provide some creditor-proofing and BPI Legacy funds also guarantee the initial investment's principal after 10 years, in the event of a market meltdown. However, the price for this is higher MERs than the under-lying BPI mutual funds. The matrix shows estimated MERs on these new funds, based on BPI's estimate that the seg-fund versions of the equity funds will have additional MERs of 25 to 40 basis points, 15 to 20 basis points for income funds, and 5 basis points for the T-Bill Fund. These extra insurance fees are lower than several competitive new entrants.

Still, in the case of the Legacy versions of its income and balanced funds, not to mention the T-bill fund, that higher price may not be worth it since it's unlikely the underlying funds would fail to return capital on their own after that long. About the only reason for choosing these particular seg funds would be the possible creditor-proofing or death benefits.

On the new-fund front, BPI launched its BPI Canadian Mid-Cap Fund in mid-1997. This Steve Misener-run fund debuts as a Noteworthy Fund in this edition. So does the new BPI Income & Growth Fund, a balanced fund that intends to have a 65 per cent weighting in high-quality, dividend-paying stocks, with the balance in bonds. BPI also unveiled a corporate bond fund at the end of 1997, which is run by Ben Cheng.

BPI made some significant additions to its Canadian portfolio management team in 1997. Robert Lyon left I.A. Michael Investment Counsel—a great training ground for seeking value in stocks—to assist the managers of BPI's Canadian Resource Fund and Canadian Small Companies Fund. Andrew Waight, M.Sc., CFA, MBA, specializes in health care, bio-tech and high-tech and assists the managers of the new BPI Canadian Mid-Cap Fund and Canadian Small Companies. Ben Cheng was hired from Sceptre Investment Counsel to manage three bond funds and to assist with the BPI High Income Fund.

BPI Global has added four research analysts to that team, including Jon Sorensen, CFA, and John Hudson, MBA. In mid-1997, it launched an EAFE (Europe, Australia, Far East) fund, the BPI International Equity Value Fund, managed by Dan Jaworski.

In summary, unless you're a schizophrenic investor, aggressive types should be investigating only half of BPI's menu; conservative investors should be looking at the other half.

Smart Funds 1999:

BPI Dividend Income, BPI High Income.

Noteworthy Funds:

BPI Canadian Mid-Cap Fund. This new mid-cap Canadian equity fund focuses on medium-sized companies with market capitalization of $250 million to $1.25 billion. It's managed by veteran BPI small-cap ace Steven Misener and technology specialist Andrew Waight. The 2.76 per cent MER is higher than the category average but at least the mid-cap arena is one in which good managers have the potential to earn their fees.

BPI Income & Growth Fund. This conservative fund invests 65 per cent in dividend-paying Canadian stocks and 35 per cent in bonds. In its first year ended June 30, 1998 it gained a promising 40.3 per cent. The 2.5 per cent MER is a bit stiff when you factor in the bond component.

Availability:

Only through brokers and discount brokers and dealers. Note that the three Opportunities funds are subject to large minimum investment requirements under regulators' sophisticated investor guidelines, which vary by province.

9. CANADA LIFE ASSURANCE COMPANY   REAR

Strengths:	Guarantees associated with seg funds
	Some long performance history
Weaknesses:	Difficult to mix with other funds unless advisor is dual licensed
	Innovation appears on hold
RESPs?:	No
Web Site:	www.canadalife.com **Toll Free:** 1-888-CLA-1847

CANADIAN	Category	Rating	Fund Name	M.E.R.%	RRSP/Foreign
Money Market:		■	Canada Life Money Market Fund	1.25	RRSP
Fixed Income:		■	Canada Life Fixed Income Fund	2.00	RRSP
	Foreign currency	■	Canada Life International Bond Fund*	2.00	RRSP
Equity:	All-cap	▲	Canada Life Canadian Equity Fund	2.25	RRSP
Tax Advantaged:	Dividend	■	Canada Life Enhanced Dividend Fund	2.00	RRSP
Mult-Asset:	Balanced	■	Canada Life Managed Fund	2.25	RRSP

FOREIGN	Category	Rating	Fund Name	M.E.R.%	RRSP/Foreign
Global Equity:		▲	Canada Life U.S. & International Equity Fund	2.40	Foreign
	Europe	■	Canada Life European Equity Fund	2.40	Foreign
	Far East	■	Canada Life Asia Pacific Fund	2.40	Foreign

* categorized a Canadian fund because it invests in Canadian bonds issued in foreign currencies..

This is Canada Life's first appearance in *Smart Funds*, reflecting our increased commitment to covering the better life insurance "segregated" fund groups.

Canada Life's history extends further back than Confederation. The company was founded in 1847 and incorporated in 1849 in the province of Upper Canada. Today it sells insurance products and services in every province and territory in Canada and has customers in the United States, Britain, and Ireland.

This group sells a family of nine segregated funds with about $3.5 billion in assets in mid-1998. Segregated funds are similar in nature to mutual funds but are managed by insurance companies and sold only by those with life licences. The primary difference between the two products is that "seg funds," as they're called, can offer investors a guarantee of their initial principal, usually between 75 and 100 per cent of the amount of the investment. Those guarantees are usually extended over 10 years. Another advantage is that seg funds are inaccessible to creditors in the event of a bankruptcy; therefore they can hold some appeal to small business owners. Mutual funds, which are regulated under the Securities Act, are not permitted to extend those guarantees, unless they are offered in conjunction with an insurance company, as is the case with Manulife's GIFs.

The Canada Life funds represent most of the common mutual fund categories but offer few specialty funds other than an Asia Pacific Fund.

The Canadian Equity Fund has a longer history than all but a handful of Canadian mutual funds. It was the company's first segregated fund, established in 1969. Over 15 years to the end of calendar 1997, it has returned an average 11.5 per cent each year with lower than average volatility over the last 10 years.

The Canada Life International Bond Fund is fully RRSP-eligible by investing in Canadian bonds denominated in foreign currencies, as well as foreign bonds.

The MERs on these funds are in line with mutual funds. For example, the Canadian Equity Fund carries an MER of 2.25 per cent compared with an average 2.2 per cent for the category. The U.S. and International Equity Funds are also competitive with an annual 2.4 per cent deducted for expenses, which is on par with the group average.

All Canada Life funds are managed by Toronto-based INDAGO Capital Management Inc. (formerly Canada Life Investment Management), owned 50 per cent by Canada Life and 50 per cent by INDAGO's partners. It also manages outside of Canada Life, for a total of $6 billion.

Smart Funds 1999:

None.

Noteworthy Funds:

Canada Life Canadian Equity. Overperformance over a long history, coupled with low volatility and an average MER make this a possible core fund. It may appeal to investors who want access to Canadian equities, but sleep better knowing much of their principal is guaranteed.

Canada Life U.S. and **International Equity Fund.** The fund was established in 1984 and has been a top-quartile performer over the two-, three-, five-, and 10-year periods ended June 30, 1998. It also beat the average over one year. Its MER is about average.

Availability:

Across Canada through agents with a life insurance licence. A minimum $1,000 initial investment per fund is required.

10. CANADA TRUST MUTUAL FUNDS   NO LOAD

Strengths:	100% RRSP-eligible global funds
	Index funds, Investment Planner Plus Asset Allocation tool
Weaknesses:	In-house equity management
RESPs?:	No
Web Site:	www.canadatrust.com **Toll Free:** 1-800-386-3757

CANADIAN	Category	Rating	Fund Name	M.E.R.%	RRSP/Foreign
Money Market:		■	Canada Trust Money Market Fund	0.98	RRSP
		■	Canada Trust Premium Money Market Fund	0.57	RRSP
Fixed Income:	Long-term	■	Canada Trust Bond Fund	1.35	RRSP
		▲	Canada Trust Canadian Bond Index Fund	0.83	RRSP
	Short-term	■	Canada Trust Short Term Bond	1.38	RRSP
	Mortgage	■	Canada Trust Mortgage Fund	1.59	RRSP
Equity:	Mid-Large Cap	■	Canada Trust Stock Fund	1.87	RRSP
		■	Canada Trust Canadian Equity Index Fund	0.75	RRSP
	Small Cap	▲	Canada Trust Special Equity Fund	2.15	RRSP
Tax Advantaged:	Dividend	■	Canada Trust Dividend Income Fund	1.90	RRSP
	Multi-Asset	■	Canada Trust Monthly Income Fund	new	RRSP
Mult-Asset:	Balanced	■	Canada Trust Balanced Fund	2.13	RRSP
		▲	Canada Trust RIF Balanced Fund	1.69	RRIF

FOREIGN	Category	Rating	Fund Name	M.E.R.%	RRSP/Foreign
Fixed Income:		■	Canada Trust International Bond Fund	2.07	RRSP
	High-yield	■	Canada Trust High-Yield Income Fund	new	Foreign
Global Equity:	All-global	▲	Canada Trust Global Growth Fund	2.05	RRSP
		■	Canada Trust International Equity Index Fund	0.53	Foreign

	EAFE	■	Canada Trust International Equity Fund	2.62	Foreign
Regional Equity:	U.S.	■	Canada Trust U.S. Equity Fund	2.34	Foreign
	U.S.	■	Canada Trust U.S. Equity Index Fund	0.85	Foreign
		▲	Canada Trust AmeriGrowth Fund	1.39	RRSP
	NAFTA/N.Am.	■	Canada Trust North American Fund	1.85	Foreign
	Emerging Market	■	Canada Trust Emerging Markets Fund	3.22	Foreign
	Far East	■	Canada Trust AsiaGrowth Fund	2.48	RRSP
	Europe	■	Canada Trust EuroGrowth Fund	2.20	RRSP
Mult-Asset:	Global	▲	Canada Trust Global Asset Allocation Fund	new	RRSP
	Global	▲	Canada Trust Balanced Index Fund	new	RRSP

Canada Trust Mutual Funds continues to beef up its fund family and delegate a portion of its investment management to regional experts. It has added five new funds in the last year and now sells 27 no-load funds through its branch network, including several fully RRSP-eligible global and regional funds.

Canada Trust continues its emphasis on index products, an arena it pursued aggressively in 1997. A new U.S. Equity Index Fund and Balanced Index Fund brings the total to five. The balanced fund invests in the holdings of the other four index funds and the Canada Trust Money Market Fund. The asset mix is not based on a particular index but is adjusted periodically within certain ranges of target weightings. Ideally it will hold about 50 per cent fixed-income securities and 50 per cent equities. It may also buy foreign securities, up to 20 per cent.

Index funds are gaining in popularity in Canada, following on the heels of the United States. One of the attractions is that their MERs are lower than actively managed portfolios.

Also new in the last year are the Canada Trust Monthly Income Fund and Canada Trust High Yield Income Fund. The latter is only eligible for the foreign-content portion of RRSPs. Monthly Income is designed for taxable portfolios, investing in a variety of income-producing securities—not just interest-bearing instruments taxed at the highest rate. High Yield Income also provides income, as the name suggests, but also aims to appreciate its assets.

Besides the index products, Canada Trust Mutual Funds remains one of the leading no-load groups to offer ways of beating the RRSP/RRIF 20 per cent foreign-content limit. It has five 100 per cent RRSP-eligible global funds: the former Smart Fund, AmeriGrowth, plus Asia-Growth, EuroGrowth funds, and Global Growth. They are managed by State Street Global Advisors Ltd., which also manages the index funds.

The newest product is Canada Trust Global Asset Allocation Fund, which was launched in January 1998. It gives investors access to a combination of stocks, bonds, and cash in a fully RRSP-eligible portfolio.

As with most of the other banks, Canada Trust has a program to help simplify the process of choosing among so many funds. Its Investment Planner Plus program recommends an appropriate mix of CT funds based on a questionnaire filled out by the investor. This program is comparable to BMO's Matchmaker. Over $2 billion is currently invested in the IPP program.

Smart Funds 1999:

None.

Noteworthy Funds:

Canada Trust Special Equity Fund. Canada Trust uses a multi-manager approach for this aggressive small- to mid-cap Canadian equity fund. The three external managers are Guardian Capital and Bissett Associates for Canadian mid- and small-cap stocks, and Warburg Pincus for U.S. equities returned 4.79 per cent over one year to June 30, 1998. Its MER is lower than average.

Canada Trust AmeriGrowth Fund. Former Smart Fund gets nudged out by the new CIBC RRSP fund, which has an MER 50 basis points lower.

Canada Trust Global Asset Allocation Fund. New 100 per cent RRSP-eligible fund debuts as a noteworthy fund, based on the reputation of its multi-manager team: Mellon Capital, J.P. Morgan, and Canada Trust Investment Management.

Canada Trust GlobalGrowth. Canada Trust has long experience with derivative-based index funds that beat foreign content. Its earlier funds focused on the United States, Asia, and Europe; this fund does all three in one, arguably the best approach for investors who don't want to make regional decisions themselves.

Canada Trust Canadian Bond Index Fund. This new entry is one of the few bond index funds available in Canada. If anything, the argument for indexing is more powerful in bond funds than for equities.

Canada Trust Balanced Index Fund. This unusual fund combines Canada Trust's four other index funds with the manager having some discretion over asset allocation. Because it is a new fund, the MER is not yet available, but the maximum management fee of 0.80 per cent suggests that, like most index funds, this will be a relative bargain.

Canada Trust RIF Balanced Fund. This product provides retirees some growth to beat inflation, as well as spinning off enough income to meet the government's yearly withdrawal schedules on RRIFs.

Availability:

Sold direct through Canada Trust branches and EasyLine and CT Securities' One Stop Fund Solutions. Not available in the Northwest Territories. Some brokers may sell on request.

11. CENTREPOST MUTUAL FUNDS NO LOAD

Strengths:	Low MERs
	Conservative core fund approach
Weaknesses:	Visibility
	Few aggressive foreign funds
RESPs?:	No
Web Site:	www.centrepost.com

Toll Free: 1-800-268-9597

CANADIAN	Category	Rating	Fund Name	M.E.R.%	RRSP/Foreign
Money Market:	Short Term	■	CentrePost Short Term	0.75	RRSP
Fixed Income:	Medium Term	■	CentrePost Bond	1.00	RRSP
Equity:	Mid to Large Cap	▲	CentrePost Canadian	1.00	RRSP
Mult-Asset:	Balanced	▲	CentrePost Balanced	1.00	RRSP

FOREIGN	Category	Rating	Fund Name	M.E.R.%	RRSP/Foreign
Global Equity:					
	Mid to Large Cap	■	CentrePost Foreign	1.75	Foreign

The name CentrePost is new to the public and to *Smart Funds*, but the firm behind it is not. Formerly the OHA Group of Funds, its roots go back to 1974, when it was a division of the Ontario Hospital Association. CentrePost managed the Hospitals of Ontario Pension Plan, and over the years, added more than 100 health-care foundations and institutions as clients.

In early 1997, OHA Investment Management Ltd. became independent and soon changed its fund family name to CentrePost, which is supposed to evoke the image of a solid, core, balanced approach to investments.

That's about what you'll get with this family, along with some aggressively low management expense ratios. Like several other "Smart" no-load outfits in this book, you may not hear the CentrePost name advertised much, which allows it to keep its marketing costs down.

The MERs on its Canadian Equity Fund and Balanced Fund are a stingy 1 per cent, about 50 per cent below the category averages. The MERs of its three other funds are 20 to 30 per cent below their peer groups.

Unlike the MD Management Funds, however, the CentrePost funds are not restricted to the health-care community. Any Ontario investor can buy them directly, or, if you live in any province except Quebec, they can be purchased through brokers and discount brokers and dealers.

It's interesting that CentrePost management invokes the fund family approach to mutual funds in its own industry positioning statement. Naturally, it suggests that its own funds serve for the 50 per cent of a portfolio that should be conservative, steady, and secure—with low MERs. Then it suggests that investors can look outside the CentrePost family for specialty funds and higher-risk vehicles.

Since many large-cap equity funds perform like the indexes, why pay 2 per cent plus? These funds are priced like passively managed index funds and should perform about the same in bull markets. In down markets, the investor will take comfort that a human manager is around to make defensive adjustments.

Smart Funds 1999:

None.

Noteworthy Funds:

CentrePost Canadian Equity. If you want large-cap Canada with a low (1 per cent) MER, this fund is an alternative to comparably priced index funds. Don't expect manager Rick Hutcheon to shoot out the lights–the fund returned just 2.65 per cent to June 30, 1998 when the index was 16.22 per cent. The Fund has a 13.43 per cent compounded return over three years. Predictable portfolio includes most of the big banks, BCE, and the usual mines and pipelines.

CentrePost Balanced Fund. If you're a CentrePost-style investor (conservative, balanced, and fee-conscious) you may as well be consistent and load up on its core Canadian balanced fund. The 1 per cent MER is well below the industry average of 1.79 per cent. The Fund had a modest 4.27 per cent return to June 30, 1998 and the five-year CAGR is 8.45 per cent, a figure below what most people would expect. Asset mix was 46 per cent Canadian equities, 48 per cent Canadian bonds, and 6 per cent cash.

Availability:

Directly by Ontario residents on a no-load basis. Also available through brokers and discount brokers and dealers in all provinces but Quebec and the Territories, with sales charges negotiable. $1,000 minimum investment.

12. CIBC SECURITIES INC. NO LOAD

Strengths:	Eight 90 bps index funds
	New high-net-worth products
Weaknesses:	Quebec-based management by T.A.L.
	Hard to choose from 34 funds
RESPs?:	No
Web Site:	www.cibc.com/MutualFunds **Toll Free:** 1-800-465-3863

CANADIAN	Category	Rating	Fund Name	M.E.R.%	RRSP/Foreign
Money Market:		■	CIBC Canadian T-Bill Fund	0.99	RRSP
		■	CIBC Premium Canadian T-Bill Fund	0.55	RRSP
		■	CIBC Money Market Fund	0.99	RRSP
Fixed Income:	Index/Short-term	■	CIBC Canadian Short-term Bond Fund	0.9	RRSP
	Mortgage	▲	CIBC Mortgage Fund	1.69	RRSP
	Index/Long-term	■	CIBC Canadian Bond Index Fund	0.9	RRSP
	Long-term	■	CIBC Canadian Bond Fund	1.55	RRSP
Equity:	Index/Large-cap	▲	CIBC Canadian Index Fund	0.9	RRSP
	Mid-Large Cap	■	CIBC Canadian Equity Fund	2.2	RRSP
	Small Cap	■	CIBC Capital Appreciation Fund	2.4	RRSP
Sector Equity:	Financial	▲	CIBC Financial Companies Fund	2.45	RRSP
	Gold/precious metal	■	CIBC Precious Metals Fund	2.2	RRSP
	Resource	■	CIBC Canadian Resources Fund	2.3	RRSP
	Energy	▲	CIBC Energy Fund	2.3	RRSP
	Real estate	■	CIBC Canadian Real Estate Fund	2.25	RRSP
Tax Advantaged:	Dividend	■	CIBC Dividend Fund	1.88	RRSP
Mult-Asset:	Balanced	■	CIBC Balanced Fund	2.24	RRSP

FOREIGN	Category	Rating	Fund Name	M.E.R.%	RRSP/Foreign
Money Market:		■	CIBC U.S. Dollar Money Market Fund	1.08	RRSP
Fixed Income:	Index/All-global	■	CIBC Global Bond Index Fund	0.9	RRSP
	All-global	■	CIBC Global Bond Fund	1.95	RRSP
Global Equity:	All-global	■	CIBC Global Equity Fund	2.5	Foreign
	Index/All-global	■	CIBC International Index Fund	0.9	Foreign
	Index/All-global	■	CIBC International Index RRSP Fund	0.9	RRSP
	Small-cap	■	CIBC International Small Companies Fund	2.8	Foreign
	Technology	▲	CIBC Global Technology Fund	2.6	Foreign
Regional Equity:					
	Index/US large-cap	★	**CIBC U.S. Index RRSP Fund**	0.9	RRSP
	U.S. Mid-Large-cap	▲	CIBC U.S. Equity Fund	0.9	Foreign
	U.S. Small-cap	■	CIBC U.S. Small Companies Fund	2.45	Foreign
	Specialty	★	**CIBC North American Demographics Fund**	2.5	Foreign
	Latin American	■	CIBC Latin American Fund	2.7	Foreign
	Emerging Market	■	CIBC Emerging Economies Fund	2.7	Foreign
	Far East	■	CIBC Far East Prosperity Fund	2.69	Foreign
	Japan	■	CIBC Japanese Equity Fund	2.5	Foreign
	Europe	■	CIBC European Equity Fund	2.5	Foreign

Over the last year, CIBC Securities Inc. has been blasting away on all fronts. Newly appointed president and CEO Ted Cadsby has extended the basic no-load family to 34 funds, and led all banks in introducing or revamping eight passively managed index funds with MERs. Add to that its third-party funds available through its CIBC Choices "junior wrap" program and the innovative wealth management services of CIBC Trust, and there's no lack of vision at the helm.

A strong possibility is a combined fund family of CIBC and TD GreenLine, which would occur if the two bank parent companies receive approval for their proposed blockbuster merger. Combined, investors could choose between excellent managed global equity funds from TD, low-fee passive index investing from both CIBC and TD, and a growing handful of sector funds from both banks. There would, of course, be much fund consolidation since there is duplication, for example, with the science and technology funds of both families.

All eight CIBC index funds now have MERs of 0.9 per cent—a far sight better than active funds' MERs and among the most aggressive of index funds in Canada. TD GreenLine has projected that its North American index funds will have MERs of 0.8 per cent and international index funds of 0.9 per cent. CIBC's Cadsby says a further reduction of 10 basis points in CIBC's index fund MERs is likely as assets grow.

What's clear is that with either family, the services of a qualified investment adviser will be necessary to help investors create well-structured fund portfolios. At CIBC, for example, you need $50,000 in assets to have a CIBC "investment specialist."

Investors and their advisers must now factor in the tradeoffs of actively managed funds and their associated high costs, and of low-cost passive management. CIBC believes that indexing pays off in certain areas, such as the United States, and that active management is needed in other places, perhaps small-caps or in industry sectors.

In this context, it's interesting to note that CIBC has abandoned active management altogether on its U.S. Equity Fund, replacing it with a fund that matches the Wilshire 5000 index (a broad index of large- and small-cap stocks). It has done a similar thing with its CIBC Canadian Short-Term Bond Fund, which matches the Scotia Capital Markets Short-Term Bond Index.

CIBC still offers actively managed funds for those who prefer it, both in-house and in its third-party offerings. Canadian investment adviser TAL Investment Counsel Ltd. has been tinkering with its Canadian equity team, now led by Denis Ouellet. Globally, CIBC Emerging Economies and Latin American Fund now use Nicholas Applegate as subadviser; Kevin Doyle is the new leader of the European Equity Fund; and Wellington Investment Management now manages CIBC U.S. Small Companies and the U.S. portion of CIBC Balanced Fund. Morguard Investment Management advises the real estate fund; Pictet Investment Management manages the international small companies fund; and Mellon Capital Management advises the CIBC U.S. Equity Fund.

CIBC Trust's Professional Investment Management Services division has developed a suite of discretionary investment management services for investors with $100,000 to $1 million in combined household investable assets.

The first service was unveiled in 1996: PPS, or Personal Portfolio Services, which are actively managed private pooled funds advised by TAL. On the first $250,000, annual fees are 2 per cent for the conservative portfolios, moving up to 2.25 per cent for the most aggressive versions. After the first $250,000 and up to $1 million, the annual fee drops to 0.75 per cent. Fees on income portfolios are lower.

In February 1998, CIBC Trust announced a new investment management service targeted to baby-boom investors that combines low-cost passive "indexing" style investing with the same discretionary approach to asset allocation. Called Index Portfolio Services (IPS), the CIBC brings together index investing and discretionary investment management. Annual fees are 1.5 per cent on the first $250,000—about 0.5 per cent cheaper than the actively managed pooled funds. The IPS fees drop to 0.75 per cent for the next $750,000.

CIBC also addresses the low end of the mass mutual fund market with its CIBC Choices, which chooses third-party mutual funds selected by author Gordon Pape, with performance monitored by TAL and pension consultants William M. Mercer Ltd. Choices requires only a $25,000 minimum investment. It is costlier than the CIBC Trust services or CIBC's no-load index funds because an annual management fee is imposed above the management fees of the underlying funds.

Add it all up and CIBC provides an interesting low-cost entry level point for cost-conscious beginning investors, as well as a growth path for affluent investors who want to leave such high-level decisions as asset allocation and fund selection to professionals.

If and when CIBC becomes CIBC-TD, this bank no-load complex will become a formidable alternative to the well-known load fund companies.

Smart Funds 1999:

CIBC U.S. Index RRSP Fund, CIBC North American Demographics Fund.

Noteworthy Funds:

CIBC Canadian Index Fund. If you can't beat the TSE index with a manager, then why not match it through indexing and cut costs to a barebones 0.9 per cent? There's something to be said for using an index fund for your core Canadian large-cap portfolio and using managed funds for specialties such as resources or small-cap.

CIBC U.S. Equity Fund. This new index fund replaces the former actively managed version, which had an MER of 2.3 per cent, with a 0.9 per cent-MER passively managed fund that tracks the Wilshire 5000. If there is any caveat, it's that index funds do not protect investors from market downturns as much as actively managed or balanced funds do. This fund uses up the 20 per cent RRSP foreign-content room; there is a 100 per cent RRSP-eligible U.S. equity fund.

CIBC Global Technology. CIBC saw a good thing when rival TD cleaned up with the GreenLine Science & Technology Fund and launched its own version in November 1995. Run by TAL's Stephen Kahn, the fund returned 32 per cent for the year ended June 30, 1998, largely on the back of U.S. technology stocks. Fund has been seeking to minimize indirect Asian exposure.

CIBC Mortgage Fund. A Smart Fund in the 1998 edition, but returned only 3.06 per cent for the year ended June 30, 1998. With interest rates poised to start rising, you don't want to be overcommitted to this asset class. MER of 1.69 per cent really eats away at the return.

CIBC Energy. Paul Wong's geology background couldn't help this fund as it suffered a negative 17 per cent return for the year ended June 30, 1998. Focus on oil and gas may be too narrow.

CIBC Financial Companies Fund. New fund uses the same idea as AIC's hugely successful Advantage Fund, and the portfolio is similar: holdings in other mutual fund companies and banks. Such funds are sector funds and normally shouldn't represent more than a 5 or 10 per cent position in your total portfolio. The fund company stocks are relatively illiquid and in a major stock correction would fall back more than more diversified holdings.

Availability:

CIBC branches across Canada. Also through some brokers and discount brokers and dealers, including CIBC Wood Gundy and CIBC Investor's Edge Discount Brokerage. CIBC's "At Your Request Direct Trading" service allows investors to switch funds by calling the 1-800 number shown in the matrix.

13. C.I. MUTUAL FUNDS

FRONT OR REAR

Strengths:	New Segregated Funds
	BEA & Associates
Weaknesses:	Too many funds to choose from
	MERs on the high side
RESPs?:	No
Web Site:	www.cifunds.com

Toll Free: 1-800-268-9374

CANADIAN	Category	Rating	Fund Name	M.E.R.%	RRSP/Foreign
Money Market:		■	C.I. Money Market Fund	0.75	RRSP
		■	C.I. Money Market Seg Fund	1.5	RRSP
		■	C.I. Sector Short Term	0.05	Foreign
Fixed Income:	Long-term	▲	C.I. Canadian Bond Fund	1.65	RRSP
Equity:	Small Cap	▲	Harbour Explorer Fund	2.33	RRSP
		■	Harbour Sector Explorer	2.33	Foreign
	Mid-Large Cap	■	C.I. Canadian Growth Fund	2.35	RRSP
		■	C.I. Sector Canadian	2.4	Foreign
		★	**Harbour Fund**	2.33	RRSP
		■	Harbour Sector	2.33	Foreign
		■	C.I. Harbour Seg Fund	3.05	RRSP
	Labor-sponsored	■	C.I. Covington Fund	4.4	RRSP
Mult-Asset:	Balanced	■	C.I. Canadian Balanced Fund	2.3	RRSP
		■	Harbour Growth & Income	2.33	RRSP
		■	C.I. Harbour Growth & Income Seg Fund	2.97	RRSP
	Dividend/Bonds	■	C.I. Canadian Income Fund	1.82	RRSP

FOREIGN	Category	Rating	Fund Name	M.E.R.%	RRSP/Foreign
Money Market:		■	C.I. U.S. Money Market Fund	0.51	Foreign
Fixed Income:		■	C.I. World Bond Fund	2.05	Foreign
		■	C.I. New World Income Fund	2.15	Foreign
		■	C.I. Global Bond RSP	2.05	RRSP
Global Equity:	All-global	■	C.I. Global Fund	2.45	Foreign
		■	C.I. Sector Global	2.5	Foreign
		■	C.I. Global Equity RSP	2.43	RRSP
		■	C.I. Global Seg Fund	3.3	Foreign
		▲	Hansberger Value Fund	2.44	Foreign
		■	C.I. Sector Hansberger Value	2.49	Foreign
		■	C.I. Hansberger Value Seg Fund	3.3	Foreign
	Multi-asset	★	**C.I. International Balanced RSP**	2.4	RRSP
		■	C.I. International Balanced	2.4	Foreign
	EAFE	▲	Hansberger International Fund	2.44	Foreign
		■	C.I. Sector Hansberger International	2.49	Foreign
	Small-cap	■	Hansberger Global Small Cap Fund	2.67	Foreign
		■	C.I. Sector Hansberger Global Small Cap	2.72	Foreign
	Specialty	▲	C.I. Sector Health Sciences	2.42	Foreign
		▲	C.I. Sector Financial Services	2.42	Foreign
		■	C.I. Sector Resource	2.42	Foreign
		■	C.I. Sector Technology	2.42	Foreign
		▲	C.I. Sector Telecommunications	2.42	Foreign
		■	C.I. Sector Global Consumer Products	2.42	Foreign
Regional Equity:	U.S.	▲	C.I. American Fund	2.38	Foreign
		■	C.I. Sector American	2.43	Foreign

	■ C.I. American Seg Fund	3.16	Foreign
	▲ C.I. American RSP Fund	2.35	RRSP
Latin American	■ C.I. Latin American	2.75	Foreign
	■ C.I. Sector Latin American	2.8	Foreign
Emerging Market	■ C.I. Emerging Markets	2.71	Foreign
	■ C.I. Sector Emerging Markets	2.76	Foreign
	■ Hansberger Developing Markets	2.73	Foreign
	■ C.I. Sector Hansberger Developing Markets	2.78	Foreign
Far East	▲ C.I. Pacific Fund	2.5	Foreign
	■ C.I. Sector Pacific	2.55	Foreign
	■ Hansberger Asian	2.75	Foreign
	■ C.I. Sector Hansberger Asian	2.8	Foreign
Europe	▲ Hansberger European	2.43	Foreign
	■ C.I. Sector Hansberger European	2.48	Foreign

This monster fund family now includes 59 different funds as of mid-year 1998. Examining the complex fund matrix would be an excellent introductory lesson in mutual fund marketing for a young person trying to break into the business.

In July, C.I. announced the introduction of yet another fund, the C.I. Global Boomernomics Fund. The fund, which will emulate CIBC's comparable fund, will invest in companies around the world that are likely to benefit from demographic trends. Highly regarded strategist Bill Sterling will be the lead manager of the fund. His co-manager, Stephen Waite, also co-authored the recently published book *Boomernomics* (Random House).

Six different fund families now exist at C.I., depending on how you count them, with various permutations and combinations. If you can keep track of all these funds and their names, there is a logical consistency to the line-up, but average investors will need the services of a financial adviser to get it all straight.

The biggest innovation that C.I. made in the past year was its entry into the segregated fund business, through its C.I. Segregated Funds, launched in concert with Toronto Mutual Life Insurance Company. Seg funds have long been the life insurance industry's equivalents of mutual funds, but with certain return-of-principal guarantees in the event of death or maturity. The other benefits are potential creditor protection and no probate fees.

However, the problem in C.I.'s case is that the investor pays a hefty 80 or 90 basis point (0.8 to 0.9 per cent) annual premium to receive these benefits. That's on top of fairly hefty management expense ratios (MERs) in the first place, putting most of the new seg funds past the 3 per cent MER mark.

It's not surprising that a marketing-driven fund company such as C.I. has above-average MERs. Still, C.I. always manages to have several funds that justify those MERs in any given year. For example, four of its six specialized global sector funds had spectacular performance numbers for the year ended June 30, 1998: ranging from 17 per cent for the 1998 Smart Fund—C.I. Sector Health Sciences—to 71 per cent for C.I. Sector Global Telecommunications.

So how do you assemble a coherent family of C.I. funds from this surfeit of choices? The fund family approach used throughout this book should help you focus on these families within a family. A global value-oriented investor might gravitate to the Hansberger funds, managed by former Templeton boss Thomas Hansberger, who has hired away a few Templeton researchers. The only problem here is that the original Templeton funds have noticeably lower MERs, which may tilt some investors to the real McCoy (Templeton).

If you're a top-down active investor with strong opinions about investing, then C.I.'s global industry funds may appeal to you. Perhaps you've tried your hand at stock-picking and are adept at picking industries but have been burned with individual securities. Like Fidelity and GT Global, C.I. now lets you bet on technology, health sciences, telecommunications, natural resources, and even the financial services industry itself. The funds are managed by BEA Associates of New York, which manages several of the older C.I. Funds.

If you're a top-down global investor with a feel for which regions of the world will boom, then C.I.'s original global and regional funds or the Hansberger regional funds may appeal. C.I. has added two new managers: Krishnamurthy (Nandu) Narayanan on the Emerging Markets Fund and Hemant Shah on C.I. Global Health Sciences Sector Shares.

If you're a frequent switcher with a large taxable portfolio, the Sector Fund approach minimizes the capital gains taxes incurred by switching. There are now 22 "classes" (essentially funds) within the C.I. Sector umbrella, including the C.I. as well as Hansberger regional funds, the theme funds (Global Industry Shares), and some of the Monarch and Harbour funds.

Harbour Fund manager Gerry Coleman is now a fixture at C.I. In 1997, he established C.I. Capital Management. In its first year, the Harbour Funds attracted $1 billion in assets. In addition to the flagship Harbour Fund, C.I. has added an asset-allocation fund, Harbour Growth & Income, and a small-cap fund, Harbour Explorer.

In 1998 Jonathan Baird departed as manager of the Monarch Funds. They are being merged into other similar C.I. funds.

Smart Funds 1999:

C.I. Harbour Fund, C.I. International Balanced RSP.

Noteworthy Funds:

Hansberger Value Fund. This Templeton wannabe disappointed investors and has been dropped from Smart Fund status.

C.I. Sector Global Health Sciences. Dropped as we reduced the number of specialty funds and went with the longer track record of AIM Global Health Sciences.

Harbour Explorer Fund. If you like the Harbour Fund philosophy of owning just 30 to 40 low-volatility stocks and low portfolio turnover, this new small-cap version of Harbour Fund could merit some of your growth dollars. Manager Stephen Jenkins will maximize the foreign content with U.S. small to mid caps.

C.I. Pacific. While more broadly diversified than most Asian funds, this prematurely reinstated Smart Fund is back to Noteworthy status after losing 49 per cent in the year ended June 30, 1998. That was better than the 60 per cent loss of Hansberger Asian Fund, however.

Hansberger International Fund. Similar to Hansberger Value but it excludes North America, making a good complement to C.I. American.

Hansberger European. Most Europe funds have thrived the past year, but this one-year-old Hansberger entry returned only 25 per cent for the year ended June 30, 1998.

C.I. Sector Telecommunications. This fund got off to the fastest start of the several new C.I. sector funds, with a 71 per cent return in the year ended June 30, 1998.

C.I. Sector Financial Services. Now two years old, this sector fund has a portfolio that looks like AIC Advantage and offers comparable performance: 40 per cent for the year ended June 30, 1998.

C.I. American, C.I. American RSP. The 20 per cent portion of the 100 per cent RRSP-eligible version of the fund that can be invested directly in U.S. stocks mirrors the successful C.I. American Fund, also run by Priest. The other 80 per cent, according to Canadian RRSP/RRIF foreign-content laws, will invest in stock index futures and customized basket forwards. Fund's 27.9 per cent return for the year ended June 30, 1998 slightly beat C.I. American's 24.7 per cent for the same period. There is no MER difference between the two.

C.I. Canadian Bond. Demoted along with many other bond funds in this edition, partly because the MER is high.

Availability:

Through brokers and discount brokers and dealers.

14. CLARINGTON CAPITAL MANAGEMENT INC. FRONT OR REAR

Strengths:	Broker loyalty to Terry Stone
	Small-cap specialty funds
Weaknesses:	High expense ratios
	No 100% RRSP-eligible global equity funds
RESPs?:	No
Web Site:	None **Toll Free:** 1-888-860-9888

CANADIAN	Category	Rating	Fund Name	M.E.R.%	RRSP/Foreign
Money Market:		■	Clarington Money Market Fund	0.75	RRSP
Fixed Income:		■	Clarington Canadian Income Fund	2.09	RRSP
Equity:	Mid-Large Cap	■	Clarington Canadian Equity Fund	2.75	RRSP
	Small Cap	■	Clarington Canadian Small Cap Fund	2.75	RRSP
	Micro Cap	■	Clarington Canadian Micro Cap	2.95	RRSP
Mult-Asset:	Balanced	▲	Clarington Canadian Balanced Fund	2.75	RRSP

FOREIGN	Category	Rating	Fund Name	M.E.R.%	RRSP/Foreign
Global Equity:	Small Cap	■	Clarington Global Opportunities Fund	2.95	Foreign
	Technology	★	Clarington Global Communications Fund	2.95	Foreign
Regional Equity:					
	U.S. mixed cap	▲	Clarington US Equity Fund	2.95	Foreign
	U.S. small cap	■	Clarington US Smaller Company Growth Fund	2.95	Foreign
	Far East	■	Clarington Asia Pacific Fund	2.95	Foreign

Clarington Capital added two new specialty funds to its small family in the past year and continues its strategy of hiring external managers with a specific expertise. In total, five management firms in different regions of North America now manage the 11 Clarington funds.

Founder Terry Stone is well known in the fund industry. The former president of Bolton Tremblay Funds Inc. continues to carve out a niche for this smaller fund company in a sea of big players.

The use of subadvisers has worked well in the past for companies such as C.I. Mutual Funds, Global Strategy, and many others. As with those families, Clarington investors get a broad cross-section of money managers who can be replaced occasionally if they fail to perform. The downside, however, is the slightly higher management expense ratios that generally accompany external advisory services. Clarington's higher than average MERs did not budge last year.

The new Clarington Canadian Micro-Cap Fund is one of only a handful in this category that targets early-stage companies with lots of growth potential. The fund is managed by QVGD Investors Inc. of Calgary, which also manages Clarington's Canadian Small Cap Fund. QVGD was started by Leigh Pullen, former manager of the Mawer New Canada Fund. Its focus is on companies with a market capitalization of less than $400 million.

All other Canadian funds continue to be managed by Seamark Asset Management of Halifax. Seamark is headed by Peter Marshall, another Bolton Tremblay alumnus who spent some of his 13 years working with Trimark co-founder Robert Krembil. Seamark is known for combining competitive performance with low volatility.

The other new addition is the Clarington Asia Pacific Fund. The timing was not ideal for this fund, launched in September 1997, early on in the Asian storm. Not surprisingly the fund had attracted only about $4.6 million by June 30, 1998. It is managed by Montgomery Asset Management of San Francisco, which also manages the Clarington Global Communications Fund. Global Communications is a Smart Fund again in 1999, after returning 43.1 per cent for the year ended June 30, 1998 under the guiding hand of Oscar Castro.

Clarington sells two U.S. equity funds: a large cap version managed by Fleming Capital Management of New York, and a small-cap U.S. equity fund managed by Boston's Keystone Investments. Keystone has invested in small caps since 1935 and that experience shone through in the last year. The fund returned an impressive 32.9 per cent to June 30, 1998. But it is a small portfolio, with only $10 million at the end of June. Keystone also manages the global small-cap fund, Clarington Global Opportunities Fund. Keystone engages Credit Lyonnais Asset Management to help choose small caps outside the Western Hemisphere.

In August 1998, Clarington announced the addition of two new global funds managed by U.S.-based Oppenheimer Funds. There will be an all-global fund and an ex-North America fund. These should be the ones to watch as Oppenheimer has received accolades from Morningstar and the Nelson's *Money Manager Directory.*

With the latest additions, Clarington offers conservative core Canadian funds, plus interesting special equity and regional funds.

Smart Funds 1999:

Clarington Global Communications Fund.

Noteworthy Funds:

Clarington US Equity Fund. Modelled after Fleming's American Fund, this fund provides the combination of performance and low volatility that Terry Stone looks for. The formula paid off with a 36.1 per cent gain in one year to June 30, 1998, putting the fund far ahead of the median 28.5 per cent gain.

Clarington Canadian Balanced Fund. A conservatively managed, low-volatility fund that can act as a core offering with exposure to both Canadian stocks and bonds. Portfolio turnover is 12 or 13 per cent for a long average hold of seven to eight years, making this a tax-efficient fund even outside the RRSP.

Availability:

Some brokers and discount brokers and dealers.

15. CLEAN ENVIRONMENT MUTUAL FUNDS LTD.
FRONT OR REAR

Strengths: Profits in the environment business
Ethical/socially conscious investing
Weaknesses: Limited family of funds; high MERs
RESPs?: No
Web Site: www.cleanenvironment.com **Toll Free:** 1-800-461-4570

CANADIAN	Category	Rating	Fund Name	M.E.R.%	RRSP/Foreign
Equity:	All-Cap	★	**Clean Environment Equity Fund**	2.75	RRSP
Mult-Asset:	Balanced	▲	Clean Environment Balanced Fund	2.70	RRSP
	Income/Bonds	■	Clean Environment Income Fund	1.95	RRSP

FOREIGN	Category	Rating	Fund Name	M.E.R.%	RRSP/Foreign
Global Equity:	All-global	▲	Clean Environment International Equity Fund	2.77	Foreign

Clean Environment Mutual Funds continues to turn out top performers while maintaining its mandate to be environmentally friendly and help investors profit from the growth of the business of the environment. The Canadian and International equity funds and the balanced fund are top-quartile performers over the last five years. It is little wonder then that investors have noticed this once-small fund family. Its assets have risen dramatically in the last year, particularly in the Canadian equity fund, designated a Smart Fund.

President Ian Ihnatowycz founded the company in 1992 and continues to be the main stock picker but all the funds are managed with a team approach. Manager Hugh McAuley, a former engineer, plays an integral part and all funds benefit from recommendations from a scientific advisory council.

These funds are run just like any other mutual fund, except certain "screens" are used to eliminate choosing certain stocks that are judged to be destructive to the environment. But Clean Environment is a little broader than that and objects to being categorized with "ethical" funds: rather, it seeks companies that can grow and profit from the environment business itself.

As the matrix shows, there continue to be just four funds in the Clean Environment line-up but they cover a fairly wide scope: Canadian stocks, bonds, and global equities, as well as a balanced fund that has outstripped many better-known competitors in recent years.

Although management expense ratios have dropped in the last year, they are still higher than average. But the past performance of the funds has more than compensated for high fees.

Smart Funds 1999:

Clean Environment Equity Fund.

Noteworthy Funds:

Clean Environment Balanced. This unorthodox balanced fund continues to outperform its peers. Its approach to asset allocation is unique among balanced funds; in the spring of 1998 it was most heavily weighted in equities, followed by income-generating royalty trusts.

Clean Environment International Fund. This is newer than Clean Environment's original Canadian funds but it too has outperformed peers over three years. Not much "international" exposure here.

Availability:

Brokers and discount brokers and planners.

16. DYNAMIC MUTUAL FUNDS   FRONT OR REAR

Strengths:	Geological and gold expertise
	Bonds and asset allocation
	Global specialty funds
Weaknesses:	Canadian performance in recent years
RESPs?:	Yes
Web Site:	www.Dynamic.ca **Toll Free:** 1-800-268-8186

CANADIAN	Category	Rating	Fund Name	M.E.R.%	RRSP/Foreign
Money Market:		■	Dynamic Money Market Fund	0.8	RRSP
Fixed Income:	Long-term	■	Dynamic Income Fund	1.55	RRSP

	Category	Rating	Fund Name	M.E.R.%	RRSP/Foreign
	Short-term	■	Dynamic Government Income Fund	0.85	RRSP
Equity:	Mid-Large Cap	■	Dynamic Fund of Canada	2.24	RRSP
	Small-large cap	■	Dynamic Canadian Growth Fund	2.31	RRSP
	Small-Mid cap	■	Dynamic Small Cap Fund	2.99-4.08*	
	Gold/precious metal	■	Dynamic Precious Metals Fund	2.47	RRSP
	Regional	▲	Dynamic Quebec Fund	2.49	RRSP
Tax Advantaged:	Dividend	▲	Dynamic Dividend Fund	1.51	RRSP
		■	Dynamic Dividend Growth Fund	1.57	RRSP
		▲	Dynamic Canadian Real Estate Fund	2.73-3.89*	RRSP
Mult-Asset:	Asset Allocation	■	Dynamic Partners Fund	2.3	RRSP
	Portfolio of Funds	■	Dynamic Team Fund**	0.52	RRSP
		▲	Dynamic Dollar-Cost Averaging Fund	N/A	RRSP

FOREIGN	Category	Rating	Fund Name	M.E.R.%	RRSP/Foreign
Fixed Income:		■	Dynamic Global Bond Fund	1.78	RRSP
Global Equity:	All-global	■	Dynamic International Fund	2.57	Foreign
	Specialty	■	Dynamic Global Resource Fund*	2.63	Foreign
		■	Dynamic Global Precious Metals Fund	2.85	Foreign
		★	**Dynamic Real Estate Equity Fund**	2.72	Foreign
		■	Dynamic Global Millennia Fund	2.41	Foreign
Regional Equity:	NAFTA/N.Am.	▲	Dynamic Americas Fund	2.37	Foreign
	Latin/Emerging	■	Dynamic Latin American Fund	3.48	Foreign
	Far East	■	Dynamic Far East Fund	2.78	Foreign
	Europe	★	**Dynamic Europe Fund**	2.5	Foreign
	Other	▲	Dynamic Israel Growth Fund	N/A	Foreign
Global Balanced:	Asset Allocation	■	Dynamic Global Partners Fund	2.47	Foreign
		■	Dynamic Global Income & Growth	2.7	Foreign

* MER higher after performance fees
** Plus MERs of underlying funds

It wasn't all smooth sailing the past year for the rowing team at Dynamic Mutual Funds, with apologies for the mixed metaphor.

Dynamic has a knack for identifying interesting investment trends early and bringing to market funds that capitalize in time for investors to share the spoils. Their real estate funds are currently benefiting from that innovative tendency, and the Quebec Fund is off to a fine start. The unique Israel Growth Fund, formerly a closed-end fund, has been converted to an open-end fund.

Unfortunately, seaweed seems to be clogging the oars of some former Smart Funds. Some past Dynamic strengths, such as precious metals, fixed income and asset allocation, and even Canadian equities, have been less evident recently. Tellingly, when asked to suggest some candidates for Smart Funds, Dynamic itself did not offer up such former winners as Dynamic Income, Dynamic Precious Metals, or Dynamic Partners.

Some of its funds no longer justify their hefty management expense ratios, although it's only fair to point out that Dynamic has also knocked some of its higher MERs down a peg since the last edition of this book.

As we've previously noted, Dynamic is completely different from fund companies that subcontract fund management to external advisers. With Dynamic, you're buying a small, tightly knit team of seasoned in-house stock-picking and bond-trading talent, and a coherent classic value-oriented investment philosophy across an entire family of funds. The approach is of bottom-up value investment of companies, not a top-down approach to choosing countries or sectors.

After 40 years in the business, Dynamic has earned its status in the broker-sold channel, with $6 billion in assets under management. Chairman Ned Goodman is a vociferous advocate of the need for professional advice. Presumably, Dynamic's 350,000 unitholders have found excellent investment advisers to steer them away from the few shoals in Dynamic's 26-fund line-up, and toward the deep pools of what its advertisements call "Dynamic performance."

Never a company to follow the crowd, in early 1998 Dynamic decided to cancel its membership in fund industry association, the Investment Funds Institute of Canada (IFIC). About 95 per cent of fund companies are still IFIC members.

The past year involved mostly tinkering with the line-up. Three new funds were added in 1997: Dynamic Small Cap (with emphasis on oil and gas, environmental services, and transportation); Dynamic Latin American Fund; and the Dollar-Cost Averaging Fund (see Noteworthy for discussion of the last fund).

Dynamic also reopened the Dynamic Dividend Fund early in 1998, and added the word Global to the former Dynamic Income & Growth Fund.

Some manager movement also occurred in 1997-98. Founding partner Lesley Beech retired in 1997, while three new managers joined the firm. Oscar Belaiche co-manages the returning Smart Fund—Dynamic Real Estate Equity Fund—and its all-Canadian version. Noah Blackstein helps the global equity team choose U.S. and Latin stocks, and Todd Beallor co-manages the two dividend funds and Dynamic Global Income and Growth Fund. In 1998, Rohit Sehgal joined as partner and vice president and will head up the new Power Mutual Funds series launched in July 1998. Sehgal was the manager of the London Life Canadian Fund.

While on the topic of insurance, three Dynamic funds are part of the Manulife Guaranteed Investment Fund (GIF) program: Dynamic Global Bond, Partners, and Dividend Growth.

It remains to be seen when Dynamic's broadly based core funds will start firing on all cylinders again. For the time being, the family's strengths appear to be the several specialty funds identified as Smart or Noteworthy Funds.

Note that a few Dynamic funds also pay the managers a performance bonus that can add to the stated MERs in the matrix.

Smart Funds 1999:

Dynamic Real Estate Equity Fund, Dynamic Europe Fund.

Noteworthy Funds:

Dynamic Dollar-Cost Averaging Fund. Marketing gimmick or brilliant innovation? The former, to the extent that all funds can be dollar cost-averaged through pre-authorized chequing plans. The twist is this fund is designed to appeal to squeamish investors by gradually transferring money over 52 weeks from short-term bonds to selected equity and asset-allocation funds. Dynamic classifies this as a money market fund; we tend to view it as a multi-asset fund. Many studies have discredited this form of dollar-cost averaging. It has been proven that if you have investable money, you're better off putting it all in the market now.

Dynamic Americas Fund. One-year return of 28 per cent to June 30, 1998 justifies dropping this fund as a Smart Fund, given how competitive the U.S. category continues to be. Formerly the Dynamic American Fund, it is still more than half invested in the United States, with names such as Ford Motor Co., Bristol Myers Squibb, Hilton Hotels Corp., and Lucent Technologies Inc.

Dynamic Canadian Real Estate Fund. A newer, 100 per cent RRSP-eligible version of the "Smart" Dynamic Real Estate Equity fund. It has a 6.1 per cent return for the year ended June 30, 1998, not quite as good as the 13 per cent of the all-global version.

Dynamic Dividend Fund. Reopened on January 2, 1998. An 11 per cent one-year return to June 30, 1998. Includes income trusts. Dynamic classifies this as an income fund, although its 11 per cent one-year return to June 30, 1998 beat the similarly named Dynamic Dividend Growth Fund's 6 per cent, which Dynamic classifies as a Canadian equity fund.

Dynamic Quebec Fund. Launched in February 1997, this unique regional Canadian equity fund is a contrarian fund targeting Quebec stocks that have become undervalued because of the constant separatist agitation in Quebec. So far, this fund has outpaced the other domestic equity funds in Dynamic's stable, returning 11.68 per cent in the year ended June 30, 1998. Many holdings get revenues outside Quebec or indeed Canada, such as Alcan, BCE Inc., and Molson's.

Dynamic Israel Growth Fund. Formerly a closed-end fund trading on the TSE as DIF.UN, this was converted to a regular open-end fund in

May 1998. A little too country-specific for Smart Fund status, but Israel has some promising technology firms.

Availability:

Funds are sold by 10,000 stockbrokers and discount brokers, mutual fund dealers and financial planners across Canada. Minimum initial investment is $1,000. Pre-authorized purchase plans may begin with $100.

17. ELLIOTT & PAGE LTD.   FRONT, REAR & LOW

Strengths:	Canadian equities
	Low MERs for a load family
Weaknesses:	Low visibility
	No 100% RRSP-eligible global funds
RESPs?:	No
Web Site:	www.fundlib.com/ellpag.html **Toll Free:** 1-800-363-6647

CANADIAN	Category	Rating	Fund Name	M.E.R.%	RRSP/Foreign
Money Market:		▲	E&P Money Fund	0.24	RRSP
		■	E&P T-Bill Fund	1.72	RRSP
Fixed Income:	Long-term	■	E&P Bond Fund	1.92	RRSP
Equity:	Mid-Large Cap	▲	E&P Equity Fund	1.92	RRSP
		■	E&P Value Equity Fund	2.1	RRSP
Tax Advantaged:		▲	E&P Monthly High Income Fund	2.11	RRSP
Mult-Asset:	Balanced	■	E&P Balanced Fund	1.78	RRSP

FOREIGN	Category	Rating	Fund Name	M.E.R.%	RRSP/Foreign
Fixed Income:		■	E&P Global Bond Fund	2.07	Foreign
Global Equity:	All-global	■	E&P Global Equity Fund	1.95	Foreign
Regional Equity:					
	U.S. Large-cap	★	**E&P American Growth Fund**	1.39	Foreign
	U.S. Mid-Cap	▲	E&P U.S. Mid Cap Fund	3.5	Foreign
	Emerging Market	■	E&P Emerging Markets Fund	3.49	Foreign
	Far East	■	E&P Asian Growth Fund	3.33	Foreign
Global Balanced:		■	E&P Global Balanced Fund	2.82	Foreign

Elliott & Page Ltd. may not be quite as much of a household name as some of the larger fund families in this book, but its North American funds sport significantly lower MERs than many of its better-known broker-sold rivals.

E&P, as fund cognoscenti like to call this family, has roots going back to 1949, when it was the first investment counsellor registered in Ontario. Today it is a member of the Manulife Group of financial service companies, managing $10 billion for corporations, unions, pension funds, foundations, and individual investors.

Its domestic funds use a combination of in-house management and a firm consisting of former E&P employees: PCJ Investment Counsel. While its domestic equity and balanced funds have been Smart Funds in the past, they have been flat performers of late, as the sector-rotation style seems to have been out of favor.

The real winners over the past year have been some of E&P's externally managed global funds, notably Smart Fund E&P American Growth (36 per cent return for the year ended June 30, 1998), which shared in the spoils of the U.S. bull market and has a stingy 1.39 per cent MER. It's managed by New York's Goldman Sachs Asset Management. E&P's other global subadvisers include London-based Flemings, Hong Kong's Jardine Fleming, and Buffalo's M&T Bank.

After a couple of years of standing pat with its fund line-up, E&P took the wraps off three new funds in September 1997, bringing the total to 14 funds. The new U.S. Mid-Cap fund, managed by M&T Bank, has an MER that is more than double that of the older U.S. equity fund.

The new Monthly High Income Fund invests in bonds, royalty trusts, real estate investment trusts, and common stocks.

The new Value Equity fund puts an 80 per cent weighting on bottom-up, fundamental value criteria, and 20 per cent in top-down economic-cycle considerations.

Investors should take care in choosing the load structure. In addition to the unusual low-load option of 0 to 2 per cent (typically with higher trailer fees), E&P's rear-load option features a novel negotiable declining-redemption schedule that can be started anywhere from 2 to 6 per cent redemption in the first year, declining to nil after seven years.

Smart Funds 1999:

Elliott & Page American Growth.

Noteworthy Funds:

Elliott & Page Equity Fund. Fund has had a tough time of late with its sector-rotation style but when it comes back into vogue, this fund's below-average MER should help performance.

Elliott & Page Money. Consistent first-quartile money-market fund for most of the last 10 years. Manager has been vice president Maralyn Kobayashi since its inception in 1984. She uses an interest rate anticipation style. MER is an extremely low 0.26 per cent, but that can be misleading, since planners must add their fee to that.

Elliott & Page U.S. Mid-Cap Growth Fund. Former executive John Vivash found his old U.S. manager, John Moore, from the Hyperion U.S. equity fund working at M&T Bank and brought him back to Canada to run this fund. Focus is on stocks below the sizzling S&P large caps. Six-month return of 4.89 per cent pales in comparison to the large-cap index return of 17.69 per cent.

Elliott & Page Monthly High Income Fund. Internally managed fund seeks high yields from resource-based royalty trust units, real estate investment trusts, and high dividend-paying Canadian stocks. MER of 1.55 per cent is competitive.

Availability:

Brokers and discount brokers, dealers, and planners across Canada; $500 minimum purchase per fund.

18. ETHICAL FUNDS INC.   NO LOAD*, FRONT & REAR

Strengths: Funds for investors with a conscience
North American equities managed by Alliance Capital
Weaknesses: MERs above averages
Distribution
RESPs?: No
Web Site: www.ethicalfunds.com   Toll Free: 1-800-267-5019

CANADIAN	Category	Rating	Fund Name	M.E.R.%	RRSP/Foreign
Money Market:		■	Ethical Money Market Fund	1.24	RRSP
Fixed Income:	Medium-term	■	Ethical Income Fund	1.63	RRSP
Equity:	Mid-Large Cap	▲	Ethical Growth Fund	2.1	RRSP
	Small Cap	▲	Ethical Special Equity Fund	2.71	RRSP
Mult-Asset:	Balanced	■	Ethical Balanced Fund	2.08	RRSP

FOREIGN	Category	Rating	Fund Name	M.E.R.%	RRSP/Foreign
Fixed Income:		■	Ethical Global Bond Fund	2.56	RRSP
	NAFTA/N.Am.	★	**Ethical North American Equity Fund**	2.47	Foreign
	Far East	■	Ethical Pacific Rim Fund	3.15	Foreign

* No load through credit unions; varies with funds

There were no additions to the eight Ethical funds in the past year, but more investors have been attracted to the commendable concept of "ethical investing," which promises to let investors sleep well at night both morally and financially. Assets under management at

Ethical Funds have passed $2 billion, after almost doubling in 1997. That maintains Ethical Funds as the largest group of "socially responsible" mutual funds in Canada.

The biggest change has been not in content but in style: Ethical Funds now has a slogan—"Do the right thing"—and a marketing campaign to go with it. The managers continue to seek out companies that are progressive in their labor relations or attitude to racial equality, or ones that embrace positive environmental practices. They also avoid investments in companies that derive "a significant portion" of their revenue from tobacco, nuclear power, or military goods.

The management at Ethical Funds claim that profits and principles can co-exist. In fact, they take a fair share of the profits for themselves—management expense ratios are slightly above the industry averages. Despite this, and to borrow from the company's sometimes overblown rhetoric, high ideals can also lead to high performance for unitholders: four of the eight funds had double-digit returns in 1997 and its Canadian equity funds outperformed the TSE. The big winner was Ethical North American Equity, which chalked up a 56 per cent return for the year ended June 30, 1998. This made the Smart Funds short list last year, and we belatedly promote it to a Smart Fund with this edition.

The Canadian equity funds are managed externally. Connor, Clark & Lunn Investment Management Inc. of Vancouver, B.C. runs the flagship Ethical Growth Fund, which returns as Noteworthy, while Co-operators Investment Counselling Ltd. runs the domestic fixed-income and balanced funds.

The small-cap Ethical Special Equity Fund has changed managers and remains Noteworthy. Replacing Howson Tattersall Investment Counsel Ltd. on the fund is QVGD Investors Inc. of Calgary. Global managers include Alliance Capital Management L.P. and Guinness Flight Hambro Asset Management Ltd.

The load/no-load structure is a bit quirky. The five original funds are no-load if purchased from participating credit unions. No front- or rear-load fees are applicable to the three new funds, including those executed through brokers and discount brokers or dealers.

In the end, ethical investing is a private matter, and it's unlikely that the screens chosen by any one mutual fund manager will correspond to an individual's. For example, there are some who may not believe in investing in stocks that profit from alcohol, yet the Ethical Funds own Seagrams Co. Ltd. The funds also faced criticism when it briefly invested in TIPs: the Toronto 35 Index Participation Units, which includes several companies that don't fit its screens. It no longer invests in TIPs but the moral is to check the portfolio holdings to ensure that these funds really do live up to your personal moral worldview as well as your financial one.

Smart Funds 1999:

Ethical North American Equity.

Noteworthy Funds:

Ethical Growth. This quality fund is managed by Connor, Clark and Lunn.

Ethical Special Equity. QVDG replaced Saxon and has performed admirably.

Availability:

Primarily through local credit unions and discount brokers and discount brokers. Not available for sale in Quebec.

19. FIDELITY INVESTMENTS CANADA LTD. FRONT, REAR OR LOW

Strengths:	Clout of world's largest fund company
	Massive research capabilities
Weaknesses:	Size of some funds
	MERs high on equity funds
RESPs?:	No
Web Site:	www.fidelity.ca **Toll Free:** 1-800-387-0074

CANADIAN	Category	Rating	Fund Name	M.E.R.%	RRSP/Foreign
Money Market:		■	Fidelity Canadian Short-Term Asset Fund	1.25	RRSP
Fixed Income:	Long-term	■	Fidelity Canadian Bond Fund	1.35	RRSP
	Short-term	■	Fidelity Canadian Income Fund	1.25	RRSP
Equity:	All Cap	▲	Fidelity True North Fund	2.49	RRSP
	Mid-Large Cap	■	Fidelity Capital Builder Fund	2.46	RRSP
	Small-Mid Cap	★	**Fidelity Canadian Growth Company**	2.49	RRSP
	Asset Allocation	★	**Fidelity Canadian Asset Allocation Fund**	2.48	RRSP

FOREIGN	Category	Rating	Fund Name	M.E.R.%	RRSP/Foreign
Money Market:		■	Fidelity U.S. Money Market Fund - $US	1.25	Foreign
Fixed Income:		■	Fidelity North American Income Fund	1.75	Foreign
		▲	Fidelity Emerging Markets Bond Fund	2.24	Foreign
Global Equity:	All-global	★	**Fidelity International Portfolio Fund**	2.70	Foreign
	Sector	■	Fidelity Focus Consumer Industries Fund	2.50	Foreign
		■	Fidelity Focus Financial Services Fund	2.50	Foreign

	▦	Fidelity Focus Health Care Fund	2.50	Foreign
	▦	Fidelity Focus Natural Resources Fund	2.50	Foreign
	▦	Fidelity Focus Technology Fund	2.50	Foreign
Regional Equity: U.S.	★	**Fidelity Growth America Fund**	2.34	Foreign
U.S. Small-cap	■	Fidelity Small Cap America Fund	2.51	Foreign
Latin American	▲	Fidelity Latin American Growth Fund	3.14	Foreign
Emerging Market	▦	Fidelity Emerging Markets Portfolio Fund	3.53	Foreign
Far East	▲	Fidelity Far East Fund	2.79	Foreign
Japan	▦	Fidelity Japanese Growth Fund	3.03	Foreign
Europe	★	**Fidelity European Growth Fund**	2.74	Foreign
Global Balanced:				
Asset Allocation	★	**Fidelity Global Asset Allocation Fund**	2.71	Foreign

Fidelity's Boston-based parent company is the largest mutual fund company in the world, with almost C$830 billion under management in mid-1998. Last year, subsidiary Fidelity Canada made considerable strides in its quest to gain comparable stature within the Canadian market. At June 30, 1998 it had $17 billion in 24 funds, a significant jump from a year earlier.

That growth occurred amid changes at the firm in the last year. Fidelity Canada's top two executives, Kevin Kelly and Dan Geraci, were reassigned to other areas in the company and David Denison has taken the reins as president.

Fidelity's in-house global stock-picking research machine makes it a tempting choice for global equity funds for investors who prefer the broker channel and the slightly higher MERs that accompany it. With hundreds of Fidelity analysts on the ground around the world, this is truly a bottom-up outfit. (See profile of Richard Habermann on page 35 for more on the Fidelity process.)

Fidelity has proved it is equally proficient at choosing good Canadian stocks as foreign ones. One of the top-selling funds in 1998 has been the Fidelity True North Fund, managed by Fidelity veteran Alan Radlo. In less than two years since its inception, the fund has more than $1.41 billion in assets. Its one-year performance to the end of June 1998 puts it in the top quartile versus similar funds. Though not a native Canadian, Radlo is familiar with the Canadian market through the small-cap Fidelity Canadian Growth Company Fund. All funds, including the Canadian portfolios, are managed from outside of Canada, primarily from Boston.

Fidelity started selling five sector funds under the Fidelity Focus umbrella in June 1997. These are all 20 per cent foreign-content funds for RRSP or RRIF purposes. The funds cover consumer industries, financial services, health care, natural resources, and high technology, and are overseen by Bob Haber, a 13-year Fidelity veteran who is director of equity research. While the funds can invest worldwide, they continue to be heavily concentrated in the United States, which investors should keep in mind when making geographical and asset-allocation decisions.

Although interesting funds, none of the Fidelity Focus funds are designated as Smart Funds in this year's edition, reflecting the authors' caution about sector and regional funds. But for the more aggressive investor, these may be suitable as a slice (say 5 or 10 per cent) of some portfolios. The usual demographic arguments for the aging of the baby boom make Fidelity Focus Health Care Fund an intriguing one.

Fidelity continues to perform well in the U.S. market. Given the volatility of the Nasdaq exchange, Brad Lewis's Fidelity Small Cap America and Fidelity Growth America are a better bet for the average investor than the sector funds.

Also in the last year, Fidelity renamed its Asset Manager Fund the Fidelity Global Asset Allocation Fund to reflect its global equities emphasis. The Fidelity RSP Global Bond Fund was merged into the Fidelity Canadian Bond Fund in April 1998.

Smart Funds 1999:

Fidelity Canadian Growth Company, Fidelity European Growth Fund, Fidelity Canadian Asset Allocation, Fidelity Growth America Fund, Fidelity Global Asset Allocation Fund, Fidelity International Portfolio Fund.

Noteworthy Funds:

Fidelity True North Fund. Alan Radlo has steered this fund to a 16.1 per cent return in one year, ended June 30, 1998, well above the category average. We continue to prefer Radlo's Canadian Growth Company Fund with its longer track record.

Fidelity Far East Fund. A former Smart Fund, but we recommend investing in broad-based international funds (such as Fidelity International Portfolio Fund) over highly volatile regional funds.

Fidelity Latin American Growth. For those who want exposure to this volatile region, this fund continues to perform as one of the best in the category but with a high MER. Demoted because of its regional focus.

Fidelity Emerging Markets Bond Fund. This 1998 Smart Fund got knocked down as we reduced the number of funds in total and dropped the count on bond funds and volatile regions. Former first-quartile performer has dropped to fourth quartile for the year ended June 30, 1998.

Availability:

Only through brokers and discount brokers and dealers.

20. GBC ASSET MANAGEMENT INC.   NO LOAD

Strengths:	Low fees; no-load
	Small- and medium-cap growth
Weaknesses:	$100,000 minimum
	Limited menu of funds
RESPs?:	No
Web Site:	www.gbc.ca **Toll Free:** 1-800-668-7383

CANADIAN	Category	Rating	Fund Name	M.E.R.%	RRSP/Foreign
Money Market:		■	GBC Money Market Fund	0.75	RRSP
Fixed Income:	Long-term	▲	GBC Canadian Bond Fund	1.1	RRSP
	Small-med Cap	★	**GBC Canadian Growth Fund**	1.87	RRSP

FOREIGN	Category	Rating	Fund Name	M.E.R.%	RRSP/Foreign
Global Equity:	EAFE	■	GBC International Growth Fund	1.81	Foreign
	NAFTA/N.Am.	■	GBC North American Growth Fund	1.89	Foreign

GBC is another high-performance no-load group, but something of an anomaly. GBC makes no attempt to cater to the average small investor; instead it targets a very specific individual: someone with at least $100,000 to invest with the firm, and who is willing to take on the risk of small- and mid-cap North American stocks in return for the opportunity for extra returns.

GBC's small five-fund portfolio is the same as in previous editions of this book. All of its funds enjoyed solid returns the past year, with the best one being new Smart Fund, GBC Canadian Growth. Because it pays no trailer fees, these funds are more likely to be recommended by a fee-only planner than a commission-oriented one.

We have also designated one of the five funds as Noteworthy this year. GBC's management expense ratios are reasonable. Unitholders enjoy access to management, with regular face-to-face meetings with the people managing the money. However, while the MERs are slightly below those of the average broker-sold load fund, many investors who can afford the $100,000 entry ticket to the GBC funds could ultimately find cheaper alternatives in pooled funds and other high-net-worth vehicles offered by investment counselling firms. So, while it is elite as a mutual fund group, GBC occupies somewhat of a narrow niche between mass-market mutual funds and high-net-worth alternatives.

GBC is evidently addressing this issue, as evidenced by a new policy for unitholders of the GBC Canadian Bond Fund. Effective April 1, 1998, GBC announced a 0.25 per cent (25 basis points) management fee rebate for investors with at least $500,000 in the fund.

The GBC initials originally stood for Great Britain and Canada Corp., a closed-end fund established 71 years ago for British investors wishing to invest in North America. The key in-house investment management team, Pembroke Management of Montreal, was founded in 1968 by veterans Ian Soutar and Scott Taylor, who remain in place today. November 1998 marks the tenth anniversary of Smart Fund GBC Canadian Growth Fund as well as Pembroke's thirtieth anniversary. Their philosophy has remained consistent over those three decades: picking growth stocks by seeking out and supporting at an early stage good companies run by good people. Pembroke manages the North American stock picking, while the respected Greydanus, Boeckh & Associates Inc. runs fixed-income funds.

Three years have now passed since Babson Stewart Ivory International took over management of the former weak duckling in the line-up: GBC International Growth Fund. This EAFE (Europe, Australia and Far East) fund had a one-year number to June 30, 1998 of 12 per cent. Much of the lacklustre five-year CAGR of 6.3 per cent was, of course, generated by the previous manager.

Smart Funds 1999:

GBC Canadian Growth.

Noteworthy Funds:

GBC Canadian Bond. See overview above regarding 0.25 per cent management fee rebate. Invests exclusively in Government of Canada and provincial or provincially guaranteed securities. Duration is neutral at 6.3 years.

Availability:

Directly from GBC on a no-load basis in Ontario and Quebec. Also available nationally through brokers/dealers, with front loads negotiable up to 3 per cent. GBC pays no trailer fees. GBC has a minimum family portfolio requirement for accounts and funds to total $100,000, with a minimum of $15,000 held in each family member's account.

Strengths: Streamlined fund line-up
Canadian equity managers
Weaknesses: Challenge of handling many external advisers
High MERs, but coming down
RESPs?: No
Web Site: www.globalstrategyfunds.com Toll Free: 1-800-387-1229

CANADIAN	Category	Rating	Fund Name	M.E.R.%	RRSP/Foreign
Money Market:		■	Global Strategy Money Market Fund	0.84	RRSP
Fixed Income:	Short-term	■	Global Strategy Bond Fund	1.50	RRSP
Equity:	Mid-Large Cap	■	Global Strategy Canada Growth Fund	2.57	RRSP
	Mid-cap	★	**Global Strategy Canadian Opportunities Fund**	2.57	RRSP
	Small Cap	★	**Global Strategy Canadian Small Cap Fund**	2.71	RRSP
	Gold/precious metal	■	Global Strategy Gold Plus Fund	2.75	RRSP
Mult-Asset:	Balanced	★	**Global Strategy Income Plus Fund**	2.40	RRSP

FOREIGN	Category	Rating	Fund Name	M.E.R.%	RRSP/Foreign
Fixed Income:		▲	Global Strategy Diversified Bond Fund	2.20	RRSP
		▲	Global Strategy World Bond Fund	2.10	Foreign
Global Equity:	All-global	■	Global Strategy World Equity	2.79	Foreign
		★	**Global Strategy World Companies**	2.79	Foreign
		■	Global Strategy Diversified World Equity	2.37	RRSP
Regional Equity:	U.S.	■	Global Strategy U.S. Equity Fund	2.59	Foreign
	Europe	▲	Global Strategy Europe Plus Fund	2.79	Foreign
		▲	Global Strategy Diversified Europe Fund	2.51	RRSP
Global Balanced:		■	Global Strategy World Balanced	2.32	Foreign

Global Strategy may have pioneered the 100 per cent RRSP-eligible global bond and equity funds, a category since adopted by many other fund companies, but it has also proven it has the right stuff in the Canadian category. The team of Tony Massie and John Sartz continues to be a powerful combination, strengthened by Sartz's decision in mid-1997 to join Global Strategy as an in-house manager.

Sartz's mid-cap Canadian Opportunities Fund lived up to expectations in its first year, performing well with 14.6 per cent at June 30, 1998. It continues to be a Smart Fund for its second year. The Canadian Small Cap Fund, reopened to new investment when Sartz joined the firm, has performed above the median at June 30, 1998 over the two- and three-year periods. It is once again a Smart Fund.

Massie's Income Plus Fund also returns as a Smart Fund. It continues to outperform peers, returning 16.6 per cent in one year to June 30, 1998 compared with the median 9.86 per cent. It is also first quartile over two, three, and five years.

On the global side, Global Strategy continues to be one of the few families that provides 100 per cent RRSP-eligible (they use the prefix "Diversified") funds. The company has also been efficient at cleaning up its fund family, which it continued in September 1998. The Asia, Japan, and Latin America funds will be merged into World Companies, a returning Smart Fund. Its RRSP-eligible "Diversified" sisters are merged into Diversified World Equity. At the same time, the Diversified Foreign Bond Fund is merged into Diversified Bond Fund. With this clean-up, Global reduced the management fee on the continuing equity funds by 25 basis points. We applaud such moves and wish more companies could simplify their line-ups and lower fees.

Global Strategy has also moved to simplify the number of managers on its funds. With the consolidation, Jardine Fleming, Platinum Asset Management, and Prospect Asset Management will no longer be required. In addition, GS has dropped AIM Capital Management from the U.S. Equity Fund and Perpetual Asset Management from the World Companies Fund.

The line-up now comprises just 15 funds, half the 30 funds it had a few years ago. The name of the World Emerging Companies Fund has been changed to World Companies Fund to clarify that it is not an emerging-markets fund.

While Global Strategy's management expense ratios are still higher than we'd like, they have dropped in the last year and will likely continue to fall as the funds grow. The difficulty of driving down MERs on some of the smaller funds was the major reason for the consolidation mentioned above. Higher MERs can be justified in its multi-adviser global equity funds, advised by three managers with different styles. Unlike the Diversified funds, these can only be held within the foreign-content portion of an RRSP or RRIF, or in taxable portfolios. The multi-adviser funds are unique in that each one has three managers, each responsible for 33.3 per cent of the portfolio. That simplifies the task of having value, growth, and small-cap versions of funds, since you can have all three approaches in single funds. In many cases, performance continues to be average or above-average with less volatility.

An investor nervous about the Canadian market could create a portfolio of all-international funds within the confines of an RRSP or RRIF by using Multi-Advisor funds for the 20 per cent portion and Diversified funds for the balance. The effects that this strategy might have on asset allocation, and the increased risk exposure generated by foreign currency fluctuations, should be discussed with your financial planner.

MAJOR FUND FAMILIES

Smart Funds 1999:

Global Strategy Income Plus, Global Strategy World Companies, Global Strategy Canadian Opportunities, Global Strategy Canadian Small Cap.

Noteworthy Funds:

Global Strategy World Bond and **Diversified Bond.** Global Strategy was an early advocate of global bonds as an asset class, one that has been perhaps too much out of favor since the setbacks of 1994. These make an interesting diversification option given the current high valuations of equity markets and can buffer a declining Canadian dollar.

Global Strategy Europe Plus. This fund is managed using Global Strategy's trademark multi-adviser approach, which has made its volatility the lowest in the category over three years to June 30, 1998. Its performance is slightly above average for the same period.

Global Strategy Diversified Europe. This 100 per cent RRSP-eligible version of Europe Plus gives investors exposure to the MSCI Europe 14 index and a 10 per cent exposure to the Europe Plus fund. It has performed just slightly below average for like funds over five years, but with lower volatility.

Availability:

Brokers and discount brokers and dealers across Canada. $500 minimum investments.

22. GREAT WEST LIFE SEGREGATED FUNDS
NO LOAD OR REAR LOAD

Strengths:	Traditional insurance guarantees
	Choice of five strong advisors
Weaknesses:	MERs average to high
	Unspectacular performance
RESPs?:	No
Web Site: www.gwl.ca	**Telephone:** 1-204-946-1190

CANADIAN	Category	Rating	Fund Name	M.E.R.%	RRSP/Foreign
Money Market:		■	GWL Money Market Fund	1.38	RRSP
Fixed Income:		■	GWL Canadian Bond Fund	1.82	RRSP
		■	GWL Bond Fund (Beutel Goodman)	2.08	RRSP
		■	GWL Bond Fund (Sceptre)	2.12	RRSP
		■	GWL Government Bond Fund	1.84	RRSP

	Category		Fund Name	M.E.R.%	RRSP/Foreign
		■	GWL Income Fund	1.93	RRSP
	Mortgage	■	GWL Mortgage Fund	2.16	RRSP
Equity:	Large-Cap	■	GWL Canadian Equity Fund	2.4	RRSP
		■	GWL Larger Company Fund (Mackenzie)	2.69	RRSP
		■	GWL Equity Fund (Mackenzie)	2.63	RRSP
		■	GWL Equity Fund (Sceptre)	2.61	RRSP
	Index	▲	GWL Equity Index Fund	2.33	RRSP
	Mid-Cap	■	GWL Mid Cap Canada Fund	2.4	RRSP
	Small-cap	■	GWL Smaller Company Fund (Mackenzie)	2.66	RRSP
		▲	GWL Growth Equity Fund (AGF)	3	RRSP
	Specialty	■	GWL Canadian Opportunity Fund (Mackenzie)	2.58	RRSP
	Resource	■	GWL Canadian Resources Fund (AGF)	3.05	RRSP
	Real estate	■	GWL Real Estate Fund	2.7	RRSP
Tax Advantaged:	Dividend	■	GWL Dividend Fund	2.28	RRSP
		■	GWL Dividend/Growth Fund (Mackenzie)	2.46	RRSP
Mult-Asset:	Balanced	■	GWL Diversified RS Fund	2.4	RRSP
		■	GWL Balanced Fund (Mackenzie)	2.7	RRSP
		■	GWL Balanced Fund (Beutel Goodman)	2.56	RRSP
		▲	GWL Balanced Fund (Sceptre)	2.64	RRSP
		■	GWL Growth & Income Fund (Mackenzie)	2.52	RRSP
		■	GWL Growth & Income Fund (AGF)	2.62	RRSP
		■	GWL Equity/Bond Fund	2.4	RRSP
		■	GWL Income Fund (Mackenize)	2.22	RRSP
	Fund of Funds	■	GWL Conservative Portfolio RS Fund	2.47	RRSP
		■	GWL Moderate Portfolio RS Fund	2.52	RRSP
		■	GWL Balanced Portfolio RS Fund	2.58	RRSP
		■	GWL Advanced Portfolio RS Fund	2.64	RRSP
		■	GWL Aggressive Portfolio RS Fun	2.7	RRSP

FOREIGN	Category	Rating	Fund Name	M.E.R.%	RRSP/Foreign
Fixed Income:		■	GWL International Bond Fund (Putnam)	2.8	Foreign
		■	GWL Global Income Fund (AGF)	2.53	RRSP
Global Equity:	EAFE	★	**GWL International Equity Fund (Putnam)**	2.69	Foreign
		■	GWL International Opportunity (Putnam)	2.52	Foreign
Regional Equity:	U.S.	■	GWL U.S. Equity fund	2.55	Foreign
		▲	GWL American Growth (AGF)	2.73	Foreign
	NAFTA/N.A.	■	GWL North American Equity Fund (Beutel Goodman)	2.56	RRSP
	Europe	■	GWL European Equity Fund (Sceptre)	2.64	Foreign
	Asia	■	GWL Asian Growth (AGF)	2.61	Foreign

** MERs are for DSC versions: add 0.24% for no-loads

Although Great-West Life Assurance Co. is 107 years old, its segregated funds only make their debut in Smart Funds with this edition.

In the past two years, traditional mutual fund companies have started taking the life insurance industry's "segregated funds" seriously. So-called "seg" funds are life insurance products governed by life insurance regulations, but are, for all intents and purposes, just like mutual funds from an investment point of view.

As stock markets sagged in 1998, investors started to rediscover the benefits of seg funds, the main one being that you can guarantee all or 75 per cent of your initial capital if markets stay down for 10 years, or, in the event of death, your beneficiary would have that initial capital guaranteed. Seg funds also provide potential creditor-proofing benefits and can allow assets to be transferred to a beneficiary without probate fees.

Several fund companies, such as BPI, C.I. Mutual Fund, Trimark, and Templeton, have made alliances with insurance companies to put an "insurance wrapper" around their own funds. Manulife Securities Inc. has taken a slightly different approach, putting a number of brand-name mutual funds under its "GIF" or Guaranteed Investment Fund umbrella.

The ability to sleep at night carries with it a price; in all these cases, the net MER is higher than the underlying funds. For this reason, investors may also want to consider the original seg fund families, such as GWL, although their "all-in" MERs don't appear to be any lower than the mutual fund/life hybrids.

Great-West Life merits special attention, for at least three reasons. GWL offers the largest selection of seg funds among the traditional seg suppliers, with 42 at last count (Manulife's GIF would be close). Second, it is a sister company to Investors Group Inc., which is Canada's largest mutual fund company. IGI has stuck to traditional mutual funds, while GWL has concentrated on seg funds. Third, GWL's funds include several well-known mutual fund managers, including AGF Management Ltd., Mackenzie Financial Corp., Beutel Goodman and Co. Ltd., Sceptre Investment Counsel Ltd., and U.S.-based Putnam Investments.

Beutel Goodman and Sceptre, both pension managers with their own mutual funds, are also subadvisers to Investors Group. But while Investors went with Rothschild and Merrill Lynch for their global subadvisers, GWL opted for Putnam. Established in 1937, Putnam is one of the largest money management firms in the United States and runs almost $200 billion in assets worldwide. Because of this relation-ship, which is unique to GWL, we made the GWL International Equity Fund a 1999 Smart Fund.

In 1994, GWL also created its own internal investment management subsidiary, known as GWL Investment Management Ltd., which it describes as a "top-down, growth-oriented manager." Perhaps so, but there are a lot of income and balanced funds in GWLIM's line-up, plus five Portfolio funds composed of other GWL funds. A glance at the GWL fund matrix shows that the all-in MERs are slightly higher than the average MERs of traditional load funds, but comparable to, or slightly below, the new fund company/life hybrid products. Note also that the MERs in the matrix are for the DSC (rear-load funds). If you want the same funds on a no-load basis, you will have to add 0.24 per cent to the MERs shown in the matrix.

Generally, our Noteworthy designations derive from the corresponding funds in the other fund families, although in some cases the extra MER precluded the equivalent ranking. Thus, the GWL Balanced Fund (Sceptre) is a Noteworthy in this edition. (See also profile of Sceptre's Lyle Stein on page 24.) Some underlying AGF funds are Noteworthy (see below).

GWL unveiled eight new seg funds late in 1997, including versions of AGF's American Growth Fund and Asian Growth Fund, Mackenzie's Dividend Growth and Canadian Opportunity Fund, Sceptre's Europe Equity Fund, and Putnam's International Opportunity Fund.

As with other fund families with more than 40 funds, it's a bit of a challenge sorting out the line-up so you'll likely need a good adviser. The matrix reveals plenty of duplication in Canadian equities, bonds and balanced funds, while the global line-up tends to have only one entry in each category.

GWL also has an asset-allocation service called Discovery.

Smart Funds 1999:

GWL International Equity Fund.

Noteworthy Funds:

GWL Equity Index Fund. For years, this was one of the few Canadian equity index funds available in the market. But the banks have entered this domain aggressively over the past year and this fund's MER of 2.33 per cent is much too high for an index fund.

GWL Balanced (Sceptre). With Lyle Stein's Sceptre Balanced Growth being a returning Smart Fund, you might want to pay the extra MER for a guarantee. Then again, with a total MER on this fund of 2.69 per cent and the Sceptre fund bought directly at Sceptre of 1.44 per cent, that is a huge cost of insurance over your holding period.

GWL American Growth (AGF). The U.S. equity market is major asset class but fraught with risk at today's valuations. Here, the extra MER to get an AGF Smart Fund (AGF American Growth) and some downside protection may be worth it.

GWL Growth Equity (AGF). The corresponding AGF small-cap fund has almost the same MER. As with GWL American Growth, the small MER premium might be worth it to get some hedged exposure to an asset class—Canadian small caps—that can more than earn its fees.

Availability:

Only through brokers and dealers.

23. GUARDIAN GROUP OF FUNDS   **FRONT OR REAR**

Strengths:	Canadian funds
	100% RRSP-eligible global funds
Weaknesses:	Classic series lower MERs but high minimums
RESPs?:	Yes
Web Site:	www.guardianfunds.com **Toll Free:** 1-800-668-7327

CANADIAN	Category	Rating	Fund Name	M.E.R.%	RRSP/Foreign
Money Market:		■	Guardian Canadian Money Market Fund	0.84-1.55	RRSP
	Short-term	■	Guardian Canadian Income Fund	1.11-1.92	RRSP
Equity:	Mid-Large Cap	▲	Guardian Growth Equity Fund	2.09-2.75	RRSP
	Small-Cap	★	**Guardian Enterprise Fund**	2.07-2.75	RRSP
Tax Advantaged:	Dividend	▲	Guardian Monthly Dividend Fund	1.25-1.85	RRSP
		▲	Guardian Monthly High Income Fund	1.46-2.07	RRSP
Mult-Asset:	Balanced	▲	Guardian Canadian Balanced Fund	1.70-2.67	RRSP
		▲	Guardian Growth & Income	2.00-2.60	RRSP

FOREIGN	Category	Rating	Fund Name	M.E.R.%	RRSP/Foreign
Money Market:		■	Guardian US Money Market Fund	0.89-1.53	RRSP
Fixed Income:		▲	Guardian International Income Fund	2.04-2.73	RRSP
		★	**Guardian Foreign Income Fund**	1.69-2.66	RRSP
Global Equity:	All-global	■	Guardian Global Equity Fund	1.02-2.75	Foreign
Regional Equity:	U.S.	★	**Guardian American Equity Fund**	2.20-2.79	Foreign
	Emerging Market	▲	Guardian Emerging Markets Fund	0.80-2.93	Foreign
	Far East	■	Guardian Asia Pacific Fund	1.68-2.96	Foreign
Global Balanced:		▲	Guardian International Balanced Fund	2.12-2.93	Foreign

Guardian has done a good job of distinguishing itself from the masses in the mutual fund world. A clever advertising campaign during the past two RRSP seasons has emphasized that the top priority of most Guardian portfolio managers is risk management—timely given the increasing volatility seen after August 1998.

Guardian has honed its singular risk-control strategies, which allow for exceptional performance in good times and capital-preserving defensive stances in bad times over many years as an institutional money manager. Many of its fixed-income funds and others such as Guardian Canadian Balanced Fund have the below-average volatility to prove it.

Guardian continues its core business of managing money for pension funds and high-net-worth individuals through the pooled funds of Guardian Capital Advisers. Retail mutual fund investors benefit from the same seasoned investment in-house investment team of John Priestman on Canadian equities (profile in S*mart Funds 1998*) and Larry Kennedy on fixed income.

Outside Canada, Guardian has made a significant change in the last year. In February 1998, it replaced Dietche & Field Advisors with Lazard Asset Management, a division of Lazard Freres and Co. Michael Rome, who is well known as the former manager of the U.S. equity funds for BPI Mutual Funds, is a welcome addition to the Guardian team. He is highly respected as a top U.S. money manager and, based on his past track record with BPI, we have promoted Guardian American Equity to "Smart Fund" status this year. Guardian is scheduled to launch a large-cap American Equity fund later in 1998, also managed by Rome.

The Guardian Group's reputation as a conservative money manager should not deter more aggressive investors. Several funds, such as the small-cap Guardian Enterprise, have more aggressive mandates. Manager Gary Chapman has done better over the longer term than the most recent year. Priestman's mid-large cap Guardian Growth Equity Fund is another conservative choice. Although it underperformed over one year to June 30, 1998, hence its departure from the Smart Funds list, it has a good long-term record, reasonable volatility, and a low MER if purchased with a front load.

Dresdner RCM, which acquired Kleinwort Benson, manages the other foreign funds.

For more conservative investors, Guardian's new balanced fund, Guardian Growth and Income, had a good first year. The Guardian Monthly Dividend Fund is still closed but for large taxable portfolios Guardian's Monthly High Income Fund compares favorably with GICs and other guaranteed products on an after-tax basis.

Investors should note that Guardian has restructured its funds in renaming the front and deferred versions: Guardian Classic Funds units are sold on a front-load basis, usually to investors with $50,000 or more. Guardian Mutual Funds are sold with a deferred or front-load option and carry higher MERs. Because the former carries lower MERs, we have recommended those as the Smart Funds in the appropriate cases.

Smart Funds 1999:

Guardian Enterprise Fund Classic, Guardian Foreign Income Classic, Guardian American Equity Classic.

Noteworthy Funds:

Guardian Canadian Balanced Classic. This long-time Smart fund has never lost money but has underperformed of late and, facing tough competition, we demoted it to Noteworthy.

Guardian Monthly High Income Classic. Former Smart Fund did not earn income; in fact, it has lost unitholders money since inception.

Guardian Growth Equity Classic. Decent, if inconsistent Canadian equity fund; 18.77 three-year CAGR is nothing to sneeze at, but puts it in the second quartile in a tough category.

Guardian Growth & Income. With John Priestman as manager, this fund had a fourth quartile first year.

Guardian Monthly Dividend Fund. Remains closed to new investors and therefore still off the Smart Funds list. Existing unitholders and those buying on pre-authorized chequing plans continue to receive monthly dividend payments.

Guardian International Income. This fund has a higher MER than the "Smart" Guardian Foreign Income but has outperformed the average international bond group over one, three, and five years to June 30, 1998.

Guardian International Balanced. This fully RRSP-eligible fund could be a good choice for a conservative investor who wanted some exposure to foreign securities.

Guardian Emerging Markets Fund. This fund performed lost 29 per cent in the past year, placing it firmly in the third quartile. Bargain MER of 0.80 per cent seems too good to be true.

AVAILABILITY:

Through brokers and discount brokers and dealers.

24. HONGKONG BANK MUTUAL FUNDS   NO LOAD

Strengths:	Far East equities		
	HSBC on fixed income		
Weaknesses:	No 100% RRSP-eligible global funds		
RESPs?:	Under development		
Web Site:	www.hksi.com	**Toll Free:**	1-800-830-8888

CANADIAN	Category	Rating	Fund Name	M.E.R.%	RRSP/Foreign
Money Market:		■	HKB Money Market Fund	0.92	RRSP
	U.S. denominated	■	HKB U.S. Dollar Money Market	new	RRSP
Fixed Income:	Long-term	■	HKB Canadian Bond Fund	1.12	RRSP
	Mortgage	▲	HKB Mortgage Fund	1.45	RRSP
Equity:	Mid-Large Cap	▲	HKB Equity Fund	1.87	RRSP
	Small-Cap	■	HKB Small Cap Growth Fund	2.15	RRSP
Tax Advantaged:	Dividend	▲	HKB Dividend Income Fund	1.85	RRSP
Mult-Asset:	Balanced	■	HKB Balanced Fund	1.81	RRSP

FOREIGN	Category	Rating	Fund Name	M.E.R.%	RRSP/Foreign
Fixed Income:		■	HKB Global Bond Fund	2.10	Foreign
Regional Equity:					
	NAFTA/N.Am.	■	HKB U.S. Equity Fund	2.17	Foreign
	Emerging Market	■	HKB Emerging Markets Fund	2.61	Foreign
	Far East	▲	HKB Asian Growth Fund	2.3	Foreign
	Europe	■	HKB European Growth Fund	2.16	Foreign
Mult-Asset:	Balanced	■	HKB Global Equity	new	Foreign

This Vancouver-based no-load group is probably best known for the strength of its investing in the Far East. But it continues to round out its fund family by adding two more funds in the last year, bringing its total to 14. Growth has been consistent. Over the last two years, the group's assets have grown from $1.8 billion to $3.7 billion.

The firm's origins go back to 1989, when Lloyds Bank of Canada had three basic mutual funds: Balanced, Money Market, and Equity Index. In May 1990, Hongkong Bank of Canada purchased Lloyds Bank of Canada from Lloyds Bank plc in Britain, along with the funds. They were renamed by adding the prefix Hongkong Bank and were administered by Hongkong Bank Securities Inc. In 1996, the Hongkong Bank of Canada purchased M.K. Wong & Associates Ltd. It was renamed HSBC Asset Management Canada Ltd on June 30, 1998, to reflect the globalization of the firm's money management services.

For investors who can't stomach the inevitable volatility that accompanies regional investing, HKB launched a global equity fund in January 1998. Rather than buy securities directly, this is a "fund of funds" that buys units in the HKB's four regional equity funds: Emerging Markets, Asian Growth, U.S. Equity, and European Growth. It may also buy units of the money market fund. The manager is restricted to minimum and maximum holdings with each fund. For example, the fund must have 32.5 to 37.5 per cent of its assets invested in the European Growth Fund. The fund charges a maximum annual management fee of 2.25 per cent (plus expenses charged to the fund), which includes the MERs charged by the underlying funds. Therefore, investors are not charged twice.

The other new fund is a U.S. dollar money market fund. This is fully RRSP-eligible because it invests in Canadian securities such as T-Bills and corporate notes. These securities just happen to be issued in U.S. dollars, which makes it convenient for investors who need regular access to U.S. dollars.

HKB portfolio managers generally take a top-down approach, analyzing economic conditions before they choose their securities. Although no funds were designated Smart this year, several were considered Noteworthy.

Smart Funds 1999:

None.

Noteworthy Funds:

Hongkong Bank Asian Growth. Given the extensive resources of the portfolio manager in Asia, this fund should do well for investors over the long term. But expect some volatility along the way.

Hongkong Bank Mortgage Fund. A little behind over one year but this fund has the second best CAGR in the category over five years to June 30, 1998 and a lower than average MER of 1.45 per cent.

Hongkong Bank Dividend Income. Launched in 1995, the fund has performed slightly better than average over the three years to June 30, 1998, with a slightly below-average MER for the group. It is weighted to preferred shares, pays quarterly distributions, and is suitable for taxable portfolios.

Hongkong Bank Equity. This large-cap Canadian equity fund has performed well over the long term and will have a 10-year track record by the end of 1998. Over the five years to June 30, 1998, it has a CAGR of 12.1 per cent, versus the 12.5 per cent median for similar funds over the same period

Availability:

Hongkong Bank branches, their discount brokerage office, and a limited number of full-service and discount brokerages.

25. INVESTORS GROUP INC.

Strengths:	Conservative, long-term approach
	Now extensive choice globally
Weaknesses:	Hard to mix with other fund families
	Complexity of 5 families & 50 funds
RESPs?:	Yes
Web Site:	www.investorsgroup.com **Toll Free:** 1-888-746-6344

CANADIAN	Category	Rating	Fund Name	M.E.R.%	RRSP/Foreign
Money Market:		■	Investors Money Market Fund	1.07	RRSP
Fixed Income:	Long-term	■	Investors Government Bond Fund	1.89	RRSP
		■	Investors Corporate Bond Fund	1.88	RRSP
		■	IG Sceptre Canadian Bond Fund	2.29	RRSP
	Mortgage	■	Investors Mortgage Fund	1.90	RRSP
Equity:	Mid-Large Cap	■	Investors Canadian Equity Fund	2.46	RRSP
	Small-Large Cap	■	Investors Canadian Enterprise	2.55	RRSP
		■	Investors Retirement Mutual	2.42	RRSP
		■	Merrill Lynch Canadian Equity	2.83	RRSP
		■	Rothschild Select GS Canadian Equity Fund	2.79	RRSP
		▲	IG Sceptre Canadian Equity Fund	2.84	RRSP
		■	IG Beutel Goodman Canadian Equity Fund	2.90	RRSP
	Small Cap	▲	Investors Canadian Small Cap Fund	2.57	RRSP
		▲	Investors Canadian Small Cap II	2.55	RRSP
		■	IG Beutel Goodman Canadian Small Cap	2.89	RRSP
	Resource	■	Investors Canadian Natural Resource Fund	2.48	RRSP
	Ethical	▲	Investors Summa Fund	2.47	RRSP
Tax Advantaged:	Dividend	■	Investors Dividend Fund	2.36	RRSP
	Real Estate	■	Investors Real Property Fund	2.37	RRSP
Mult-Asset:	Balanced	■	Investors Mutual of Canada Fund	2.36	RRSP
		▲	Rothschild Select GS Canadian Balanced	2.68	RRSP
		★	**IG Sceptre Canadian Balanced Fund**	2.81	RRSP
		■	IG Beutel Goodman Canadian Balanced Fund	2.79	RRSP
	Asset Allocation	▲	Investors Asset Allocation Fund	2.73	RRSP
	Portfolio of Funds*	▲	Investors Growth Portfolio	2.61	Foreign
		▲	Investors Growth Plus Portfolio	2.45	Foreign
		■	Investors Income Portfolio	2.06	RRSP
		■	Investors Income Plus Portfolio	2.29	RRSP
		■	Investors World Growth Portfolio	2.62	Foreign
		■	Investors Retirement Plus Portfolio	2.41	RRSP
		■	Investors Retirement Growth Portfolio	2.62	RRSP

FOREIGN	Category	Rating	Fund Name	M.E.R.%	RRSP/Foreign
Money Market:	U.S.	■	Investors U.S. Money Market Fund	1.19	Foreign
Fixed Income:		■	Investors Global Bond Fund	2.19	Foreign
		■	Investors North American High Yield Bond Fund	2.23	Foreign
		■	Merrill Lynch World Bond Fund	2.26	RRSP
		■	Rothschild Select GS International Bond	2.79	RRSP
Global Equity:	All-global	■	Investors Global Fund	2.48	Foreign
		■	Rothschild Select GS International Equity	2.83	Foreign
Regional Equity:	U.S.	▲	Investors U.S. Growth Fund	2.40	Foreign
		■	Rothschild Select GS American Equity	2.94	Foreign
	U.S. small cap	■	Investors U.S. Opportunities Fund	2.56	Foreign

NAFTA/N.Am.	■	Investors North American Growth Fund	2.38	Foreign
NAFTA small-cap	■	Investors Special Fund	2.39	Foreign
Latin American	■	Investors Latin American Growth Fund	3.10	Foreign
Emerging Market	■	Merrill Lynch Emerging Markets	3.28	Foreign
Far East	■	Investors Pacific International Fund	2.55	Foreign
Japan	■	Investors Japanese Growth Fund	2.46	Foreign
Europe	■	Investors European Growth Fund	2.47	Foreign
Global Balanced:	▲	Merrill Lynch World Allocation	2.91	Foreign
U.S. Balanced	■	Merrill Lynch Capital Asset Fund	2.85	Foreign

* No-load on equity funds if more than $10,000 with Investors Group

---

Investors Group Inc. (IG) of Winnipeg continues its reign as the largest mutual fund firm in Canada, with assets now spread among at least 50 funds. It is also the oldest fund company in Canada, founded in 1894 as Investors Diversified Services. Its sales operation was first launched in 1926. However, it wasn't until 1950 that Investors Group's first mutual fund was introduced: Investors Mutual of Canada.

Investors Group is unique in that its funds are available only through its proprietary group of advisers. That's just as well, given that most would need an adviser to differentiate among all these funds. Investors now has three years under its belt selling five fund families. Since 1996, when it "opened up its shelf" of 3,300 agents to four outside families run by external subadvisers, the number of funds has more than doubled. As the matrix shows, considerable duplication occurs in certain fund categories. Confusion can be minimized by taking a "fund family" approach—first selecting the families appropriate to your personal risk profile and objectives, and only then choosing the individual funds.

The choice comes down to the IG Beutel Goodman and IG Sceptre families for Canadian content; the Merrill Lynch Asset Management family or Rothschild Select Funds globally; or Investors' own proprietary funds both domestically and globally.

There were several changes at IG in the last year, some of them affecting Smart Funds. In January 1998, the Investors Canadian Small Cap Fund and IG Beutel Goodman Canadian Small Cap Fund were both closed to new unitholders. Existing unitholders are permitted to continue investing in the fund.

IG also lost Larry Sarbit, its top U.S. equity manager to fund distributor Berkshire Investments, the sister company to AIC Ltd. Berkshire plans to launch its own product sometime in 1998 and Sarbit will spearhead that effort. With Sarbit gone, oversight of Investors U.S. Growth Fund and Investors U.S. Opportunities Fund has been assumed by Scott Penman and the eight members of his North American Equity Team. As of June, Terry Wong has taken over as the lead manager. This is a busy group, collectively managing 13 funds for IG. Based on the departure of Sarbit, Investors U.S. Growth has been downgraded from Smart to Noteworthy.

The Merrill Lynch World Bond Fund had a change of management from Sean Casey to Alex Bouzakis at Merrill Lynch Asset Management And the Merrill Lynch Canadian Equity Fund Portfolio moved from Ken Done to Robert Mulligan, also at Merrill.

There continues to be no fee to switch among the five fund families. The funds are no-load if you have a minimum $10,000 with Investors Group. Otherwise, there is a 2.5 per cent commission on equity funds payable at time of purchase.

While the various Investors "Portfolios" have always provided asset allocation through various combinations of Investors' in-house funds, the "Personal Asset Allocation" program provides customized asset allocation across the entire spectrum of funds.

Smart Funds 1999:

IG Sceptre Canadian Balanced.

Noteworthy Funds:

Investors Canadian Small Cap II. Should be a clone to the closed Small Cap I, a 1998 Smart Fund.

IG Sceptre Canadian Equity. Should be a clone of the newly launched Sceptre Large cap fund.

IG Rothschild Select. GS Canadian Balanced. Has the solid Smart Fund, Global Strategy Income Plus, as its core underlying investment, but with a higher MER.

Investors Canadian Small Cap Fund. This 1998 Smart Fund managed by Scott Penman has been a top-quartile performer in one year to June 1998. It was closed to new unitholders in January 1998 because of its large size and Canadian Small Cap II, with the same investment mandate as the first, was launched.

Investors U.S. Growth Fund. This former Smart Fund has been demoted to Noteworthy to reflect the departure of manager Larry Sarbit, who left the firm in early 1998. Management of the portfolio was moved onto the already full plate of Scott Penman and his team.

Investors Growth Portfolio and **Investors Growth Plus Portfolio.** These are both "fund of funds" offerings composed of underlying Investors funds. Growth is a global equity fund and Growth Plus is an international balanced fund. Performance has been above average over one and three years to June 30, 1998.

Investors Asset Allocation. This asset-allocation fund now has a solid three-year performance record: an average CAGR of 16.9 per cent for the three years ended June 30, 1998, well above the category average.

Investors Summa. This equity fund targets socially and environmentally responsible companies, with an emphasis toward Canadian investing. At June 30, 1998, it is a top-quartile performer over one, two, three, and five years.

Merrill Lynch World Allocation. This demoted Smart Fund had a disappointing year with a 5.7 per cent return to June 30, 1998, putting it in the fourth quartile for the category, and an MER that is above the category average at 2.75 per cent.

Availability:

Exclusively from Investors reps.

26. JONES HEWARD GROUP OF FUNDS FRONT OR REAR

Strengths:	Half a century of pension experience
	Low-MER money market fund
Weaknesses:	No global funds (except U.S.)
	Relatively high MERs
RESPs?:	No
Web Site:	www.jonesheward.com **Toll Free:** 1-800-361-1392

CANADIAN	Category	Rating	Fund Name	M.E.R.%	RRSP/Foreign
Money Market:		▲	Jones Heward Money Market Fund	0.5	RRSP
Fixed Income:	Long-term	■	Jones Heward Bond Fund	1.75	RRSP
	Small-Large cap	▲	Jones Heward Fund Ltd.	2.5	RRSP
Mult-Asset:	Balanced	■	Jones Heward Canadian Balanced Fund	2.4	RRSP

FOREIGN	Category	Rating	Fund Name	M.E.R.%	RRSP/Foreign
Regional Equity:	U.S.	▲	Jones Heward American Fund	2.5	Foreign

With no new funds added in the past year, the Jones Heward group of funds remains a tightly focused five-fund family. There has, however, been a change at the top: Rick Knowles is now CEO of Jones Heward Investment Management Inc. and also president of the Jones Heward Fund Ltd.

While its MERs are comparable to any of the big load groups, the firm has aggressively cut the MER of its Money Market fund in half (from 1.0 to 0.5 per cent). This fund has now been designated Noteworthy.

Although it has instituted no such action on its equity funds, the continued superior performance of the Jones Heward American Fund almost earned it Smart Fund status. This noteworthy fund returned almost 36 per cent for the year ended June 30, 1998 and has a three-year CAGR of 25 per cent. Harris Bretall Sullivan & Smith of San Francisco took over the fund three years ago. HBSS believes that growth follows earnings and once a stock makes it through several screens of fundamentals, it tends to be held for the longer term.

The five funds are regular load funds, with an optional front load negotiable to 9 per cent or a rear load of 5 per cent, declining to nil after seven years. Its Canadian funds are average performers, except the money market fund, but we see little evidence that their fairly high MERs have created extra value added. Perhaps recognizing this, in 1997 the firm shook up the venerable Jones Heward Fund, which is approaching its sixtieth birthday. The fund remains Noteworthy until we see the results of these changes.

The family remains part of the Bank of Montreal group of companies. It remains to be seen how Jones Heward will fit into the proposed merger of BMO and the Royal Bank of Canada.

Smart Funds 1999:

None.

Noteworthy Funds:

Jones Heward American. This blue-chip American equity fund is nicely diversified across consumer products, technology, financial services, merchandising, and industrial products. Plenty of household names, such as Pfizer, Gillette, GE, and Wal-Mart.

Jones Heward Money Market Fund. A cut in management fees from 1.0 to 0.5 per cent should put this fund into the high second quartile or first quartile. The minimum purchase level of $1,000 has been retained.

Jones Heward Fund Ltd. Manager James Lawson has departed for Guardian. Formerly invested in small emerging growth stocks, many of them high-tech issues, the firm's flagship has changed its mandate to invest in all market caps, but particularly those above $100 million. One-third of the fund is invested in small- to mid-cap Canadian stocks, chosen through a "bottom-up" process. The balance is in large cap stocks picked through a GARP—Growth at a Reasonable Price—approach.

Availability:

Through brokers and discount brokers and dealers, primarily Nesbitt Burns. $1,000 minimum initial purchase.

27. LEITH WHEELER INVESTMENT COUNSEL LTD.
NO LOAD

Strengths:	Low MERs
	Route to high-net-worth products
Weaknesses:	Limited number of funds
	Not available in all provinces
RESPs?:	No
Web Site:	none **Toll Free:** 1-888-292-1122

CANADIAN	Category	Rating	Fund Name	M.E.R.%	RRSP/Foreign
Money Market:		■	Money Market Fund	0.6	RRSP
Fixed Income:	Long-term	■	Fixed Income Fund	0.75	RRSP
Equity:	Large-cap	▲	Canadian Equity Fund	1.4	RRSP
Mult-Asset:	Balanced	★	**Balanced Fund**	1.1	RRSP

FOREIGN	Category	Rating	Fund Name	M.E.R.%	RRSP/Foreign
Regional Equity:	U.S.	▲	U.S. Equity Fund	1.25	Foreign

New to Smart Funds this year is this 17-year-old Vancouver-based, employee-owned investment counselling firm. The addition was made on the strength of its low-MER no-load funds. While there are only five funds in the family and assets are but a tiny combined $141 million, the firm also manages another $2.5 billion for pension funds, wealthy individuals, charities, and foundations.

Not everyone can gain access to this small family: the initial minimum investment is $50,000, which can be invested in any combination of the funds. Availability is restricted to British Columbia, Alberta, Ontario, Saskatchewan and Manitoba only.

But for those who qualify, the MERs are tough to beat: the Balanced Fund, with a 1.1 per cent MER, debuts as a Smart Fund. It's also the oldest Leith Wheeler Fund, having been created in 1987: the other four were started up in 1994. The Canadian Equity Fund, with a 1.4 per cent MER, and U.S. Equity Fund, at 1.25 per cent, are designated Noteworthy.

The Leith Wheeler funds also provide an entry level and growth path to the even lower-fee "High Net Worth" products normally offered by investment counselling firms. At Leith Wheeler, discretionary "Segregated" portfolio management is available at a $1 million minimum, while a "Portfolio of Funds" service is available at a $500,000 threshold. For a full explanation of these terms, investors in this category can refer to the *National Post*'s new companion volume to the Smart Funds guides: *The Wealthy Boomer: Life After Mutual Funds.*

Leith Wheeler's approach is to eschew attempts to "time" the stock market. It looks for stocks that it believes are undervalued and will grow; the managers typically expect to hold a stock for two to four years.

Smart Funds 1999:

Leith Wheeler Balanced Fund.

Noteworthy Funds:

Leith Wheeler Canadian Equity Fund. MER of 1.4 per cent is well below the category average. Created in 1994, this mostly large-cap fund is broadly spread across the major economic sectors: 25 per cent resources, 24 per cent in financial services, 11 per cent utilities, 10 per cent industrials, 9 per cent consumer products, and lesser amounts in media, merchandising, and real estate companies.

Leith Wheeler U.S. Equity Fund. An MER of 1.25 per cent is lower than most comparable retail-level funds. The managers are cautious about record valuations and seek companies in industries where sentiment has turned negative, or which have encountered a short-term difficulty that can be overcome, or stocks that the managers believe other analysts have overlooked or misunderstood.

Availability:

Direct from the company, in Ontario, Alberta and British Columbia.

FRONT OR REAR

Strengths: Ivy and Universal families
STAR asset-allocation service
Weaknesses: Industrial family
MERs could be lower
RESPs?: Yes
Web Site: www.mackenziefinancial.com **Toll Free:** 1-800-387-0614

CANADIAN	Category	Rating	Fund Name	M.E.R.%	RRSP/Foreign
Money Market:		■	Industrial Cash Management	0.5	RRSP
		■	Industrial Short Term	1.25	RRSP
Fixed Income:	Long-term	■	Industrial Bond	1.87	RRSP
	Mortgage	■	Industrial Mortgage Securities	1.86	RRSP
		■	Ivy Mortgage	1.89	RRSP
Equity:	Mid-Large Cap	■	Industrial Growth	2.37	RRSP
		■	Industrial Horizon	2.37	RRSP
		▲	Ivy Canadian	2.38	RRSP
		■	Cundill Security	2.04	RRSP
		★	**Universal Canadian Growth**	2.39	RRSP
	Small Cap	■	Industrial Equity	2.42	RRSP
		★	**Ivy Enterprise**	2.39	RRSP
	Gold/precious metal	■	Universal Precious Metals	2.42	RRSP
	Resource	▲	Universal Canadian Resource	2.39	RRSP
	Technology & Resources	▲	Universal Future*	2.38	RRSP
Tax Advantaged:	Dividend	▲	Industrial Dividend Growth	2.38	RRSP
Mult-Asset:	Balanced	■	Industrial Balanced	2.37	RRSP
		■	Industrial Income	1.86	RRSP
		★	**Industrial Pension**	2.4	RRSP
		■	Ivy Growth & Income	2.12	RRSP
		▲	Universal Canadian Balanced Fund	2.41	RRSP
	Asset Allocation	■	STAR service		RRSP & Foreign

FOREIGN	Category	Rating	Fund Name	M.E.R.%	RRSP/Foreign
Money Market:		■	Universal U.S. Money Market	1.25	Foreign
Fixed Income:		■	Universal World Income RRSP	2.15	RRSP
		■	Universal World Tactical Bond Fund	2.32	Foreign
		■	Universal World High Yield Fund	new	Foreign
Global Equity:	All-global	★	**Ivy Foreign Equity****	2.39	Foreign
		▲	Cundill Value	2.01	Foreign
		▲	Universal World Growth RRSP	2.44	RRSP
		■	Universal World Value Fund	new	Foreign
	Specialty	★	**Universal World Science & Technology Fund**	2.41	Foreign
		■	Universal World Real Estate	new	Foreign
Regional Equity:	U.S. Large-cap	■	Industrial American	2.38	Foreign
	U.S. Small-cap	▲	Universal U.S. Emerging Growth	2.4	Foreign
	NAFTA/N.Am.	■	Universal Americas	2.55	Foreign
	EAFE	■	Universal International Stock Fund***	2.41	Foreign
	Emerging Market	■	Universal World Emerging Growth	2.54	Foreign
	Far East	■	Universal Far East	2.58	Foreign
	Japan	■	Universal Japan	2.54	Foreign
	Europe	★	**Universal European Opportunities**	2.48	Foreign

Global Balanced:	■	Universal World Asset Allocation	2.47	Foreign
	★	**Universal World Balanced RRSP**	2.41	RRSP

* formerly Industrial Future
** Universal Growth merged into Ivy Foreign Equity
*** formerly Universal World Equity

After a year of standing pat, relatively speaking, Mackenzie Financial Corp. kicked its fund-creation machinery into high gear again over the past 18 months. Most of the innovation and tinkering involved the global-oriented Universal family, which launched three new funds. In addition, one of the funds from the moribund Industrial family, Industrial Future, was renamed the Universal Future Fund, while Bill Kanko's Universal Growth Fund was merged into Ivy Foreign World Equity following unitholder approval in June 1998. The two funds had a similar investment philosophy, reflected by a 90 per cent overlap in their stock holdings.

Universal World Equity Fund has been recast as an EAFE fund (investing outside North America, as it had increasingly been doing since 1993). It was therefore renamed Universal International Stock Fund (a philosophy and name reminiscent of the successful Templeton International Stock Fund).

In all, then, there are just shy of 40 funds spread over Mackenzie's three fund families, all with distinct styles. Investors who find it difficult to choose a few entrees from this feast can give up the task and delegate it to Gordon Garmaise's STAR fund portfolio optimization service, which now holds a few billion dollars worth of Mackenzie funds and has been extended to include funds of other families as well.

Regular Smart Funds readers will be aware the Universal family has long had the lion's share of Smart Funds and the Industrial family almost none. The one Industrial Fund we picked last year, Industrial Future, is now also in the Universal family, as noted above.

The STAR service similarly overweights the Universal funds in its foreign and non-registered portfolios, but includes all three families in the category that counts: registered portfolios. For example, the Registered Balanced Growth & Income portfolio has one Industrial fund, two Ivy funds, and four Universal funds; the Registered Maximum Long-Term Growth portfolio has one Ivy fund, two Industrial, and four Universal funds.

Minor reshufflings of portfolio managers have occurred in all three families. Following the departure of Gerry Coleman to C.I. Mutual Funds, Jerry Javasky took over the lead management role for Ivy Canadian and Ivy Growth & Income Fund. Javasky now focuses on Canadian large caps, since he has been joined by two other strong managers. Bill Kanko moved to the Ivy family, following the merger of his Universal Growth Fund into Ivy Foreign Equity. He is now assisted by Sarah Khoo, formerly of Royal Mutual Funds. Chuck Roth, who managed small- and large-cap Canadian equity portfolios for Ultravest Counsellors and ran small caps on the Colonia Special Growth Fund, joined Mackenzie in December 1997 to manage the small-cap Ivy Enterprise Fund.

The Industrial family has now been under Bill Proctor for more than a year, following the move upstairs by Neil Lovatt, as noted in last year's edition. Proctor runs Industrial Dividend Growth Fund, Industrial Pension, and Industrial Horizon. New Industrial managers include Chris Kresic on Industrial Bond and Industrial Mortgage Securities, and Ian Osler on the small-mid cap Industrial Equity Fund.

In the Universal family, subadviser Bluewater Investment Management Inc. added Sukyong Yang, formerly of TD GreenLine, to the successful team of Dina DeGeer and Dennis Starritt. They manage Universal Canadian Growth and Universal Canadian Balanced. Raymond Chan joined Thornton Investment Advisors to assist on Universal Far East Fund.

And now, the envelopes please for the latest funds, all launched in October 1997.

Universal World High Yield Fund invests in corporate bonds of high-growth companies, special situations in mature markets, and corporate and government debt in emerging markets. Most of the high-yield bonds represent senior debt: the bondholders have first claim on a corporation's assets in the event of default. The funds are managed by Mackenzie Investment Management Inc., which runs Universal World Income RRSP Fund.

Universal World Real Estate Fund, managed by the Henderson Real Estate Strategy Group, invests in liquid, publicly listed real estate securities from around the world. The managers seek to exploit the fact that property market cycles tend to be out of phase with underlying domestic equity cycles.

Universal World Value Fund uses strict value criteria to uncover companies with stock prices it believes are more depressed than warranted. The fund does not use "top-down" geographic criteria but goes wherever in the world valuations direct it. Again, like the new EAFE fund, this is a Templeton-style philosophy.

In July 1998, Mackenzie announced it had reached a strategic alliance with Peter Cundill to market the Cundill funds. It is expected the funds will be made available through multiple broker/dealers, but with a higher MER to pay for the trailers. Stay tuned for more developments from the new Mackenzie brand name: "Cundill."

Smart Funds 1999:

Ivy Enterprise Fund, Universal Canadian Growth, Ivy Foreign Equity, Universal European Opportunities, Universal World Balanced RRSP Fund, Universal World Science & Technology Fund, Industrial Pension Fund.

Noteworthy Funds:

Universal U.S. Emerging Growth. Demoted after several years as a Smart Fund. We still like James Broadfoot but his picks may show up in the more diversified Universal World Science & Technology Fund, which has been promoted to Smart Funds status with this edition. Not only did U.S. small caps take a beating, but this fund also fell to the 97th fund out of 100 U.S. funds with a two-year performance number.

Universal Canadian Balanced. Would have been promoted from Noteworthy status, but we felt that Mackenzie didn't need to have two balanced funds deemed Smart. This is a good fund and should be a keeper for most people. New Bluewater-managed fund far out-stripped the Trimark balanced funds on which it was modelled, returning a sparkling 19.4 per cent for the year ended June 30, 1998.

Universal World Growth RRSP Fund. Still not a bad way to circumvent the foreign-content restrictions. Former Smart Fund has now dropped into the third quartile. Do not hold this fund in your taxable account since all realized returns are taxed as interest income.

Cundill Value. Former Smart Fund is now offered as part of the Mackenzie family. Our international pick from Mackenzie is Ivy Foreign Equity. Cundill has huge weighting in Japan, which has killed the fund's performance, dropping it to fourth quartile across the one-, two-, three-, five-, and 10-year CAGR periods to June 30, 1998.

Ivy Canadian. Huge fund with $5.8 billion in assets makes it questionable if it can justify its 2.38 per cent MER. We picked the Universal Canadian Growth as Mackenzie's Smart Fund for the Canadian equity category. But Ivy Canadian holds up well in volatile or falling markets.

Universal Canadian Resource. Demoted after a tough year for natural resources.

Universal Future Fund. Formerly Industrial Future, this fund continues to be one of the few 100 per cent RRSP-eligible technology funds, with the added diversification of an equal weighting of natural resource stocks. Five-year average CAGR to June 30, 1998 of 13.6 and 12.7 per cent in the past year. It remains a better alternative to the moribund Industrial Growth Fund.

Industrial Dividend Growth. This fund sizzled with a 22 per cent one-year return to June 30, 1998. Continues to be appropriate for taxable portfolios or conservative RRSP portfolios.

Availability:

Available through brokers and discount brokers, dealers and a growing list of life insurance agents.

29. MANULIFE GUARANTEED INVESTMENT FUNDS
NO LOAD

Strengths:	Hedge against market losses
	Choice of major families
Weaknesses:	MERS stiff
	No need for GIFs on bond, balanced funds
RESPs?:	No
Web Site: www.manulife.com	**Toll Free:** 1-888-626-8543

CANADIAN	Category	Rating	Fund Name	M.E.R.%	RRSP/Foreign
Money Market:		■	Manulife Elliott & Page Money Market GIF	1.35	RRSP
		■	Manulife Elliott & Page Money Market GIF	1.25	RRSP
Fixed Income:	Long-term	■	Manulife AGF Canadian Bond GIF	2.35	RRSP
		■	Manulife AGF High Income GIF	2.35	RRSP
		■	Manulife Fidelity Canadian Bond GIF	2.15	RRSP
	Short-term	■	Manulife Talvest Income GIF	2.25	RRSP
Equity:	Mid-Large Cap	■	Manulife AGF Canadian Equity GIF	3.20	RRSP
		■	Manulife C.I. Harbour GIF	3.00	RRSP
		■	Manulife Elliott & Page Equity GIF	2.75	RRSP
		■	Manulife Elliott & Page Value Equity GIF	2.80	RRSP
		■	Manulife Fidelity Capital Builder GIF	3.00	RRSP
		▲	Manulife Fidelity True North GIF	3.00	RRSP
		■	Manulife GT Global Canada Fund, Canada Growth Class GIF	3.00	RRSP
		■	Manulife O'Donnell Canadian GIF	3.00	RRSP
		▲	Manulife O'Donnell Select GIF	3.00	RRSP
		■	Manulife Trimark Select Canadian Growth GIF	2.98	RRSP
	Index	▲	Manulife Canadian Equity Index GIF	1.75	RRSP
Tax Advantaged:	Dividend	■	Manulife AGF Dividend GIF	2.80	RRSP
		■	Manulife Dynamic Dividend Growth GIF	2.94	RRSP
Mult-Asset:	Balanced	■	Manulife AGF Growth + Income GIF	2.95	RRSP
		■	Manulife C.I. Harbour Growth & Income GIF	2.95	RRSP
		■	Manulife Dynamic Partners GIF	3.37	RRSP
		■	Manulife Elliott & Page Balanced GIF	2.75	RRSP
		■	Manulife Fidelity Canadian Asset Allocation GIF	2.95	RRSP
		■	Manulife Talvest Canadian Asset Allocation GIF	2.95	RRSP
		■	Manulife Trimark Select Balanced GIF	2.98	RRSP

FOREIGN	Category	Rating	Fund Name	M.E.R.%	RRSP/Foreign
Fixed Income:		■	Manulife AGF Global Government Bond GIF	2.35	Foreign
		■	Manulife Dynamic Global Bond GIF	2.45	RRSP
Global Equity:	All-global	■	Manulife Fidelity International Portfolio GIF	3.38	Foreign
		■	Manulife Trimark Select Growth GIF	3.33	Foreign
Regional Equity:					
	U.S Large-cap	▲	Manulife AGF American Growth Class GIF	3.25	Foreign
		▲	Manulife Elliott & Page American Growth GIF	3.05	Foreign
		▲	Manulife Fidelity Growth America GIF	3.15	Foreign
		■	Manulife GT Global Fund, America Growth Class GIF	3.15	Foreign
		■	Manulife Talvest/Hyperion Value Line U.S. Equity GIF	3.15	Foreign
	Index - U.S.	■	Manulife U.S. Equity Index GIF	1.80	Foreign

With close to $3 billion of its new GIFs sold since inception two years ago, the Manulife Guaranteed Investment Funds have sparked a revolution across the fund industry. Trimark, BPI, Templeton, Talvest and C.I. have all subsequently introduced "segregated" or "seg" versions of their in-house funds and many more fund majors are talking to insurance firms to announce similar alliances.

With this edition, we have dropped coverage of the Manulife Cabot Funds to make room for the 36—and growing—brand-name mutual funds covered under the GIF umbrella.

Take a look at the revised fund matrix for Manulife and you'll notice two things: first, there are no Smart Funds; second, there are high MERs.

What's going on here? The fact that prudent firms such as Trimark and Templeton have jumped on the seg fund bandwagon clearly indicates a lot of unease with stock valuations on the part of mutual fund industry executives. The public is voting with their feet, and telling them they're willing to pay more to protect their initial capital against market loss. Given the 20 per cent "corrections" of 1998, their timing seems perfect.

But investors must ask themselves if it's realistic that stock markets would go down and stay down a decade, which is how long it would have to be for the seg fund guarantees (100 per cent maturity benefit or 100 per cent death benefit) to apply. The 10-year clock can also be "reset," meaning that you can lock in market gains after a few years so you redefine your initial capital investment at the new higher level. The flipside, however, is that the time for the benefit to apply is also set back to the 10-year time horizon. More useful may be the 3- and 5-year guarantee periods of the banks' index-linked GICs.

There are two other reasons you might check out seg funds. If you died, your spouse would be guaranteed at least the initial capital even if stocks crashed. And second, it's somewhat easier to protect your assets from creditors with seg funds—but not if you're already in financial problems and being harried by creditors.

We don't think it makes sense to pay higher MERs for this so-called "protection" on money market funds, bond funds, or even balanced funds. The extra premium may be worth it in the case of U.S. stock funds or certain aggressive equity funds, which is why we have designated some of the GIF funds as "Noteworthy." These correspond to equivalent funds that may be "Smart" or "Noteworthy" in the fund family treatments located elsewhere in this book.

In addition, Manulife has its own in-house Cabot Funds, a group of seven no-load funds launched in February 1994. This family is predominantly Canadian equity, with one pure global fund, Global Equity. Manulife Cabot offers a "fund-on-fund" strategy on two of its domestic funds for investors who wish to maximize foreign content. Manulife International Fund Management Ltd., a Manulife subsidiary based in Britain, chooses the foreign stocks.

Smart Funds 1999:

None.

Noteworthy Funds:

Manulife Fidelity True North GIF. The underlying fund was originally managed by Veronika Hirsch. We believe that investors got a break when Alan Radlo took it over. If anyone can justify a 3 per cent MER it may be Radlo, since he is able to add some small-cap and medium-cap stocks to the large-cap names in this fund. A 15.5 per cent return for year ended June 30, 1998, good enough for first quartile.

Manulife O'Donnell Select GIF. New fund headed by former Trimark manager Wally Kusters. Although it makes no sense to pay a 3 per cent MER on the large-cap O'Donnell Canadian GIF, at least this fund has a shot at earning its fees with the small- and mid-cap stocks it can also invest in.

Manulife Canadian Index GIF. If managers can't beat the TSE 300 index, why pay for them? This should do as well as any actively managed large-cap Canadian equity fund, the MER of 1.75 per cent isn't back-breaking, and you receive some downside protection. Managed by Elliott & Page.

Manulife AGF American Growth Class GIF. Underlying AGF fund is a Smart Fund but 3.25 per cent is a hefty MER. Consider the Manulife U.S. Equity Index GIF at 1.8 per cent.

Manulife Elliott & Page American Growth GIF. Goldman Sachs runs this for E&P's version, which is designated a Smart Fund. Again, are they likely to beat the index version enough to justify the stiff MER?

Manulife Fidelity Growth America GIF. The underlying fund run by Fidelity's Brad Lewis is a Smart Fund. See above comments.

Availability:

Life insurance agents and "dual-licensed" brokers and discount brokers and dealers.

30. MAWER INVESTMENT MANAGEMENT   NO LOAD

Strengths:	Low MERs (but inching up)
	Mawer New Canada Fund
Weaknesses:	Limited distribution
	Low profile
RESPs?:	No
Web Site: www.mawer.com	**Toll Free:** 1-800-889-6248

CANADIAN	Category	Rating	Fund Name	M.E.R.%	RRSP/Foreign
Money Market:		■	Mawer Canadian Money Market Fund	0.69	RRSP
Fixed Income:	Long-term	■	Mawer Canadian Bond Fund	1.01	RRSP
	Short-term	■	Mawer Canadian Income Fund	1.01	Not RRSP eligible
	Corporate	▲	Mawer High Yield Bond Fund	1.54	RRSP
Equity:	Mid-Large Cap	■	Mawer Canadian Equity Fund	1.27	RRSP
	Small Cap	▲	Mawer New Canada Fund	1.47	RRSP
Mult-Asset:	Balanced	■	Mawer Canadian Balanced Retirement Savings Fund	1	RRSP

FOREIGN	Category	Rating	Fund Name	M.E.R.%	RRSP/Foreign
Global Equity:	EAFE	■	Mawer World Investment Fund	1.4	Foreign
Regional Equity:	US.	▲	Mawer U.S. Equity Fund	1.32	Foreign
Mult-Asset:	Balanced	■	Mawer Canadian Diversified Investment Fund	1.12	Foreign

This Calgary-based no-load firm, like its fellow Albertan-based competitor Bissett, does minimal marketing and passes along the savings with low management expense. The MERs of both its Canadian and global equity funds are at the low end of their category averages, although several have edged slightly higher since the last edition of this book. There are no switching charges.

As of mid-1997 the firm's 10 mutual funds were registered in all provinces and territories. No new funds have been added since the last edition.

The firm was founded in 1974 as a high-net-worth investment counsellor, expanded into pensions, and, in 1987, into mutual funds. It does not subcontract subadvisers, even in its international funds (which also helps keep fees down.) It now employs nine in-house investment managers, with an average of 15 years each in the business. The latest addition to the Canadian equity team is James Hall, who is an equity analyst on both the Canadian Equity Fund and the New Canada Fund.

Mawer describes itself as having a "value" approach to equity investing. The Canadian funds, also like Bissett, tend to have strong Western Canada representation, particularly in oil and gas and other natural resources. That may make it attractive to investors concerned about possible Quebec separation. Several of the funds have reached their 10-year anniversaries.

Asset allocation is handled by partner Don Ferris, a 20-year veteran who manages the Canadian Balanced Retirement Savings Fund and Canadian Diversified Investment Fund.

Mawer Investment Management provides discretionary investment management for individuals with a minimum $500,000 in investable assets. Segregated portfolios are available for private clients with at least $2 million.

Smart Funds 1999:

None.

Noteworthy Funds:

Mawer New Canada Fund. Originally the North American Shares Fund, the name was changed to the New Canada Fund in 1993 to reflect its concentration on Canadian small-cap securities, defined as a market float of less than $450 million. Fund returned 16.4 per cent in 1997, about 1.5 per cent better than the TSE 300. While the large-cap Mawer Canadian Equity Fund outperformed New Canada in 1997, the small-cap version has generally outpaced it by 5 per cent over the last five years. Both funds are managed by Bill MacLachlan, but New Canada also uses Martin Ferguson.

Mawer High Yield Bond Fund. Gary Feltham invests in low-rated and unrated bonds and debentures of Canadian companies, and high-yield bonds payable in U.S. dollars. So far, the greater risk of holding these "junk" bonds has not paid off. The one-year return of

10.55 per cent for the year ended June 30, 1998 was slightly below the 10.7 per cent generated by both the ScotiaMcLeod Bond Universe Index.

Mawer U.S. Equity Fund. With a stingy 1.32 per cent MER, this consistent performer has an average CAGR of 27.71 per cent for the five years ended June 30, 1998 (albeit less than the 31.97 per cent generated by the S&P 500 over the same period). Manager Darrell Anderson invests in 40 to 50 U.S. stocks of mixed market capitalization.

Availability:

Through selected discount brokers and investment dealers in all provinces and territories, with minimum $5,000 investment per fund. Residents of Alberta and Saskatchewan can purchase directly from Mawer, with minimum initial investment of $25,000.

31. MAXXUM GROUP OF FUNDS FRONT OR REAR

Strengths:	Canadian equities
	Janus on global funds
Weaknesses:	Volatile specialty funds
	MERs no longer below average
RESPs?:	No
Web Site:	www.maxxumfund.com **Toll Free:** 1-888-462-9986

CANADIAN	Category	Rating	Fund Name	M.E.R.%	RRSP/Foreign
Money Market:		■	Maxxum Money Market of Canada	0.84	RRSP
Fixed Income:	Long-term	■	Maxxum Income Fund	1.73	RRSP
Equity:	Mid-Large Cap	▲	Maxxum Canadian Equity Growth	2.13	RRSP
	Gold/precious metal	■	Maxxum Precious Metals Fund	2.23	RRSP
	Resource	▲	Maxxum Natural Resource Fund	2.23	RRSP
Tax Advantaged:	Dividend	★	**Maxxum Dividend Fund**	1.73	RRSP
Mult-Asset:	Balanced	▲	Maxxum Canadian Balanced Fund	2.13	RRSP

FOREIGN	Category	Rating	Fund Name	M.E.R.%	RRSP/Foreign
Global Equity:	All-global	▲	Maxxum Global Equity Fund	2.48	Foreign
Regional Equity:	U.S.	★	**Maxxum American Equity Fund**	2.48	Foreign

When this family was known as Prudential Fund Management, it was ahead of its time, keeping management expense ratios low by engaging in minimal marketing overhead. Not surprisingly, performance was robust. The investment home of Veronika Hirsch before she rocketed to stardom, Prudential had a particular strength in precious metals and Canadian resource stocks.

Alas, Prudential underwent ownership change. Two years ago, London Life Insurance Co. acquired Prudential and renamed the group MAXXUM. Then, in August 1997, Great West Life purchased the London Insurance Group. GWL has confirmed continuance of the MAXXUM Group of Funds through an OSC filing.

MAXXUM has had to broaden its distribution, since it had been difficult for most investors to access its products. As a result of these distribution changes, MAXXUM has been forced to act like most other marketing-driven load fund outfits. It raised its MERs just as the issue started to become top of mind with many fund investors and, by 1997, introduced trailer (or service) fees.

Meanwhile, performance of those domestic special equity funds has sagged in recent years—not primarily because of higher MERs, however, but because of the generally negative climate for gold and resource stocks. These special equity funds were always high on the risk/reward spectrum and short-term drops are nothing to panic about. The portfolio managers running them have provided consistency throughout the changes in ownership: Head of the investing department, Martin Anstee, has been in place for 28 years, bond manager Gerry Boychuk for 11 years, and Hirsch's replacement—Canadian equities manager Jackee Pratt—for almost three years.

Nevertheless, in line with our general policy to minimize special equity funds in Smart Funds 1999, we have demoted MAXXUM Natural Resource Fund from Smart Fund status, and removed the Noteworthy designation of MAXXUM Precious Metals. Nervous investors can switch to more broadly diversified MAXXUM funds if they feel their portfolios are overly concentrated in resources and precious metals.

Pratt's top-quartile Dividend Fund retains its Smart Fund status. We believe that it or Pratt's broader Canadian Equity Growth Fund is a safer harbor for fans of the specialty funds. The latter, for example, still provides a modest (5 per cent) exposure to gold stocks and almost 20 per cent in natural resources.

While 60 per cent of MAXXUM's investment management is performed in-house—that is, in its domestic equity and fixed-income funds—a growing strength are its two global equity funds, which have been managed since 1995 by Janus Capital Corp. of Denver. *Forbes* magazine ranked Janus as the top U.S. fund company in 1997.

We flagged the MAXXUM American Equity and MAXXUM Global Equity funds as Noteworthy in the last two editions of this book, and this year we promote the American Equity Fund to a Smart Fund.

Smart Funds 1999:

Maxxum Dividend Fund, Maxxum American Equity Fund.

Noteworthy Funds:

Maxxum Global Equity Fund. The other strong Maxxum fund managed by Denver's Janus Capital. Morningstar named manager Helen Young Hayes the 1997 international fund manager of the year. Fund returned 28 per cent for year ended June 30, 1998. Some of Janus's American Equity picks (see its Smart Fund listing) show up here, as the fund had a 29 per cent U.S. weighting early in 1998. Large weighting in Europe; almost none in the Far East.

Maxxum Natural Resource Fund. A bad year for this fund—down 31 per cent for the year ended June 30, 1998—and most resources funds. More volatile than its peers, we have demoted many such overly specialized funds in this year's edition. This fund is more diversified than Maxxum Precious Metals but does have a 24 per cent weighting in gold and precious metal stocks, arguably enough of that asset class for most investors.

Maxxum Canadian Equity Growth Fund. Traditionally more volatile than others in the large-cap category, as evidenced by exposure to junior mine stocks. 6.6 per cent one-year return to June 30, 1998.

Maxxum Canadian Balanced Fund. This fund returned 9.2 per cent for the year ended June 30, 1998. As of the spring, fund was only half invested in stocks, 46 per cent in bonds, and 4 per cent in cash. Now 10 years old, the fund has an 11 per cent CAGR for the decade ended June 30.

Availability:

Through some full-service and discount brokers and financial planners, registered London Life agents and other insurance agents with a mutual fund licence.

32. MD MANAGEMENT LTD. NO LOAD

Strengths:	Performance with low fees
	Strong subadvisers
Weaknesses:	Not available to general public
RESPs?:	Soon
Web Site:	www.cma.ca **Toll Free:** 1-800-267-2332

CANADIAN	Category	Rating	Fund Name	M.E.R.%	RRSP/Foreign
Money Market:		■	MD Money Fund	0.52	RRSP
Fixed Income:	Mid-term	▲	MD Bond Fund	1.02	RRSP
	Short-term	■	MD Income Fund*		RRSP
	Short-term	■	MD Bond and Mortgage Fund	1.10	RRSP
Equity:	Mid-Large Cap	▲	MD Equity Fund	1.27	RRSP
	Mid-Large Cap	▲	MD Select Fund	1.30	RRSP
Tax Advantaged:	Dividend	■	MD Dividend Fund	1.29	RRSP
Mult-Asset:	Balanced	▲	MD Balanced Fund	1.28	RRSP

FOREIGN	Category	Rating	Fund Name	M.E.R.%	RRSP/Foreign
Fixed Income:		■	MD Global Bond Fund	1.19	Foreign
Global Equity:	All-global	★	**MD Growth Fund**	1.28	Foreign
Regional Equity:	U.S.	★	**M.D. U.S. Equity**	1.30	Foreign
	Emerging Market	■	MD Emerging Markets	3.21	Foreign

* not a fund but a deferred group annuity contract

MD Management Limited has much to offer investors but this subsidiary of the Canadian Medical Association (CMA) sells its funds exclusively to doctors and their families who form the CMA membership.

MD Management also sells a broader package of services, including GICs, financial planning, and MD Family Trust, a tax-effective way to save for family members. And it has been doing so for more than a quarter century. In the early 1950s the CMA was an early advocate of government-endorsed retirement savings plans, which were introduced in 1957 as RRSPs. It was named one of Canada's 50 best-managed private companies in 1995.

In 1969, the CMA established Lancet Management Ltd., a wholly owned financial subsidiary offering three mutual funds. Lancet was renamed MD Management Ltd. in 1971. Some funds were renamed and more added.

Today, several of the funds are top performers. They are managed externally by well-established load fund enterprises in the business, namely Guardian Capital, Mackenzie, T.A.L. Investment Counsel, and Templeton. Even better, for those who qualify for this exclusive club, the management fees are much lower than the equivalent load funds, which ultimately contributes to the bottom-line performance.

This group continues to stick with its 12-fund family—eight Canadian funds and four foreign.

On the administration front, MD has tried to improve accessibility to its product. The funds are sold through a national branch network of MD Management Consultants and through a toll-free telephone trading service.

Smart Funds 1999:

MD Growth Fund, MD U.S. Equity.

Noteworthy Funds:

MD Select. This Canadian equity fund managed by Guardian Capital fell short of the competition over one year to June 30, 1998 but is still above average over three years.

MD Equity Fund. This fund has multiple managers: Mawer and O'Donnell Investment Management on small- and mid-cap stocks, McLean Budden on large-cap growth stocks, and J.R. Senecal & Associates for a large-cap sector rotator approach, plus Templeton for the international picks. Even with all those managers getting paid, the fund has an MER of only 1.27 per cent.

MD Balanced. One-, three-, and five-year CAGRs are all above average at June 30, 1998 and an MER of 1.28 per cent is among the lowest anywhere.

MD Bond. Continues to turn in above-average performance under the guiding hand of TAL Investment Counsel, which is strong in fixed income.

Availability:

Available only to members of Canadian Medical Association and their immediate families and sold through MD Management Financial Consultants.

33. MUTUAL GROUP OF FUNDS   NO LOAD, FRONT, AND REAR LOADS

Strengths:	Several second quartile no-load funds
	Balanced funds
Weaknesses:	Confusion of old and newer families
	No 100% RRSP-eligible global funds
RESPs?:	Yes
Web Site:	www.TheMutualGroup.com **Phone:** (519) 888-3900

CANADIAN	Category	Rating	Fund Name	M.E.R.%	RRSP/Foreign
Money Market:		■	Mutual Money Market Fund	1.03	RRSP
Fixed Income:	Long-term	■	Mutual Premier Bond Fund	1.99	RRSP
	Short-term	■	Mutual Bond Fund	1.87	RRSP
	Mortgage	■	Mutual Premier Mortgage Fund	1.68	RRSP

Equity:	Mid-Large Cap	■	Mutual Equifund	1.79	RRSP
		■	Mutual Premier Blue Chip Fund	2.39	RRSP
		■	Mutual Summit Equity Fund	2.70	RRSP
		■	Mutual Summit Dividend Growth	2.70	RRSP
	Small-Mid Cap		Mutual Alpine Equity Fund	2.85	RRSP
	Small Cap	▲	Mutual Premier Growth Fund	2.38	RRSP
	Resource	■	Mutual Alpine Resources Fund	2.85	RRSP
Mult-Asset:	Balanced	■	Mutual Diversifund 40	1.77	RRSP
		■	Mutual Premier Diversified Fund	2.40	RRSP
		■	Mutual Summit Growth and Income Fund	2.70	RRSP

FOREIGN	Category	Rating	Fund Name	M.E.R.%	RRSP/Foreign
	EAFE	■	Mutual Premier International Fund	2.47	Foreign
		■	Mutual Summit Foreign Equity Fund	2.70	Foreign
Regional Equity:	U.S.	■	Mutual Premier American Fund	2.44	Foreign
		■	Mutual Amerifund	2.09	Foreign
	Emerging Market	■	Mutual Premier Emerging Markets Fund	3.87	Foreign
	Far East		Mutual Alpine Asian Fund	2.85	Foreign

The Mutual Group added seven new funds to its line-up in June 1997, giving its clients access to the external portfolio management of Mackenzie Financial Corp. and AGF Funds Inc.

Of the new funds, the four managed by Mackenzie are sold under the Summit label including Ivy Canadian, Ivy Foreign Equity, and Ivy Growth and Income. An additional three, managed by AGF, carry the Alpine label, with AGF Asian Equity, 20/20 Canadian Resource, and AGF Growth Equity as the underlying funds. Such an arrangement helps a proprietary sales force add outside managers so that Mutual Life clients can have choice.

The new funds include Canadian balanced, equity, and foreign equity, which add some more aggressive growth funds to Mutual's previously limited line-up. Unfortunately, some of these funds carry much higher MERs than the category averages.

It is a bit early to tell how these are doing, but it's easy to check the performance track record by looking at the underlying funds. The selection is not bad, and all except the Industrial Dividend fund have been Smart Funds at one time or another.

The total 20 funds now fall into four families. The long-established Mutual Leader group funds carries a front-end load of 3.75 per cent. All other funds, including the new Summit and Alpine are sold no-load. The Mutual Premier funds are now managed by Perigee Private Management Inc., replacing Mutual Asset Management Ltd.

Although the Mutual Group is affiliated with the Mutual Life Assurance Company of Canada, these were mutual funds, not insurance segregated fund products. These funds were managed by the old Mutual Asset Management, which suffered the loss of two key Canadian equity managers at the end of 1997; Suzann Pennington and Peter Hodson left to join Synergy Asset Management.

Smart Funds 1999:

None.

Noteworthy Funds:

Mutual Premier Growth. The most aggressive fund in the family, this small-cap Canadian equity fund fell below the average return over one year to June 30, 1998 with a negative 1.79 per cent compared with the median 4.89 per cent gain. But it continues to be above the median over five years.

Availability:

Distributed through agents licensed by Mutual Investco Inc., one of the Mutual Group of Companies.

34. NAVIGATOR FUND COMPANY   LOAD

Strengths:	A capital preserving Asian fund	
	A Canadian technology fund	
Weaknesses:	No broad global funds	
	High MERs	
RESPs?:	No	
Web site:	www.navigator.ca	**Toll Free:** 1-888-240-2220

CANADIAN	Category	Rating	Fund Name	M.E.R.%	RRSP/Foreign
Fixed Income:	Short-term	▲	Navigator Canadian Income Fund	2.45	RRSP
Equity:	Mid-Large Cap	■	Navigator Canadian Growth Fund	2.75	RRSP
	Small -cap	▲	Navigator Value Investment Retirement	2.99	RRSP
	Sector	▲	Navigator Canadian Technology Fund	2.85	RRSP
Mult-Asset:	Balanced	■	Navigator Canadian Growth & Income Fund	2.75	RRSP

FOREIGN	Category	Rating	Fund Name	M.E.R.%	RRSP/Foreign
Regional Equity:	US Value	■	Navigator American Value Investment Fund	2.99	Foreign
	US Growth	■	Navigator American Growth Fund	2.99	Foreign
	Far East	▲	Navigator Asia Pacific Fund	3.01	Foreign

Navigator added three new funds to its small family, providing a broader selection for investors in this Vancouver-based fund group. In the process, it brought two new subadvisers into the fold.

New in the last year are two additional Canadian funds—a mid- to large-cap equity and a balanced fund, both managed by Sterling Asset Management Inc. of Vancouver. The management of all eight Navigator funds is farmed out to subadvisers in Canada, the United States, and Hong Kong.

The other addition was more unusual—a Canadian Technology fund. It is unique because it differs from most technology funds, which are global in scope. The fund is managed by Tera Capital Corp. of Toronto, a small specialist in technology and biotechnology investing. The fund was launched based on Navigator's belief that enormous opportunity exists for investment in this sector right here in Canada. Marketing material notes this is the fastest-growing sector in Canada and technology and biotechnology represent 20 per cent of the Canadian economy.

Navigator's best-known subadviser is Wayne Deans of Marathon Equity fame. He continues to manage the Navigator Value Investment Retirement Fund, the family's inaugural offering in late 1992. Dean's fixed-income partner at Deans, Knight Capital Management of Vancouver, is also involved, as manager of the Navigator Canadian Income Fund, which was introduced in early 1993.

But it is the subadviser to the Navigator Asia Pacific Fund that really caught investors' attention in the last year. Portfolio managers Cheah Cheng Hye and V-Nee Yeh of Value Partners in Hong Kong managed to insulate the fund from a dramatic bout of the Asian flu that swept through this fund category. Value Partners moved much of the portfolio into Hong Kong shortly after they took on its management in the late summer of 1997. At June 30, 1998, the fund has a one-year loss of 26.9 per cent versus the median decline of 38.8 per cent for all funds in the same category. But this fund also has a large exposure to China at the time of writing and, with uncertainty in that market as well, the ongoing drama of Far East funds continues.

Investors looking south of the border can choose between a growth or a value style U.S. equity fund in this family. Both are managed by Roxbury Capital Management of Santa Monica, California. Former Fidelity salesman Barry Lavalley and company Nova Bancorp took over control of the company in mid-1998.

Smart Funds 1999:

None.

Noteworthy Funds:

Navigator Canadian Technology. This 100 per cent RRSP-eligible technology fund is unique in its mandate of investing in Canadian firms. Its manager is a small niche firm that specializes in technology and biotechnology investing.

Navigator Asia Pacific. This fund was demoted when we eliminated all Asia and volatile regional funds from being Smart Funds.

Navigator Canadian Income. While the fees on bond funds are often hard to justify, given the accessibility of direct investment in bonds, a high-yield bond fund offers potential for higher return and requires professional management, which justifies the fees.

Navigator Value Investment Retirement. Wayne Deans had a disappointing year as he missed out on the top performing large-cap stocks that drove the TSE300. But Deans' experience should prove itself over the longer term.

Availability:

Brokers and discount brokers and planners in Ontario and the four western provinces. $1,000 minimum initial investment in non-registered and registered plans.

35. O'DONNELL GROUP OF FUNDS   FRONT OR REAR

Strengths:	Choice of value & growth styles
	Aggressive small-mid cap growth funds
Weaknesses:	MERs a tad high
	Spotty debuts for U.S. funds
RESPs?:	No
Web Site:	None **Toll Free:** 1-800-292-5658

CANADIAN	Category	Rating	Fund Name	M.E.R.%	RRSP/Foreign
Money Market:		■	O'Donnell Money Market Fund	1.1	RRSP
Fixed Income:		■	O'Donnell Short Term Fund	1.35	RRSP
	Short-term	▲	O'Donnell High Income Fund	2	RRSP
Equity:	Large-cap/Growth	■	O'Donnell Canadian Fund	2.75	RRSP
	Large-cap/Value	■	O'Donnell Select Fund	2.75	RRSP
	Medium Cap	▲	O'Donnell Growth Fund	2.75	RRSP
	Small-mid Cap	■	O'Donnell Canadian Emerging Growth Fund	2.75	RRSP
Mult-Asset:	Balanced	■	O'Donnell Balanced Fund	2.4	RRSP

FOREIGN	Category	Rating	Fund Name	M.E.R.%	RRSP/Foreign
Global Equity:	All-global	▲	O'Donnell World Equity Fund	2.75	Foreign
	Specialty	■	O'Donnell World Precious Metals Fund	2.75	RRSP
Regional Equity:	U.S. Mid-cap	▲	O'Donnell U.S. Mid Cap Fund	2.9	Foreign
	U.S. Small-cap	▲	O'Donnell American Sector Growth Fund	2.9	Foreign

The O'Donnell Funds pass their third anniversary in December 1998. The 11 funds now have $1.5 billion in assets. If you're in this family, odds are your broker is enthusiastic about founder James (Jim) F. O'Donnell, whose contacts go back a quarter century to the marketing heyday of Mackenzie Financial Corp. That's allowed him to snare some big-name investment talent, including small-cap ace Wayne Deans, U.S. market timer Elaine Garzarelli, media/communications guru Mario Gabelli, and former Trimark manager Wally Kusters.

Such big names cost money, and the O'Donnell Fund's management expense ratios are at the top of the MER range. Gabelli has earned his fees, with his O'Donnell U.S. Mid-Cap Fund returning 34.9 per cent for the year ended June 30, 1998 (25.8 per cent for the two-year CAGR). Garzarelli has recovered from her infamous and premature call to cash out of the U.S. stock market in 1996. Now fully reinvested, her O'Donnell American Sector Growth Fund returned 21.7 per cent in the year ended June 30, 1998 (but just 13.2 per cent for the two-year CAGR, well below the index). Both U.S. funds are Noteworthy with this edition.

Deans' Canadian Emerging Growth Fund continues to be in the doldrums: it lost 21.1 per cent for the one-year period. However, investors now have several alternatives in the critical Canadian equity category: in addition to Jim Goar's mid-cap O'Donnell Growth Fund, there are two new large-cap Canadian equity funds, available in either a Value or Growth management style. The value fund is O'Donnell Select Fund, managed by Wally Kusters; the growth fund is O'Donnell Canadian, managed by Glenn Inamoto. We give the Noteworthy nod to the more established mid-cap fund.

Doug Knight's O'Donnell High Income Fund, which invests in high-yielding corporate bonds, fell from Smart Fund status because of its MER. O'Donnell Balanced Fund provides a mix of Knight on bonds with Deans in small and mid-caps.

The O'Donnell World Precious Metals Fund was launched in late 1996 and features Kjeld Thygesen, a London, U.K.-based mining analyst with a 30-year track record. That didn't stop the fund from getting hammered in 1997, just as all gold funds did as the price of gold bullion sagged.

O'Donnell World Equity Fund is an all-global equity fund but the manager, Dan Jaworski of STI Capital Management, left to work for BPI's U.S. affiliate. In June 1998, O'Donnell announced that Mario Gabelli would also take on the global fund.

For now, O'Donnell is strong in high-yield corporate bonds and North American mid-cap stocks, two places where managers may justify their high fees.

Smart Funds 1999:

None.

Noteworthy Funds:

O'Donnell High Income Fund. A former Smart Fund, but in pruning our bond fund selections, this high MER third-quartile performer got squeezed out.

O'Donnell Growth Fund. Manager Jim Goar's mid-cap mandate for Canadian stocks is more likely to justify a hefty MER than the new large-cap versions. Investors waiting for Wayne Deans to regain his magic touch on emerging growth stocks may want to try this fund in the interim. 1.3 per cent return for year ended June 30, 1998.

O'Donnell American Sector Growth Fund. If you believe in market timing, Elaine Garzarelli may be your manager. She's famous for calling the 1987 crash, infamous for making a premature call to exit the market in 1996. Now back to being almost fully invested (8 per cent cash as of the spring) the fund is up nicely. Garzarelli figures the Dow should reach 9500 before becoming "overextended." Large-cap, top-down approach to S&P 500 firms.

O'Donnell U.S. Mid-Cap Fund. Mario Gabelli is an oft-quoted guru on communications and media stocks and this fund rode that wave to a 34.9 per cent return for the year ended June 30, 1998. U.S. mid-caps are companies between US$2 billion and US$5 billion. Note that son Marc Gabelli assists father Mario on this fund.

O'Donnell World Equity Fund. As noted above, this fund has undergone management changes and a period in which it rested mostly in cash. Now managed by Mario Gabelli, the opportunity to put the cash to work during the periodic corrections of 1998 is viewed by some advisers as an opportunity to access Gabelli's stock-picking prowess worldwide.

Availability:

Through financial planners, independent dealers, and full-service stockbrokers and discount brokers in all provinces. Minimum investment $500.

36. PHILLIPS, HAGER & NORTH LTD. NO LOAD

Strengths:	Performance
	Low MERs
Weaknesses:	Marketing
	$25,000 minimum
RESPs?:	No
Web Site:	www.phn.ca

Toll Free: 1-800-661-6141

CANADIAN	Category	Rating	Fund Name	M.E.R.%	RRSP/Foreign
Money Market:		■	PH&N Canadian Money Market Fund	0.44	RRSP
Fixed Income:	Long-term	★	**PH&N Bond Fund**	0.57	RRSP
	Short-term	■	PH&N Short Term Bond & Mortgage Fund	0.63	RRSP
Equity:	Mid-Large Cap	★	**PH&N Canadian Equity Fund**	1.1	RRSP
		■	PH&N Canadian Equity Plus Fund	1.16	RRSP
	Small Cap	■	PH&N Vintage Fund*	1.75	RRSP
Tax Advantaged:	Dividend	★	**PH&N Dividend Income Fund**	1.16	RRSP
Mult-Asset:	Balanced	★	**PH&N Balanced Fund**	0.89	RRSP

FOREIGN	Category	Rating	Fund Name	M.E.R.%	RRSP/Foreign
Money Market:		■	PH&N $U.S. Money Market Fund	0.52	RRSP
Global Equity:	EAFE	▲	PH&N International Equity Fund	1.49	Foreign
Regional Equity:	U.S.	★	**PH&N U.S. Equity Fund**	1.09	Foreign
	NAFTA/N.Am.	■	PH&N North American Equity Fund	1.12	Foreign

* closed

Growing consumer awareness of the importance of low management expense ratios (MERs) has played into the hands of Vancouver-based Phillips, Hager & North Ltd. This employee-owned no-load outfit may not advertise, but after 30 years, it hardly constitutes a secret anymore. Its consistent strong long-term performance and low MERs mean PH&N continues to garner more than its fair share of "Smart Funds."

Whether the accompanying popularity forces its larger funds into a "regression to the mean" syndrome remains to be seen. On the one hand, PH&N is taking steps to retain its elite status: effective June 1, 1998, it raised the minimum initial investment for RRSP accounts for clients dealing directly with the firm from $5,000 to $10,000. On the other hand, it decreased the minimum investment for third-party accounts to $10,000 from the previous $25,000. Thus, the minimum investment is $10,000 whether you buy direct or through a third party. It has also lowered the minimum initial investment for RRIF accounts to $50,000, down from $100,000, also as of June 1.

No new funds were added in the past year. The investment management team remains solid, although co-founder Rudy North retired in December 1997 as part of a planned transition. Over the past year, PH&N added two new Canadian equity fund managers— Dale Harrison (formerly a fund company stock analyst at Nesbitt Burns Inc.) and Dan Lewan—and two new bond fund managers— Christine Hu and Hanif Mamdani. On the administrative front, PH&N introduced pre-authorized chequing (PAC) accounts effective June 1, 1998, provided the $10,000 minimum purchase requirement has been met. The minimum for subsequent automatic purchases is $500, with the minimum transaction involving any one fund set at $100.

PH&N's core business is pension investing and running segregated management and pooled funds for high-net-worth individuals. Due in part to the funds' low MERs, even its wealthy clients use the same family of no-load funds. That tells you one of the most respected independent investment counsellors in Canada thinks the diversification and other benefits of mutual funds are appropriate for almost anyone.

PH&N's investment style is focused on finding good North American companies, based on specific criteria, such as a consistently above-average rate of return on shareholder equity, and companies that are industry leaders and in the growth phase of their life cycles.

Nevertheless, PH&N may not be for everyone. An Altamira investor, for example, may happily pay slightly higher MERs for a package of services that PH&N does not provide, such as extensive seminars, educational material, and other intangibles.

The proven funds that PH&N does have are ideal for building a low-cost, above-average core holding in North American stocks and bonds. As of the end of 1997, PH&N held the opinion that Canadian stocks were 20 per cent undervalued, while the U.S. market was roughly 20 per cent overvalued.

But if you want to beat RRSP or RRIF foreign-content limitations or want regional equity funds concentrated in such exotic locales as the Far East or Latin America, PH&N may not be the place to be.

Smart Funds 1999:

Simply hard to deny these great no-loads, low-MER, and above-median performers. All five return for their fourth year as Smart Funds!!

PH&N Bond Fund, PH&N Canadian Equity Fund, PH&N Dividend Income Fund, PH&N Balanced Fund, PH&N U.S. Equity Fund.

Noteworthy Funds:

PH&N International Equity Fund. This EAFE (Europe, Australia, and Far East) index fund has a lower than normal expense ratio for its category because PH&N acts on the premise that most of the performance from global equity funds comes primarily from country selection, which can be achieved through local stock indexes. It calls this approach "active country allocation/passive stock selection." The fund is exposed to about 20 industrial economies, with all industry groups in the chosen countries represented. Its total stock exposure is between 300 and 700 companies, and the fund has full exposure to foreign currencies.

Availability:

Directly from PH&N or through some brokers and discount brokers. Funds available across Canada: a prospectus had been filed in every province as of May 1998. $10,000 minimum initial investment, whether purchased directly or through third parties.

37. ROYAL MUTUAL FUNDS INC.   NO LOAD

Strengths:	Low-MER strategic index funds
	Style diversification
Weaknesses:	Billion-dollar funds,
	One merger down, one to go?
RESPs?:	Yes
Web Site:	www.royalbank.com **Toll Free:** 1-800-463-3863

CANADIAN	Category	Rating	Fund Name	M.E.R.%	RRSP/Foreign
Money Market:		■	Royal Canadian T-Bill Fund	0.92	RRSP
		■	Royal Canadian Money Market Fund	0.95	RRSP
		▲	Royal Premium Money Market Fund*	0.3	RRSP
Fixed Income:	Long-term	■	Royal Bond Fund	1.39	RRSP
	Mortgage	■	Royal Mortgage Fund	1.79	RRSP
		▲	Royal Monthly Income Fund	1.12	RRSP
Equity:	Mid-Large Cap	■	Royal Canadian Equity Fund	2.1	RRSP

		Fund Name	M.E.R.%	RRSP/Foreign
	■	Royal Canadian Growth Fund	2.3	RRSP
	■	Royal Canadian Value Fund	2	RRSP
Small Cap	■	Royal Canadian Small Cap Fund	2.27	RRSP
Gold/precious metal	▲	Royal Precious Metals Fund	2.21	RRSP
Resource	▲	Royal Energy Fund	2.32	RRSP
Index	▲	Royal Canadian Strategic Index Fund	1.5	RRSP
Tax Advantaged: Dividend	★	**Royal Dividend Fund**	1.84	RRSP
Mult-Asset: Balanced	■	Royal Balanced Fund	2.25	RRSP
	■	Royal Balanced Growth Fund	2.25	RRSP
	■	Royal Trust Advantage Income Fund	1.65	RRSP
	■	Royal Trust Advantage Balanced Fund	1.78	RRSP
	■	Royal Trust Advantage Growth Fund	1.92	RRSP

FOREIGN	Category	Rating	Fund Name	M.E.R.%	RRSP/Foreign
Money Market:		■	Royal $U.S. Money Market Fund	1.12	Foreign
Fixed Income:		■	Royal Global Bond Fund	1.87	RRSP
Global Equity:	EAFE	■	Royal International Equity Fund	2.49	Foreign
	Technology	▲	Royal Life Science and Technology Fund	2.81	Foreign
Regional Equity:					
	U.S. Large-cap	▲	Royal U.S. Equity Fund	2.18	Foreign
		▲	Royal U.S. Value Strategic Index Fund	1.5	Foreign
		■	Royal U.S. Growth Strategic Index Fund	1.5	Foreign
	U.S. Small-cap	▲	Zweig Strategic Growth Fund	2.59	Foreign
	Latin American	■	Royal Latin American Fund	3	Foreign
	Far East	■	Royal Asian Growth Fund	2.84	Foreign
	Japan	■	Royal Japanese Stock Fund	2.95	Foreign
	Europe	▲	Royal European Growth Fund	2.66	Foreign
Global Balanced:		■	Zweig Global Managed Assets	2.99	Foreign

* $250,000 minimum

One merger down, one to go? It's taken the better part of four years for Royal Mutual Funds to integrate its old RoyFund family of funds with the Royal Trust line-up. Already Canada's largest no-load family, the proposed merger of the Royal Bank of Canada with the Bank of Montreal would create a giant no-load group of more than 50 funds and another four-year period of painful fund consolidation. In theory, the creation of even more multibillion-dollar funds would bring with it greater economies of scale and a driving-down of management expense ratios (MERs). However, there's been little evidence so far of that occurring at Royal Mutual Funds. The mammoth ($7 billion) Royal Balanced Fund has an MER of 2.25 per cent, down only a few basis points from the previous year.

On the other hand, like CIBC Securities Inc., Royal Mutual has taken the MER bull by the horns by introducing the lower-MER passively managed "Strategic Index" funds, championed by none other than the Wealthy Barber himself, author/speaker David Chilton.

The maximum MER of these funds has been set at 1.5 per cent, which is no screaming bargain but a far sight better than the cost of

Royal's fully managed funds or many actively managed funds in the broker channel. Such an intermediate-level MER is appropriate, since these passively managed funds do have a component of active management. Royal has trademarked the phrase "strategy indexing" to describe an investment approach developed by James P. O'Shaughnessy, who runs the Greenwich, Connecticut investment advisory firm bearing his name. A computer-based set of screens select promising stocks that are held for a year, after which the portfolio is rebalanced and stocks reselected. This could end up making these highly taxable distributions unlike a low-turnover fund such as AIC Diversified.

Note that in strong equity markets, pure index funds often outperform actively managed funds, partly because they remain completely invested in the market. On the other hand, actively managed funds generally do a better job of protecting investors in "bear" markets. Even Royal's own marketing material concedes that "in falling equity markets, index funds often lose relatively more value." It's also worth noting that outside registered plans, traditional index funds generate fewer capital gains.

One of the aspects of the new funds is style diversification: investors can choose between "value" and "growth" approaches to stock selection in the U.S. market. In June 1998, Royal launched the Royal Canadian Value Fund and Royal Balanced Growth Fund (not to be confused with the Royal Trust Advantage Balanced or Advantage Growth funds!). The Balanced Growth Fund is a "single-decision" asset-allocation fund with a growth orientation; the Canadian Value Fund is an equity fund that tries to identify undervalued Canadian stocks.

Also new since our last edition is the Royal Monthly Income Fund, launched in August 1997. Less than a year later, this conservative income fund, which invests in bonds, common, and preferred shares, and aims to provide a monthly payout (4.5 cents a unit as we write), gathered more than $850 million. Outside registered plans, the after-tax income may be superior to pure-interest products, because some of the fund's proceeds will be taxed as dividends and capital gains. Its MER is a reasonable 1.12 per cent. The manager is vice president, Canadian equities John Kellet manager of Royal Dividend, a Smart Fund again this year.

Most of Royal's Canadian and some U.S. funds are managed internally by Royal Bank Investment Management (RBIM). RBIM also has a Global Investment Group, so the international funds are managed partly through its internal resources and partly through externally contracted subadvisers. However, some of the global funds have moved to in-house management. RBIM's Yoji Takeda now heads the Royal Japanese Stock Fund, formerly managed by Nikko

International Capital Management Co. Ltd. of Tokyo. RBIM's Philip Chiu now manages the Royal Asian Growth Fund.

Still in place are Delaware International Advisers Ltd. of the U.K. for the International Equity Fund; Bankers Trust Co. of the U.S. for European Growth, BBV LatInvest Investment Management Ltd. for Latin American Fund, and Zweig/Glaser Advisers for the two Zweig funds. Elizabeth Cheung became manager of the Royal Canadian Small Cap Fund in late 1997.

Investors with more than $50,000 also have the option of a discretionary investment management service called Personal Asset Management Services, which is managed by Royal Trust Investment Counsel (RTIC). The service holds $1 billion in Royal Mutual Funds. RTIC also provides other discretionary products for larger-sized portfolios.

Smart Funds 1999:

Royal Dividend.

Noteworthy Funds:

Royal U.S. Equity. 20 per cent return for year ended June 30, 1998. Formerly RoyFund U.S. Equity, this large-cap U.S. equity fund now has a solid 10-year track record of 16 per cent CAGR, for the 10 years ended June 30, 1998. Manager Jim Young, who also manages the Royal Life Science & Technology Fund, has a 12 per cent technology weighting in this broader fund. Reasonable MER of 2.18 per cent, although investors can beat that with the more passively managed Royal U.S. Value Strategic Index Fund.

Royal Canadian Strategic Index Fund, Royal U.S. Value Strategic Index Fund. See also comments in above overview. If large-cap actively managed funds can't beat the indexes, then why pay high MERs? These funds provide a lower-cost alternative that may out-perform in bull markets, but may offer less downside protection in extensive market downdrafts.

Royal Monthly Income Fund. See comments in above overview. Conservative fund pays monthly income with a better after-tax treatment than five-year GICs. Reasonable 1.1 per cent MER.

Royal Premium Money Market Fund. Those with hefty portfolios can "park" a minimum $250,000 in this low-MER (0.3 per cent) money-market fund. Subsequent investments are minimum $5,000.

Royal Energy Fund. This demoted Smart Fund had a poor year and is generally too specialized and volatile for most investors who would gravitate to this fund family.

Royal Precious Metals. Demoted, albeit reluctantly, Smart Fund. Like Royal Energy, specialized funds investing in gold are probably too volatile for the average bank no-load investor.

Royal European Growth. Shared in the general European bull market, returning 42 per cent for the year ended June 30, 1998, and a healthy 22 per cent five-year CAGR as of the same date, for a solid second-quartile performance. Manager Ross Youngman of BT Fund Managers (International) Ltd. concedes, "Valuations are no longer cheap across the board," but says he can still find value. *The Economist* thinks otherwise: that as of the spring of 1998, the European economy is a "bubble."

Royal Life Science & Technology. 14 per cent return for the year ended June 30, 1998, not quite as good as the 20 per cent achieved by the same manager—Jim Young—in the more diversified U.S. Equity Fund.

Zweig Strategic Growth Fund. The fund for cautious bulls. In 1997, even though the fund was only 68 per cent invested, this gained 22 per cent (and 28 per cent for year ended June 30, 1998). A market timing fund, this will move 100 per cent to cash if deemed advisable. The Zweig Global Managed Asset Fund expands this concept globally and across asset classes.

Availability:

Royal Bank and Royal Trust branches; RBC Dominion Securities and Action Direct.

38. SAXON FUNDS   NO LOAD

Strengths:	No frills, low fees, no-load
	Small-cap value niche
Weaknesses:	Limited range of funds
	Profile and marketing
RESPs?:	No
Web site:	www.saxonfunds.com/~saxon **Toll Free:** 1-888-287-2966

CANADIAN	Category	Rating	Fund Name	M.E.R.%	RRSP/Foreign
Equity:	Mid-Large Cap	▲	Saxon Stock Fund	1.75	RRSP
	Small Cap	★	**Saxon Small Cap**	1.75	RRSP
Tax Advantaged:	Income Trust	▲	Saxon High Income Fund	1.25	RRSP
Mult-Asset:	Balanced	▲	Saxon Balanced Fund	1.75	RRSP

Saxon Funds is a small, but fast-growing no-frills, no-load company, and has passed the $100 million mark in assets. It now has five funds in its stable.

After standing pat for the better part of 12 years, Saxon added the Saxon High Income Fund in November 1997. The fund will invest 70 per cent of its money in income trust units, with the balance in fixed-income products. The objective is to provide a consistent cash flow along with the tax advantages of return of capital.

The other change in the last year is that brokers and discount brokers and planners now have the option of charging up to a 2 per cent acquisition fee (front load.)

On the marketing front, the arrival last year of Ed Kwan has started to show itself in more sophisticated marketing materials. Saxon now sports a color brochure to go along with its delightfully plain quarterly reports and prospectus.

But the essence of the company continues to be investment management by its two principals, who remain in place. The in-house manager is Howson Tattersall Investment Counsel Ltd., which also does pension and private client investment management, with pooled accounts for investors with $250,000 or more. Bob Tattersall has been a Saxon principal since the firm's founding 12 years ago. Rick Howson has been on board nine years and also handles segregated portfolio management for private clients with investible assets of more than $1 million.

As sole owners, both managers can be expected to stick around. Both employ a value approach that insists that stocks—primarily small cap—be statistically cheap. The search for value brings them to stocks with low financial leverage, low market to book ratio, low price to cash flow ratio, and low price to sales. Similar in approach to Trimark, Saxon views themselves as investors in companies, not traders in shares. That results in low portfolio turnover, which is especially attractive for taxable portfolios.

The management fee for all funds is 1.75 per cent, which is also the MER, since the managers absorb all other expenses.

Three of the four original funds have been Smart Funds previously, and the other debuts as a Smart Fund this year. The new High Income Fund rates a Noteworthy designation out of the starting blocks.

Smart Funds 1999:

Saxon Small Cap.

Noteworthy Funds:

Saxon Stock. Managed by Richard Howson, this Canadian equity fund mixes some small caps with large caps. Fund has been well above average the last five years and returned 13 per cent for the year ended June 30, 1998.

Saxon Balanced (Former Smart Fund). It has slipped a bit last year amid some greater competition. Still it is second quartile over the one-, two-, three-, five-, and 10-year periods to June 30, 1998, so it remains a keeper.

Saxon World Growth. Another former Smart Fund up against a tough category. Fund has dropped down to fourth quartile over the one-, two-, and three-year periods ending June 20, 1998.

Saxon High Income Fund. This new tax-advantaged income trust fund will pay out distribution income every quarter, including some return of capital. Saxon projects the fund will generate a pre-tax return of 6 to 7 per cent, or as much as 5.5 per cent after taxes. The fund was launched at a difficult time for this sector, since commodity prices such as oil were weak early in 1998. It also owns mining, pipelines, and utilities; REITs; and other types of income trusts. Managed by Richard Howson.

Availability:

Directly from Saxon at no load, discount brokers, or though dealers and financial planners at a 2 per cent front load. The funds are available only in Ontario, British Columbia, and Alberta. There is a $5,000 minimum initial purchase.

39. SCEPTRE MUTUAL FUNDS   NO LOAD

Strengths:	High performance with low MERs		
	No-frills marketing		
Weaknesses:	No specialty funds		
	Low profile		
RESPs?:	No		
Web Site:	www.sceptre.ca	**Toll Free:**	1-800-265-1888

CANADIAN	Category	Rating	Fund Name	M.E.R.%	RRSP/Foreign
Money Market:		■	Sceptre Money Market Fund	0.75	RRSP
Fixed Income:	Short-term	★	**Sceptre Bond Fund**	0.98	RRSP
Equity:	Small-Mid Cap	★	**Sceptre Equity Growth Fund**	1.42	RRSP
	Mid-Large Cap	▲	Sceptre Canadian Equity	new	RRSP
Mult-Asset:	Balanced	★	**Sceptre Balanced Growth Fund**	1.44	RRSP

FOREIGN	Category	Rating	Fund Name	M.E.R.%	RRSP/Foreign
U.S. Equity:	Large-Cap	▲	Sceptre U.S. Equity	new	Foreign
	All-global	▲	Sceptre International Fund	2.07	Foreign
	Far East	▲	Sceptre Asian Growth Fund	2.45	Foreign

Sceptre Mutual Funds finally broke through $1 billion in assets in June 1998, a testament to its growing popularity among retail investors. It has taken time for fund buyers to notice Toronto-based Sceptre, a low-profile, no-load group. But consistent performance and low fees have merited the belated attention.

Sceptre Investment Counsel's reputation in the pension fund business, on the other hand, is well established. It has been in that business since 1955, and today manages more than $19.3 billion.

Sceptre Mutual Funds added two new funds in the past year, bringing its total fund group to eight. It added a mid-large cap Canadian equity fund and a U.S. fund in July 1998. The Sceptre U.S. Equity fund and the Sceptre Canadian Equity Fund represent mutual fund offerings of investment mandates already performed for institutional and high-net-worth clients.

If you're looking for a firm with definite investment opinions and the courage to stick with them, Sceptre may well fit the bill. Two funds return as Smart Funds this year and the Bond fund has been added. We have designated the two new offerings as Noteworthy. Sceptre continues to excel at its Canadian funds. Under Allan Jacobs, Sceptre Equity Growth is a small- to mid-cap Canadian equity fund, which boasts a 21.7 per cent average three-year CAGR at June 30, 1998. Jacobs has been managing the fund since 1993. Its MER has fallen to 1.42 per cent as fund assets increased to $449 million at the end of June.

Sceptre considers itself a balanced fund manager, so it is appropriate that Sceptre Balanced was named "Best Balanced Fund" at the Canadian Mutual Funds Awards in December 1996 and again in 1997. Managed by Lyle Stein since 1993, Sceptre Balanced has been a consistent outperformer for 10 years. (See profile of Lyle Stein on page 24.)

Sceptre is committed to low fees and its MERs continue to score among the 25 per cent least expensive of all funds. Although it has started to pay a small service fee to brokers and discount brokers who sell the funds, the company did not raise MERs to subsidize that cost. Sceptre capped the MER on its balanced fund at 0.95 per cent, down from 1.25 per cent a year earlier. That decision was based on Sceptre's expectation that returns for bonds and equities would be less robust in coming years and in that environment, low MERs are more important than ever to the net return.

Although Sceptre is no longer a well-kept secret, the company has not changed its winning formula. It continues to shy away from big-budget ad campaigns and road shows aimed at wooing brokers and planners. It remains focused on what it does best: money management.

Smart Funds 1999:

Sceptre Balanced Growth, Sceptre Equity Growth, Sceptre Bond.

Noteworthy Funds:

Sceptre U.S. Equity and **Sceptre Canadian Equity.** Given the company's tradition of money management excellence and low MERs, we are recognizing these two new funds as Noteworthy.

Sceptre International. Demoted from Smart Fund status as Lennox McNeely continues to take unitholders through a roller-coaster ride. Fund is now fourth quartile from one year through the five-year CAGR periods ending June 30, 1998.

Sceptre Asian Growth. This broadly diversified Asia Pacific Fund continues to suffer from the troubled Asian markets along with all funds that invest here. But if you want to invest in this region it is worth considering with its lower than average MER.

Availability:

Ontario residents can purchase directly from Sceptre. Other investors must buy through brokers and discount brokers or dealers, at a negotiable 0 to 2 per cent acquisition charge. Minimum in any province is $5,000 per new account.

Strengths: Balanced funds
100% RRSP eligible global funds
Weaknesses: Some global funds still finding their way
Few small-cap offerings
RESPs?: No
Web Site: www.Scotiabank.ca   **Toll Free:** 1-800-268-9269

CANADIAN	Category	Rating	Fund Name	M.E.R.%	RRSP/Foreign
Money Market:		■	Scotia Excelsior T-Bill Fund	1.00	RRSP
		■	Scotia Excelsior Premium T-Bill Fund	0.52	RRSP
		■	Scotia Excelsior Money Market Fund	1.00	RRSP
Fixed Income:	Long-term	■	Scotia Excelsior Income Fund	1.37	RRSP
	Short-term	■	Scotia Excelsior Defensive Income Fund	1.37	RRSP
	Mortgage	▲	Scotia Excelsior Mortgage Fund	1.56	RRSP
Equity:	Large Cap	■	Scotia Excelsior Canadian Blue Chip Fund	2.01	RRSP
		▲	Scotia Excelsior Canadian Growth Fund	2.09	RRSP
	Gold/precious metal	■	Scotia Excelsior Precious Metals Fund	2.19	RRSP
Tax Advantaged:	Dividend	▲	Scotia Excelsior Dividend Fund	1.07	RRSP
Mult-Asset:	Balanced	■	Scotia Excelsior Balanced Fund	1.97	RRSP
	Asset Allocation	▲	Scotia Excelsior Total Return Fund	2.27	RRSP
	Asset Allocation Service	■	Autopilot service		

FOREIGN	Category	Rating	Fund Name	M.E.R.%	RRSP/Foreign
Money Market:		■	Scotia CanAm Money Market Fund	1.00	RRSP
Fixed Income:		■	Scotia CanAm Income Fund	1.60	RRSP
		■	Scotia Excelsior Global Bond Fund	1.86	Foreign
Global Equity:	All-global	■	Scotia Excelsior International Fund	2.20	Foreign
Regional Equity:	U.S.	▲	Scotia CanAm Growth Fund	1.34	RRSP
		■	Scotia Excelsior American Growth Fund	2.19	Foreign
	Latin American	▲	Scotia Excelsior Latin American Fund	2.32	Foreign
	Far East	■	Scotia Excelsior Pacific Rim Fund	2.37	Foreign
	Europe	■	Scotia Excelsior European Growth Fund	2.16	Foreign

The Scotia Excelsior funds continue to offer some innovative products and many funds have consistent long-term track records. The fact that the 21 funds carry slightly lower than average MERs is also an advantage, and some MERs were further reduced in the last year.

Scotia has not added any new funds or changed its portfolio managers since our last edition. (But uncertainty remains in connection with the Bank of Nova Scotia's acquisition of National Trust Company in August 1997. At the time of writing, Scotia says it is still contemplating a merger of the National Trust Funds with the Excelsior Funds.) A decision on combining the two fund groups is expected by the end of 1998.

Most of the funds are managed in-house by Scotia Cassels Investment Management Ltd., which also manages money for pension and "high-net-worth" private investors. Together with the full-service brokerage ScotiaMcLeod Inc., the discount brokerage and Scotiatrust, many investors may find it convenient to combine these multiple services with the Scotia Excelsior no-load funds.

Scotia Excelsior has both a 100 per cent RRSP-eligible U.S. Equity fund (CanAm Growth) and a 100 per cent RRSP-eligible global bond fund (CanAm Income, a U.S.dollar-denominated fund). It also has a free foreign-content monitoring service for RRSP customers. Accounts are monitored monthly and automatically adjusted to ensure that the 20 per cent foreign limit is not exceeded.

Asset allocation is becoming an almost obligatory value-added service for bank fund groups. Scotia was relatively early with its Autopilot Service in 1993, which does not impose any fees or commissions for its quarterly rebalancing service: a minimum $5,000 is needed to set up this account. Another worthwhile service is its Reality Check Report, which helps investors with their retirement planning.

Smart Funds 1999:

None.

Noteworthy Funds:

Scotia Excelsior Latin American Fund. This fund has a three-year CAGR of 13.57 at June 30, 1998 versus –0.77 per cent for the median fund. Loss of lead manager Tony Genoa dropped this from Smart Fund status.

Scotia Excelsior Total Return. For investors who want growth potential and one-stop shopping, this balanced fund could be a wise choice. The manager decides on asset allocation for the fund by selecting the weightings in stocks, bonds, and other securities. It may also hold up to 20 per cent foreign content. It has performed above average over three and five years and has a lower than average MER.

Scotia Excelsior Dividend Fund. This fund, which invests in common and preferred shares that guarantee dividend payment, has done a solid job over the long term. It has achieved a CAGR of 11.84 per cent over 10 years to June 30, 1998, with volatility and an MER well below the group average. This was a Smart Fund in 1997 when Denis Ouellet was running it.

Scotia Excelsior Canadian Growth. This fund has a consistent track record going back to 1961. It underperformed over one year to June 30, 1998, following the departure of its former manager Denis Ouellet.

Scotia CanAm Growth. If you want an index fund, this has a lower MER than managed U.S. equity funds (1.34 per cent); it is 100 per cent

RRSP-eligible so it doesn't take up the precious 20 per cent foreign-content space in RRSPs or RRIFs. It underperformed in one year to June 30, 1998, but has proved itself over the longer term.

Scotia Excelsior Mortgage Fund. Banks are the place to go for mortgage funds and this one has been an above-average performer over three years. It fell slightly short over one year to June 30, 1998.

Availability:

Through branches of the Bank of Nova Scotia, Scotiabank and Trust, Montreal Trust, Scotia Discount Brokerage and ScotiaMcLeod, and some discount brokerages. Premium T-bill fund has minimum $100,000 investment requirement; the other money market funds have a $2,500 minimum each. Most other funds are $500 minimum.

41. SCUDDER FUNDS OF CANADA   NO LOAD

Strengths:	Global equities
	Low MERs, though rising
Weaknesses:	Brokers not motivated to sell family
RESPs?:	Yes
Web Site:	www.scudder.ca	Toll Free: 1-800-850-3863

CANADIAN	Category	Rating	Fund Name	M.E.R.%	RRSP/Foreign
Money Market:		■	Scudder Canadian Money Market	0.25	RRSP
Fixed Income:	Short-term	★	**Scudder Canadian Short Term Bond Fund**	0.61	RRSP
	Long-term	■	Scudder Canadian Bond Fund	1.0	RRSP
Equity:	Mid-Large Cap	★	**Scudder Canadian Equity Fund**	1.35	RRSP
	Small-cap	■	Scudder Canadian Small Company	new	RRSP

FOREIGN	Category	Rating	Fund Name	M.E.R.%	RRSP/Foreign
Global Equity:	All-global	★	**Scudder Global Fund**	1.75	Foreign
Regional Equity:					
	U.S. Large cap	▲	Scudder U.S. Growth & Income Fund	1.25	Foreign
	Emerging Market	★	**Scudder Emerging Markets Fund**	2.11	Foreign
	Far East	■	Scudder Pacific Fund	1.91	Foreign
	Europe	▲	Scudder Greater Europe Fund	1.91	Foreign

With three years under its belt in the Canadian market, Scudder Funds of Canada now has some alluring performance numbers to show investors. As consumer awareness of the benefits of low management expense ratios grows, and despite its MERs creeping a little higher, Scudder will prove an attractive alternative no-load offering for do-it-yourselfers who are disillusioned with the banks or Altamira.

Scudder Canada is a subsidiary of Scudder Kemper, the tenth-largest mutual fund company in the United States. In 1997, Scudder, Stevens & Clark Inc. joined with the Zurich Group. Zurich subsidiary Zurich Kemper Investments was combined with Scudder to form Scudder Kemper Investments, Inc.

Scudder's formidable global research team delivers original thinking on macro global equity trends. Scudder Global Fund, for example, has developed a "secure streams of income" theme based on its perception that baby boomers will start to snap up the short supply of utility stocks and bonds as they shift from a growth mode to a focus on secure retirement income. Its global managers also seem to have a keener awareness than many Canadian-based global managers of the deepening problems of deflationary trends evidenced in Asia and Japan. Scudder doesn't believe that those problems are limited to those regions of the world.

If global equity markets do slow to single-digit growth rates—or worse—Scudder's reasonable MERs should give its funds some performance edge. And in the event of major and protracted stock-market corrections, Scudder's value focus and evident caution could prove to be even more valuable to investors.

Compared to the 50-fund-plus portfolios of some of the families in this book, Scudder's 10-fund line-up is refreshingly modest. Each year it has added a couple of worthwhile new offerings. The latest is the Scudder Canadian Small Company Fund, launched in July 1998, and managed by the same team as returning Smart Fund Scudder Canadian Equity Fund. It will be managed in the quantitative style of the Canadian Equity fund by Phil Fortuna. The fund will carry a management fee of 1.50 per cent. See also profile of manager Phil Fortuna on page 37.

Also new since the last edition of this book, Scudder introduced the now one-year-old Canadian Money Market Fund and Canadian Bond Fund. The latter is managed by Adam Greshin and Gary Johnson, who also run the Canadian Short-Term Bond Fund. The Canadian Bond Fund has no minimum or maximum average term to maturity, but normally invests in intermediate to longer-term bonds.

We reiterate the closing paragraphs of last year's edition: "With no-loads, reasonable MERs, a 75-year history of strong fiduciary responsibility to investors and a think-for-yourself approach to portfolio creation, Scudder Canada deserves to be on the short list for no-load portfolios."

Smart Funds 1999:

Scudder Canadian Equity Fund, Scudder Short-Term Income, Scudder Global Fund, Scudder Emerging Markets Fund.

Noteworthy Funds:

Scudder Greater Europe Fund. The U.S. version of this fund is also a five-star Morningstar fund. A hard-to-ignore 54 per cent one-year return to June 30, 1998—well above the 22 per cent of the more broadly diversified Scudder Global Fund. Normally, we prefer the broader funds, and those who have large gains in Europe may want to switch to the Global fund if Europe shows signs of topping out.

Scudder U.S. Growth & Income Fund. Another strong performer with a well below-average MER (of 1.25 per cent) for the U.S. equity category. The fund buys stocks with dividend yields 20 per cent higher than the yield on the unmanaged S&P 500. Focus on companies with prospects for continued earnings growth. Managed by same team as the U.S.-based Growth & Income Fund ranked five-star by Morningstar. A 27 per cent one-year return to June 30, 1998.

Availability:

Directly from Scudder Canada in Alberta, British Columbia, Saskatchewan, and Ontario, and now Manitoba. Also available across Canada through major discount brokerages and some full-service brokers and mutual fund dealers, and some financial planners. $1,000 minimum investment; $500 for registered accounts. There are no account set-up fees.

42. SPECTRUM UNITED MUTUAL FUNDS FRONT OR REAR

Strengths:	Small-cap funds in U.S., Canada and Europe
	Relationship with McLean Budden
Weaknesses:	Some funds sub-par
RESPs?:	Yes
Web Site:	www.spectrumunited.ca **Toll Free:** 1-800-263-1851

CANADIAN	Category	Rating	Fund Name	M.E.R.%	RRSP/Foreign
Money Market:		■	Spectrum United Canadian Money Market Fund	0.92	RRSP
Fixed Income:	Long-term	■	Spectrum United Long-Term Bond Fund	1.66	RRSP
	Medium-term	■	Spectrum United Mid-Term Bond Fund	1.59	RRSP

			Fund Name	M.E.R.%	RRSP/Foreign
	Short-term	■	Spectrum United Short-Term Bond Fund	1.45	RRSP
Equity:	Large-cap	★	**Spectrum United Canadian Equity Fund**	2.35	RRSP
		■	Spectrum United Canadian Investment Fund	2.33	RRSP
		■	Spectrum United Canadian Stock Fund	2.33	RRSP
	Small-mid Cap	■	Spectrum United Canadian Growth Fund	2.35	RRSP
		■	Spectrum United Canadian Small-Mid Cap Fund	2.36	RRSP
	Resource	■	Spectrum United Canadian Resource Fund	2.35	RRSP
	Portfolio	■	Spectrum United Canadian Maximum Growth Portfolio	2.22	RRSP
Tax Advantaged:	Dividend	■	Spectrum United Dividend Fund	1.61	RRSP
Mult-Asset:	Balanced	■	Spectrum United Diversified Fund	2.08	RRSP
	Asset Allocation	■	Spectrum United Asset Allocation Fund	2.22	RRSP
	Portfolio of Funds	■	Spectrum United Canadian Income Portfolio	1.85	RRSP
		■	Spectrum United Canadian Conservative Portfolio	2.00	RRSP
		■	Spectrum United Canadian Balanced Portfolio	2.16	RRSP
		■	Spectrum United Canadian Growth Portfolio	2.22	RRSP

FOREIGN	Category	Rating	Fund Name	M.E.R.%	RRSP/Foreign
Money Market:	U.S.	■	Spectrum United U.S. Dollar Money Market	1.2	Foreign
Fixed Income:		■	Spectrum United Global Bond Fund	2.03	Foreign
		■	Spectrum United RRSP International Bond Fund	1.98	RRSP
Global Equity:	Large-cap	■	Spectrum United Global Equity Fund	2.3	Foreign
	Small-cap	■	Spectrum United Global Growth Fund	2.3	Foreign
	Telecom	■	Spectrum United Global Telecommunications Fund	2.55	Foreign
Regional Equity:					
	U.S. Large-cap	■	Spectrum United Optimax USA Fund	2.35	Foreign
	US Mixed cap	▲	Spectrum United American Equity Fund	2.35	Foreign
	U.S. Small-mid cap	★	**Spectrum United American Growth Fund**	2.35	Foreign
	Emerging Market	▲	Spectrum United Emerging Markets Fund	2.66	Foreign
	Far East	■	Spectrum United Asian Dynasty Fund	2.58	Foreign
	European	▲	Spectrum United European Growth Fund	2.6	Foreign
Global Balanced:		■	Spectrum United Global Diversified Fund	2.30	Foreign
	Portfolio	■	Spectrum United Global Growth Portfolio	2.43	Foreign

The last year brought more changes for Spectrum United Mutual Funds, just when things were supposed to have settled down following the integration of the Spectrum and United fund groups.

President Allen Marple has left the firm. Meanwhile, Spectrum United's parent company, insurance giant Sun Life, purchased a 60 per cent interest in McLean Budden, a well-established Canadian money manager founded in 1947. That move brought a team of highly regarded growth-style managers into the Sun Life fold.

Through the acquisition, 100 per cent of Sun Life Investment Management was absorbed by McLean Budden, creating one more diversified portfolio management group. McLean Budden is a bottom-up stock picker, with an approach similar to the way many

Spectrum portfolios were already managed. The result of the merger is reflected in a couple of funds that are managed with a combination of growth and value styles.

The Spectrum United Canadian Stock Fund, managed by Brian Dawson since November 1997 and Susan Shuter of McLean Budden, is one such example. The idea is to achieve a happy medium: this fund should be more aggressive than a pure value portfolio but the value stocks should remove some of the volatility inherent in most pure growth portfolios. The equity portfolio of the Spectrum United Diversified Fund is also managed with a blend of styles.

The Canadian side is the only place you'll find a value component. International equities are all managed with a growth style. The one global sector fund sold by the company experienced a management change last year. Maura Shaughnessy of MFS Institutional Advisors became manager of the Spectrum United Global Telecommunications Fund in November 1997.

Further to the style diversification and based on client requests, the Spectrum United Small-Mid Cap Fund was launched in December 1997. It is managed by John Mulvihill of Mulvihill Capital with a bottom-up growth style. That approach differs from the small-cap value approach of Lynn Miller.

Kiki Delaney continues to manage the flagship, Spectrum United Canadian Equity, the large-cap Canadian equity portfolio, which is designated a Smart Fund again this year.

The fixed-income funds continue to be managed by Stuart Pomphrey with the help of McLean Budden's bond team of which he is now a part.

Also in the last year, the Portfolio Series was launched in December 1997. The Spectrum United Portfolio of Funds was renamed the Canadian Balanced Portfolio and five other portfolios were created: Canadian Income, Canadian Conservative, Canadian Growth, Canadian Maximum Growth, and Global Growth. The six portfolio funds each combine several Spectrum United funds.

Smart Funds 1999:

Spectrum United Canadian Equity, Spectrum United American Growth.

Noteworthy Funds:

Spectrum United Emerging Markets. In a very ugly year for emerging markets, this fund's 31 per cent loss was worse than most.

Spectrum United American Equity. This former Smart Fund has been burdened with its small- and mid-cap mix to compete against the big large-cap herd. Still, this is a solid if unspectacular fund, worthy of consideration for those who have had a run with the U.S. index stocks.

Spectrum United European Growth. This fund has had some good years. This was a Smart Fund in 1997 and was dropped last year. It remains one of the better ones in this category.

Availability:

Brokers and discount brokers, financial planners, and Sun Life insurance agents.

43. STANDARD LIFE SEGREGATED FUNDS
NO LOAD & REAR

	Strengths:	Seg fund guarantees
	Weaknesses:	Limited product line
	RESPs?:	No
	Web Site:	None	Toll Free: N/A

CANADIAN	Category	Rating	Fund Name	M.E.R.%	RRSP/Foreign
Money Market:		■	Standard Life Ideal Money Market	1.00	RRSP
Fixed Income:		■	Standard Life Ideal Bond Fund	2.00	RRSP
Equity:		▲	Standard Life Ideal Equity Fund	2.00	RRSP
Mult-Asset:	Balanced	■	Standard Life Ideal Balanced Fund	2.00	RRSP

The Canadian division of this global insurance company sells both mutual funds and segregated funds, all managed by Standard Life Portfolio Management. In the last year, SLPM became part of Standard Life Investment Management, the Edinburgh-based investment manager for the worldwide Standard Life Group.

In this edition we introduce the group's small segregated fund offerings. It also has some solid-performing mutual funds. The funds are managed with a bottom-up, research-driven approach. The managers focus on individual stock picking, as opposed to allocations based on macroeconomic forecasts.

The four funds cover the bases for Canadian content, although there are no specialty or foreign funds in this group. MERs are variable: below average on the equity and balanced funds and above average on the bond fund.

For investors considering this seg fund group for the guarantee feature, it is worth noting that the guarantee is backed by the company, which is the only major life insurance company in Canada to be rated AAA by both Moody's and Standard & Poor's.

Smart Funds 1999:

None.

Noteworthy Funds:

Standard Life Ideal Equity Fund. This portfolio has a long performance history and is a first-quartile performer over one, two, three, and five years ended June 30, 1998, and has a lower than average MER at 2 per cent versus the average 2.2 per cent. Add to that the guarantee of principal, and it is a good deal.

Availability:

Through life agents and investment advisers with life insurance licences.

44. STONE & CO. LTD.   FRONT OR REAR

Strengths:	McLean Budden as adviser
Weaknesses:	No foreign products
RESPs?:	No
Web Site:	www.stoneco.com

Toll Free: 1-800-336-9528

CANADIAN	Category	Rating	Fund Name	M.E.R.%	RRSP/Foreign
Money Market:		■	Flagship Money Market Fund Canada	1.00	RRSP
Equity:		▲	Flagship Stock Fund Canada	2.88	RRSP
Mult-Asset:	Balanced	▲	Flagship Growth & Income Fund Canada	2.85	RRSP

Richard Stone, a former executive with the Guardian Group of Funds, created this start-up firm in 1994. Although Stone did not launch any new funds last year, he intends to add to the line-up by the end of 1998, which will make it more attractive.

For now, this remains a small limited group with only three funds. The three "Flagship" portfolios, as they are called, continue to be managed by highly regarded McLean Budden Ltd., which is now majority owned by Sun Life (see Spectrum United entry). Investors who don't have enough assets to engage McLean Budden's private client service can do so through this fund family, as well as some Spectrum funds. The Canadian equity and balanced funds have had good results but continue to carry higher than average MERs. It is interesting to note that the Flagship Stock Fund is labelled a "pure growth" fund, as it avoids cyclicals such as resource stocks. If that strategy appeals, so may this fund.

Smart Funds 1999:

None.

Noteworthy Funds:

Flagship Stock Fund Canada. Stone calls this a "pure growth" fund because it avoids cyclicals—"no trees, no rocks," as Stone likes to say. The fund focuses on mid- and large-cap stocks and has performed better than average over the year ended June 30, 1998.

Flagship Growth & Income Fund Canada. Conservative investors looking for a balanced fund sold through the advice channel may like this fund. As opposed to some that try to time the market by actively moving between asset classes, this fund maintains a classic balanced split of 60 per cent equity to 40 per cent bonds. The growth component is managed like Flagship Stock Fund Canada. Stone & Co. is paid a performance fee of 10 per cent of the amount by which the fund beats a benchmark that is 45 per cent the TSE 300, 15 per cent MSCI world index, and 40 per cent Scotia Capital Markets Universe bond index. The maximum performance fee is 0.3 per cent of the fund's net asset value.

Availability:

Brokers and discount brokers and dealers with a $500 minimum investment.

45. STRATEGIC VALUE CORP.   FRONT OR REAR

Strengths:	Value approach of Mark Bonham		
	Hambros global connections		
Weaknesses:	High MERs		
RESPs?:	No		
Web Site:	www.strategicvalue.com	**Toll Free:**	1-800-408-2311

CANADIAN	Category	Rating	Fund Name	M.E.R.%	RRSP/Foreign
Money Market:		■	Strategic Value Money Market	1.19	RRSP
Fixed Income:	Long-term	■	Strategic Value Income Fund	2.18	RRSP
	Short-term	■	Strategic Value Government Bond Fund	2.18	RRSP
Equity:	Large Cap	■	Strategic Value Canadian Equity	2.68	RRSP
	Mid-Large Cap	■	Strategic Value Canadian Equity Value Fund	3.1	RRSP
	Small Cap	■	Strategic Value Canadian Small Companies Fund	2.69	RRSP
	Specialty	▲	Strategic Value RSP Fund	new	RRSP
Tax Advantaged:	Dividend	■	Strategic Value Dividend Fund	2.68	RRSP
Mult-Asset:	Balanced	■	Stratgeic Value Canadian Balanced Fund	2.69	RRSP
		■	Strategic Value Global Balanced RSP	5.16	RRSP

FOREIGN	Category	Rating	Fund Name	M.E.R.%	RRSP/Foreign
Global Equity:	All-global	■	Strategic Value International Fund	2.69	Foreign
	Specialty	▲	Strategic Value Fund	3.19	Foreign
Regional Equity:					
	US Large Cap	■	Strategic Value American Equity	2.68	Foreign
	Europe	■	Strategic Value Europe Fund	2.68	Foreign
	Asia Pacific	■	Strategic Value Asia Pacific Fund	2.57	Foreign
	Emerging Markets	■	Strategic Value Emerging Markets	2.94	Foreign
Global Balanced:		■	Strategic Value Commonwealth Fund	2.69	Foreign
		■	Strategic Value Global Balanced Fund	2.65	Foreign

Strategic Value Corp. has completed the integration of the Laurentian Funds and has emerged with a more streamlined family of 18 funds, all renamed under the Strategic Value brand.

Founder Mark Bonham was the entrepreneur who engineered BPI's famous "minnow that swallowed the whale" acquisition of Bolton Tremblay Funds Inc. in 1994. After leaving BPI and founding his own firm, Bonham repeated history in May 1997 when he acquired Laurentian Funds Management from Imperial Life Financial, one of the oldest mutual fund operators in Canada, including the global balanced Commonwealth Fund, launched in 1932.

The acquisition instantly vaulted tiny Strategic to $1.8 billion in assets and 19 funds, although many of Laurentian's 14 funds were third- or fourth-quartile performers. The group is now turning around and Strategic has been adding assets to many of its funds. Its main fault remains its higher than average MERs on many funds, which is in part why none received the "Smart" designation this year.

Unlike many fund executives who left top-level sales and marketing jobs at established fund firms to start their own shops, Bonham is a money manager first and foremost. Although relinquishing lead manager status on the Canadian Equity Funds, he still manages the Strategic Value Dividend Fund and the Strategic Value Canadian Balanced Fund in addition to the Strategic Value Fund for high-net-worth investors. A 100 per cent RRSP-eligible version of that fund with a lower minimum was launched in December 1997: the Strategic Value RSP Fund.

Bonham has hired three other managers to oversee portfolios managed in-house. Among them is Michael Labanowich, director of fixed income, who manages the Income Funds. Several international portfolios are managed by the Guiness Flight Hambro team out of London, England.

To pare down to 18 funds, Strategic Value merged several similar funds last year. The Strategic Value American Equity Value Fund and Strategic Value Global Equity Fund were closed and dissolved as of April 30, 1998.

Smart Funds 1999:

None.

Noteworthy Funds:

Strategic Value Fund. Bonham's original offering is a high-net-worth fund available through offering memorandum only, with a minimum investment of $150,000 in Ontario and Saskatchewan, and $97,000 in the other western provinces. The fund is similar in concept to one of the last funds that Bonham conceived for BPI: the BPI Canadian Opportunities Fund. Thus it invests in emerging and "pre-emerging" markets—industries or sectors under consolidation and even illiquid situations and short sales. The fund had a negative return over the two-year period ending June 30, 1998.

Strategic Value RSP Fund. Also managed by Bonham, this fund is similar to the above but is fully RRSP-eligible.

Availability:

Through independent brokers and discount brokers and dealers with a $500 minimum with the exception of Strategic Value Fund.

46. SYNERGY ASSET MANAGEMENT　　FRONT OR REAR

Strengths:	Unique style approach
Weaknesses:	Only equity funds in family
RESPs?:	No
Web Site:	www.info@synergyasset.com **Toll Free:** 1-888-664-4784

CANADIAN	Category	Rating	Fund Name	M.E.R.%	RRSP/Foreign
Equity:		■	Synergy Canadian Value Class	new	RRSP
		■	Synergy Canadian Growth Class	new	RRSP
		▲	Synergy Canadian Momentum Class	new	RRSP
		★	**Synergy Canadian Style Management Class**	new	RRSP
	Small Cap	■	Synergy Canadian Small Cap Class	new	RRSP
Fixed Income:	Short-term	■	Synergy Canadian Short-Term Income Class	new	RRSP

FOREIGN	Category	Rating	Fund Name	M.E.R.%	RRSP/Foreign
Equity:	Global	■	Synergy Global Equities	new	Foreign

When fund industry veteran Joe Canavan left GT Global, we noted his departure as one of the weaknesses for the firm. True to his word, Canavan resurfaced in December 1997 with his own fund group. Although it is new, we have included it among the 50 fund families, based on his experience and track record, and a unique concept.

In an overcrowded fund arena, Canavan knew he had to come up with something different to get noticed. The Synergy Funds are based on the concept that investors benefit from diversifying their portfolios on the basis of investment style, as well as the more common strategies of diversifying by region and asset class. Many investors look for funds with strict style mandates, but until now had to shop around among fund groups. Synergy's group of equity funds offers strict style funds within one family. Synergy Canadian Fund Inc. is composed of six classes, each sold as a separate fund. There are four Canadian equity funds that each use a different style: growth, value, momentum, and small-cap. A fifth fund, Canadian Style Management Class, combines the best picks from the other four portfolios, giving investors style diversification within that portfolio. The theory is that when one style is out of favor, another does well.

The sixth portfolio within the Canadian Fund Inc. is Canadian Short-Term Income Class. Synergy offers no long-term bond funds and only one global equity fund.

Smart Funds 1999:

Synergy Canadian Style Management Class.

Noteworthy Funds:

Synergy Canadian Momentum Class. The momentum style is not widely used in Canada but offers an interesting alternative to growth and value. This new fund managed by Dave Picton should benefit over the long term by a strict adherence to the style.

Availability:

Through brokers and discount brokers and dealers. Minimum investment is $500.

47. TALVEST FUND MANAGEMENT INC.   **FRONT OR REAR**

Strengths: Fixed income and asset allocation
Technology & health funds
Weaknesses: High MERs, weak marketing
RESPs?: No
Web Site: www.talvest.com   **Toll Free:** 1-800-268-8258

CANADIAN	Category	Rating	Fund Name	M.E.R.%	RRSP/Foreign
Money Market:		■	Talvest Money Fund	0.75	RRSP
Fixed Income:	Long-term	▲	Talvest Bond Fund	1.99	RRSP
		★	**Talvest/Hyperion High Yield Bond Fund**	2.1	RRSP
	Short-term	▲	Talvest Income Fund	1.5	RRSP
Equity:	Mid-Large Cap	■	Talvest Canadian Equity Value Fund	2.4	RRSP
		★	**Talvest/Hyperion Canadian Equity Growth Fund**	2.6	RRSP
	Small Cap	▲	Talvest/Hyperion Small Cap Canadian Equity Fund	2.5	RRSP
	Other	■	Talvest New Economy	2.5	RRSP
		■	Talvest/Hyperion Canadian Resource Fund		RRSP
Tax Advantaged:	Dividend	■	Talvest Dividend Fund	1.99	RRSP
	Labor-sponsored	■	Canadian Medical Discoveries Fund	5.8	RRSP
		▲	Canadian Science & Technology Growth Fund Inc.		RRSP
Mult-Asset:	Balanced	■	Talvest Diversified Fund		RRSP
	Asset Allocation	■	Talvest Canadian Asset Allocation Fund	2.42	RRSP

FOREIGN	Category	Rating	Fund Name	M.E.R.%	RRSP/Foreign
Money Market:		■	Talvest Global Cash Management Fund		RRSP
Fixed Income:		■	Talvest Foreign Pay Cdn. Bond Fund	2.15	RRSP
Global Equity:	All-global	■	Talvest/Hyperion Global Equity Fund		Foreign
		■	Talvest Global RRSP Fund	2.5	RRSP
	Specialty	▲	Talvest/Hyperion Global Science & Technology Fund	2.25	Foreign
		▲	Talvest/Hyperion Global Health Care Fund	3.3	Foreign
	Small-cap	■	Talvest/Hyperion Global Small Cap Fund		Foreign
Regional Equity:	U.S.	▲	Talvest/Hyperion Value Line U.S. Equity Fund	3	Foreign
	U.S. Index	▲	Talvest/Hyperion U.S. Index Small-cap Fund		Foreign
	Europe	■	Talvest/Hyperion European Fund	3	Foreign
	Far East	■	Talvest/Hyperion Asian Fund	3.25	Foreign
	China	■	Talvest/Hyperion China Plus Fund		Foreign
Global Balanced:		■	Talvest Global Asset Allocation Fund	2.75	Foreign

Talvest is a broker-sold sister company of the Canadian Imperial Bank of Commerce, which acquired Talvest's parent company, TAL Investment Counsel Ltd., in 1994. However, the operating shareholders retain management control, and the company intends to go public.

TAL itself manages $20 billion in pension funds and also acts as subadviser to some of the no-load funds at CIBC Securities Inc. The company decided to leverage its pension expertise to mutual funds and launched Talvest in 1985 as traditional broker-sold funds (front load of 5 per cent, or rear load of 5.5 per cent, declining to nil after seven years). Many of the TAL portfolio managers also manage similar funds for CIBC's no-load funds.

With so many billions to manage, TAL's challenge is to beat the indexes. Perhaps that's why the Talvest funds are more specialized. Both in Canada and globally, it has developed real expertise in science and technology funds and health sciences. This extends to the venture capital level, through Dr. Calvin Stiller's Canadian Medical Discoveries Fund and a newer labor-fund spin-off, Canadian Science & Technology Growth Fund Inc.

While the first open-end domestic tech fund, Talvest New Economy, has yet to deliver on its early promise (Nuala Beck, who coined the phrase New Economy, has withdrawn from the fund), Talvest has started to make an impact with its global versions. It's hard not to notice the 45 per cent one-year return (to June 30, 1998) of its new Talvest/Hyperion Global Science & Technology Fund.

Talvest is also strong in fixed income but its MERs keep it from making our Smart Fund list this year. Both Talvest Bond and Talvest Income continue to be solid long-term performers. The new Talvest/Hyperion High Yield Fund debuts as a Smart Fund. Talvest also talks a good game in asset allocation. Its Benchmarker software, available for PCs, uses strategic asset-allocation portfolios that Talvest designed with pension firm William M. Mercer Ltd. Talvest research showed that most investors do not know the target returns they need to meet their long-term goals.

While Talvest's tactical asset-allocation funds have had a good year, over the longer term they are just as ordinary as the rest of the industry's asset-allocation products. It's interesting to note that the derivative-based, all-equity 100 per cent RRSP-eligible Talvest Global RRSP Fund, now managed by vice president asset mix Guy Normandin, has done far better than the global asset-allocation fund. Derivatives are another CIBC/TAL strength that you can expect to hear more about.

Talvest has added six funds since the last edition of this book, most of them fairly specialized funds. The new Talvest/Hyperion

Canadian Resource Fund is managed by Paul Wong, a geologist/fund manager who also manages CIBC Energy Fund. The Talvest/Hyperion Global Equity Fund is a global large-cap fund, eligible as 20 per cent foreign content in an RRSP, which supplements the Global RRSP Fund. The Talvest/Hyperion Global Small Cap Fund uses Nicholas-Applegate Capital Management of San Diego, but almost two-thirds of the global small-cap names are North American. The Talvest/Hyperion Global Health Care Fund uses Edward Owens, manager of the successful Vanguard Health Care Fund in the United States.

An interesting small-cap addition is the Talvest/Hyperion U.S. Index Small Cap Fund, which is described in the Noteworthy section.

Investors who believe China will be to the twenty-first century what Japan was to the twentieth may be enticed by the new Talvest/Hyperion China Plus Fund, managed in-house by TAL subsidiary CEF-TAL Investment Management Ltd. Talvest also unveiled a 100 per cent RRSP-eligible global money-market fund.

Like all Europe funds, Talvest/Hyperion European Fund had a good year, returning 39 per cent in the year ended June 30, 1998. It has a new manager, Sarah Caygill of TAL Asset Management (Europe) s.a.

Smart Funds 1999:

Talvest/Hyperion Canadian Growth, Talvest/Hyperion High Yield Bond.

Noteworthy Funds:

Talvest Income Fund. Continued high MER of 1.69 per cent caused this one to be demoted in addition to its straight fourth-quartile performance across all periods out to 10 years as of June 30, 1998.

Talvest/Hyperion Small Cap Equity Fund. Winner of the small-cap fund of the year at the 1997 Canadian Mutual Fund Awards. Managed by Sebastian van Berkom. Fund is expected to be closed when it reaches $300 million. Therefore, is demoted from Smart Fund status.

Talvest/Hyperion U.S. Index Small Cap Fund. New fund takes a unique passive investing approach to U.S. small caps, by investing in futures, options, and forward contracts on small-cap indices. Counts as foreign content. MER not yet available but the underlying management fee is 1.75 per cent.

Hyperion Value Line U.S. Equity Fund. This is managed by Value Line Inc., a well-respected research firm that ranks more than 1,700 U.S. growth stocks. Manager Nancy Bendig was formerly a technology stock analyst with Shearson Lehman. Overweights promising industries, which it considers finance, technology, and health care. A 26.5 per cent return for year ended June 30, 1998; 24 per cent three-year CAGR.

Talvest/Hyperion Global Science & Technology Fund. A spectacular start for this new global specialty fund, with a huge 45 per cent return to the year ended June 30, 1998. Managed in-house by TAL's Stephen Kahn, the fund includes large-cap tech blue chips such as Microsoft and Northern Telecom, as well as lesser-known small caps. Kahn tries to limit the number of names to a manageable 40. Despite the global moniker, most of the stocks are U.S.

Talvest/Hyperion Global Health Care Fund. A change of manager here, as Talvest has moved to an external manager, Edward Owens of Wellington Management Co., which is also a subadviser for a comparable Vanguard fund. For "global," read U.S., since more than 80 per cent of the health care and medical products picks are from the United States, 10 per cent from Japan, and about 5 per cent from Europe. A 16.7 per cent return for year ended June 30, 1998, not as impressive as the broader-focused, but also U.S.-centric, Global Science & Tech fund. Fund rated highly by U.S. rating service Morningstar.

Canadian Science & Technology Growth Fund. Labor-sponsored fund modelled after the $276 million Canadian Medical Discoveries Fund. This one is broader in scope than health care, although it slightly underperformed CMDF last year. It's sponsored by the Canadian Air Traffic Controllers Association and partners with three sci-tech government agencies. What you gain in the federal and provincial tax credits (and now including New Brunswick) you may lose on high MERs.

Talvest Bond. Under John Braive, this core bond fund has been consistently in the second quartile over the past 10 years. Braive is considered one of the country's most astute fixed-income managers. His style of spread trading is less aggressive than those who try to anticipate interest rate moves. The 8.9 per cent one-year return to June 30, 1998 beat former Smart Fund, Talvest Income, also run by Braive.

Availability:

Brokers and discount brokers and dealers across Canada.

48. TD GREEN LINE FUNDS

Strengths: Low-MER index funds
T. Rowe Price foreign funds
Education & support
Weaknesses: Choosing from 43+ funds
RESPs?: Yes
Web Site: www.greenlinefunds.com   **Toll Free:** 1-800-268-8166

CANADIAN	Category	Rating	Fund Name	M.E.R.%	RRSP/Foreign
Money Market:		■	Green Line Canadian Money Market Fund	0.84	RRSP
		■	Green Line Canadian T-Bill Fund	0.86	RRSP
		■	Green Line Premium Money Market Fund	0.3	RRSP
Fixed Income:	Long-term	★	**Green Line Canadian Bond Fund**	0.94	RRSP
		■	Green Line Real Return Bond Fund	1.53	RRSP
	Short-term	■	Green Line Short Term Income Fund	1.1	RRSP
	Index	▲	Green Line Canadian Government Bond Index	0.8	RRSP
	Mortgage	■	Green Line Mortgage Fund	1.59	RRSP
		■	Green Line Mortgage Backed Fund	1.55	RRSP
Equity:	Mid-Large Cap	▲	Green Line Blue Chip Equity Fund	2.25	RRSP
	Mixed cap	■	Green Line Canadian Equity Fund	2.1	RRSP
		■	Green Line Canadian Small-Cap Equity	2.35	RRSP
		▲	Green Line Value Fund	2.09	RRSP
	Index	★	**Green Line Canadian Index Fund**	0.8	RRSP
Sector:	Gold/precious metal	■	Green Line Precious Metals Fund	2.12	RRSP
	Resource	■	Green Line Resource Fund	2.12	RRSP
	Other	▲	Green Line Energy Fund	2.1	RRSP
Tax Advantaged:	Dividend	■	Green Line Dividend Fund	2	RRSP
		■	Green Line Monthly Income Fund		RRSP
Mult-Asset:	Balanced	■	Green Line Balanced Growth Fund	1.95	RRSP
		▲	Green Line Balanced Income Fund	1.95	RRSP

FOREIGN	Category	Rating	Fund Name	M.E.R.%	RRSP/Foreign
Money Market:		■	Green Line U.S. Money Market Fund	1.24	RRSP
Fixed Income:		▲	Green Line Global Government Bond Fund	2.07	Foreign
		▲	Green Line Global RSP Bond	2	RRSP
Global Equity:	All-global	▲	Green Line Global Select Fund	2.34	Foreign
	EAFE	■	Green Line International Equity Fund	2.32	Foreign
	EAFE Index	■	Green Line International RSP Index	0.9	RRSP
	Specialty	★	**Green Line Science & Technology Fund**	2.58	Foreign
		■	GL Entertainment & Communications Fund	2.57	Foreign
		▲	Green Line Health Sciences Fund	2.58	Foreign
Regional Equity:					
	U.S. Large-cao	▲	Green Line U.S. Blue Chip Equity	2.34	Foreign
	U.S. Mid-cap	▲	Green Line Mid-Cap Growth Fund*	2.33	Foreign
	U.S. Small-cap	■	Green Line U.S. Small-Cap Equity Fund	2.35	Foreign
	U.S. Index	■	Green Line Dow Jones Industrial Average Index	0.8	Foreign
		★	**Green Line U.S. Index Fund**	0.66	Foreign
		■	Green Line U.S. RSP Index Fund	0.8	RRSP
	Latin American	■	Green Line Latin American Growth Fund	2.66	Foreign
	Emerging Market	▲	Green Line Emerging Markets Fund	2.69	Foreign
	Far East	▲	Green Line Asian Growth Fund	2.6	Foreign

Japan	■	Green Line Japanese Growth Fund	2.59	Foreign
Japan Index	■	Green Line Japanese Index Fund	0.9	Foreign
Europe	■	Green Line European Growth Fund	2.58	Foreign
	■	GL European Index Fund	0.9	Foreign

* formerly North American Growth Fund

TD Green Line Funds have always had a disproportionate share of Smart Funds. This year is no exception, although we must confess to experiencing the same kind of confusion the average investor must feel, when confronting the massive 43-fund line-up.

TD cranked up the fund-creation machinery in 1997-98, with low-MER index funds being the chief additions. The MERs for North American index funds are projected to be 0.8 per cent in 1998, and 0.9 per cent for the global index funds, which are the figures used in the matrices. The 1997 MERs on those funds were closer to 1.0 per cent.

If the merger of the TD Bank with the Canadian Imperial Bank of Commerce proceeds, the combined CIBC-TD no-load family would present investors with a massive choice of funds, and particularly index funds, which have also been targeted by CIBC Securities Inc. (we'd have to call the CIBC-TD index funds the "massive passive" family). CIBC's MERs on its index funds are 0.9 per cent but will no doubt be adjusted to come into line with TD's new 0.8 per cent standard for passively managed equity funds.

Two of the new TD GreenLine index funds allow RRSP or RRIF investors to beat the 20 per cent foreign content, the first time that TD has offered 100 per cent RRSP-eligible global equity funds. The two funds are the U.S. RSP Index Fund and the International RSP Index Fund.

TD has even introduced index funds specific to Europe, Japan, and even the Dow Jones Industrial Average. TD really pushes the MER envelope on its U.S. Index Fund, which has just a 0.66 per cent MER—about the closest you can get in Canada to the low-MER index funds of U.S. no-load, not-for-profit giant Vanguard Group Inc.

Keeping in mind that TD also sells some brand-name, actively managed load funds, TD investors are confronted with something of a dilemma in creating their fund portfolios. Do they believe that human fund managers can beat the indexes and justify higher MERs, or do they cut costs by going with the indexes? To some extent, the answer will be determined by the direction of the markets. Generally, index funds can outperform in bull markets because they remain fully invested; on the other hand, in bear markets, human managers may be able to preserve capital better than a blind commitment to the indexes.

MAJOR FUND FAMILIES

Such a wealth of choices will be tough for the individual do-it-yourselfer; this is the kind of fund line-up that almost begs for the services of a competent adviser. A CIBC-TD merger would only intensify these dilemmas. The days are long gone when critics of bank no-load funds could dismiss them with the phrase, "No load, no advice," but investors should ensure that their bank representative has certain financial planning qualifications—preferably a CFP (Certified Financial Planner) or RFP (Registered Financial Planner).

Fortunately, TD boasts one of the industry's more sophisticated staff-education programs, which includes an annual exam that all TD representatives must pass, and some innovative work on asset allocation. Marketing Solutions has ranked TD's Investment Specialists as number one in dispensing mutual fund advice from a financial institution. TD is also making it easier to tweak portfolios, with detailed quarterly statements and a free rebalancing service.

As for Smart Fund selections, we rank many of the new index funds as Noteworthy, particularly since markets retrenched from their early-1998 highs.

TD's actively managed domestic funds are managed either internally by TD Asset Management Inc., or externally by Sceptre Investment Counsel Ltd. and McLean, Budden Ltd. Generally, our Smart Fund and Noteworthy picks are managed by external managers, particularly in its global funds. TD was among the first banks to recognize that the quickest way to build competent foreign funds is to set up a number of outside subadvisers. It has 10 external advisers around the world, including such respected firms as Morgan Stanley Asset Management Inc. of New York (a pioneer in Emerging Markets); T. Rowe Price Associates Inc. of Baltimore (manager of the top-performing Green Line Science & Technology Fund and now a health sciences and blue-chip U.S. equity fund: see Noteworthy); Schroder Capital Management International, and Perpetual Portfolio Management of the U.K. True, as is the case with their load counterparts, external management does not come cheap: management expense ratios for most of these funds tend to be more than 2.50 per cent. Overall, TD Bank may have the best fund family for its breadth of quality funds across active and passive strategies, a variety of management styles, and a full selection of sector and regional funds. You may not need any other fund family than TD Green Line.

TD's Asset Accumulator Account allows consolidation of all money market, fixed income and mutual fund investments: mixing and matching various funds from multiple companies along with direct investments in stocks, bonds, GICs, and other products. TD's new Goal Planner and Retirement and Education Savings Planner are new financial planning tools available to Green Line customers.

Smart Funds 1999:

Green Line Canadian Bond Fund, Green Line Canadian Index Fund, Green Line Science & Technology, Green Line U.S Index Fund.

Noteworthy Funds:

Green Line Blue Chip Equity. Replicates the new Sceptre Canadian Equity Fund. Buy the Sceptre fund direct and save on the MER. However, if you are in the no-load TD fund family, this is a solid core holding for your RRSP and was a Smart Fund in 1998. MER of 2.25 per cent is a bit high, but the returns have been above average to compensate.

Green Line Value Fund. This one is managed internally by Bonnie Bloomberg. Fund has fallen into the fourth quartile for the year ended June 30, 1998, but has a three-year return of 21.28 per cent, well ahead of the TSE300's 19.86 per cent and solidly in the first quartile. MER of 2.09 per cent is getting more competitive, but still could come down.

Green Line Energy Fund. Resource-based sector funds have proven too volatile to be Smart Funds anymore. Losing 39 per cent in one year is not our idea of "Smart" investing, although we mistakenly made it a Smart Fund in 1998.

Green Line Health Sciences Fund. A solid competitor to AIM's and Talvest/Hyperion's offering managed by T. Rowe Price with a 25 per cent one-year return number through June 30, 1998. Still AIM outperformed it and has a longer track record. Brian Stansky has replaced departed Skip Klein.

Green Line Global RSP Bond Fund. This is a solid international bond fund with first-quartile performance and a 2.00 per cent MER. A Smart Fund in 1998 that got squeezed off the list as we pared down the number of funds and the number of bond funds.

Green Line U.S. Blue Chip Equity. Another solid fund managed by T. Rowe Price. Begun in September 1996, it soared to first-quartile ranking with its 36 per cent return for the year ended June 30, 1998.

Green Line Mid-Cap Growth. Former Smart Fund, managed by T. Rowe Price, has suffered a little inconsistency relative to others in the U.S. category because of its mandate to be in mid-cap stocks. Don't give up on it yet—it's still a solid hold with a 27 per cent three-year compounded return. A Smart Fund from 1996 to 1998, it was tough to knock it down and make room for some great competitors.

Green Line Balanced Income Fund. A Smart Fund last year, but we recommend buying the Sceptre Balanced Growth Fund directly or through a broker and save on the MER of 1.95 per cent versus the 1.44 per cent for Lyle Stein's fund. This has been a solid above-average performer for the past three years.

Green Line Canadian Government Bond Index Fund. The 0.96 per cent MER makes this one noteworthy. Why not go passive and avoid the expenses of active management? The approach has generated solid second-quartile performance for this fund.

Green Line Global Select Fund. A Smart Fund in 1996 and 1997, we always thought renowned manager Perpetual would generate better than second and third quartile performance. This is a competitive category and TD needs to work on getting this fund up there with AGF International Value, Fidelity International Portfolio, and Templeton Growth.

Green Line Emerging Markets. This was a Smart Fund in 1996 and 1997, managed by Morgan Stanley Asset Management, one of the pioneers in emerging market investing. The fund has lost money for the three years ended June 30 and ranks in the third quartile.

Green Line Global Government Bond Fund. This is managed by J.P. Morgan and counts as foreign content. It was a Smart Fund in 1996 and has returned 7 per cent compounded for the five years ending on June 30, 1998.

Green Line Asian Growth Fund. This 1996 Smart Fund has experienced a couple of manager changes since then. The fund lost 50 per cent for the year ended June 30, 1998. Remember when Asian funds returned 90 per cent in 1993? Did anyone warn you about volatility?

Availability:

TD Bank branches; through the Investment Centre and many dealers and brokers and discount brokers.

49. TEMPLETON MANAGEMENT LTD. FRONT OR REAR

Strengths:	All-global equities
	New seg funds (not shown below)
Weaknesses:	Canadian funds
	Loss of Michael Price
RESPs?:	Yes
Web Site: www.templeton.ca	**Toll Free:** 1-800-387-0830

CANADIAN	Category	Rating	Fund Name	M.E.R.%	RRSP/Foreign
Money Market:		■	Templeton Treasury Bill Fund	0.75	RRSP
Fixed Income:	Long-term	■	Templeton Canadian Bond Fund	1.65	RRSP
Equity:	Mid-Large Cap	■	Templeton Canadian Stock Fund	2.44	RRSP
Mult-Asset:	Balanced	■	Templeton Balanced Fund	2.44	RRSP
	Asset Allocation	■	Templeton Canadian Asset Allocation Fund	2.15	RRSP

FOREIGN	Category	Rating	Fund Name	M.E.R.%	RRSP/Foreign
Fixed Income:		■	Templeton Global Bond Fund	2.25	Foreign
Global Equity:	All-global	★	**Templeton Growth Fund Ltd.**	2	Foreign
		▲	Templeton Growth Fund Linked Notes*		RRSP
	EAFE	★	**Templeton International Stock Fund**	2.49	Foreign
	Small-cap	■	Templeton Global Smaller Companies Fund	2.61	Foreign
Regional Equity:	U.S.	▲	Mutual Beacon Fund	2.5	Foreign
	U.S. small cap	▲	Franklin U.S. Small Cap Growth Fund	2.5	Foreign
	Emerging Market	★	**Templeton Emerging Markets Fund**	3.24	Foreign
Global Balanced:		■	Templeton International Balanced Fund	2.55	Foreign
		■	Templeton Global Balanced Fund	2.55	Foreign

* issued by TD Bank

Regular *Smart Funds* readers who are also Templeton investors won't find much new in this edition. And that's a good thing! (Apologies to Martha Stewart.) The Smart Funds philosophy is to find stable, consistent, long-term performing funds that can be held over decades.

In this respect, Templeton fits the bill, particularly for global investing. For most investors, that means the 20 per cent foreign-content portion of an RRSP or RRIF, or the unconstrained taxable portfolios.

For the benefit of new readers, we'll repeat what we've said in earlier editions: "When it comes to international equity investing, Templeton seems like an obvious and easy decision. Good as many of the newcomers are, it's hard to make a case why the average investor shouldn't just buy Templeton Growth and maybe a dash of Templeton Emerging Markets or Templeton Smaller Companies and be done with agonizing regional equity decisions."

Templeton's value approach to stock-picking means it doesn't make "top-down" country-specific decisions at all. It just seeks bargain-priced stocks wherever in the world they might be. As a result, Templeton investors were largely spared the angst of investors who bought all-Asian regional funds, and then watched their investments be cut in half in 1997. The Templeton investor who had the above-mentioned "dash" of emerging markets would have suffered a huge 31 per cent drop in the Templeton Emerging Markets Fund, but that would have been offset somewhat by the 9 per cent gain in Templeton Growth and the 15 per cent rise in Templeton International (year ended June 30, 1998). All three funds return as Smart Funds. See also profile of Templeton Growth Fund manager Mark Holowesko on page 32.

In its rookie year, we awarded the Mutual Beacon Fund Smart Fund status, largely on the track record of fabled value investor Michael Price of Franklin Mutual Advisers Inc. Mutual Beacon was up 22 per cent for the year ended and would have remained a Smart Fund. However, in July 1998, Michael Price announced he would step down from managing the fund and the U.S. versions of the same, effective November 1, 1998. This is too great a loss, no matter how good the team replacing him allegedly is. The small-cap Franklin U.S. Small Cap Fund stays in the Noteworthy category.

In past editions, we have noted the absence of Templeton global funds designed to beat the 20 per cent foreign-content limit in Canadian RRSPs and RRIFs. Templeton Growth fans will be delighted to note the new Templeton Growth Fund Ltd. Linked Notes, issued by TD Bank in March 1998. The notes are structured to provide holders with comparable rates of return to TGF, but are not considered to be foreign property under the Income Tax Act. For more details, see the "Noteworthy" section below.

Most of Templeton's core global equity funds are perennial Smart Funds. Why then do we continue to ignore Templeton's Canadian offerings? From time to time, we are tempted, since the rigorous Templeton approach to securities analysis and its value orientation became more and more valuable as the bull market ascended ever higher. With the global funds, the investor gets the benefit of a giant research team located in dozens of countries. With a reasonable 2 per cent MER on Templeton Growth, this is a prudent way to access 97 per cent of the world's stock markets.

For Canadian securities, however, there are so many competing fund families, that Templeton appears to us merely average on the performance front. Their Canadian MERs are, however, no bargain.

Outside the core global funds, the rest of the Templeton funds essentially allow you to do two things: to add bond exposure through balanced or asset-allocation funds or to provide Canadian funds that maximize their permitted 20 per cent foreign content.

Generally, the U.S. Templeton organization offers a wider selection of funds than the Toronto-based Templeton Management Ltd. Some of these are closed-end regional and single-country funds traded on the New York Stock Exchange, which can be purchased by Canadians. Cost-conscious investors may find the closed-end fund, Templeton Emerging Markets Appreciation Fund, a viable alternative to the open-end version. Both are managed by Mark Mobius. The fund is available on the Toronto and Montreal Stock Exchanges. In July, Trimark announced it would offer "seg" or "segregated" versions of several funds, including TGF but not Templeton Emerging Markets.

Smart Funds 1999:

Templeton Growth, Templeton International, Templeton Emerging Markets.

Noteworthy Funds:

Templeton Growth Fund Ltd. Linked Notes. As noted above, these TD Bank-issued deposit notes allow note-holders to receive interest payments proportional to, but slightly less than, Templeton Growth Fund. The advantage is the notes are not considered to be foreign content. Outside the RRSP, it is taxed unfavorably as interest; therefore you'd want to hold this in a registered plan, and TGF in taxable plans.

The notes are sold out but industry insiders would not be surprised if a second issue were made. The interest payments will be slightly less than TGF distributions; there is an annual reduction of 55 basis points, so in effect the MER is 2.55 per cent compared to TGF's 2.00 per cent. The minimum investment is $1,000 with what amounts to a 1.0 per cent front load. Redemption fees of 6 per cent declining to 0 per cent after six years.

Unlike the banks' index-linked GICs, this product does pass along dividends. However, there is no guarantee of initial principal.

Original offering was available through all stockbrokers and discount brokers.

Mutual Beacon Fund is demoted with the announced departure of superstar Michael Price.

Franklin U.S. Small Cap Growth Fund. Managed by Edward Jamieson at Franklin Advisers Inc. and had a 24 per cent return in a tough small-cap market.

Availability:

Brokers and discount brokers and planners across Canada, TD Bank, CT Securities, e-trade and imoney. London Life distributes Templeton International, Emerging Markets and the Treasury Bill funds. $500 minimum initial purchase per fund; $2,500 for the Treasury Bill fund.

50. TRIMARK INVESTMENT MANAGEMENT INC. FRONT OR REAR LOAD

Strengths: Reasonable MERs
Consistent long-term performance
New Seg Funds (not shown below)
Weaknesses: Size of Canadian equity funds
RESPs?: Yes
Web Site: www.trimark.com   **Toll Free:** 1-800-387-9845

CANADIAN	Category	Rating	Fund Name	M.E.R.%	RRSP/Foreign
Money Market:		■	Trimark Interest Fund	0.75	RRSP
Fixed Income:	Long-term	▲	Trimark Canadian Bond Fund	1.25	RRSP
		★	**Trimark Advantage Bond Fund**	1.25	RRSP
	Short-term	■	Trimark Government Income Fund	1.25	RRSP
Equity:	Mid-Large Cap	▲	Trimark Canadian Fund	1.52	RRSP
		■	Trimark RSP Equity Fund	2.0	RRSP
		■	Trimark Select Canadian Growth Fund	2.3	RRSP
	Small-cap	▲	Trimark Canadian Small Companies Fund	2.25	RRSP
	Resources	■	Trimark Canadian Resources Fund	2.25	RRSP
Mult-Asset:	Balanced	★	**Trimark Income Growth Fund**	1.57	RRSP
		▲	Trimark Select Balanced Fund	2.24	RRSP

FOREIGN	Category	Rating	Fund Name	M.E.R.%	RRSP/Foreign
Global Equity:	All-global	★	**Trimark Fund**	1.52	Foreign
		▲	Trimark Select Growth Fund	2.32	Foreign
	Specialty	▲	Trimark Discovery Fund	2.55	Foreign
Regional Equity:					
	NAFTA/N.Am.	▲	The Americas Fund	2.6	Foreign
	Far East	▲	Trimark Indo-Pacific Fund	2.95	Foreign
	Europe	■	Trimark Europlus Fund	2.75	Foreign

How fickle mutual fund investors can be! Two years ago, Trimark ruled as the brokers' favorite. The media acclaimed the family and the public opened its wallets to it.

In 1998, the consensus changed and the strong net sales turned into net redemptions for the first time since 1991. What should have been a problem in just a single asset class—Canadian equities—has been used as an excuse to leave the Trimark family altogether.

Regular readers of the *Smart Funds* books know the Fund Family approach to Mutual Funds means minimizing redemption charges and making every possible effort to stay in your chosen family (or families) until there is solid evidence such a drastic departure is warranted.

The Smart Funds Selection Committee has long been concerned about the amount of money contained in Trimark's three almost identical mid-large cap funds. Lead manager Vito Maida has found it difficult to beat the TSE 300 and smaller, nimbler rivals. He seems more of a value manager than a growth manager and his prudent value stance on, for example, the pricey Canadian banks had hurt him as the rampaging bull market continued to rage. The profile of Trimark chairman Robert Krembil on page 29 contains more insights as to why we don't believe the Trimark philosophy has changed as significantly as some of its critics suggest. Maida no longer manages the Trimark RSP Equity Fund, which is now managed by the newly appointed managers of the Resource and Small Companies funds.

With some reluctance and despite its low MER, we have demoted former Smart Fund, Trimark Canadian, to Noteworthy status, and stripped the two higher-MER mirror funds of their Noteworthy designations. But we would not be surprised if Trimark Canadian confounds us all with strong performance for the balance of the century.

We do not, however, advocate throwing the fund-family baby out with the "laggard fund" bath water. The previously designated "Smart" Trimark Advantage bond fund retains its status. So does the flagship global equity Trimark remain a Smart Fund? With its 1.52 per cent MER, we regard Trimark Fund as one of the high-performing, cost-effective bargains in the global equity universe. We have demoted Trimark Indo-Pacific Fund and increasingly view high-MER regional equity funds like the new Trimark Europlus Fund as inferior to a good all-global, low-MER fund such as Trimark Fund. Trimark Fund has some, albeit modest, exposure to Europe and Asia (in fact Trimark already had $1.3 billion invested in Europe through its various funds). It seems to us that the better picks identified by the Indo-Pacific and EuroPlus managers will end up in Trimark Fund anyway and there's less danger of overweighting a volatile region such as Asia. We note that, like Templeton, Trimark does not make top-down geographic calls: regional exposure is merely an after-fact of stocks picked because of good valuations.

For those who want a little more jump to their Trimark global equity portfolios, we note the high-tech-oriented Discovery Fund has started to perform, mostly on the back of the U.S. market. It has been promoted to Noteworthy status in this edition.

As for those with significant holdings in Trimark Canadian, there are several alternatives, all still within the Trimark family. Trimark has launched two new Canadian specialty funds: Trimark Canadian Small Companies, which starts out as Noteworthy, and Trimark Resources, which seems to us somewhat of a departure from the core Trimark investment philosophy. They are managed by Keith Graham and Geoff MacDonald.

These new funds begin their lives with the advantage of small size, but both have higher MERs (2.25 per cent) than Trimark Canadian. A combination of Trimark Canadian and one of these specialty funds might be the prudent course for the average Trimark investor. Another alternative is a switch to the "Smart" balanced fund, Trimark Income Growth, keeping in mind that such a switch alters your asset allocation by putting more weight in fixed income. That fund also has one of the lowest MERs in the Canadian balanced fund universe.

Should the reader think we are belaboring the point about MERs, this is what Trimark's official Smart Funds submission says about the subject: "As competition intensifies, we expect to see downward pressure on fees...fees now associated with many funds will not be sustainable if returns revert to historical norms of 10 per cent or less."

While Trimark has never believed in timing the market, it was becoming more cautious about stock valuations even before the August correction. It has introduced several new products that allow investors to hedge their bets a bit—such as Trimark Trust's new equity-linked Stock Market GIC and Trimark Convertible GIC.

Along the same lines, Trimark has also launched a new family of segregated funds, which allow investors to combine investments in Trimark funds and also receive the benefits of the life insurance industry's seg funds: normally return-of-principal guarantees after 10 years or the death of a spouse, plus greater flexibility in creditor-proofing. At the time we went to press, there were few details on the Trimark seg funds, but normally one expects to pay a premium of 30 to 80 basis points on the MER to gain such peace of mind.

So is it time to jump off the Trimark bandwagon? Many will have done so by the time this book hits the market: net redemptions as of June 30, 1998, were significant. We see no reason to encourage those who have held the course from following their example. The adjustments suggested above should be all that is necessary.

Smart Funds 1999:

Trimark Fund, Trimark Income Growth Fund, Trimark Advantage Bond Fund.

Noteworthy Funds:

Trimark Canadian Fund. A low MER and a consistent value approach made us reluctant to remove this fund from the Smart Fund list. But the sheer quantity of money under management here makes it hard to beat the underlying index. We hope Vito Maida proves us wrong on this call. This fund will do spectacularly well versus the competition if two things happen: resource stocks come back and the high-flying banks and utilities get clobbered.

The Americas Fund former Smart Fund ran into stiff competition and is demoted.

Trimark Indo-Pacific Fund. Another demoted Smart Fund, not so much because this fund did badly on a relative basis but because of our criterion change for Smart Funds generally. The Asian crisis is not over. Why pay high MERs to make regional bets when the low-MER Trimark Fund continues to outperform?

Trimark Canadian Small Companies Fund. In the early years, this fund should get off to a fast start because of two advantages it holds over Trimark Canadian: far less money to invest and a large universe from which to find undervalued, undiscovered small-cap stocks.

Trimark Discovery Fund. Upgraded to Noteworthy status this year. Rick Serafini's focus on U.S. technology firms—and even Canada's Mortice Kern Systems—generated a 12 per cent return in the year ended June 30, 1998. But there are several "Smart" competitors that have done better still.

Trimark Select Growth. The DSC version, with a higher MER, of the Trimark Fund. This version has underperformed Trimark Fund by 2 or 3 per cent a year over the last five years, no doubt because of the MER disadvantage.

Trimark Selected Balanced. The DSC version, with a higher MER, of the Trimark Income Growth Fund. Despite the higher MER, this fund beat Trimark Income Growth by almost 4 per cent in the year ended June 30, 1998. With almost 10 times more money invested in it, cash flows and different entry points may account for the disparity.

Trimark Canadian Bond Fund. A 10.64 per cent three-year average CAGR through June 30, 1998 but a few points below the Advantage Bond fund. MERs are better than many rival bond funds.

Availability:

Brokers and discount brokers and financial planners across Canada, and through some insurance sales agents.

The 100 Smart Funds

Once an investment strategy is in place, the investor is faced with the difficult task of selecting the individual funds that will make up his or her portfolio. This section contains details of the 100 funds that we, along with the selection committee, would feel comfortable recommending to family and friends. We call these Smart Funds.

There are six criteria for selecting a Smart Fund. Although performance is a key criterion, it is not the only one. Furthermore, absolute performance is not that important. It is relative performance that is critical. We have represented this by quartile—ranking the Smart Funds against other funds in that asset category. This apples-to-apples comparison allows us to assemble the more than 1,800 funds sold in Canada into manageable groups. We can then maintain a watch over money managers with similar styles and mandates to determine who emerges as the best of the bunch.

We are renowned for our inclusion of funds with less than three years' performance history. In certain instances, this has forced a compromise of the criteria used on the more mature funds. However, we would be remiss if we did not identify some of the extraordinary money management talent that Canadian fund companies have developed or hired in recent years. Securities regulations make it difficult for fund companies to advertise the past track records of managers without including reams of disclaimers. This is appropriate because past performance is not a guarantee of future returns, and the investing circumstances surrounding the new fund may be different from the old fund's. Still, we cannot ignore a manager's successful past, and we do have a bias towards managers who have proven track records.

SELECTION CRITERIA

Quartile ranking is the prime performance measure. Examining performance relative to a fund's category peers, both in compound and in annual returns, allows for a more broad-based evaluation than the use of raw return numbers. Consistent, top-quartile performance over several periods is sought. Quartile rankings are determined by ranking the funds by their return numbers and then grouping the top 25 per cent into the first category, or quartile, the next 25 per cent into the second quartile, and so on. A mutual fund that can consistently achieve first- or second-quartile rankings will generate superior long-term returns for its unit holders.

Management expense ratio (MER) is calculated by dividing the total annual expenses of the fund by the fund's assets. Currently, there is a wide range of MERs, even within the same asset classes. Good-quality management must come at a reasonable price. These expenses are always deducted from the fund before the returns are calculated.

Asset size is considered relative to the fund's asset type and its mandate. For example, small bond funds face a price disadvantage against larger bond funds, which, because of their size, can negotiate lower commissions. Likewise, small-cap funds with a large asset pool may find it difficult to move in and out of the stocks they want.

When funds are being selected for income-oriented portfolios, the distribution of income and capital gains is a key criterion. Monthly distributions are preferred.

The authors conduct interviews with hundreds of money managers a year. These meetings are designed to confirm stated positions on style, explore the reasons behind past success (or lack of it) and ensure adherence to a stated methodology. This qualitative process balances the other quantitative aspects of fund selection.

SMART FUND LEGEND

There are many different pieces of information that are important to an investor when he or she is selecting a fund. We have included only the most important in each Smart Fund overview. Most do not need an explanation, but we'd like to touch on a few.

Fund manager: The person or team listed is the principal decision maker on the fund—the individual responsible for achieving the fund's performance. You could call these the Smart Managers. These managers are the best in Canada and should be on anyone's all-star team. The individual named is in-house, unless a subadviser is noted.

RRSP eligibility: 100 per cent indicates that the fund is fully eligible; 20 per cent means it can be in an RRSP or RRIF as part of one's foreign content.

Management style: *Equity style can be one of the following:*
• Bottom-up, growth. The manager selects stocks based on their growth potential.
• Bottom-up, value. The manager selects stocks based on price.
• Top-down, growth. The manager selects for the growth potential of an industry, sector or geographic region.
• Sector rotator. The manager moves between industry sectors to capture growth.
• Growth at a reasonable price, or GARP. This is a blend of growth and value.

Fixed income managers can adopt one of two styles, or a blend of the two:
• Interest rate anticipation. Managers endeavor to predict the direction of interest rates, and structure the fund to take advantage of this movement.
• Spread trading. Managers trade bonds to capture the differences between the interest rates of bonds of different credit qualities.

Risk: Although many investors are uncomfortable with a fund that is volatile, one that changes in value frequently and dramatically, it is really the loss of money that is disturbing. Therefore, we look at the maximum loss that has been experienced by a fund over a three-month period. These quarters are not calendar quarters; they are rolling three-month periods: January, February, March would be the first quarter of the year; February, March, April would be the second rolling quarter; March, April, May the third rolling quarter. There are 10 of these rolling quarters in a year. REMEMBER: these only show paper losses. Actual losses for an individual only occur when a sale is realized and could also be affected by taxes and commissions. We have also indicated how the fund has done over any 12-month holding period. Keep in mind that these are short periods for holding equity funds, but still useful for demonstrating volatility.

We've also used the three-month time period to look at a fund's worst and best performances. The worst three-month performance for an older fund is often the three months ended in September 1990. This risk indicator lets you see the fund at its worst and at its best.

Performance: The graph compares the growth of a $1,000 investment in the fund to an appropriate benchmark and Canada Savings Bonds. The dots on the graph represent the fund's quartile performance in each calendar year. Beneath the graph are the fund's annual returns for each of the past nine calendar years and for the nine months ending September 30, 1998. We have also calculated the compound returns for the period ending September 30, 1998.

Notice on the graphs where sometimes the index outperforms the fund. This usually means the fund has recovered or made a manager change. When we talk long term it can be enlightening to see performance over long-term time periods.

CANADIAN EQUITY FUNDS

For most Canadians, a significant portion of their core portfolio should be in mid- to large-cap Canadian equity funds. This is not because the Canadian market has outperformed other markets (it has not), but because:

* most Canadian investors are investing ultimately to spend in Canadian dollars;
* there is a familiarity with the companies that are chosen for investment; and
* most investors are saving in their RRSPs, which are governed by foreign-content rules.

Over the longer term, Canadian equities have outperformed Canadian bonds, so a core equity base is essential for long-term wealth accumulation.

Small-cap stocks are not for the conservative investor, or at least not as a significant portion of a portfolio. Although they have a history of outperforming large-cap stocks over the long term, when they move down, they can go down a lot. However, Canada is becoming internationally recognized for its small-cap opportunities. Once dominated by junior oils, the sector is diversifying as our expertise in computer systems and software grows. But small-cap investing is a skill. The managers often rely on their own research, culled from a wide variety of services that help them find that company or niche that is still largely undiscovered. The attraction is the huge potential for growth when the manager is right. Mutual funds are a natural vehicle for most investors who want to participate in this area of the market. The stocks are volatile, and owning a diversified portfolio will lessen the impact.

CANADIAN DIVIDEND FUNDS

Generally, dividend funds should be considered only by those investors who need to generate income from their non-RRSP portfolios. This is because dividends are taxed at 75 per cent of the rate that applies to interest income from bonds and GICs. The major difference between dividend funds is the percentage of dividends coming from preferred stock. Preferred stock is issued with a fixed dividend rate, making it possible for an investor to determine what the return will be. And there is greater security in preferred stock. A company must first pay its debt (bond) holders, and next in line are the preferred shareholders. Common equity holders are last in this hierarchy. In slower economic times, companies can suspend common equity payments without any obligation to make these payments in the future. Rarely do they suspend preferred equity payments. If they do, they must pay the preferred dividends in arrears before any payments can be made to common shareholders. The trade-off is that, in good times, you could enjoy capital gains from common equity. The funds with a higher percentage of dividends from preferred stock will underperform in rising markets, but they are the choice for those who want a higher degree of income certainty and less price volatility.

SPECIALTY FUNDS

These funds must be considered only in the context of a diversified portfolio. They are volatile, but investing in these funds wisely can enhance performance and reduce risk, since many behave differently from broader market funds.

We have moved all regional and sector funds into one category. We are benchmarking these for a Canadian investor to the TSE300. These are personal risky asset allocations made by the investor, who could have just as easily bought a low-cost index fund.

BALANCED FUNDS

Holding balanced funds is convenient. Ideally, investors should make their own decisions about asset mix, and then invest with managers who specialize in equity or fixed income. If you do not have the time to do this, put the decision in the hands of those who do it for a living.

There are two types of balanced funds. Most are strategic asset-allocation funds. These have fixed minimum and maximum percentages of stock and bond holdings. This type of fund is best suited to the more conservative investor. The tactical asset-allocation funds can make more extreme bets. Their managers can be 100 per cent in an asset class if they believe in it strongly enough to make such a decision. This type of balanced fund is clearly for the more risk-tolerant investor. International balanced funds have the same benefits as their domestic counterparts but include the benefit of geographic and currency diversification.

U.S. EQUITY FUNDS

Too often Canadians feel they have to look across an ocean to get international investing exposure. The truth is that just south of the border is the largest capital market in the world. For many, this market should represent a first step in global investing and serve as a significant portion of their international allocation over time.

The U.S. economy, in global terms, is not as big as it once was. However, it still represents approximately 40 per cent of the global economy. Many of the world's largest and most successful companies are headquartered in the United States. Many are multinational and derive much of their revenue from international activity. By investing in them, managers get international exposure without having to invest in less-regulated markets.

In addition, the United States has a fertile small-cap market. The entrepreneurial spirit in the United States is such that good ideas and talented people find the money to develop business propositions.

INTERNATIONAL EQUITY FUNDS

Global equity funds should be in almost everyone's portfolio. The Canadian equity market represents only 3 to 4 per cent of world capital markets, and it is prudent to look outside Canada when building a properly diversified portfolio. Yet with the potential for increased return comes the potential for increased risk. Therefore, we favour globally diversified funds rather than regionally specific funds. Investors can enhance their portfolio returns while minimizing their reliance on any one region. Another reason to invest internationally is to diversify away from the Canadian dollar. Many people are concerned about the loonie losing its competitiveness; international investing is one way of protecting against that loss.

Ideally, every growth-oriented portfolio should include some emerging market exposure. However, the volatility that will be experienced by these funds means that anyone who finds such movement unsettling should steer clear. Broad-based emerging market funds, rather than their region-specific cousins, are the best way to take advantage of the areas around the world that will experience greater economic growth than more mature economies. The political instability and economic crises that exist in these regions will continue to cause short- to mid-term performance to remain uncertain.

EUROPEAN EQUITY FUNDS

Europe is a region familiar to most investors; there is a sense of comfort with business practices and cultures there. We believe Europe represents the most conservative international step outside of North America. These countries are not in the same economic cycle at the same time. There is an opportunity to invest during times when the other mature markets are out of cycle, and thereby enhance a portfolio's return and lower its risk. Most of the funds in this section have looked at the eastern European markets and are at various stages of investing in them. However, these countries are considered emerging markets, and the area is still seen as risky. Europe itself is undergoing tremendous changes that bode well for investors. We don't know what the impacts of the EMU and a recent movement toward running companies in the interest of shareholders will mean, but it should be positive.

CANADIAN BOND FUNDS

Most of the excitement and glamour in mutual funds surrounds equity funds. But investing in bonds, mortgages and other fixed-income products can also be lucrative. This was certainly the case as rates came down in the early 1990s. The reverse is also true, as too many found out the hard way in 1994.

Just as there are many different types of equity funds, there are also differences among bond funds. The three key considerations are term to maturity, credit quality and style.

Average term to maturity measures a bond portfolio's sensitivity to interest rate fluctuations. The longer the bond fund's term to maturity, the more sensitive the fund is to these moves. Most bond fund managers have the flexibility to shorten or lengthen their term. There are a growing number that simply focus on short-term (five years and under), and a few that have remained committed to longer-term (eight years and more).

The second consideration is credit quality. Credit quality is expressed in terms of As and Bs. The highest quality is AAA. National governments often get this top rating. Most Canadian mutual funds invest across the range of A- to AAA-rated bonds.

Finally, there is style. There are two main styles in bond management: interest rate anticipation and spread trading. An interest rate anticipator has an opinion on where interest rates are headed. If the manager believes that rates are going up, he or she will shorten the average term to maturity. A spread trader focuses on credit quality and the prices of the bonds. The lower the credit rating, the higher the interest rate the issuer pays to compensate the investor for the increased risk.

In looking for a Smart Bond Fund, there are two more considerations: size and price. In fact, price (MER) usually goes down as the size goes up. The debt market is huge. Those who trade bonds make a little on each transaction. Those with bigger amounts to buy and sell can demand better prices. As a rule of thumb, a bond fund under $100 million is going to find it hard to compete. Ideally, a bond fund should have $500 million or more under management. Bond funds charging more than 2 per cent are not competitive; 1 per cent is ideal.

INTERNATIONAL BOND FUNDS

The criteria reviewed in the Canadian bond funds section are also applicable to international bond funds. Currency is an important fourth variable. Today's securities markets make it possible to buy bonds issued in German marks or British pounds, without exposure to either of these currencies, through hedging. If, in the opinion of the manager, the currency of the bond is likely to be weak against the unit holder's currency, the international bond fund manager will try to manage the currencies defensively. The benefits of international bond investing are similar to those of international equity investing. Economic markets around the world are at different stages and hence will have interest rates that differ from Canada's. Global bond managers can take advantage of many more investment opportunities to hedge the return, or reduce the risk, in their portfolios.

MONEY MARKET FUNDS

For most investors, these funds should be used as a temporary parking place for money to be spent or invested in the near term. Often investors will sit on the sidelines, waiting for the right time to invest. We believe, and a number of studies in the United States confirm this view, that rather than trying to assess the right time, it is best just to make a move and get into the market. Market timing is a mug's game. Alternatively, for the cautious, a dollar-cost-averaging, automatic investment program could be used to gradually invest cash. If cash is to be spent within two years, a money market fund is a low-risk investment vehicle until the purchase date arrives.

Money market funds generally invest in the highest quality, Government of Canada treasury bills. The net asset value per share (NAVPS) is fixed at $10, and the total return is from interest earned. Barring a sudden and severe shift in interest rates, the NAVPS should not fluctuate.

There are two things to keep in mind when shopping for a money market fund. If investing on a deferred sales charge (DSC) basis, use that fund family's money market fund to avoid redemption charges.

On the other hand, if you are looking only for a money market fund to hold some money prior to purchase, shop for the one that has the lowest fee, but that is still convenient to purchase. If this is the only investment you are making, you should not pay more than 0.75 per cent in annual fees.

Money market funds can also represent the cash component of a portfolio. Cash plays two important roles in building an investment portfolio. First, cash, or money market, is the safest mutual fund investment, and its low volatility will add stability to a portfolio that includes riskier funds. Second, money market funds provide liquidity. Investors can be left unprepared when an event occurs that requires a part of their portfolio to be sold. Money market funds can be sold quickly with no loss of principal, and when other investments may be temporarily down in price. Additionally, they will not generate a taxable capital gain. Without a money market fund, the alternative may be selling a fund with a good unrealized gain, only because of the emergency, leaving the investor exposed to a potential tax bill.

For most investors, the money market fund they use will be determined by the other mutual fund investments they make and by the major fund families they have selected. Therefore, *we do not recommend any specific money market funds* as Smart Funds. However, if you are shopping only for a money market fund, consider it a form of bond fund and pay attention to the size and MER of the fund.

THE TOP SIX FUND FAMILIES

There are a few fund families that stand out from the competition. Within the fund companies that sell through the load channel, the companies we feel deserve special recognition are **AIM GT Canada**, **Fidelity Investments Canada** and **Mackenzie Financial**. Among the no-load families, we select **Bissett & Associates**, **Phillips**, **Hager & North** and **Scudder Canada**.

Our choices were based not only on the number of Smart or Noteworthy Funds each company held, although this was a significant factor, but also on the scope of funds in all asset classes, the range of management styles, the level of support to clients as determined by outside consultants, the depth of management talent and experience, and the extent of communications with clients and advisers.

Of the no-load fund families, Bissett and Phillips Hager and North bring superior performance, low MERs and solid long-term management teams. Scudder is new this year to our Top 6 Families list with four Smart Funds and a strong performance in its other funds. Its low MERs make it an attractive fund company for the future.

Mackenzie returns as one of our top three load fund families. The breadth of this fund family enabled it to withstand the loss of Gerry Coleman, which was more than offset by the return to top-quartile performance of the funds managed by Dina DeGeer and Dennis Starritt.

Fidelity continues to build its fund family leveraging off its strength as the largest mutual fund company in the world. Fidelity has demonstrated strong performance across core asset classes like Canadian equities, Canadian balanced, International equities, U.S. equities and European equities. It has started to bring down many of the MERs to be comparable to, if not slightly ahead, of its load competitors. The company may now be the number one choice for financial planners and brokers.

Our hats go off again to Fred Pynn, of Bissett & Associates. He is the 1999 Smart Fund Manager of the Year, retaining his title from last year's edition. Pynn is the manager of the Bissett Dividend, Atlas Canadian Large-Cap and Bissett Multi-National funds, and the co-manager of the Bissett Canadian Equity Fund.

ABC FUNDAMENTAL VALUE

NO LOAD

Primary Objective:	Growth
Sponsor:	I.A. Michael Investment Counsel
Fund Manager:	Irwin A. Michael
Style:	Bottom-up, Value
Size (MMs):	$233.200
RRSP:	100%
Management Expense Ratio:	2% (Average: 2.22%)

COMMENTS

The ABC funds require a minimum investment of $150,000 and are generally unavailable from dealers and discount brokerages. Still, outstanding performance must be recognized and Irwin Michael has not disappointed. With no money spent on marketing, the low number of unitholders and no trailers paid to brokers, the MER seems a bit high at 2%. A top-quartile performer in almost every calendar year since 1990, this could be a core holding for the affluent. Fund has experienced rough going with the recent volatility in the Canadian market, but we have long-term faith in Mr. Michael. Smart Fund 1998, 1997, 1996

RISK

How Often Money Was Lost:....40 of 114 Months
....34 of 112 Quarters
.....................................16 of 103 Rolling 12 Months
Worst 3 Months: ....-26.87% (1998)
Best 3 Months: 40.09% (1993)

ASSET ALLOCATION

Industrial products	19.2%
Forest products	17.7%
Financial services	10.8%
Merchandising	10.6%
Metals and minerals	9.8%
Other	31.9%

COMPARISON OF FUND TO INDEXES

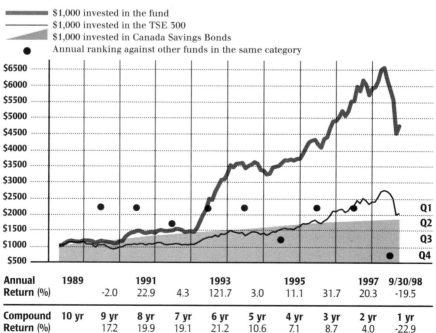

- $1,000 invested in the fund
- $1,000 invested in the TSE 300
- $1,000 invested in Canada Savings Bonds
- Annual ranking against other funds in the same category

Annual Return (%)	1989		1991		1993		1995		1997	9/30/98
		-2.0	22.9	4.3	121.7	3.0	11.1	31.7	20.3	-19.5

Compound Return (%)	10 yr	9 yr	8 yr	7 yr	6 yr	5 yr	4 yr	3 yr	2 yr	1 yr
		17.2	19.9	19.1	21.2	10.6	7.1	8.7	4.0	-22.9

AIC DIVERSIFIED CANADA   LOAD

Primary Objective:	Growth
Sponsor:	AIC Limited
Fund Manager:	Jonathan Wellum
Style:	Bottom-up, Growth
Size (MMs):	$1,936.635
RRSP:	100%
Management Expense Ratio:	2.39% (Average: 2.22%)

COMMENTS

AIC has made its mark by investing in financial services firms and especially mutual fund companies. The funds have done spectacularly with declining interest rates and increasing mutual fund sales. This fund shows the management team is capable of picking stocks in other sectors. The tax-efficient buy-and-hold philosophy works well, as Wellum buys solid companies for the long term. The fund's $2 billion size has forced Wellum to look at more liquid stocks, and in other industry groups. Sizzling 31.9% three-year return makes it number two in the category. But be realistic: just because it has not yet had a year below 26% return does not mean it can sustain this level in the future. Smart Fund 1998, 1997

RISK

How Often Money Was Lost: ......11 of 45 Months
....5 of 43 Quarters
......................1 of 24 Rolling 12 Months
Worst 3 Months:..............................-18.85% (1998)
Best 3 Months: 24.77% (1996)

ASSET ALLOCATION

Industrial products....................7.6%
Consumer products................11.9%
Financial services....................42.3%
Gold and precious 5.6%
Communications......................16.0%
Other..16.6%

COMPARISON OF FUND TO INDEXES

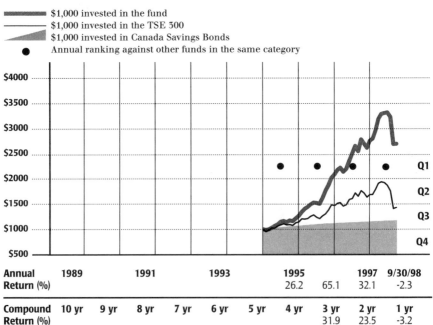

- ▰▰▰ $1,000 invested in the fund
- ——— $1,000 invested in the TSE 300
- ◢ $1,000 invested in Canada Savings Bonds
- ● Annual ranking against other funds in the same category

Annual Return (%)	1989		1991		1993		1995		1997	9/30/98
							26.2	65.1	32.1	-2.3

Compound Return (%)	10 yr	9 yr	8 yr	7 yr	6 yr	5 yr	4 yr	3 yr	2 yr	1 yr
								31.9	23.5	-3.2

AIM GT GLOBAL CANADA GROWTH CLASS   LOAD

Primary Objective:	Growth
Sponsor:	AIM GT Investments
Fund Manager:	Derek Webb
Style:	Momentum
Size (MMs):	$648.007
RRSP:	100%
Management Expense Ratio:	2.42% (Average: 2.22%)

COMMENTS

This fund uses a disciplined security selection process that focuses on corporate growth. Incorporated in Webb's analysis are corporate growth projections, analyst expectations and price momentum. Negative moves in any of these areas often lead to a holding being sold. The model has been back-tested with favourable results. A fund mandate is to have a minimum of 15% foreign content and it is often closer to the maximum 20%. The fund has bopped around a bit and returns after a year off the Smart Fund list, after dropping to third quartile. This is our choice for momentum-style investing. Fund was riding a 30% position in financial services as of June 30, 1998. Smart Fund 1997

RISK

How Often Money Was Lost: ......17 of 44 Months
....14 of 42 Quarters
..........................2 of 33 Rolling 12 Months
Worst 3 Months: ....-23.54% (1998)
Best 3 Months: 22.38% (1997)

ASSET ALLOCATION

Consumer products 7.4%
Merchandising 9.1%
Financial services 30.7%
Technology 7.0%
Communications 18.4%
Other 27.4%

COMPARISON OF FUND TO INDEXES

━━━━━ $1,000 invested in the fund
───── $1,000 invested in the TSE 300
▱▱▱▱▱ $1,000 invested in Canada Savings Bonds
● Annual ranking against other funds in the same category

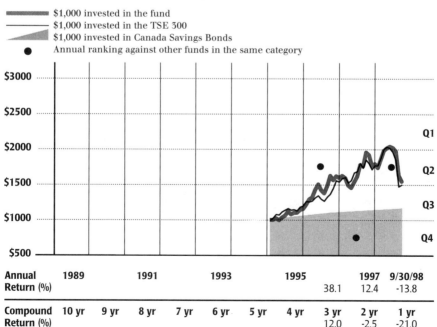

Annual Return (%)	1989		1991		1993		1995			1997	9/30/98
									38.1	12.4	-13.8

Compound Return (%)	10 yr	9 yr	8 yr	7 yr	6 yr	5 yr	4 yr	3 yr	2 yr	1 yr
								12.0	-2.5	-21.0

ATLAS CANADIAN LARGE-CAP GROWTH **LOAD**

Primary Objective:	Growth
Sponsor:	Atlas Asset Management
Fund Manager:	Fred Pynn, Bissett & Associates (7/94)
Style:	Bottom-up, Growth
Size (MMs):	$539.996
RRSP:	100%
Management Expense Ratio:	2.44% (Average: 2.22%)

COMMENTS

This used to be one of the only ways of acquiring, on a national basis, the investment management team of Bissett & Associates. Fred Pynn, Smart Fund Manager of the Year in 1998 and 1999, manages this fund and also co-manages the Bissett Canadian Equity Fund (also a Smart Fund). It may be more convenient to buy this fund, depending on your relationship with your adviser. It has been a top-quartile performer since Pynn took over in July 1994. A solid RRSP choice from the Atlas family. Fund pays broker dealers a trailer, hence its wider availability in the advice channel. For small investors, this may be the only way to get Bissett. Smart Fund 1998

RISK

How Often Money Was Lost:....48 of 117 Months
....39 of 115 Quarters
....................................27 of 106 Rolling 12 Months
Worst 3 Months:..............................-23.65% (1998)
Best 3 Months....................................17.97% (1997)

ASSET ALLOCATION

Industrial products..................26.8%
Utilities 4.3%
Financial services....................19.3%
Oil and gas...................................9.9%
Consumer products..................4.5%
Other...35.2%

COMPARISON OF FUND TO INDEXES

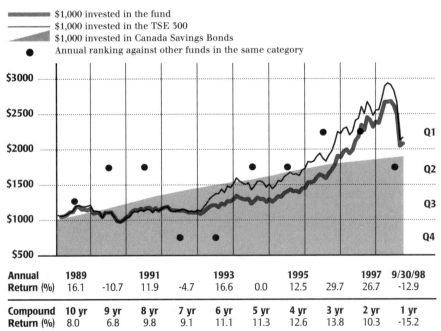

- $1,000 invested in the fund
- $1,000 invested in the TSE 300
- $1,000 invested in Canada Savings Bonds
- Annual ranking against other funds in the same category

Annual Return (%)	1989		1991		1993		1995		1997	9/30/98
	16.1	-10.7	11.9	-4.7	16.6	0.0	12.5	29.7	26.7	-12.9

Compound Return (%)	10 yr	9 yr	8 yr	7 yr	6 yr	5 yr	4 yr	3 yr	2 yr	1 yr
	8.0	6.8	9.8	9.1	11.1	11.3	12.6	13.8	10.3	-15.2

BISSETT CANADIAN EQUITY

NO LOAD

Primary Objective:	Growth
Sponsor:	Bissett & Associates
Fund Manager:	Michael Quinn and Fred Pynn
Style:	Bottom-up, Growth
Size (MMs):	$403.803
RRSP:	100%
Management Expense Ratio:	1.33% (Average: 2.22%)

COMMENTS

The authors have always been fans of the investment management team that David
Bissett has assembled. But in the past, limited distribution made it difficult to include
them as Smart Funds. Now available in most provinces, we again include this managed
fund as a Smart Fund. A low MER combined with top-quartile performance over
several periods make this a solid choice. This no-load fund is available from many
dealers, who are entitled to charge an up-front commission. That's money well spent if
your RRSP is with an adviser. Despite minimum $10,000 investment and no trailers
to brokers (enabling Bissett to keep the MER low) the fund has caught on, with assets
more than doubling since the end of 1997 to over $400 million. Smart Fund 1998, 1997

RISK

How Often Money Was Lost:	....43 of 117 Months
	..........33 of 115 Quarters
	......13 of 106 Rolling 12 Months
Worst 3 Months:	-23.38% (1998)
Best 3 Months:	20.80% (1997)

ASSET ALLOCATION

Industrial products	25.3%
Consumer products	8.2%
Financial services	18.9%
Oil and gas	12.6%
Merchandising	7.3%
Other	27.7%

COMPARISON OF FUND TO INDEXES

▬▬▬ $1,000 invested in the fund
───── $1,000 invested in the TSE 300
◤ $1,000 invested in Canada Savings Bonds
● Annual ranking against other funds in the same category

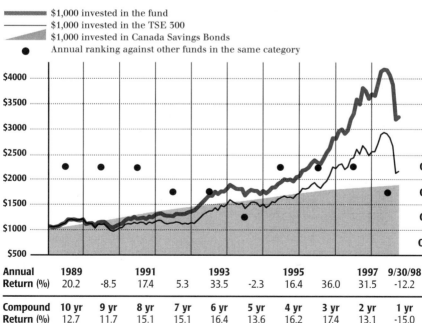

Annual	1989		1991		1993		1995		1997	9/30/98
Return (%)	20.2	-8.5	17.4	5.3	33.5	-2.3	16.4	36.0	31.5	-12.2

Compound	10 yr	9 yr	8 yr	7 yr	6 yr	5 yr	4 yr	3 yr	2 yr	1 yr
Return (%)	12.7	11.7	15.1	15.1	16.4	13.6	16.2	17.4	13.1	-15.0

C.I. HARBOUR FUND

LOAD

Primary Objective:	Growth
Sponsor:	CI Mutual Funds
Fund Manager:	Gerald Coleman
Style:	Bottom-up, Value
Size (MMs):	$690.505
RRSP:	100%
Management Expense Ratio:	2.33% (Average: 2.22%)

COMMENTS

Smart Funds traditionally identifies strong new funds for investors. Manager Gerry Coleman has an outstanding track record, first at United, then at Mackenzie. His former fund, Ivy Canadian, was a Smart Fund in 1996 and 1997 and we see no reason why he won't continue his successful buy-and-hold, value philosophy. Considering his classic low-volatility performance, and Coleman's ownership stake in the firm, we expect him to be managing this fund for many years. Should appeal to low-risk investors seeking a quality equity fund. Fund has raised approximately $700 million in its first year. Smart Fund 1998

RISK

How Often Money Was Lost:	........8 of 15 Months
	..............8 of 13 Quarters
	..........3 of 4 Rolling 12 Months
Worst 3 Months:	-18.86% (1998)
Best 3 Months:	9.49% (1998)

ASSET ALLOCATION

Cash	33.9%
Canadian equities	49.2%
U.S. equities	16.5%
Global equities	0.4%

COMPARISON OF FUND TO INDEXES

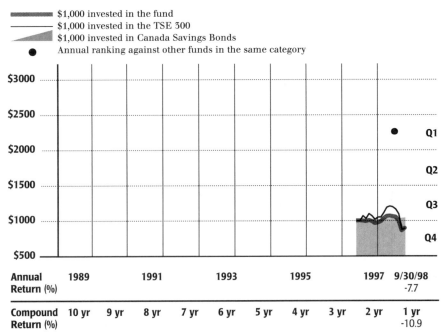

- $1,000 invested in the fund
- $1,000 invested in the TSE 300
- $1,000 invested in Canada Savings Bonds
- Annual ranking against other funds in the same category

Annual Return (%)	1989		1991		1993		1995		1997	9/30/98
										-7.7

Compound Return (%)	10 yr	9 yr	8 yr	7 yr	6 yr	5 yr	4 yr	3 yr	2 yr	1 yr
										-10.9

GLOBAL STRATEGY CANADIAN OPPORTUNITIES LOAD

Primary Objective:	Growth
Sponsor:	Global Strategy Financial
Fund Manager:	John Sartz
Style:	Bottom-up, Mid-cap growth
Size (MMs):	$120.238
RRSP:	100%
Management Expense Ratio:	2.50% (Average: 2.22%)

COMMENTS

John Sartz has been a top-quartile performer, and one you can hold onto for the long run, through thick and thin. This mid-cap fund was created to enable Sartz to move higher up the capitalization level without compromising the mandate of the other small-cap fund. There are few funds that intend to focus on mid-cap companies. This could be a great growth area after the large-cap play has finished. Smart Fund 1998

RISK

How Often Money Was Lost: ....9 of 21 Months
....8 of 19 Quarters
....2 of 10 Rolling 12 Months
Worst 3 Months: ....-20.61% (1998)
Best 3 Months: 17.77% (1997)

ASSET ALLOCATION

Industrial products..................38.5%
Oil and gas 21.6%
Merchandising 17.1%
Consumer products..................9.3%
Communications and media 8.6%
Other 4.9%

COMPARISON OF FUND TO INDEXES

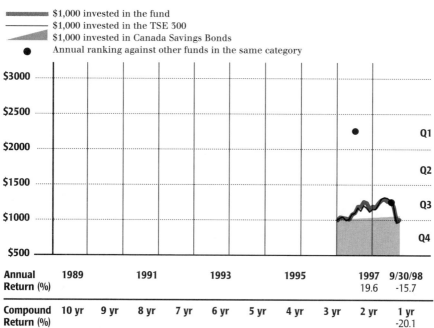

- $1,000 invested in the fund
- $1,000 invested in the TSE 300
- $1,000 invested in Canada Savings Bonds
- Annual ranking against other funds in the same category

Annual Return (%)	1989		1991		1993		1995		1997 19.6	9/30/98 -15.7

Compound Return (%)	10 yr	9 yr	8 yr	7 yr	6 yr	5 yr	4 yr	3 yr	2 yr	1 yr -20.1

GREEN LINE CANADIAN INDEX **NO LOAD**

Primary Objective:	Growth
Sponsor:	TD Asset Management
Fund Manager:	TD Asset Management
Style:	Passive
Size (MMs):	$325.461
RRSP:	100%
Management Expense Ratio:	0.80% (Average: 2.22%)

COMMENTS

If you can't beat the index, why not own it? Low MER, tax efficiency and guaranteed to be fully invested in bull markets. The downside: being fully invested in bear markets. But over history the market is up more often than it is down and you can never time when to get back in the market, so stay fully invested. The major differentiation on index funds is the costs, loads and MERs. This is one of the cheapest.

RISK

How Often Money Was Lost: ....47 of 117 Months
....45 of 115 Quarters
....30 of 106 Rolling 12 Months
Worst 3 Months:..............................-26.94% (1998)
Best 3 Months:...................................17.33% (1996)

ASSET ALLOCATION

Industrial products.................17.2%
Utilities.......................................11.3%
Financial services...................23.6%
Oil and gas................................9.7%
Consumer products..................5.8%
Other..32.4%

COMPARISON OF FUND TO INDEXES

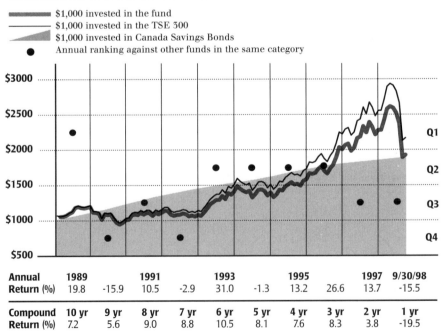

━━━ $1,000 invested in the fund
──── $1,000 invested in the TSE 300
▨▨▨ $1,000 invested in Canada Savings Bonds
● Annual ranking against other funds in the same category

Annual	1989		1991		1993		1995		1997	9/30/98
Return (%)	19.8	-15.9	10.5	-2.9	31.0	-1.3	13.2	26.6	13.7	-15.5

Compound	10 yr	9 yr	8 yr	7 yr	6 yr	5 yr	4 yr	3 yr	2 yr	1 yr
Return (%)	7.2	5.6	9.0	8.8	10.5	8.1	7.6	8.3	3.8	-19.5

MCLEAN BUDDEN EQUITY GROWTH NO LOAD

Primary Objective:	Growth
Sponsor:	McLean Budden Ltd.
Fund Manager:	Mary Hallward and Team
Style:	Bottom-up, Growth
Size (MMs):	$13.482
RRSP:	100%
Management Expense Ratio:	1.75% (Average: 2.22%)

COMMENTS

This fund demonstrates that slow and steady wins the race. It has been a dependable, if unspectacular, performer year in and year out. Since 1989, it has been second quartile every year, with the odd third-quartile showing mixed in with an occasional first. This no-load fund comes with a 1.75% MER and average volatility but may not be conveniently purchased from your financial adviser. Otherwise this team of managers is available with traditional loads through Stone & Co. Acquisition of firm by Sun Life in 1997 has had no impact on investment management department. Smart Fund 1998

RISK

How Often Money Was Lost: ....52 of 117 Months
....41 of 115 Quarters
....................................21 of 106 Rolling 12 Months
Worst 3 Months: ....-25.92% (1998)
Best 3 Months: 23.55% (1996)

ASSET ALLOCATION

Industrial products 27.6%
Utilities 8.7%
Financial services 23.1%
Oil and gas 12.8%
Consumer products 6.2%
Other 21.6%

COMPARISON OF FUND TO INDEXES

$1,000 invested in the fund
$1,000 invested in the TSE 300
$1,000 invested in Canada Savings Bonds
● Annual ranking against other funds in the same category

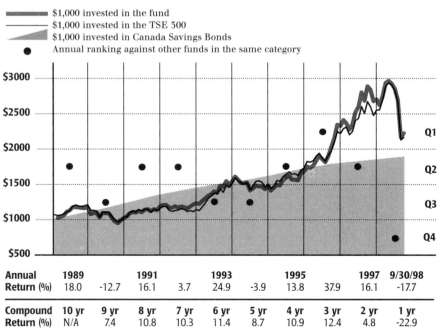

Annual	1989		1991		1993		1995		1997	9/30/98
Return (%)	18.0	-12.7	16.1	3.7	24.9	-3.9	13.8	37.9	16.1	-17.7

Compound	10 yr	9 yr	8 yr	7 yr	6 yr	5 yr	4 yr	3 yr	2 yr	1 yr
Return (%)	N/A	7.4	10.8	10.3	11.4	8.7	10.9	12.4	4.8	-22.9

PH&N CANADIAN EQUITY

NO LOAD

Primary Objective:	Growth
Sponsor:	Phillips, Hager & North Investment Management
Fund Manager:	Team
Style:	Bottom-up, Growth
Size (MMs):	$623.865
RRSP:	100%
Management Expense Ratio:	1.09% (Average: 2.22%)

COMMENTS

Top-quartile performance over five and ten-year periods ending June 30, 1998 from a team of managers with a miniscule MER and no-load to boot. So what's the catch? You must invest a healthy minimum and unless dealing directly with PH&N you will be charged by brokers. Consistent style of picking growth stocks from the mid- and large-cap universe. The managers keep volatility low while generating solid above-average returns. Put this one in your RRSP, if you can. Smart Fund 1998, 1997, 1996

RISK

How Often Money Was Lost:....45 of 117 Months
....42 of 115 Quarters
.......................22 of 106 Rolling 12 Months
Worst 3 Months:..............................-25.27% (1998)
Best 3 Months: 18.18% (1996)

ASSET ALLOCATION

Industrial products..................21.0%
Utilities 7.7%
Financial services...................25.5%
Oil and gas 13.0%
Communications.......................6.3%
Other...26.5%

COMPARISON OF FUND TO INDEXES

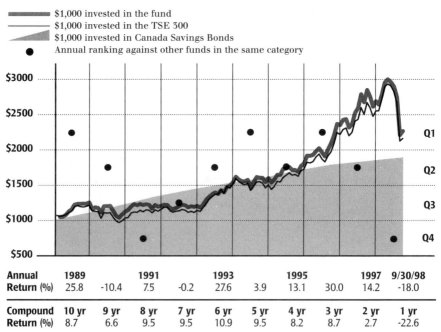

- $1,000 invested in the fund
- $1,000 invested in the TSE 300
- $1,000 invested in Canada Savings Bonds
- Annual ranking against other funds in the same category

Annual Return (%)	1989		1991		1993		1995		1997	9/30/98
	25.8	-10.4	7.5	-0.2	27.6	3.9	13.1	30.0	14.2	-18.0

Compound Return (%)	10 yr	9 yr	8 yr	7 yr	6 yr	5 yr	4 yr	3 yr	2 yr	1 yr
	8.7	6.6	9.5	9.5	10.9	9.5	8.2	8.7	2.7	-22.6

SCUDDER CANADIAN EQUITY

NO LOAD

Primary Objective:	Growth
Sponsor:	Scudder Canada Investor Services
Fund Manager:	Phil Fortuna and Mac Eysenbach
Style:	Quantitative, Bottom-up
Size (MMs):	$243.764
RRSP:	100%
Management Expense Ratio:	1.25% (Average: 2.22%)

COMMENTS

We had our doubts when this fund debuted, since most foreign money managers do poorly in the Canadian equity market. But back-to-back first-quartile returns for 1996 and 1997 can hardly be ignored. Scudder managers Fortuna and Eysenbach use rigorous quantitative screens to generate a short-list of Canadian names. The fund's low MER of 1.25% gives it about a 1% per year competitive advantage in the performance game. Scudder has worked hard to make the funds more accessible, so check with your dealer or broker, who may get a small fee for selling the fund. But the word is out—fund is up from $72 million at July 31, 1997 to $314 million at June 30, 1998. Fund will have a three-year performance number as of November 1998 and may finally be recognized by other fund guides. Smart Fund 1998

RISK

How Often Money Was Lost:	12 of 35 Months
	6 of 33 Quarters
	2 of 24 Rolling 12 Months
Worst 3 Months:	-20.82% (1998)
Best 3 Months:	20.86% (1996)

ASSET ALLOCATION

Industrial products	16.0%
Utilities	13.9%
Financial services	15.5%
Oil and gas	9.3%
Merchandising	14.8%
Other	30.5%

COMPARISON OF FUND TO INDEXES

- $1,000 invested in the fund
- $1,000 invested in the TSE 300
- $1,000 invested in Canada Savings Bonds
- Annual ranking against other funds in the same category

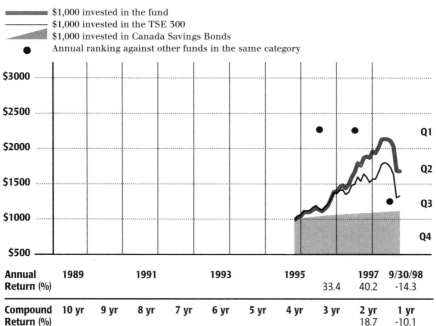

Annual Return (%)	1989		1991		1993		1995			1997	9/30/98
							33.4			40.2	-14.3

Compound Return (%)	10 yr	9 yr	8 yr	7 yr	6 yr	5 yr	4 yr	3 yr	2 yr	1 yr
									18.7	-10.1

SPECTRUM UNITED CANADIAN EQUITY LOAD

Primary Objective:	Growth
Sponsor:	Spectrum United Mutual Funds
Fund Manager:	Kiki Delaney, C.A. Delaney Capital Mgmt (10/92)
Style:	Bottom-up
Size (MMs):	$1,289.154
RRSP:	100%
Management Expense Ratio:	2.35% (Average: 2.22%)

COMMENTS

Kiki Delaney continues to provide consistent returns for this returning Smart Fund, using a growth-at-a-reasonable-price style that emphasizes fundamental stock picking combined with broad economic themes. Delaney keeps volatility low and still generates competitive returns. The fund's size is still at a level that enables her to outperform on a risk-adjusted basis. A solid, long-term RRSP holding from this highly regarded money manager. Smart Fund 1998, 1997, 1996

RISK

How Often Money Was Lost:....45 of 117 Months
....36 of 115 Quarters
....................................16 of 106 Rolling 12 Months
Worst 3 Months:...............................-24.33% (1998)
Best 3 Months:....................................17.32% (1993)

ASSET ALLOCATION

Industrial products.................12.2%
Merchandising...........................7.1%
Financial services...................15.3%
Oil and gas 14.8%
Foreign 7.9%
Other..42.7%

COMPARISON OF FUND TO INDEXES

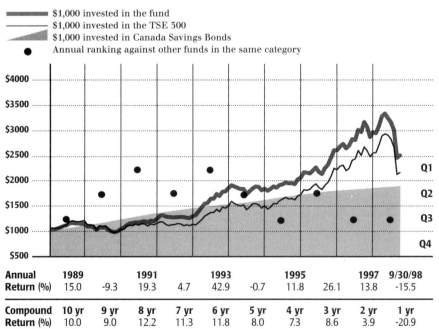

$1,000 invested in the fund
$1,000 invested in the TSE 300
$1,000 invested in Canada Savings Bonds
● Annual ranking against other funds in the same category

Annual Return (%)	1989		1991		1993		1995		1997	9/30/98
	15.0	-9.3	19.3	4.7	42.9	-0.7	11.8	26.1	13.8	-15.5

Compound Return (%)	10 yr	9 yr	8 yr	7 yr	6 yr	5 yr	4 yr	3 yr	2 yr	1 yr
	10.0	9.0	12.2	11.3	11.8	8.0	7.3	8.6	3.9	-20.9

SYNERGY CANADIAN STYLE MANAGEMENT CLASS LOAD

Primary Objective:	Growth
Sponsor:	Synergy Asset Management
Fund Manager:	Dave Picton
Style:	Multiple
Size (MMs):	$25.731
RRSP:	100%
Management Expense Ratio:	2.50% estimated (Average: 2.22%)

COMMENTS

A unique fund, since style diversification can reduce volatility over the long term. President Canavan claims that many managers are guilty of style drift; strict adherence makes this fund different. Manager David Picton is responsible for ensuring that the underlying managers stick to their individual mandates of value, growth, momentum and small-cap. The unique blending of different styles makes this theoretically less volatile, so we have put it on the Smart Funds list in its debut year.

RISK

How Often Money Was Lost:	4 of 9 Months
	4 of 7 Quarters
	0 of 0 Rolling 12 Months
Worst 3 Months:	-22.75% (1998)
Best 3 Months:	13.00% (1998)

ASSET ALLOCATION

Industrial products	30.3%
Utilities	3.6%
Financial services	15.3%
Oil and gas	7.4%
Consumer products	6.9%
Other	36.5%

COMPARISON OF FUND TO INDEXES

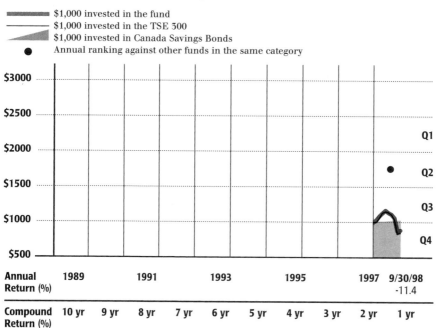

- $1,000 invested in the fund
- $1,000 invested in the TSE 300
- $1,000 invested in Canada Savings Bonds
- Annual ranking against other funds in the same category

Annual Return (%)	1989	1991	1993	1995	1997	9/30/98 -11.4

Compound Return (%)	10 yr	9 yr	8 yr	7 yr	6 yr	5 yr	4 yr	3 yr	2 yr	1 yr

TALVEST/HYPERION CANADIAN GROWTH LOAD

Primary Objective:	Growth
Sponsor:	Talvest Fund Management
Fund Manager:	Denis Ouellet, TAL Investment Counsel
Style:	Bottom-up, Growth
Size (MMs):	$328.149
RRSP:	100%
Management Expense Ratio:	2.62% (Average: 2.22%)

COMMENTS

"One of the jewels in the Montreal Trust fund family, this fund is the exception to the vanilla large-cap bank-run funds. Credit manager Ouellet, whose bottom-up value-based style has made this fund a consistent top-quartile performer since its inception." From Smart Funds 1997 on Scotia Excelsior Canadian Growth. Denis Ouellet returns to Smart Fund status at his new firm with superior performance once again. His move demonstrates the importance of keeping up with manager changes.

RISK

How Often Money Was Lost: ....7 of 21 Months
....8 of 19 Quarters
.........................2 of 10 Rolling 12 Months
Worst 3 Months:..............................-27.09% (1998)
Best 3 Months:..................................19.88% (1997)

ASSET ALLOCATION

Industrial products.................18.5%
Utilities.....................................17.1%
Financial services...................15.2%
Oil and gas 11.6%
Communications.......................7.8%
Other...29.8%

COMPARISON OF FUND TO INDEXES

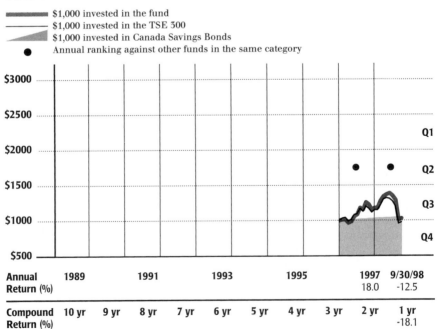

- ▬▬▬ $1,000 invested in the fund
- ——— $1,000 invested in the TSE 300
- ◢ $1,000 invested in Canada Savings Bonds
- ● Annual ranking against other funds in the same category

Annual Return (%)	1989	1991	1993	1995	1997	9/30/98
					18.0	-12.5

Compound Return (%)	10 yr	9 yr	8 yr	7 yr	6 yr	5 yr	4 yr	3 yr	2 yr	1 yr
										-18.1

UNIVERSAL CANADIAN GROWTH LOAD

Primary Objective:	Growth
Sponsor:	Mackenzie Financial
Fund Manager:	Dina DeGeer and Dennis Starritt, Bluewater
Style:	Bottom-up, Growth
Size (MMs):	$1,768.726
RRSP:	100%
Management Expense Ratio:	2.34% (Average: 2.22%)

COMMENTS

The authors have watched this Trimark clone since inception. The former Trimark team of Dina DeGeer and Dennis Starritt have outperformed their old company's Trimark Canadian fund by a country mile. This fund can be considered a core RRSP holding. The fund has attracted approximately $2 billion in assets and has proven to be a solid first-quartile performer. Dennis and Dina buy good growth companies at attractive prices and hold them for several years. Their favourite stocks, such as TD Bank, Methanex and Nova, are well represented. Smart Fund 1998

RISK

How Often Money Was Lost: ......13 of 37 Months
....6 of 35 Quarters
....2 of 26 Rolling 12 Months
Worst 3 Months: ....-18.24% (1998)
Best 3 Months: 16.73% (1997)

ASSET ALLOCATION

Canadian equities 56.0%
Cash 23.0%
U.S. equities..............................11.0%
Fixed income 10.0%

COMPARISON OF FUND TO INDEXES

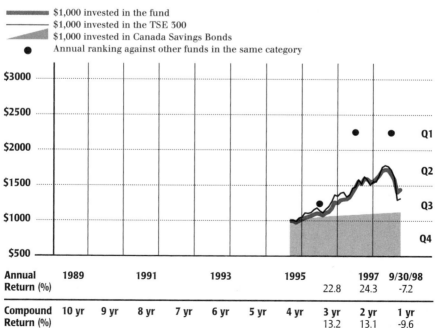

- $1,000 invested in the fund
- $1,000 invested in the TSE 300
- $1,000 invested in Canada Savings Bonds
- Annual ranking against other funds in the same category

Annual Return (%)	1989		1991		1993		1995		1997	9/30/98
								22.8	24.3	-7.2

Compound Return (%)	10 yr	9 yr	8 yr	7 yr	6 yr	5 yr	4 yr	3 yr	2 yr	1 yr
								13.2	13.1	-9.6

BISSETT SMALL-CAP

Primary Objective:	High Growth
Sponsor:	Bissett & Associates Investment Management
Fund Manager:	David Bissett and Gene Vollendorf
Style:	Bottom-up, Growth
Size (MMs):	$88.467
RRSP:	100%
Management Expense Ratio:	1.90% (Average: 2.40%)

COMMENTS

David Bissett's passion is small-cap investing. He's a stock-picking fundamentalist with some Western Canadian flair thrown in. This is not, however, merely a play on resource stocks. Bissett has an extraordinary track record in picking basic businesses that produce real products and generate real cash flow. Since 1992, this fund has been either first or second quartile in every full calendar year. That string adds up to first-quartile performance over five years compounded to September 30, 1998. He is getting the recognition, including being an award winner at last year's Mutual Fund Awards Dinner. Smart Fund 1998

RISK

How Often Money Was Lost:	24 of 81 Months
	25 of 79 Quarters
	11 of 70 Rolling 12 Months
Worst 3 Months:	-30.94% (1998)
Best 3 Months:	44.86% (1993)

ASSET ALLOCATION

Industrial products	39.8%
Consumer products	15.3%
Oil and gas	12.6%
Merchandising	8.7%
Financial services	7.1%
Other	16.5%

COMPARISON OF FUND TO INDEXES

■■■■■ $1,000 invested in the fund
———— $1,000 invested in the Nesbitt Burns Small Cap Index
▨▨▨▨ $1,000 invested in Canada Savings Bonds
● Annual ranking against other funds in the same category

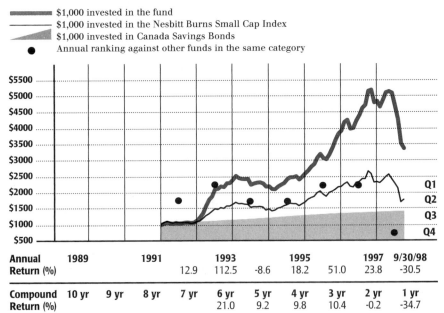

Annual Return (%)	1989			1991		1993		1995		1997	9/30/98
					12.9	112.5	-8.6	18.2	51.0	23.8	-30.5

Compound Return (%)	10 yr	9 yr	8 yr	7 yr	6 yr	5 yr	4 yr	3 yr	2 yr	1 yr
					21.0	9.2	9.8	10.4	-0.2	-34.7

CANADIAN SMALL-CAP EQUITY

CLEAN ENVIRONMENT EQUITY

LOAD

Primary Objective:	High Growth
Sponsor:	Clean Environment Mutual Funds
Fund Manager:	Ian Ihnatowycz, Acuity Investment Mgmt
Style:	Bottom-up, Growth
Size (MMs):	$248.241
RRSP:	100%
Management Expense Ratio:	2.60% (Average: 2.40%)

COMMENTS

When your fund has names like Open Text, Zenon Environmental, CFM Majestic, Cinram and Yogen Fruz in its top 10 holdings, we feel it is only fair to categorize the fund as a small-mid-cap fund. To be in the large-cap group, people expect to own TSE 35-type names. That clarified, the fund has a strong performance history with a three-year compound return of 13.4% through September 30, 1998. MER of 2.6% has come down from several years ago and should inch down a bit more as the fund grows. Manager Ian Ihnatowycz has a disciplined approach and finds solid companies. These names do not have to be environment or green companies. It is a "negative" selection process. A solid stock will be denied if it has potential environmental downside. Fund has outperformed the TSE with almost the same volatility.

RISK

How Often Money Was Lost: ......29 of 80 Months
......................................22 of 78 Quarters
......................11 of 69 Rolling 12 Months
Worst 3 Months:..............................-25.04% (1998)
Best 3 Months:..................................19.38% (1997)

ASSET ALLOCATION

Industrial products..................35.4%
Environment.............................13.7%
Financial services...................11.9%
Merchandising...........................9.2%
Oil and gas................................6.7%
Other......................................23.1%

COMPARISON OF FUND TO INDEXES

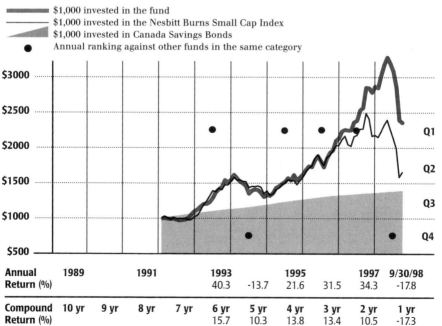

- $1,000 invested in the fund
- $1,000 invested in the Nesbitt Burns Small Cap Index
- $1,000 invested in Canada Savings Bonds
- ● Annual ranking against other funds in the same category

Annual Return (%)	1989		1991		1993		1995		1997	9/30/98
					40.3	-13.7	21.6	31.5	34.3	-17.8

Compound Return (%)	10 yr	9 yr	8 yr	7 yr	6 yr	5 yr	4 yr	3 yr	2 yr	1 yr
					15.7	10.3	13.8	13.4	10.5	-17.3

FIDELITY CANADIAN GROWTH COMPANY LOAD

Primary Objective:	High Growth
Sponsor:	Fidelity Investments Canada
Fund Manager:	Alan Radlo, Fidelity Mgmt & Research
Style:	Bottom-up, Growth
Size (MMs):	$1,344.798
RRSP:	100%
Management Expense Ratio:	2.45% (Average: 2.40%)

CANADIAN SMALL-CAP EQUITY

COMMENTS

Manager Alan Radlo continues to do what he does best—picking solid growth companies and holding them. He and his analysts do their homework, visiting and interviewing company management teams to ensure that stated profits and cash flows are real. This diligence helped them avoid Bre-X and YBM Magnex, but he did get stung by Livent's accounting problems. This fund has one of the best risk-adjusted returns in the category. The fund continues to grow with more than $1.5 billion in assets, making it more difficult for Radlo to generate outlandish returns. It also means the fund won't get torpedoed by single names. There is no evidence yet that he can't outperform many large-cap funds with reasonable risk. Fund is first quartile for three, two, and one-year returns ending September 30, 1998. Smart Fund 1998, 1997, 1996

RISK

How Often Money Was Lost: ......12 of 50 Months
....10 of 48 Quarters
....2 of 39 Rolling 12 Months
Worst 3 Months: ....-20.87% (1998)
Best 3 Months: 18.05% (1997)

ASSET ALLOCATION

Cash	21.1%
Industrial products	17.9%
Communications	12.4%
Oil and gas	9.9%
Consumer products	7.5%
Other	31.2%

COMPARISON OF FUND TO INDEXES

▬▬▬▬ $1,000 invested in the fund
——— $1,000 invested in the Nesbitt Burns Small Cap Index
◢ $1,000 invested in Canada Savings Bonds
● Annual ranking against other funds in the same category

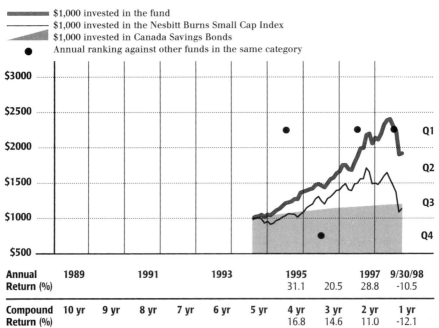

Annual Return (%)	1989		1991		1993		1995		1997	9/30/98
							31.1	20.5	28.8	-10.5

Compound Return (%)	10 yr	9 yr	8 yr	7 yr	6 yr	5 yr	4 yr	3 yr	2 yr	1 yr
							16.8	14.6	11.0	-12.1

GBC CANADIAN GROWTH

Primary Objective:	High Growth
Sponsor:	GBC Asset Management
Fund Manager:	Ian Soutar and Nicolas Chevalier
Style:	Bottom-up, Growth
Size (MMs):	$183.287
RRSP:	100%
Management Expense Ratio:	1.85% (Average: 2.40%)

COMMENTS

Sometimes performance makes a fund undeniable. Since 1993, this fund has been first
or second quartile in every calendar year. That string equates to first-quartile performance for the five, three, two and one-year periods ending September 30, 1998. This
solid fund comes at a price and we don't just mean the 1.85% MER. GBC requires a
$100,000 minimum investment.

RISK

How Often Money Was Lost:	....35 of 117 Months
	...................33 of 115 Quarters
	.................20 of 106 Rolling 12 Months
Worst 3 Months:	..............-24.72% (1990)
Best 3 Months:	..................22.47% (1997)

ASSET ALLOCATION

Industrial products	.................15.0%
Technology	..............................23.0%
Oil and gas	..............................10.0%
Drugs and healthcare	............10.0%
Communications	....................10.0%
Other	....32.0%

CANADIAN SMALL-CAP EQUITY

COMPARISON OF FUND TO INDEXES

- $1,000 invested in the fund
- $1,000 invested in the Nesbitt Burns Small Cap Index
- $1,000 invested in Canada Savings Bonds
- Annual ranking against other funds in the same category

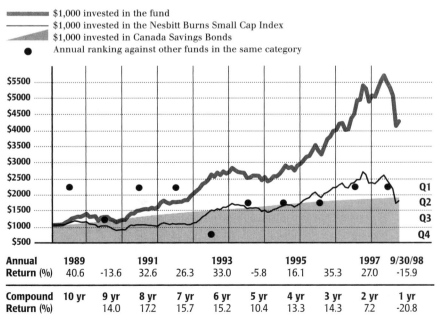

Annual	1989		1991		1993		1995		1997	9/30/98
Return (%)	40.6	-13.6	32.6	26.3	33.0	-5.8	16.1	35.3	27.0	-15.9

Compound	10 yr	9 yr	8 yr	7 yr	6 yr	5 yr	4 yr	3 yr	2 yr	1 yr
Return (%)		14.0	17.2	15.7	15.2	10.4	13.3	14.3	7.2	-20.8

GLOBAL STRATEGY CANADIAN SMALL-CAP   LOAD

Primary Objective:	Growth
Sponsor:	Global Strategy Financial Inc.
Fund Manager:	John Sartz
Style:	Bottom-up, Growth
Size (MMs):	$278.882
RRSP:	100%
Management Expense Ratio:	2.60% (Average: 2.4%)

COMMENTS

We sometimes look in the rear-view mirror on this fund. After we prematurely removed this from the Smart Fund list, it blew the doors off in performance. Reinstated last year, it dropped to fourth quartile. During that period it has been closed and then reopened. We have decided to leave it a Smart Fund and to watch it over longer periods. The fund's performance came despite being handcuffed with a punitive 2.6% MER, one of the highest in the class. Sartz has a track record in Canadian small caps that exceeds 20 years. He buys solid companies with consistent earnings and cash-flow streams, often in simple businesses, then holds them for what seems like forever. Smart Fund 1998, 1996

RISK

How Often Money Was Lost: ......17 of 45 Months
....13 of 43 Quarters
....4 of 34 Rolling 12 Months
Worst 3 Months:................................-27.44% (1998)
Best 3 Months:....................................21.15% (1997)

ASSET ALLOCATION

Industrial products.................41.5%
Oil and gas 22.9%
Consumer products................11.2%
Merchandising 10.2%
Communications and media...4.4%
Other...9.8%

COMPARISON OF FUND TO INDEXES

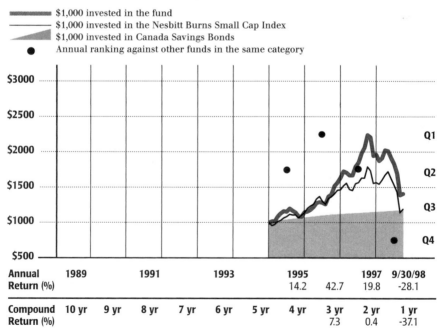

■■■■■ $1,000 invested in the fund
────── $1,000 invested in the Nesbitt Burns Small Cap Index
▨▨▨ $1,000 invested in Canada Savings Bonds
● Annual ranking against other funds in the same category

Annual Return (%)	1989	1991	1993	1995		1997	9/30/98
				14.2	42.7	19.8	-28.1

Compound Return (%)	10 yr	9 yr	8 yr	7 yr	6 yr	5 yr	4 yr	3 yr	2 yr	1 yr
								7.3	0.4	-37.1

CANADIAN SMALL-CAP EQUITY

GUARDIAN ENTERPRISE CLASSIC **LOAD**

Primary Objective:	Growth
Sponsor:	Guardian Mutual Funds
Fund Manager:	Gary Chapman, Guardian Capital, since 12/94
Style:	Bottom-up, Growth
Size (MMs):	$41.387
RRSP:	100%
Management Expense Ratio:	2.10% (Average: 2.40%)

COMMENTS

Chapman has struggled the past 18 months dropping to third quartile. The disciplined stock selection process has rewarded investors in the past. The addition of James Lawson to the team should help. Lawson previously ran the First Canadian Special Growth fund, a Smart Fund in 1998. Chapman will continue to hold quality stocks as they grow from small-cap to large-cap status. His research in small stocks also contributes to Guardian Growth Equity Fund, which is run more conservatively than Enterprise. Smart Fund 1998, 1997

RISK

How Often Money Was Lost: ....45 of 117 Months
......................................40 of 115 Quarters
.....................................28 of 106 Rolling 12 Months
Worst 3 Months: ....-28.14% (1998)
Best 3 Months: 23.30% (1996)

ASSET ALLOCATION

Industrial products.................28.1%
Consumer products................14.8%
Oil and gas 12.6%
Financial services.....................7.8%
Real Estate..................................6.7%
Other...30.0%

COMPARISON OF FUND TO INDEXES

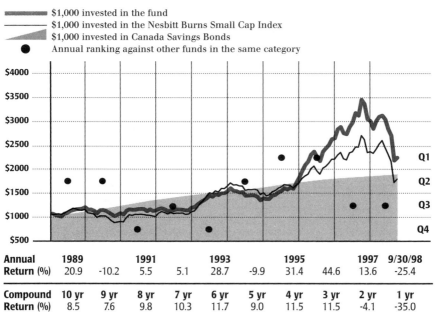

$1,000 invested in the fund
$1,000 invested in the Nesbitt Burns Small Cap Index
$1,000 invested in Canada Savings Bonds
● Annual ranking against other funds in the same category

Annual	1989		1991		1993		1995		1997	9/30/98
Return (%)	20.9	-10.2	5.5	5.1	28.7	-9.9	31.4	44.6	13.6	-25.4

Compound	10 yr	9 yr	8 yr	7 yr	6 yr	5 yr	4 yr	3 yr	2 yr	1 yr
Return (%)	8.5	7.6	9.8	10.3	11.7	9.0	11.5	11.5	-4.1	-35.0

IVY ENTERPRISE

Primary Objective:	Growth
Sponsor:	Mackenzie Financial
Fund Manager:	Chuck Roth since 12/97
Style:	Bottom-up, Growth
Size (MMs):	$338.734
RRSP:	100%
Management Expense Ratio:	2.33% (Average: 2.40%)

COMMENTS

Manager Chuck Roth came on board in December 1997 after knocking the ball out of the park with blistering performance numbers in the Colonia Special Growth fund, including 70% for calendar 1996. A bottom-up stock-picker who loves good companies, with good managements and clean balance sheets. The nature of this fund will change, as Roth may move to be more fully invested than his predecessors, Coleman and Javasky, had been. As of June 30, 1998, the fund had 25% cash so it still is the most conservative fund in the category.

RISK

How Often Money Was Lost: ......11 of 48 Months
....6 of 46 Quarters
....2 of 37 Rolling 12 Months
Worst 3 Months: ....-22.2% (1998)
Best 3 Months: 8.87% (1997)

ASSET ALLOCATION

Cash 25.0%
U.S. 11.0%
Other...64.0%

COMPARISON OF FUND TO INDEXES

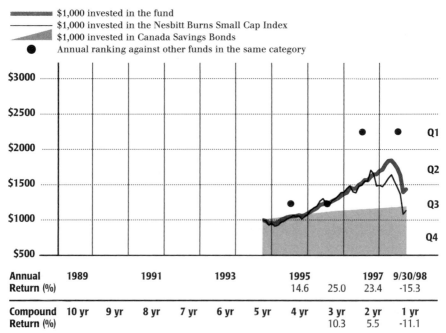

| ▰▰▰ $1,000 invested in the fund |
| ─── $1,000 invested in the Nesbitt Burns Small Cap Index |
| ◣ $1,000 invested in Canada Savings Bonds |
| ● Annual ranking against other funds in the same category |

Annual	1989		1991		1993		1995		1997	9/30/98
Return (%)							14.6	25.0	23.4	-15.3

Compound	10 yr	9 yr	8 yr	7 yr	6 yr	5 yr	4 yr	3 yr	2 yr	1 yr
Return (%)								10.3	5.5	-11.1

CANADIAN SMALL-CAP EQUITY

SAXON SMALL CAP

Primary Objective:	High Growth
Sponsor:	Saxon Funds
Fund Manager:	Rick Howson, Howson Tattersall Investment Counsel
Style:	Bottom-up, Growth
Size (MMs):	$19.045
RRSP:	100%
Management Expense Ratio:	1.75% (Average: 2.40%)

COMMENTS

Saxon has a history of funds showing up in the Smart Funds list. Their funds do a respectable job of performing, but never seem to gather many assets in this booming fund industry. This one appears on the Smart Fund list for the first time, after strong returns in 1997 and early 1998 pulled the fund into the first-quartile rankings across most compound periods. Manager Bob Tattersall is a bottom-up stock picker who has a portfolio of industrial products firms. Fund has an outstanding risk/return profile and sports one of the lower MERs in the small-cap class.

RISK

How Often Money Was Lost: ....51 of 117 Months
....44 of 115 Quarters
......................................27 of 106 Rolling 12 Months
Worst 3 Months:.............................-20.08% (1998)
Best 3 Months:....................................16.48% (1997)

ASSET ALLOCATION

Industrial products...................50.3%
Consumer products.................24.6%
Metals and minerals 10.5%
Oil and gas..................................8.2%
Interest sensitive 6.4%

CANADIAN SMALL-CAP EQUITY

COMPARISON OF FUND TO INDEXES

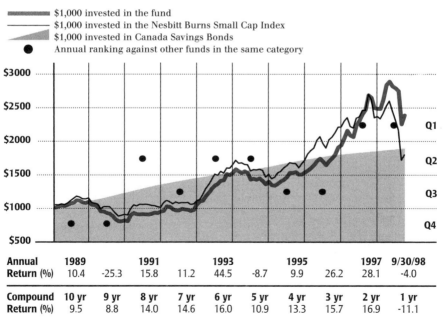

- $1,000 invested in the fund
- $1,000 invested in the Nesbitt Burns Small Cap Index
- $1,000 invested in Canada Savings Bonds
- Annual ranking against other funds in the same category

Annual	1989		1991		1993		1995		1997	9/30/98
Return (%)	10.4	-25.3	15.8	11.2	44.5	-8.7	9.9	26.2	28.1	-4.0

Compound	10 yr	9 yr	8 yr	7 yr	6 yr	5 yr	4 yr	3 yr	2 yr	1 yr
Return (%)	9.5	8.8	14.0	14.6	16.0	10.9	13.3	15.7	16.9	-11.1

SCEPTRE EQUITY GROWTH

NO LOAD

Primary Objective:	High Growth
Sponsor:	Sceptre Investment Counsel Limited
Fund Manager:	Allan Jacobs
Style:	Bottom-up, Growth
Size (MMs):	$305.256
RRSP:	100%
Management Expense Ratio:	1.42% (Average: 2.40%)

COMMENTS

Allan Jacobs used to be the most unsung manager in Canada. The South African-born accountant has been putting up great numbers since leaving Canada Life. Jacobs is a fundamental bottom-up stock picker who selects stocks when their P/E multiple is less than the company's growth rate. An above average performer with a low MER and reasonable volatility, this fund is appropriate for most equity investors. Fund returns for its third appearance in the Smart Funds list, although it slumped in the past year and was hurt by YBM Magnex. Jacobs is free to move his selections freely across the capitalization range. Top holdings of BCE, CIBC, BMO and RBC at of June 30, 1998 show that he will move around. Smart Fund 1998, 1997

RISK

How Often Money Was Lost:	....41 of 117 Months
	....41 of 115 Quarters
	....25 of 106 Rolling 12 Months
Worst 3 Months:	-30.12% (1998)
Best 3 Months:	21.37% (1995)

ASSET ALLOCATION

Industrial products	23.5%
Financial services	16.6%
Oil and gas	14.6%
Consumer products	10.4%
Merchandising	5.8%
Other	29.1%

COMPARISON OF FUND TO INDEXES

- $1,000 invested in the fund
- $1,000 invested in the Nesbitt Burns Small Cap Index
- $1,000 invested in Canada Savings Bonds
- ● Annual ranking against other funds in the same category

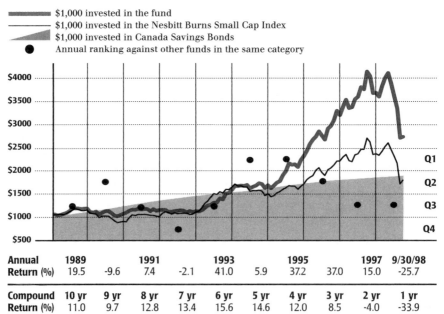

Annual Return (%)	1989		1991		1993		1995		1997	9/30/98
	19.5	-9.6	7.4	-2.1	41.0	5.9	37.2	37.0	15.0	-25.7

Compound Return (%)	10 yr	9 yr	8 yr	7 yr	6 yr	5 yr	4 yr	3 yr	2 yr	1 yr
	11.0	9.7	12.8	13.4	15.6	14.6	12.0	8.5	-4.0	-33.9

AIC VALUE

Primary Objective:	Growth
Sponsor:	AIC Limited
Fund Manager:	Neil Murdoch
Style:	Bottom-up, Growth
Size (MMs):	$1,268.805
RRSP:	100%
Management Expense Ratio:	2.44% (Average: 2.16%)

COMMENTS

With the addition of AIC American Advantage fund, Murdoch is expected to make this a more diversified U.S. fund. This was the top U.S. equity fund at the Annual Mutual Funds awards dinner the past two years. It owns stock classics like Gillette, Johnson & Johnson, Coca-Cola and Warren Buffett's Berkshire Hathaway. U.S. financial services stocks, such as Franklin Resources, Merrill Lynch, American Express and T. Rowe Price, have helped fuel this fund to a strong 20% five-year return. Fund also has low turnover, making it a good one to hold in taxable accounts. Smart Fund 1998

RISK

How Often Money Was Lost:....31 of 103 Months
....24 of 101 Quarters
.........................6 of 92 Rolling 12 Months
Worst 3 Months:............................-21.44% (1990)
Best 3 Months: 30.41% (1991)

ASSET ALLOCATION

Financial services...................42.9%
Consumer products................18.5%
Other..38.6%

COMPARISON OF FUND TO INDEXES

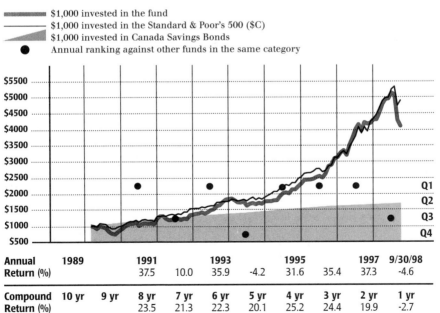

- $1,000 invested in the fund
- $1,000 invested in the Standard & Poor's 500 ($C)
- $1,000 invested in Canada Savings Bonds
- Annual ranking against other funds in the same category

Annual Return (%)	1989		1991		1993		1995		1997	9/30/98
			37.5	10.0	35.9	-4.2	31.6	35.4	37.3	-4.6

Compound Return (%)	10 yr	9 yr	8 yr	7 yr	6 yr	5 yr	4 yr	3 yr	2 yr	1 yr
			23.5	21.3	22.3	20.1	25.2	24.4	19.9	-2.7

U.S. EQUITY

AGF AMERICAN GROWTH CLASS   LOAD

Primary Objective:	Growth
Sponsor:	AGF Funds Inc
Fund Manager:	Stephen Rogers, since 3/93
Style:	Bottom-up, Growth
Size (MMs):	$663.101
RRSP:	20%
Management Expense Ratio:	2.78% (Average: 2.16%)

COMMENTS

The American Growth Fund is where AGF got its name. Steve Rogers was able to ride the technology and pharmaceutical stocks to continue the top-quartile performance on this fund. AGF has a stiff 2.78% MER for a fund that uses in-house money management and has more than $600 million in assets. Fund has been first or second quartile every calendar year since 1992. It is first quartile for every compound period out to 10 years ended September 30, 1998 and sports a 21.7% compounded annual return for the five-year period. Fund's top holdings at June 30th were Dell Computer, Microsoft, Cisco, GE, and Pfizer—just the kind of growth stocks you expect from this fund. Smart Fund 1998

RISK

How Often Money Was Lost:....42 of 117 Months
....32 of 115 Quarters
......................................7 of 106 Rolling 12 Months
Worst 3 Months:...........................-15.55% (1990)
Best 3 Months:................................24.48% (1997)

ASSET ALLOCATION

Technology 31.6%
Health care 18.0%
Consumer products................11.0%
Financial services.....................9.5%
Capital goods............................7.0%
Other..22.9%

COMPARISON OF FUND TO INDEXES

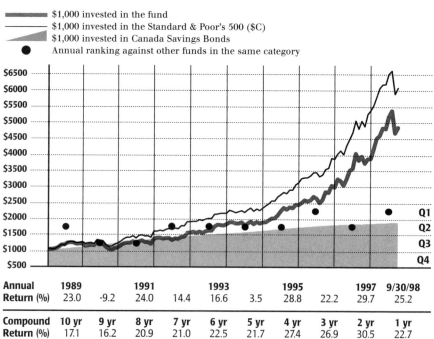

■■■■■■ $1,000 invested in the fund
——— $1,000 invested in the Standard & Poor's 500 ($C)
▨ $1,000 invested in Canada Savings Bonds
● Annual ranking against other funds in the same category

Annual Return (%)	1989		1991		1993		1995		1997	9/30/98
	23.0	-9.2	24.0	14.4	16.6	3.5	28.8	22.2	29.7	25.2

Compound Return (%)	10 yr	9 yr	8 yr	7 yr	6 yr	5 yr	4 yr	3 yr	2 yr	1 yr
	17.1	16.2	20.9	21.0	22.5	21.7	27.4	26.9	30.5	22.7

U.S. EQUITY

BPI AMERICAN EQUITY VALUE

LOAD

Primary Objective:	Growth
Sponsor:	BPI Mutual Funds
Fund Manager:	Paul Holland, BPI Global Asset, since 4/97
Style:	Bottom-up, Growth
Size (MMs):	$103.200
RRSP:	100%
Management Expense Ratio:	2.42% (Average: 2.16%)

COMMENTS

Our hats go off to BPI. We were skeptical of the switch from highly regarded Lazard Freres to BPI's new U.S. affiliate. Former Lazard manager Dan Jaworski has built an energetic young team that has generated stellar performance. The fund is now top quartile across the compound periods to five years ended September 30, 1998, where it has achieved a 19% CAGR. GE, Microsoft, American Express, Cisco, Bristol Myers, Warner Lambert holdings indicate that this fund has been misnamed. It should be a growth fund not a value fund. MER is competitive for category, but not compelling.

RISK

How Often Money Was Lost:	....41 of 112 Months
	....21 of 110 Quarters
	....4 of 101 Rolling 12 Months
Worst 3 Months:	-9.56% (1990)
Best 3 Months:	17.85% (1997)

ASSET ALLOCATION

Consumer products	3.4%
Financial services	3.2%
Industrial products	2.7%
Technology	2.3%
Communications	2.2%
Other	86.2%

COMPARISON OF FUND TO INDEXES

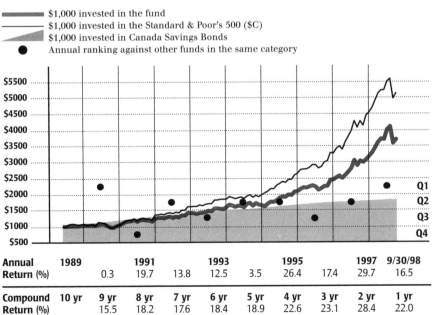

- $1,000 invested in the fund
- $1,000 invested in the Standard & Poor's 500 ($C)
- $1,000 invested in Canada Savings Bonds
- Annual ranking against other funds in the same category

Annual Return (%)	1989		1991		1993		1995		1997	9/30/98
		0.3	19.7	13.8	12.5	3.5	26.4	17.4	29.7	16.5

Compound Return (%)	10 yr	9 yr	8 yr	7 yr	6 yr	5 yr	4 yr	3 yr	2 yr	1 yr
		15.5	18.2	17.6	18.4	18.9	22.6	23.1	28.4	22.0

U.S. EQUITY

CIBC US INDEX RRSP

NO LOAD

Primary Objective:	Index
Sponsor:	CIBC Securities
Fund Manager:	Richard Pharn, TAL Investment Counsel
Style:	Passive
Size (MMs):	$272.033
RRSP:	20%
Management Expense Ratio:	0.90% (Average: 2.16%)

COMMENTS

Do not hold this one outside an RRSP or in a taxable account. All distributions in this and other RSP-eligible foreign funds are taxed as income. Still, this is a great way to gain foreign exposure without going offside on your foreign content. Since managers don't often beat the highly efficient S&P 500 index, the 0.90% MER makes it a deal over the previous Smart Fund for this type, Canada Trust's AmeriGrowth.

RISK

How Often Money Was Lost: ....5 of 26 Months
....3 of 24 Quarters
...................................0 of 15 Rolling 12 Months
Worst 3 Months: ....-6.10% (1998)
Best 3 Months:.................................18.62% (1997)

ASSET ALLOCATION

Cash 95.0%
Other 5.0%

COMPARISON OF FUND TO INDEXES

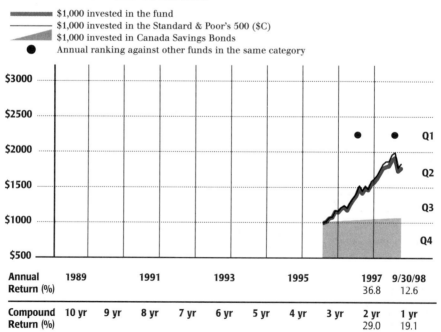

- $1,000 invested in the fund
- $1,000 invested in the Standard & Poor's 500 ($C)
- $1,000 invested in Canada Savings Bonds
- Annual ranking against other funds in the same category

Annual Return (%)	1989	1991	1993	1995	1997	9/30/98
					36.8	12.6

Compound Return (%)	10 yr	9 yr	8 yr	7 yr	6 yr	5 yr	4 yr	3 yr	2 yr	1 yr
									29.0	19.1

U.S. EQUITY

CIBC NORTH AMERICAN DEMOGRAPHICS NO LOAD

Primary Objective:	Growth
Sponsor:	CIBC Securities Inc
Fund Manager:	Kenneth Woods, TAL Investment Counsel
Style:	Top-down
Size (MMs):	$73.786
RRSP:	20%
Management Expense Ratio:	2.50% (Average 2.16%)

COMMENTS

After reading David Foot's best-selling *Boom, Bust & Echo*, many seek to invest in the demographic theme. We made this a Smart Fund last edition when it came out of the starting blocks and are happy to include it again this year. This remains one of the best offerings from a fund family that has been steadily improving. The fund uses demographic analysis to determine how the baby boomers, Generation X and other generations will impact markets as they age. Managed by TAL, with input from demographers at the RAND Corporation. At June 30, the fund invested in Disney, Pfizer, Franklin Resources and Medtronic, to name a few. The fund was up 43% in 1997 and is up 22% since inception. Smart Fund 1998

RISK

How Often Money Was Lost: ....7 of 24 Months
....2 of 22 Quarters
....0 of 13 Rolling 12 Months
Worst 3 Months:.............................-15.81% (1998)
Best 3 Months:.................................21.72% (1997)

ASSET ALLOCATION

Consumer services.................34.0%
Financial services...................17.5%
Consumer products.................7.9%
Healthcare 16.9%
Cash 9.1%
Other.......................................14.6%

COMPARISON OF FUND TO INDEXES

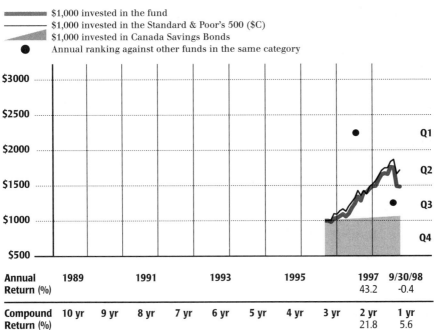

- $1,000 invested in the fund
- $1,000 invested in the Standard & Poor's 500 ($C)
- $1,000 invested in Canada Savings Bonds
- ● Annual ranking against other funds in the same category

Annual Return (%)	1989		1991		1993		1995		1997	9/30/98
									43.2	-0.4

Compound Return (%)	10 yr	9 yr	8 yr	7 yr	6 yr	5 yr	4 yr	3 yr	2 yr	1 yr
									21.8	5.6

U.S. EQUITY

ELLIOTT & PAGE AMERICAN GROWTH LOAD

Primary Objective:	Growth
Sponsor:	Elliott & Page Ltd.
Fund Manager:	Robert Jones, Goldman Sachs
Style:	Bottom-up, Growth
Size (MMs):	$140.383
RRSP:	20%
Management Expense Ratio:	1.40% (Average: 2.16%)

COMMENTS

Outstanding performance with one of the lowest MERs in the load-fund world at 1.40%. Robert Jones at Goldman Sachs continues to hold the large-cap growth stocks like GE, Coke, AIG and Merrill Lynch. These types of holdings represent a big change for the fund over the holdings of departed value manager, Jim McClure. Fund's first-quartile performance in 1997 and second-quartile for the year-to-date 1998 has pulled the overall compound returns up to 20.8% for the three years ended September 30, 1998.

RISK

How Often Money Was Lost:....39 of 117 Months
....31 of 115 Quarters
...............................5 of 106 Rolling 12 Months
Worst 3 Months:...............................-11.60% (1990)
Best 3 Months: 19.36% (1998)

ASSET ALLOCATION

Consumer products..................7.4%
Financial services....................22.7%
Capital goods 10.2%
Technology 7.8%
Healthcare 8.6%
Other.......................................43.3%

COMPARISON OF FUND TO INDEXES

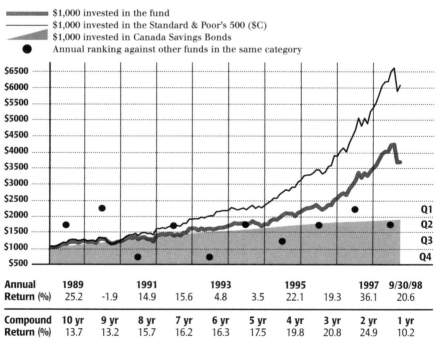

- $1,000 invested in the fund
- $1,000 invested in the Standard & Poor's 500 ($C)
- $1,000 invested in Canada Savings Bonds
- ● Annual ranking against other funds in the same category

Annual	1989		1991		1993		1995		1997	9/30/98
Return (%)	25.2	-1.9	14.9	15.6	4.8	3.5	22.1	19.3	36.1	20.6

Compound	10 yr	9 yr	8 yr	7 yr	6 yr	5 yr	4 yr	3 yr	2 yr	1 yr
Return (%)	13.7	13.2	15.7	16.2	16.3	17.5	19.8	20.8	24.9	10.2

U.S. EQUITY

ETHICAL NORTH AMERICAN EQUITY NO LOAD

Primary Objective:	Growth with Ethical Screens
Sponsor:	Ethical Funds Inc.
Fund Manager:	Cynthia Frick, Alliance Capital since 5/93
Style:	Growth
Size (MMs):	$203.584
RRSP:	20%
Management Expense Ratio:	2.47% (Average: 2.16%)

COMMENTS

Alliance Capital steered this to a 66% return for the 12 months ended March 31, 1998. That has dropped to 21.6% for the year ended September 30, 1998. Healthy exposure to computer stocks like Dell and Cisco, and to healthcare firms like Merck and Bristol Myers Squibb, drove strong returns. Cynthia Frick manages this slightly differently than star manager Al Harrison on the MD U.S. Equity (also a Smart Fund). This one has ethical screens that the fund sponsor imposes, such as no tobacco or alcohol stocks. That stance included avoiding most resource stocks and loading up on S&P stocks, and has proven to beat the market soundly.

RISK

How Often Money Was Lost: ....37 of 117 Months
....31 of 115 Quarters
...................................16 of 106 Rolling 12 Months
Worst 3 Months:...............................-10.55% (1990)
Best 3 Months:...................................23.93% (1997)

ASSET ALLOCATION

Consumer products.................32.1%
Financial services....................20.6%
Healthcare 10.3%
Technology 20.4%
Communications.......................8.6%
Other 8.0%

COMPARISON OF FUND TO INDEXES

- $1,000 invested in the fund
- $1,000 invested in the Standard & Poor's 500 ($C)
- $1,000 invested in Canada Savings Bonds
- ● Annual ranking against other funds in the same category

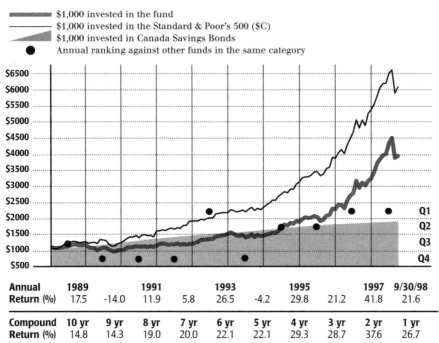

	1989		1991		1993		1995		1997	9/30/98
Annual Return (%)	17.5	-14.0	11.9	5.8	26.5	-4.2	29.8	21.2	41.8	21.6

	10 yr	9 yr	8 yr	7 yr	6 yr	5 yr	4 yr	3 yr	2 yr	1 yr
Compound Return (%)	14.8	14.3	19.0	20.0	22.1	22.1	29.3	28.7	37.6	26.7

FIDELITY GROWTH AMERICA

Primary Objective:	Growth
Sponsor:	Fidelity Investments Canada
Fund Manager:	Brad Lewis
Style:	Top-down, Quantitative
Size (MMs):	$1,552.462
RRSP:	20%
Management Expense Ratio:	2.32% (Average: 2.16%)

COMMENTS

Lewis is well known for his ability to construct and use sophisticated computer models. The models use the huge amount of statistical data Fidelity generates and, at speeds humans could never match, analyze it. The result is information that Lewis uses to pick stocks. A key part of this work is focused on avoiding stocks that will underperform. Fund currently has a value tilt and a slightly small-cap orientation to it. Fund's goal is to always be second quartile or better each calendar year. It has done that every year since 1991. The fund's seven-year CAGR of 20.2% speaks for itself. Smart Fund 1996, 1997

RISK

How Often Money Was Lost:	30 of 96 Months
	19 of 94 Quarters
	2 of 85 Rolling 12 Months
Worst 3 Months:	-11.89% (1998)
Best 3 Months:	24.18% (1992)

ASSET ALLOCATION

Finance	19.9%
Technology	9.3%
Retail and wholesale	9.0%
Utilities	7.8%
Cash	13.6%
Other	40.4%

COMPARISON OF FUND TO INDEXES

- $1,000 invested in the fund
- $1,000 invested in the Standard & Poor's 500 ($C)
- $1,000 invested in Canada Savings Bonds
- ● Annual ranking against other funds in the same category

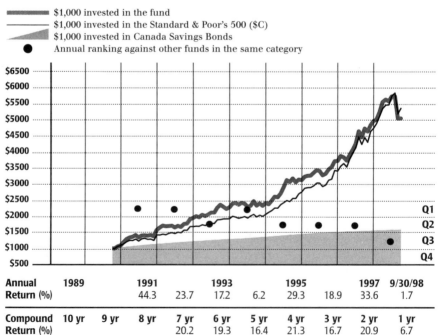

Annual Return (%)	1989		1991		1993		1995		1997	9/30/98
			44.3	23.7	17.2	6.2	29.3	18.9	33.6	1.7

Compound Return (%)	10 yr	9 yr	8 yr	7 yr	6 yr	5 yr	4 yr	3 yr	2 yr	1 yr
				20.2	19.3	16.4	21.3	16.7	20.9	6.7

GUARDIAN AMERICAN EQUITY CLASSIC LOAD

Primary Objective:	Growth
Sponsor:	Guardian Mutual Funds
Fund Manager:	Michael Rome, Lazard since 2/98
Style:	Bottom-up, Growth
Size (MMs):	$34.961
RRSP:	20%
Management Expense Ratio:	2.19% (Average: 2.16%)

COMMENTS

This former Smart Fund has had new life breathed into it. Michael Rome, well known as the former manager of the U.S. equity funds for BPI Mutual Funds, is a welcome addition to the Guardian team. He is highly respected as a top U.S. money manager and based on his past track record with the BPI American Small Companies Fund, we have promoted this to "Smart Fund" status this year. The BPI American Small Companies fund was a Smart Fund 1997, 1996. In our 1997 edition we said, "Using a bottom-up, value discipline, Michael Rome concentrates on about 60 stocks that appear to offer superior capital gains potential." This one has a value tilt and should hold up well in the volatile market of the past several months.

RISK

How Often Money Was Lost:....38 of 117 Months
...................................30 of 115 Quarters
.....................................8 of 106 Rolling 12 Months
Worst 3 Months: ....-20.13 (1990)
Best 3 Months:.......................................25.36 (1992)

ASSET ALLOCATION

Consumer products.................34.8%
Financial services....................19.3%
Capital goods...........................8.1%
Technology 8.7%
Consumer staples 7.5%
Other...21.6%

COMPARISON OF FUND TO INDEXES

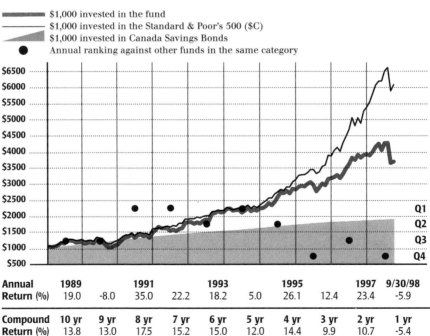

- $1,000 invested in the fund
- $1,000 invested in the Standard & Poor's 500 ($C)
- $1,000 invested in Canada Savings Bonds
- ● Annual ranking against other funds in the same category

Annual	1989		1991		1993		1995		1997	9/30/98
Return (%)	19.0	-8.0	35.0	22.2	18.2	5.0	26.1	12.4	23.4	-5.9

Compound	10 yr	9 yr	8 yr	7 yr	6 yr	5 yr	4 yr	3 yr	2 yr	1 yr
Return (%)	13.8	13.0	17.5	15.2	15.0	12.0	14.4	9.9	10.7	-5.4

GREEN LINE U.S. INDEX

NO LOAD

Primary Objective:	Growth
Sponsor:	TD Asset Management
Fund Manager:	TD Asset Management
Style:	Passive
Size (MMs):	$134.036
RRSP:	20%
Management Expense Ratio:	0.66% (Average: 2.16%)

COMMENTS

For many, the future could be index funds. MERs are significantly less, they outperform the majority of money managers and they are tax efficient. This one has been around a while and has a reasonable MER vs. some other Canadian pretenders. One confusing note on the Green Line fund—it has traditionally had its NAV quoted in U.S. dollars. No problem for Canadians: they have picked up the currency gain in addition to the soaring U.S. stock market. Other Canadian dollar-quoted U.S. equity funds or the S&P500 index reflected in Canadian dollar terms look to be outperforming the TD fund. TD is looking into disclosing performers in both currencies.

RISK

How Often Money Was Lost:....36 of 117 Months
....22 of 115 Quarters
.... 6 of 106 Rolling 12 Months
Worst 3 Months: ....-14.07% (1990)
Best 3 Months:..................................19.31% (1997)

ASSET ALLOCATION

Consumer staples 14.8%
Financial services....................17.2%
Consumer cyclicals 9.2%
Technology 14.7%
Healthcare 11.6%
Other...32.5%

COMPARISON OF FUND TO INDEXES

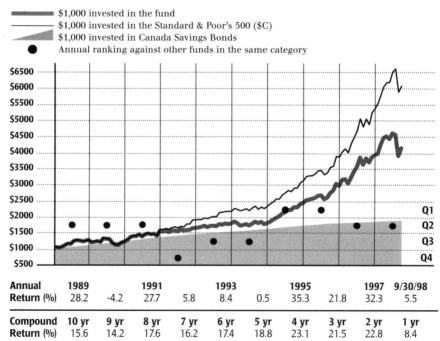

━━━━ $1,000 invested in the fund
───── $1,000 invested in the Standard & Poor's 500 ($C)
░░░░░ $1,000 invested in Canada Savings Bonds
● Annual ranking against other funds in the same category

Annual Return (%)	1989		1991		1993		1995		1997	9/30/98
	28.2	-4.2	27.7	5.8	8.4	0.5	35.3	21.8	32.3	5.5

Compound Return (%)	10 yr	9 yr	8 yr	7 yr	6 yr	5 yr	4 yr	3 yr	2 yr	1 yr
	15.6	14.2	17.6	16.2	17.4	18.8	23.1	21.5	22.8	8.4

MAXXUM AMERICAN EQUITY

LOAD

Primary Objective:	Growth
Sponsor:	London Fund Management
Fund Manager:	Warren Lammert, Janus Capital, since 11/97
Style:	Bottom-up, Growth
Size (MMs):	$33.620
RRSP:	20%
Management Expense Ratio:	2.48% (Average: 2.16%)

COMMENTS

A new addition to the Smart Funds list following 41% return for the year-ended June 30, 1998 (and 27.1% CAGR over three years). One of two MAXXUM funds managed by highly regarded, Denver-based Janus Capital Corp. Manager Warren Lammert, who manages the Janus Mercury Fund, can invest up to 30% outside the U.S. Fund had 30% technology weighting early in 1998, holding Microsoft, Cisco Systems as well as pharmaceuticals like Pfizer and Warner Lambert. The fund is first quartile over the one, two, and three-year return periods ending September 30th. You may have to ask around for MAXXUM funds because they are not well known, but watch the two managed by Janus.

RISK

How Often Money Was Lost: ......15 of 44 Months
....9 of 42 Quarters
....0 of 33 Rolling 12 Months
Worst 3 Months: ....-6.16% (1996)
Best 3 Months: 25.35% (1995)

ASSET ALLOCATION

Consumer products.................21.7%
Financial services....................10.9%
Consumer staples 14.1%
Technology 30.7%
Communications........................8.1%
Other.......................................14.5%

COMPARISON OF FUND TO INDEXES

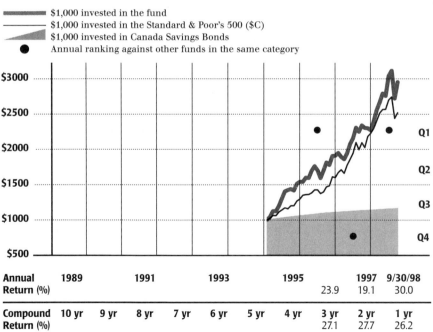

- $1,000 invested in the fund
- $1,000 invested in the Standard & Poor's 500 ($C)
- $1,000 invested in Canada Savings Bonds
- Annual ranking against other funds in the same category

Annual Return (%)	1989		1991		1993		1995		1997	9/30/98
								23.9	19.1	30.0

Compound Return (%)	10 yr	9 yr	8 yr	7 yr	6 yr	5 yr	4 yr	3 yr	2 yr	1 yr
								27.1	27.7	26.2

U.S. EQUITY

MD U.S. EQUITY

Primary Objective:	Growth
Sponsor:	MD Management
Fund Manager:	Alliance Capital
Style:	Bottom-up, Growth
Size (MMs):	$341.722
RRSP:	20%
Management Expense Ratio:	1.29% (Average: 2.16%)

COMMENTS

Alliance Capital continues to outperform. Unfortunately this excellent manager is only available to members of the medical establishment. A top-quartile performer over the five-, three-, two- and one-year periods and a regular on the Smart Funds list, this is a great long-term hold if you're eligible. The fund's 57.2% one-year number as of June 30, 1998 exceeded the S&P 500 index by 19 percentage points and made it the number one performing U.S. equity fund for that period. This is essentially a clone of manager Alfred Harrison's Alliance Premier Growth B (ranked 5-star by Morningstar) fund available to American investors. Fund scored huge gains on its holdings of Dell Computer, Nokia, Cisco and Ford. Alliance Capital is also available through the Ethical funds. Smart Fund 1998, 1996

RISK

How Often Money Was Lost:	19 of 72 Months
	12 of 70 Quarters
	1 of 61 Rolling 12 Months
Worst 3 Months:	-9.65% (1998)
Best 3 Months:	23.96% (1997)

ASSET ALLOCATION

Consumer products	25.1%
Financial services	25.2%
Utilities	8.4%
Technology	17.3%
Healthcare	12.6%
Other	11.4%

COMPARISON OF FUND TO INDEXES

- $1,000 invested in the fund
- $1,000 invested in the Standard & Poor's 500 ($C)
- $1,000 invested in Canada Savings Bonds
- ● Annual ranking against other funds in the same category

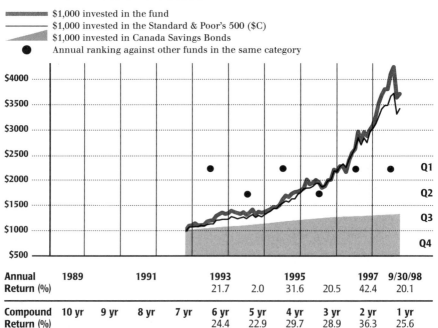

Annual Return (%)	1989		1991		1993		1995		1997	9/30/98
					21.7	2.0	31.6	20.5	42.4	20.1

Compound Return (%)	10 yr	9 yr	8 yr	7 yr	6 yr	5 yr	4 yr	3 yr	2 yr	1 yr
					24.4	22.9	29.7	28.9	36.3	25.6

U.S. EQUITY

PH&N U.S. EQUITY

Primary Objective:	Growth
Sponsor:	Phillips, Hager & North Investment Mgmt
Fund Manager:	Team
Style:	Bottom-up, Growth
Size (MMs):	$631.722
RRSP:	20%
Management Expense Ratio:	1.10% (Average: 2.16%)

COMMENTS

This perennial Smart Fund has not disappointed. Like many PH&N funds, it sports a low MER of 1.1%, is no-load and has generated first- or second-quartile performance. It hasn't had a down year since 1990, and has superior risk-adjusted returns. The team of managers seeks high-growth companies with solid balance sheets. This track record proves you don't have to reside in the U.S. to pick U.S. stocks. It lagged some of its peers because it missed some of the hot-performing technology stocks. Smart Fund 1998, 1997, 1996

RISK

How Often Money Was Lost:.....38 of 117 Months
....27 of 115 Quarters
.......................5 of 106 Rolling 12 Months
Worst 3 Months:...............................-18.82% (1990)
Best 3 Months: 25.19% (1991)

ASSET ALLOCATION

Consumer products................11.1%
Financial services...................15.1%
Healthcare 15.0%
Technology 11.6%
Retail..8.8%
Other.......................................38.4%

COMPARISON OF FUND TO INDEXES

$1,000 invested in the fund
$1,000 invested in the Standard & Poor's 500 ($C)
$1,000 invested in Canada Savings Bonds
● Annual ranking against other funds in the same category

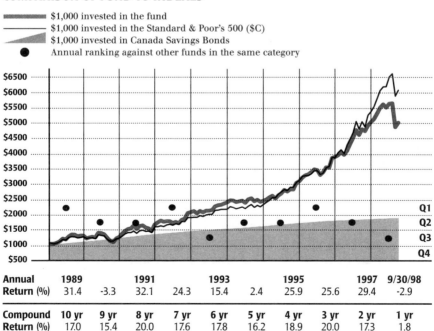

Annual	1989		1991		1993		1995		1997	9/30/98
Return (%)	31.4	-3.3	32.1	24.3	15.4	2.4	25.9	25.6	29.4	-2.9

Compound	10 yr	9 yr	8 yr	7 yr	6 yr	5 yr	4 yr	3 yr	2 yr	1 yr
Return (%)	17.0	15.4	20.0	17.6	17.8	16.2	18.9	20.0	17.3	1.8

U.S. EQUITY

SPECTRUM UNITED AMERICAN GROWTH LOAD

Primary Objective:	Growth
Sponsor:	Spectrum United Mutual Funds
Fund Manager:	John Ballen and Toni Shimura, MFS Institutional (12/95)
Style:	Bottom-up, Small- and mid-cap growth
Size (MMs):	$575.764
RRSP:	20%
Management Expense Ratio:	2.35% (Average: 2.16%)

COMMENTS

Our only U.S. small-cap fund is a first-time Smart Fund, taking the place of Universal U.S. Emerging Growth. This sector has missed out on the S&P500 bull market, but should be a component of most people's portfolios. Manager Ballen is highly acclaimed with stellar long-term numbers. Despite the handicap of playing in the small- and mid-cap arena when the big growth funds have roared ahead, Ballen has steered this to first-quartile return in the three-year period. Ballen has recently put his bets on technology with a 28% weighting with large-cap names like Cisco and Microsoft driving the year-to-date performance

RISK

How Often Money Was Lost:	....46 of 117 Months
	.................................29 of 115 Quarters
	.....................7 of 106 Rolling 12 Months
Worst 3 Months:	...............................-17.59% (1990)
Best 3 Months:	...................................25.94% (1991)

ASSET ALLOCATION

Consumer products	18.5%
Leisure	10.0%
Retail	8.8%
Technology	28.0%
Communications	12.9%
Other	21.8%

COMPARISON OF FUND TO INDEXES

$1,000 invested in the fund
$1,000 invested in the Standard & Poor's 500 ($C)
$1,000 invested in Canada Savings Bonds
● Annual ranking against other funds in the same category

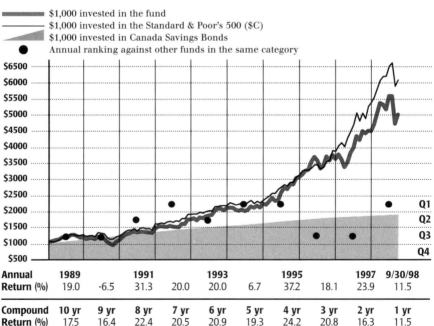

Annual Return (%)	1989		1991		1993		1995		1997	9/30/98
	19.0	-6.5	31.3	20.0	20.0	6.7	37.2	18.1	23.9	11.5

Compound Return (%)	10 yr	9 yr	8 yr	7 yr	6 yr	5 yr	4 yr	3 yr	2 yr	1 yr
	17.5	16.4	22.4	20.5	20.9	19.3	24.2	20.8	16.3	11.5

U.S. EQUITY

AGF INTERNATIONAL VALUE LOAD

Primary Objective:	Growth
Sponsor:	AGF Funds Inc.
Fund Manager:	Charles Brandes and Jeff Busby, Brandes Partners
Style:	Bottom-up, Value
Size (MMs):	$2,049.230
RRSP:	20%
Management Expense Ratio:	2.77% (Average: 2.33%)

COMMENTS

Charles Brandes and Jeff Busby have a similar style to the famous Ben Graham's value investing approach and have been just as successful as Templeton. This is a top-quartile performer, with modest volatility. Investors have noticed this three-time Smart Fund as dollars continue to flow in. The fund had assets of $106 million when we first recommended it in our 1996 edition. It had grown to $937 million in last year's edition and is now over $2 billion. We hope the flood of money will motivate AGF to lower the MER from its outrageous 2.77% and get closer to competitors such as Trimark and Templeton. Perhaps with those kind of fees, we should recommend the AGF stock rather than the AGF funds. Smart Fund 1998, 1997, 1996

RISK

How Often Money Was Lost: ......14 of 46 Months
....8 of 44 Quarters
....1 of 35 Rolling 12 Months
Worst 3 Months: ....-10.88% (1998)
Best 3 Months: 14.92% (1998)

ASSET ALLOCATION

USA...27.7%
France..11.7%
Germany 8.2%
Japan..15.2%
Hong Kong....................................8.2%
Other...29.0%

COMPARISON OF FUND TO INDEXES

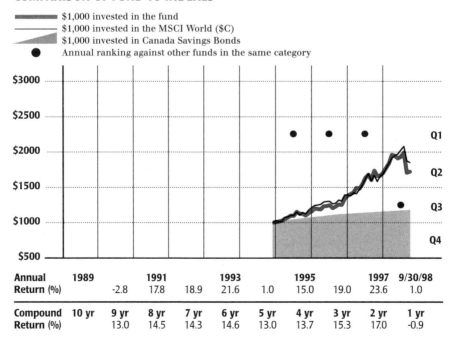

- $1,000 invested in the fund
- $1,000 invested in the MSCI World ($C)
- $1,000 invested in Canada Savings Bonds
- ● Annual ranking against other funds in the same category

Annual Return (%)	1989		1991		1993		1995		1997	9/30/98
		-2.8	17.8	18.9	21.6	1.0	15.0	19.0	23.6	1.0

Compound Return (%)	10 yr	9 yr	8 yr	7 yr	6 yr	5 yr	4 yr	3 yr	2 yr	1 yr
	13.0	14.5	14.3	14.6	13.0	13.7	15.3	17.0	-0.9

GLOBAL EQUITY

AIC WORLD EQUITY

Primary Objective:	Growth
Sponsor:	AIC Limited
Fund Manager:	Neil Murdoch
Style:	Bottom-up
Size (MMs):	$324.945
RRSP:	20%
Management Expense Ratio:	2.70% (Average: 2.33%)

COMMENTS

With the addition of the AIC World Advantage to continue the wealth management theme, Manager Neil Murdoch will be able to diversify this fund across other industries to reduce the potential volatility. A new addition to the Smart Funds list, but one that is hard to deny with first-quartile returns for 1996 and 1997 and for the first six months of 1998. Fund has some blue-chip international names like Novartis, ING and Ericsson as well as big positions in two money managers, Perpetual and Amvescap. Others are noticing the returns, as the AIC fund company continues to swell. This fund has more than tripled in a year to almost $325 million.

RISK

How Often Money Was Lost:	22 of 59 Months
	19 of 57 Quarters
	9 of 48 Rolling 12 Months
Worst 3 Months:	-19.48% (1998)
Best 3 Months:	21.40% (1998)

ASSET ALLOCATION

UK	72.2%
Far East	4.0%
Australia	0.2%
Other	23.6%

COMPARISON OF FUND TO INDEXES

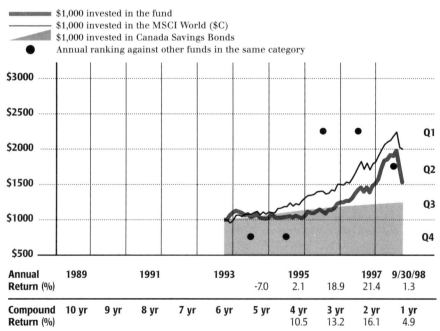

- $1,000 invested in the fund
- $1,000 invested in the MSCI World ($C)
- $1,000 invested in Canada Savings Bonds
- ● Annual ranking against other funds in the same category

Annual Return (%)	1989		1991		1993		1995		1997	9/30/98
						-7.0	2.1	18.9	21.4	1.3

Compound Return (%)	10 yr	9 yr	8 yr	7 yr	6 yr	5 yr	4 yr	3 yr	2 yr	1 yr
							10.5	13.2	16.1	4.9

GLOBAL EQUITY

BPI GLOBAL EQUITY VALUE

Primary Objective:	Growth
Sponsor:	BPI Mutual Funds
Fund Manager:	Dan Jaworski,
	BPI Asset Management
Style:	Bottom-up, Growth
Size (MMs):	$451.700
RRSP:	20%
Management Expense Ratio:	2.47% (Average: 2.33%)

COMMENTS

We mentioned in the BPI American Equity Value entry the change from Lazard Freres to the new BPI affiliate run by Dan Jaworski. This fund is managed by Jaworski himself. Solid first-quartile performance has pulled this fund into the top quartile across all compound periods through 10 years. Big weighting in the U.S. large-cap stocks like GE, Microsoft and Cisco has paid off.

RISK

How Often Money Was Lost:....38 of 117 Months
....24 of 115 Quarters
........................7 of 106 Rolling 12 Months
Worst 3 Months:..............................-11.11% (1998)
Best 3 Months:...................................17.77% (1989)

ASSET ALLOCATION

Financial services....................20.0%
Consumer products................19.0%
Communications.....................15.0%
Industrial products..................11.0%
Utilities 8.0%
Other 27.0%

COMPARISON OF FUND TO INDEXES

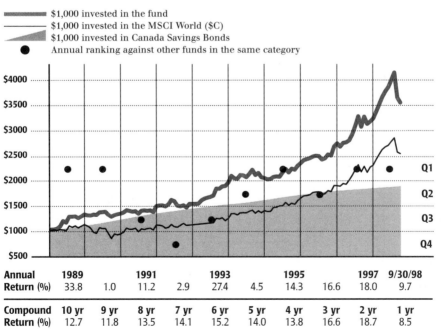

- ▬▬▬ $1,000 invested in the fund
- —— $1,000 invested in the MSCI World ($C)
- ▨ $1,000 invested in Canada Savings Bonds
- ● Annual ranking against other funds in the same category

Annual	1989		1991		1993		1995		1997	9/30/98
Return (%)	33.8	1.0	11.2	2.9	27.4	4.5	14.3	16.6	18.0	9.7

Compound	10 yr	9 yr	8 yr	7 yr	6 yr	5 yr	4 yr	3 yr	2 yr	1 yr
Return (%)	12.7	11.8	13.5	14.1	15.2	14.0	13.8	16.6	18.7	8.5

GLOBAL EQUITY

BISSETT MULTI-NATIONAL GROWTH NO LOAD

Primary Objective:	Growth
Sponsor:	Bissett & Associates
Fund Manager:	Fred Pynn since 12/96
Style:	Large-cap, Growth
Size (MMs):	$75.183
RRSP:	20%
Management Expense Ratio:	1.50% (Average: 2.33%)

COMMENTS

Bissett's version of a global equity fund features investments in companies listed on North American stock exchanges but which derive a large portion of their revenues and profits from overseas. Many of the stock picks are household names. Emphasis is on dividend-paying companies. The formula is working. Fund was third in the category for both 1996 and 1997 after being second in 1995, and is the number one global equity fund for three-year CAGR ending June 30, 1998. When you consider it's also no-load and has an MER of just 1.5%, it could stay on the Smart Fund list for many years to come. This one, like Trimark Fund, is tied to the vagaries of the U.S. stock market and missed out on the phenomenal European returns in 1998. See profile of manager Fred Pynn on page 27. Smart Fund 1998

RISK

How Often Money Was Lost: ......15 of 50 Months
....6 of 48 Quarters
....0 of 39 Rolling 12 Months
Worst 3 Months: ....-12.27% (1998)
Best 3 Months: 18.17% (1997)

ASSET ALLOCATION

USA 56.6%
Canada 28.3%
Europe...15.1%

COMPARISON OF FUND TO INDEXES

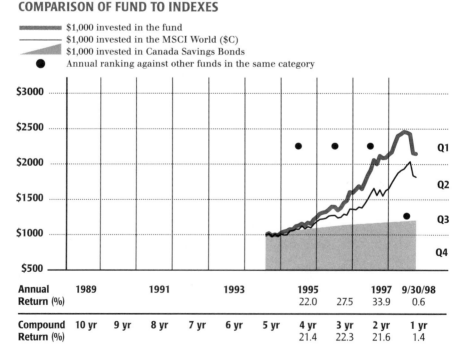

▬▬▬▬ $1,000 invested in the fund
——— $1,000 invested in the MSCI World ($C)
▨▨▨ $1,000 invested in Canada Savings Bonds
● Annual ranking against other funds in the same category

Annual Return (%)	1989		1991		1993		1995		1997	9/30/98
							22.0	27.5	33.9	0.6

Compound Return (%)	10 yr	9 yr	8 yr	7 yr	6 yr	5 yr	4 yr	3 yr	2 yr	1 yr
							21.4	22.3	21.6	1.4

GLOBAL EQUITY

CI GLOBAL

Primary Objective:	Growth
Sponsor:	CI Mutual Funds
Fund Manager:	Bill Sterling, BEA Associates
Style:	Top-down
Size (MMs):	$989.536
RRSP:	20%
Management Expense Ratio:	2.47% (Average: 2.33%)

COMMENTS

Top-down strategist Dr. Bill Sterling is a keen student of demographics with the release of his new book *Boomernomics*. Many of his themes will play out in the direction of the fund and its positioning going forward. Well diversified, its biggest holding, Medtronic, makes up just 2% of the fund. Almost 80% of the fund is split between Europe and the U.S. Since Sterling took over, it has risen from back-to-back fourth quartile years in 1994 and 1995 to a first quartile ranking over the one-, two-, three-, and five-year compound periods to September 30, 1998.

RISK

How Often Money Was Lost: ....42 of 117 Months
....30 of 115 Quarters
.......................18 of 106 Rolling 12 Months
Worst 3 Months: ....-12.66% (1990)
Best 3 Months: 17.95% (1997)

ASSET ALLOCATION

USA 37.5%
Cash 12.9%
Europe 39.5%
Japan 2.6%
Latin America 3.3%
Other 4.9%

COMPARISON OF FUND TO INDEXES

■■■■■ $1,000 invested in the fund
——— $1,000 invested in the MSCI World ($C)
▨ $1,000 invested in Canada Savings Bonds
● Annual ranking against other funds in the same category

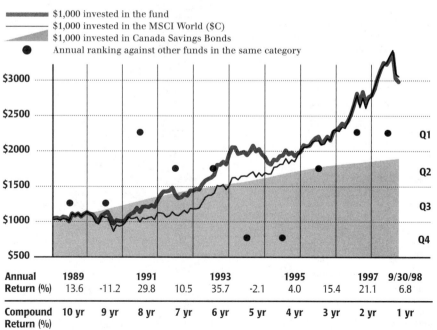

Annual Return (%)	1989		1991		1993		1995		1997	9/30/98
	13.6	-11.2	29.8	10.5	35.7	-2.1	4.0	15.4	21.1	6.8

Compound Return (%)	10 yr	9 yr	8 yr	7 yr	6 yr	5 yr	4 yr	3 yr	2 yr	1 yr

GLOBAL EQUITY

FIDELITY INTERNATIONAL PORTFOLIO LOAD

Primary Objective:	Growth
Sponsor:	Fidelity Investments Canada
Fund Manager:	Dick Habermann
Style:	Top-down
Size (MMs):	$3,494.062
RRSP:	20%
Management Expense Ratio:	2.69% (Average: 2.33%)

COMMENTS

Steady, consistent performers can appear boring in comparison with the high flyers. This fund proves slow and steady wins the race for most investors. It has first-quartile performance across all the compound periods, combined with modest volatility. Manager Dick Habermann makes the country-allocation calls and uses the selections from Fidelity's regional managers to populate the fund. For those in the Fidelity family, this fund could easily provide the only foreign content you need. It has made money every calendar year since 1991. For those seeking slightly less volatility, the Fidelity Global Asset Allocation fund, also a Smart Fund, will hold bonds and therefore offer more stability in down markets. Smart Fund 1998, 1997

RISK

How Often Money Was Lost: ....37 of 117 Months
.....................................29 of 115 Quarters
.....................................13 of 106 Rolling 12 Months
Worst 3 Months: ....-17.86% (1990)
Best 3 Months: 17.69% (1997)

ASSET ALLOCATION

USA 49.0%
France...3.8%
UK..8.9%
Japan...10.6%
Cash 4.6%
Other...23.1%

COMPARISON OF FUND TO INDEXES

$1,000 invested in the fund
$1,000 invested in the MSCI World ($C)
$1,000 invested in Canada Savings Bonds
● Annual ranking against other funds in the same category

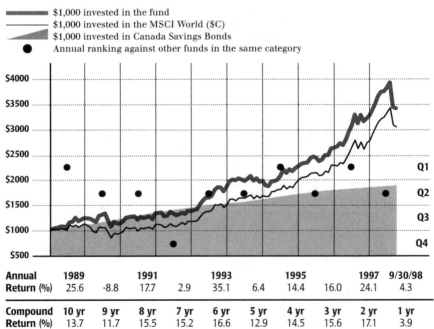

Annual	1989		1991		1993		1995		1997	9/30/98
Return (%)	25.6	-8.8	17.7	2.9	35.1	6.4	14.4	16.0	24.1	4.3

Compound	10 yr	9 yr	8 yr	7 yr	6 yr	5 yr	4 yr	3 yr	2 yr	1 yr
Return (%)	13.7	11.7	15.5	15.2	16.6	12.9	14.5	15.6	17.1	3.9

GLOBAL EQUITY

GWL INTERNATIONAL EQUITY LOAD

Primary Objective:	Growth
Sponsor:	GWL Investment Management
Fund Manager:	Putnam Investments
Style:	Bottom-up, Growth
Size (MMs):	$84.737
RRSP:	20%
Management Expense Ratio:	2.92% (Average: 2.33%)

COMMENTS

This is the only seg fund on the Smart Fund list this year. Expense ratios are high on others and we are not sure being locked in for 10 years is worth the price. We picked this one for its unique feature—it is the only way for Canadians to get the benefits of Putnam's asset management expertise. This does not invest in the United States so it suffers against funds that have benefited from the U.S. bull run. This fund is similar to the five-star-rated Putnam International Growth A fund, managed by a team led by Justin Scott. He has been there since 1991. The managers seek stocks that are cheap relative to their return on capital and generally carry holdings with lower P/E multiples. Stiff MER of 2.92% pays for Putnam, your Great West Life rep and the guarantee on the fund.

RISK

How Often Money Was Lost:.......12 of 47 Months
....11 of 45 Quarters
......................................1 of 36 Rolling 12 Months
Worst 3 Months:............................-14.65% (1998)
Best 3 Months:................................16.30% (1997)

ASSET ALLOCATION

Germany 11.0%
France...13.6%
UK 17.6%
Japan..10.9%
Switzerland................................9.2%
Other 37.7%

COMPARISON OF FUND TO INDEXES

▬▬▬▬ $1,000 invested in the fund
─────── $1,000 invested in the MSCI World ($C)
◢ $1,000 invested in Canada Savings Bonds
● Annual ranking against other funds in the same category

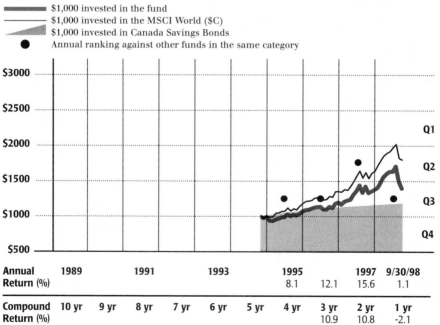

Annual Return (%)	1989		1991		1993		1995			1997	9/30/98
							8.1	12.1		15.6	1.1

Compound Return (%)	10 yr	9 yr	8 yr	7 yr	6 yr	5 yr	4 yr	3 yr	2 yr	1 yr
								10.9	10.8	-2.1

GLOBAL EQUITY

GLOBAL STRATEGY WORLD COMPANIES   LOAD

Primary Objective:	Growth
Sponsor:	Global Strategy Financial
Fund Manager:	Rothschild, Montgomery Asset
	Management
Style:	Multi-Manager
Size (MMs):	$126.129
RRSP:	20%
Management Expense Ratio:	2.70% (Average: 2.33%)

COMMENTS

Global Strategy terminated its agreement with Perpetual and now divides the portfolio between Montgomery Asset Management and Rothschild, which are free to choose stocks from anywhere around the globe. Each has its relative strengths and offers diversification for unitholders. A first-quartile performer in 1995 and 1996, the fund fell to third quartile in 1997 and has climbed back to the second quartile for the nine months ended September 30, 1998. This fund is highly diversified, so no single position or industry weighting can torpedo the net asset value. Despite our endorsement of the fund since its launch, it still has only $126 million. Smart Fund 1998, 1997, 1996

RISK

How Often Money Was Lost: ......10 of 45 Months
....8 of 43 Quarters
....1 of 34 Rolling 12 Months
Worst 3 Months:.............................-14.55% (1998)
Best 3 Months:...................................17.84% (1995)

ASSET ALLOCATION

USA...27.8%
Asia..4.4%
Europe.......................................51.3%
Japan..7.6%
Eastern Europe........................2.8%
Other..6.1%

COMPARISON OF FUND TO INDEXES

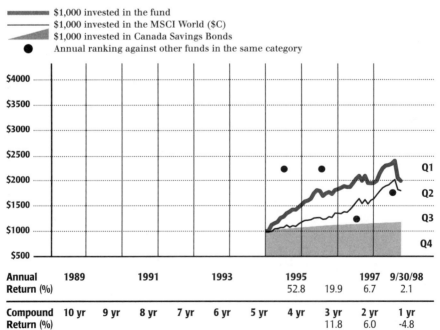

■■■■■ $1,000 invested in the fund
———— $1,000 invested in the MSCI World ($C)
◢◣ $1,000 invested in Canada Savings Bonds
● Annual ranking against other funds in the same category

Annual Return (%)	1989		1991		1993		1995		1997	9/30/98
							52.8	19.9	6.7	2.1

Compound Return (%)	10 yr	9 yr	8 yr	7 yr	6 yr	5 yr	4 yr	3 yr	2 yr	1 yr
								11.8	6.0	-4.8

GLOBAL EQUITY

IVY FOREIGN EQUITY

LOAD

Primary Objective:	Growth
Sponsor:	Mackenzie Financial
Fund Manager:	Bill Kanko since 6/97
Style:	Bottom-up, Growth
Size (MMs):	$1,097.026
RRSP:	20%
Management Expense Ratio:	2.33% (Average: 2.33%)

COMMENTS

Bill Kanko learned his craft working with Bob Krembil managing the Trimark Fund in the early 1990s. He is using the same management style he learned at Trimark—buying businesses poised to grow. While his mandate is global, like the Trimark Fund, this fund will concentrate on companies domiciled in major markets that derive significant revenues internationally. The fund is highly concentrated, holding 30 to 40 securities. Mackenzie recently merged Kanko's old Universal Growth Fund into the Ivy fund. Kanko's portion of the track record on this fund is only after mid-1997. Universal Growth was a Smart Fund in 1996

RISK

How Often Money Was Lost: ......17 of 71 Months
....9 of 69 Quarters
....0 of 60 Rolling 12 Months
Worst 3 Months: ....-9.20% (1998)
Best 3 Months: 12.85% (1997)

ASSET ALLOCATION

USA 49.0%
Cash 21.0%
Canada 5.0%
Other 25.0%

COMPARISON OF FUND TO INDEXES

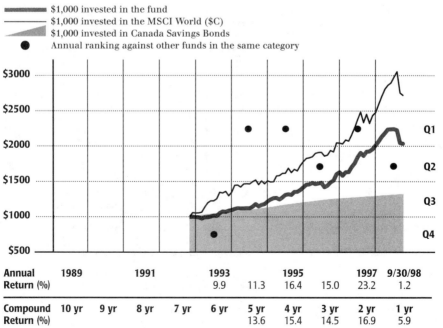

▬▬▬ $1,000 invested in the fund
——— $1,000 invested in the MSCI World ($C)
◣ $1,000 invested in Canada Savings Bonds
● Annual ranking against other funds in the same category

Annual	1989		1991		1993		1995		1997	9/30/98
Return (%)					9.9	11.3	16.4	15.0	23.2	1.2

Compound	10 yr	9 yr	8 yr	7 yr	6 yr	5 yr	4 yr	3 yr	2 yr	1 yr
Return (%)						13.6	15.4	14.5	16.9	5.9

GLOBAL EQUITY

MD GROWTH

Primary Objective:	Growth
Sponsor:	MD Management
Fund Manager:	Templeton Global Advisors
Style:	Bottom-up, Value
Size (MMs):	$3,131.397
RRSP:	20%
Management Expense Ratio:	1.28% (Average: 2.33%)

COMMENTS

Everything said about Templeton Growth Fund applies equally to this fund since it is managed by the Templeton team. The bottom-up, value-oriented stock picks from around the world that comprise the Templeton buy list have provided the performance. A great fund for those in the medical establishment, who can get it at no-load with a 1.28% MER, low volatility and consistent top-quartile returns. Smart Fund 1998, 1997, 1996

RISK

How Often Money Was Lost:....40 of 117 Months
......................................31 of 115 Quarters
....................................17 of 106 Rolling 12 Months
Worst 3 Months: ....-18.37% (1990)
Best 3 Months:....................................17.43% (1993)

ASSET ALLOCATION

Stock...74.0%
Cash 20.7%
Bonds 5.2%

COMPARISON OF FUND TO INDEXES

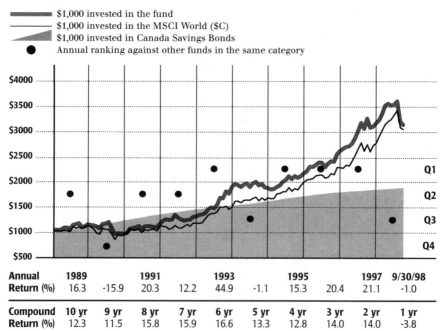

- $1,000 invested in the fund
- $1,000 invested in the MSCI World ($C)
- $1,000 invested in Canada Savings Bonds
- Annual ranking against other funds in the same category

Annual Return (%)	1989		1991		1993		1995		1997	9/30/98
	16.3	-15.9	20.3	12.2	44.9	-1.1	15.3	20.4	21.1	-1.0

Compound Return (%)	10 yr	9 yr	8 yr	7 yr	6 yr	5 yr	4 yr	3 yr	2 yr	1 yr
	12.3	11.5	15.8	15.9	16.6	13.3	12.8	14.0	14.0	-3.8

GLOBAL EQUITY

SCUDDER GLOBAL

Primary Objective:	Growth
Sponsor:	Scudder Canada
Fund Manager:	Nicolas Bratt and William Holzer
Style:	Theme-based, Bottom-up
Size (MMs):	$43.179
RRSP:	20%
Management Expense Ratio:	1.75% (Average: 2.33%)

COMMENTS

Fund has been a first-quartile performer since its inception in Canada in 1995. Holzer is the manager of the same fund in the U.S. This fund has a 10-year record of outperforming the MSCI World Index by a considerable margin. The U.S. fund is ranked five-star by Morningstar. In this fund, country and stock selection is value based and is theme driven with particular emphasis on the impact of aging populations. Holzer will move to bonds if he cannot find value. He hates to overpay for any stock. Fund is carrying a big weighting in financial services stocks in its belief they are poised to do well with baby boomers. Smart Fund 1997, our mistake in dropping it in 1998.

RISK

How Often Money Was Lost	7 of 35 Months
	6 of 33 Quarters
	0 of 24 Rolling 12 Months
Worst 3 Months:	-8.25% (1998)
Best 3 Months:	12.74% (1997)

ASSET ALLOCATION

Financial services	28.0%
Manufacturing	16.8%
Utilities	7.1%
Energy	6.7%
Services	6.7%
Other	34.7%

COMPARISON OF FUND TO INDEXES

- $1,000 invested in the fund
- $1,000 invested in the MSCI World ($C)
- $1,000 invested in Canada Savings Bonds
- Annual ranking against other funds in the same category

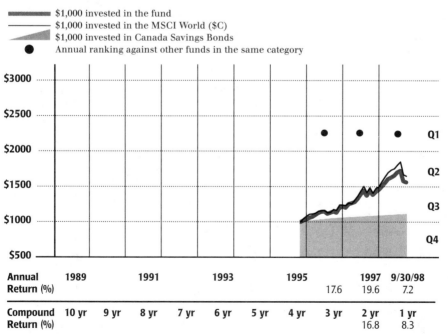

Annual Return (%)	1989		1991		1993		1995		1997	9/30/98
								17.6	19.6	7.2

Compound Return (%)	10 yr	9 yr	8 yr	7 yr	6 yr	5 yr	4 yr	3 yr	2 yr	1 yr
									16.8	8.3

GLOBAL EQUITY

TEMPLETON GROWTH

Primary Objective:	Growth
Sponsor:	Templeton Management
Fund Manager:	Mark Holowesko
Style:	Bottom-up, Value
Size (MMs):	$9,187.964
RRSP:	20%
Management Expense Ratio:	1.97% (Average: 2.33%)

COMMENTS

This perennial winner is everyone's automatic pick for the foreign-content of an RRSP: put it away and leave it there forever. It's a consistent top-quartile performer with a reasonable 1.97% MER and good risk-adjusted performance. Many use the International Stock Fund to eliminate U.S. exposure, which is frequently obtained elsewhere. The fund's large size tells us that just about every Canadian knows about it by now. It is the single largest mutual fund in Canada and has grown by $6 billion since the end of 1995. Its current 4th quarter performance might concern some. Its track record goes back to 1954, so don't let this short-term underperformance worry you. Smart Fund 1998, 1997, 1996

RISK

How Often Money Was Lost:....36 of 117 Months
....27 of 115 Quarters
......................10 of 106 Rolling 12 Months
Worst 3 Months:.............................-20.23% (1990)
Best 3 Months: 15.69% (1992)

ASSET ALLOCATION

USA 25.0%
Hong Kong..................................8.5%
UK...9.6%
Netherlands...............................4.3%
Sweden 4.3%
Other..48.3%

COMPARISON OF FUND TO INDEXES

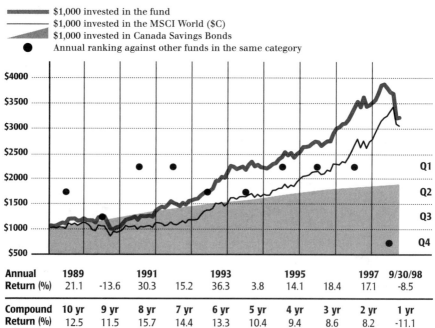

- $1,000 invested in the fund
- $1,000 invested in the MSCI World ($C)
- $1,000 invested in Canada Savings Bonds
- ● Annual ranking against other funds in the same category

Annual Return (%)	1989 21.1	-13.6	1991 30.3	15.2	1993 36.3	3.8	1995 14.1	18.4	1997 17.1	9/30/98 -8.5
Compound **Return (%)**	**10 yr** 12.5	**9 yr** 11.5	**8 yr** 15.7	**7 yr** 14.4	**6 yr** 13.3	**5 yr** 10.4	**4 yr** 9.4	**3 yr** 8.6	**2 yr** 8.2	**1 yr** -11.1

GLOBAL EQUITY

TEMPLETON INTERNATIONAL STOCK   LOAD

Primary Objective:	Growth
Sponsor:	Templeton Management
Fund Manager:	Don Reed
Style:	Bottom-up, Value
Size (MMs):	$5,014.920
RRSP:	20%
Management Expense Ratio:	2.46% (Average: 2.33%)

COMMENTS

Another mainstay from Templeton, this fund is redundant if you already have the Templeton Growth Fund. However, it adds excellent diversification for those who already have significant holdings in North American securities. Manager Don Reed has used the Templeton buy list to achieve first-quartile performance, despite being restricted from the soaring U.S. market. MER of 2.46% is a bit much on a $5 billion fund. Makes you want to own the Franklin Resources stock instead. This one has lagged the other international funds in 1998 and missed out on the huge gains in Europe in early 1998. Smart Fund 1997, 1998

RISK

How Often Money Was Lost:....38 of 116 Months
....28 of 114 Quarters
....................................13 of 105 Rolling 12 Months
Worst 3 Months:.............................-15.34% (1990)
Best 3 Months: 23.43% (1992)

ASSET ALLOCATION

Hong Kong...................................6.0%
France..12.6%
UK 17.0%
Sweden 5.0%
Netherlands.................................5.5%
Other...53.9%

COMPARISON OF FUND TO INDEXES

━━━ $1,000 invested in the fund
——— $1,000 invested in the MSCI World ($C)
▨ $1,000 invested in Canada Savings Bonds
● Annual ranking against other funds in the same category

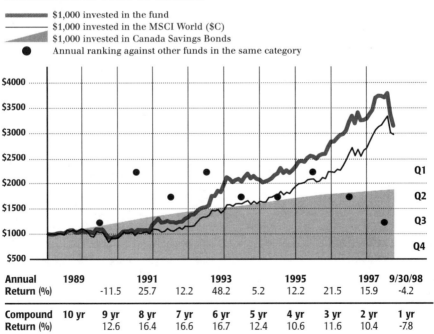

Annual Return (%)	1989		1991		1993		1995		1997	9/30/98
		-11.5	25.7	12.2	48.2	5.2	12.2	21.5	15.9	-4.2

Compound Return (%)	10 yr	9 yr	8 yr	7 yr	6 yr	5 yr	4 yr	3 yr	2 yr	1 yr
		12.6	16.4	16.6	16.7	12.4	10.6	11.6	10.4	-7.8

GLOBAL EQUITY

TRIMARK FUND

LOAD

Primary Objective:	Growth
Sponsor:	Trimark Investment Management
Fund Manager:	Bob Krembil & Angela Eaton
Style:	Bottom-up, Growth
Size (MMs):	$2,479.996
RRSP:	20%
Management Expense Ratio:	1.52% (Average: 2.33%)

COMMENTS

A regular on the Smart Fund list, this one often accompanies Templeton as an automatic foreign-content component of an RRSP. Trimark has been consistent in its investment philosophy of buying great businesses and holding them for five years. The team is led by Bob Krembil, but both Angela Eaton and Richard Jenkins play a big role. This consistent top-quartile performer has modest volatility and a low MER of 1.52%. We used to be nervous about its high exposure to the U.S. market but somehow it missed out on the bull market growth stocks of the past year. Relatively large exposure to Japan has torpedoed the fund of late. The fund has slipped into the fourth quartile during 1998. We feel it would be premature to demote this fund, given its outstanding track record dating back to 1981. Smart Fund 1996, 1997, 1998

RISK

How Often Money Was Lost:	41 of 117 Months
	30 of 115 Quarters
	9 of 106 Rolling 12 Months
Worst 3 Months:	-23.14% (1990)
Best 3 Months:	24.22% (1992)

ASSET ALLOCATION

USA	53.0%
France	2.6%
UK	2.2%
Japan	16.6%
Germany	10.1%
Other	15.5%

COMPARISON OF FUND TO INDEXES

$1,000 invested in the fund
$1,000 invested in the MSCI World ($C)
$1,000 invested in Canada Savings Bonds
● Annual ranking against other funds in the same category

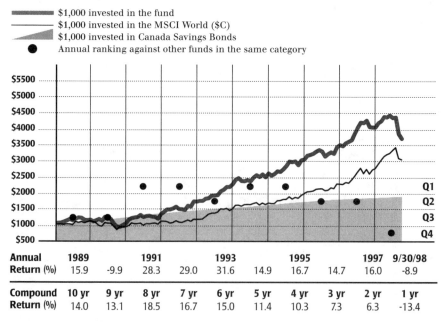

Annual Return (%)	1989		1991		1993		1995		1997	9/30/98
	15.9	-9.9	28.3	29.0	31.6	14.9	16.7	14.7	16.0	-8.9

Compound Return (%)	10 yr	9 yr	8 yr	7 yr	6 yr	5 yr	4 yr	3 yr	2 yr	1 yr
	14.0	13.1	18.5	16.7	15.0	11.4	10.3	7.3	6.3	-13.4

GLOBAL EQUITY

AGF DIVIDEND

Primary Objective:	Conservative Growth
Sponsor:	AGF Funds Inc.
Fund Manager:	Martin Gruber, Connor, Clark & Lunn
Style:	Bottom-up
Size (MMs):	$2,074.031
RRSP:	100%
Management Expense Ratio:	1.87% (Average: 1.93%)

COMMENTS

Dividend funds have been the best asset class over the recent past as investors pour money into conservative equity funds. Martin Gerber and the Connor Clark Lunn team continue their steady performance of first- or second-quartile years. Over the ten-, five-, three- and two-year periods, this fund is in the top quartile in the category. It invests more in high-yielding common stocks, so its volatility will be higher than other funds in the category. For nervous types, this could be a core RRSP holding. Like many funds in the category this has outperformed the TSE300 index, with less risk, for the three years ended June 30, 1998. Smart Fund 1998, 1997

RISK

How Often Money Was Lost:....44 of 117 Months
....32 of 115 Quarters
...................11 of 106 Rolling 12 Months
Worst 3 Months:..............................-18.60% (1998)
Best 3 Months:....................................19.77% (1996)

ASSET ALLOCATION

Financial Services....................19.2%
Industrial products.................13.4%
Oil and gas 11.3%
Utilities 5.1%
Transportation.........................10.2%
Other..40.8%

COMPARISON OF FUND TO INDEXES

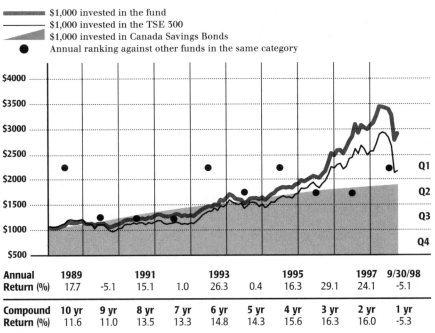

- ▬▬▬ $1,000 invested in the fund
- ——— $1,000 invested in the TSE 300
- ◢ $1,000 invested in Canada Savings Bonds
- ● Annual ranking against other funds in the same category

Annual	1989		1991		1993		1995		1997	9/30/98
Return (%)	17.7	-5.1	15.1	1.0	26.3	0.4	16.3	29.1	24.1	-5.1

Compound	10 yr	9 yr	8 yr	7 yr	6 yr	5 yr	4 yr	3 yr	2 yr	1 yr
Return (%)	11.6	11.0	13.5	13.3	14.8	14.3	15.6	16.3	16.0	-5.3

AIM GT GLOBAL CANADA INCOME CLASS   LOAD

Primary Objective:	Income
Sponsor:	AIM GT Investments
Fund Manager:	Derek Webb
Style:	Bottom-up
Size (MMs):	$774.238
RRSP:	100%
Management Expense Ratio:	2.10% (Average: 1.93%)

COMMENTS

Returns as a Smart Fund primarily for its yield focus. We have again chosen to include it in the dividend fund category, even though some measurement services prefer to classify it as a balanced fund. In the balanced category it is first quartile, but in the dividend category it is third quartile. It is the emphasis on yield that lowers its standing against the likes of AGF Dividend. The fund invests in blue-chip, high-yielding common stocks and is committed to returning a fixed payout of 3.8 cents per unit per month, roughly a 7% yield. Manager Derek Webb writes covered calls against these stocks to generate more income for the unitholders. Smart Fund 1998, 1997

RISK

How Often Money Was Lost: ....9 of 28 Months
....6 of 26 Quarters
....2 of 17 Rolling 12 Months
Worst 3 Months:..............................-20.36% (1998)
Best 3 Months:...................................18.27% (1996)

ASSET ALLOCATION

Financial services....................26.8%
Consumer products................15.0%
Energy.......................................20.0%
Communications.....................12.5%
Real estate 11.4%
Other...14.3%

COMPARISON OF FUND TO INDEXES

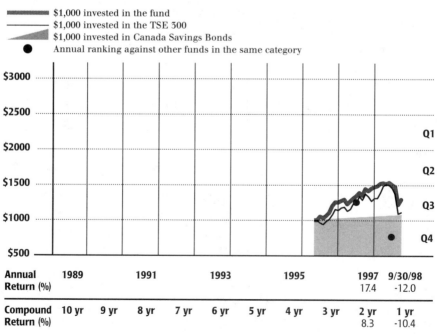

	$1,000 invested in the fund
	$1,000 invested in the TSE 300
	$1,000 invested in Canada Savings Bonds
●	Annual ranking against other funds in the same category

Annual Return (%)	1989	1991	1993	1995	1997	9/30/98
					17.4	-12.0

Compound Return (%)	10 yr	9 yr	8 yr	7 yr	6 yr	5 yr	4 yr	3 yr	2 yr	1 yr
									8.3	-10.4

ALTAMIRA DIVIDEND

NO LOAD

Primary Objective:	Growth & Income
Sponsor:	Altamira Investment Services
Fund Manager:	Ian Joseph and Frances Connelly
Style:	Bottom-up
Size (MMs):	$214.164
RRSP:	100%
Management Expense Ratio:	1.56% (Average: 1.93%)

COMMENTS

Fund started off well as a first-quartile performer in 1995 and made the 1996 Smart Funds list. After tailing off for two years, it has been revitalized and makes its way back to Smart Fund status. Managed by Frances Connelly and Ian Joseph. Holds big weighting in financial stocks and in BCE. MER of 1.56% is more competitive than others in the category. Solid second-quartile returns have outperformed the TSE 300 index with modest volatility. This could be a solid choice for Altamira customers wondering what to do as the once infallible company works on patching up its portfolio management team. Smart Fund 1996.

RISK

How Often Money Was Lost: ......12 of 48 Months
....5 of 46 Quarters
....2 of 37 Rolling 12 Months
Worst 3 Months: ....-19.79% (1998)
Best 3 Months: 14.45% (1997)

ASSET ALLOCATION

Financial services 42.5%
Industrial products 4.9%
Pipelines 4.2%
Utilities 17.8%
Real Estate 6.1%
Other 24.5%

COMPARISON OF FUND TO INDEXES

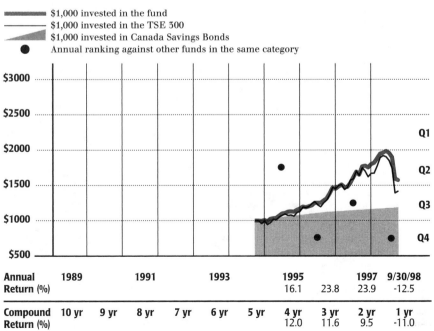

- $1,000 invested in the fund
- $1,000 invested in the TSE 300
- $1,000 invested in Canada Savings Bonds
- ● Annual ranking against other funds in the same category

Annual Return (%)	1989		1991		1993		1995			1997	9/30/98
							16.1	23.8		23.9	-12.5

Compound Return (%)	10 yr	9 yr	8 yr	7 yr	6 yr	5 yr	4 yr	3 yr	2 yr	1 yr
							12.0	11.6	9.5	-11.0

BPI DIVIDEND INCOME

LOAD

Primary Objective:	Income
Sponsor:	BPI Mutual Funds
Fund Manager:	Eric Bushell, since 1/95
Style:	Bottom-up
Size (MMs):	$603.000
RRSP:	100%
Management Expense Ratio:	1.22% (Average: 1.93%)

COMMENTS

This is the most conservative pick in this category, as it is the least volatile. Manager Eric Bushell's focus is more on yield and low volatility than on trying to capture capital gains from common equity holdings. Bushell will hold royalty trust units and preferred shares in high-yielding common stocks. He also tries to manage after-tax returns by minimizing the amount of interest income distributed. The low MER of 1% has increased to 1.22%, as BPI removed the expense cap and began charging the fund's expenses back to unitholders. The fund is committed to making monthly distributions of about 4.5 cents per unit, for a pre-tax yield of 4%. Fund has doubled in size since August 1997. Smart Fund 1998, 1997, 1996

RISK

How Often Money Was Lost:....32 of 117 Months
....22 of 115 Quarters
.....................................12 of 106 Rolling 12 Months
Worst 3 Months:...............................-11.41% (1998)
Best 3 Months: 11.23% (1996)

ASSET ALLOCATION

Preferreds 65.0%
Common 24.0%
Cash 7.0%
REITs 4.0%

COMPARISON OF FUND TO INDEXES

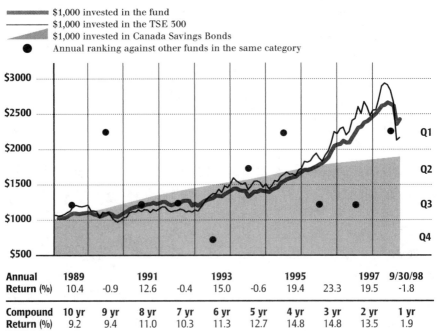

■■■■ $1,000 invested in the fund
──── $1,000 invested in the TSE 300
▨▨▨ $1,000 invested in Canada Savings Bonds
● Annual ranking against other funds in the same category

Annual Return (%)	1989		1991		1993		1995		1997	9/30/98
	10.4	-0.9	12.6	-0.4	15.0	-0.6	19.4	23.3	19.5	-1.8

Compound Return (%)	10 yr	9 yr	8 yr	7 yr	6 yr	5 yr	4 yr	3 yr	2 yr	1 yr
	9.2	9.4	11.0	10.3	11.3	12.7	14.8	14.8	13.5	1.9

BPI HIGH INCOME

LOAD

Primary Objective:	Income
Sponsor:	BPI Mutual Funds
Fund Manager:	Eric Bushell and Ben Cheng
Style:	Bottom-up
Size (MMs):	$266.900
RRSP:	100%
Management Expense Ratio:	1.48% (Average: 1.93%)

COMMENTS

Manager Eric Bushell and the BPI team have recognized the market's demand for yield. Working with co-manager Ben Cheng, Bushell is seeking high yield by investing in royalty trust units, high-yield corporate bonds and real estate investment trusts. All this in a portfolio with an MER of 1.48%. The fund distributes 6 cents per unit per month for those looking for a pre-tax yield of 6.5%. Many of the funds holding royalty trust units have suffered as the market has dropped their NAVs. Still, they yield good after-tax cash flows. Smart Fund 1998

RISK

How Often Money Was Lost: ....7 of 21 Months
....7 of 19 Quarters
....2 of 10 Rolling 12 Months
Worst 3 Months: ....-17.83% (1998)
Best 3 Months:....................................10.75% (1997)

ASSET ALLOCATION

Preferreds......................................6.0%
Cash 6.0%
Royalty trusts.............................23.0%
Corporate bonds 32.0%
Real estate 33.0%

COMPARISON OF FUND TO INDEXES

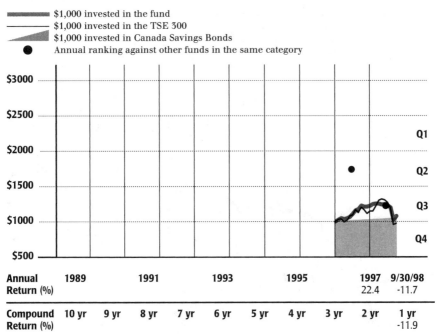

▬▬▬ $1,000 invested in the fund
──── $1,000 invested in the TSE 300
▨ $1,000 invested in Canada Savings Bonds
● Annual ranking against other funds in the same category

Annual Return (%)	1989		1991		1993		1995		1997	9/30/98
									22.4	-11.7

Compound Return (%)	10 yr	9 yr	8 yr	7 yr	6 yr	5 yr	4 yr	3 yr	2 yr	1 yr
										-11.9

BISSETT DIVIDEND INCOME

NO LOAD

Primary Objective:	Total Return
Sponsor:	Bissett & Associates
Fund Manager:	Fred Pynn since 12/91
Style:	Bottom-up
Size (MMs):	$45.321
RRSP:	100%
Management Expense Ratio:	1.50% (Average: 1.93%)

COMMENTS

Last year's Smart Fund Manager of the Year, Fred Pynn (see profile on page 27) has posted solid returns in an asset class that is increasingly sought by yield-hungry Canadians. The fund has been either first or second quartile every year since 1993. It invests in high-yielding common equities, preferred stocks and some U.S. stocks. The modest MER of 1.5% and the reasonable volatility make this a solid conservative fund for many investors. Solid compound returns have been generated with a standard deviation (measure of volatility) 30% less than most equity funds. The fund pays its modest 10 cent distribution only quarterly, so it is less attractive for those dependent on the yield. Smart Fund 1998

RISK

How Often Money Was Lost: ....37 of 117 Months
....28 of 115 Quarters
.....................................13 of 106 Rolling 12 Months
Worst 3 Months:..............................-14.50% (1998)
Best 3 Months: 16.72% (1996)

ASSET ALLOCATION

Financial services....................13.8%
Preferred shares......................26.3%
Pipelines...................................5.4%
Utilities 8.1%
Bonds 6.2%
Other..40.2%

COMPARISON OF FUND TO INDEXES

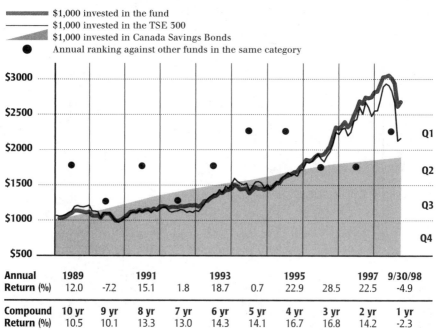

▬▬▬ $1,000 invested in the fund
——— $1,000 invested in the TSE 300
▨ $1,000 invested in Canada Savings Bonds
● Annual ranking against other funds in the same category

Annual	1989		1991		1993		1995		1997	9/30/98
Return (%)	12.0	-7.2	15.1	1.8	18.7	0.7	22.9	28.5	22.5	-4.9

Compound	10 yr	9 yr	8 yr	7 yr	6 yr	5 yr	4 yr	3 yr	2 yr	1 yr
Return (%)	10.5	10.1	13.3	13.0	14.3	14.1	16.7	16.8	14.2	-2.3

FIRST CANADIAN DIVIDEND FUND NO LOAD

Primary Objective:	Conservative Growth
Sponsor:	First Canadian Funds
Fund Manager:	Michael Stanley, Jones Heward Investment Counsel
Style:	Bottom-up
Size (MMs):	$1,043.425
RRSP:	100%
Management Expense Ratio:	1.67% (Average: 1.93%)

COMMENTS

Another conservatively managed blue-chip equity fund that generates a yield and still gives the investor an opportunity for capital gains. Bank clients seem to have caught on to this gem. The fund continues to grow rapidly growing from $470 million in last year's edition to more than $1.0 billion as of September 30, 1998. The reasonable 1.67% MER, no-load status, convenience of Bank of Montreal and the first-quartile performance add up to a compelling story. This could be your primary RRSP holding in the First Canadian family. We will not speculate on what happens to the Royal Dividend Fund (also a Smart Fund) and this fund if the Royal-BMO mega-merger is allowed but hopefully all MERs would be reduced. Smart Fund 1998

RISK

How Often Money Was Lost:.......11 of 47 Months
....5 of 45 Quarters
....0 of 36 Rolling 12 Months
Worst 3 Months:.............................-22.13% (1998)
Best 3 Months: 19.83% (1996)

ASSET ALLOCATION

Interest sensitives....................61.6%
Industrial products..................10.2%
Resources.................................8.9%
Consumer products................10.2%
Cash 9.1%

COMPARISON OF FUND TO INDEXES

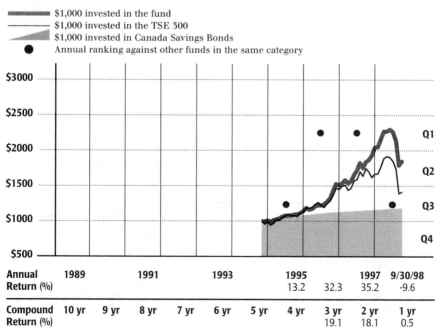

- $1,000 invested in the fund
- $1,000 invested in the TSE 300
- $1,000 invested in Canada Savings Bonds
- ● Annual ranking against other funds in the same category

Annual Return (%)	1989	1991	1993	1995		1997	9/30/98
				13.2	32.3	35.2	-9.6

Compound Return (%)	10 yr	9 yr	8 yr	7 yr	6 yr	5 yr	4 yr	3 yr	2 yr	1 yr
								19.1	18.1	0.5

MAXXUM DIVIDEND FUND OF CANADA   LOAD

Primary Objective:	Conservative Growth
Sponsor:	London Fund Management
Fund Manager:	Jackee Pratt, since 5/95
Style:	Bottom-up
Size (MMs):	$218.608
RRSP:	100%
Management Expense Ratio:	1.73% (Average 1.93%)

COMMENTS

This top-performing dividend fund traditionally had more volatility than the others in its peer group. This is now Jackee Pratt's fund and the three-year track record is hers. Veronika Hirsch's legacy exists only on the performance numbers prior to 1995. Ms. Pratt has led the fund to first-quartile performance in 1995 and 1997. She has also made it more conservative: it now has a lower three-year standard deviation than PH&N, AGF, First Canadian and Royal, all Smart Funds. Fund holds big weightings in the banks and BCE and carries a 1.73% MER. Smart Fund 1998, 1997

RISK

How Often Money Was Lost: ....44 of 117 Months
.....................................30 of 115 Quarters
....................................17 of 106 Rolling 12 Months
Worst 3 Months: ....-21.77% (1998)
Best 3 Months: 16.30% (1996)

ASSET ALLOCATION

Canadian equities 87.4%
US equities...................................6.3%
Preferreds.....................................4.1%
Debentures 0.4%
Cash 1.8%

COMPARISON OF FUND TO INDEXES

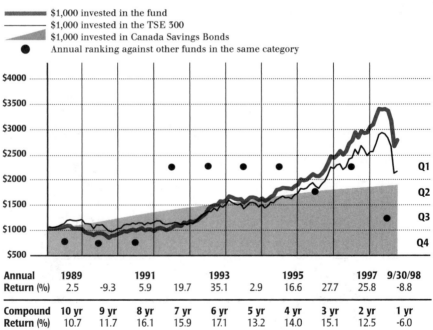

- $1,000 invested in the fund
- $1,000 invested in the TSE 300
- $1,000 invested in Canada Savings Bonds
- ● Annual ranking against other funds in the same category

Annual	1989		1991		1993		1995		1997	9/30/98
Return (%)	2.5	-9.3	5.9	19.7	35.1	2.9	16.6	27.7	25.8	-8.8

Compound	10 yr	9 yr	8 yr	7 yr	6 yr	5 yr	4 yr	3 yr	2 yr	1 yr
Return (%)	10.7	11.7	16.1	15.9	17.1	13.2	14.0	15.1	12.5	-6.0

PH&N DIVIDEND INCOME

Primary Objective:	Conservative Growth
Sponsor:	Phillips, Hager & North Investment Mgmt
Fund Manager:	Team
Style:	Bottom-up
Size (MMs):	$549.878
RRSP:	100%
Management Expense Ratio:	1.21% (Average: 1.93%)

COMMENTS

Always near the top of the class, this is another solid PH&N low-MER, top-quartile performer. If we sound like a broken record on PH&N, forgive us. This is the number one fund in the category for ten-, five-, three-, two- and one-year compounded periods ended September 30, 1998. It's a shame most brokers and planners cannot distribute it. You have to buy this on your own, with a $25,000 minimum (less inside an RRSP). This provides some uniqueness, as it is now 33% weighted to the pipelines and utilities. There are no phone companies in the top 10, but four of the big five banks are there. Smart Fund 1998, 1997, 1996

RISK

How Often Money Was Lost: ....34 of 117 Months
....27 of 115 Quarters
.....................................10 of 106 Rolling 12 Months
Worst 3 Months: ....-21.56% (1998)
Best 3 Months: 20.33% (1996)

ASSET ALLOCATION

Financial services...................27.8%
Cash 8.6%
Pipelines.......................................32.6%
Conglomerates............................9.8%
Oil and gas..................................6.5%
Other..14.7%

COMPARISON OF FUND TO INDEXES

- $1,000 invested in the fund
- $1,000 invested in the TSE 300
- $1,000 invested in Canada Savings Bonds
- ● Annual ranking against other funds in the same category

Annual	1989		1991		1993		1995		1997	9/30/98
Return (%)	21.8	-6.0	15.6	-0.9	28.0	1.3	13.9	33.3	44.5	-7.4

Compound	10 yr	9 yr	8 yr	7 yr	6 yr	5 yr	4 yr	3 yr	2 yr	1 yr
Return (%)	13.4	12.6	15.8	15.9	17.8	17.3	19.6	23.0	24.0	1.6

ROYAL DIVIDEND

CANADIAN DIVIDEND FUNDS

Primary Objective:	Conservative Growth
Sponsor:	Royal Mutual Funds
Fund Manager:	John Kellett
Style:	Bottom-up
Size (MMs):	$1,863.964
RRSP:	100%
Management Expense Ratio:	1.77% (Average: 1.93%)

COMMENTS

Most dividend funds have been on a roll since 1996, but this merged survivor of RoyFund Dividend and Royal Trust Growth and Income Fund did better than most. Manager John Kellett has rewarded bank clients with more than just a top-quartile fund. It is the number two fund over the five-year period ended September 30th. This may be the best choice for many Royal Bank "GIC refugees" outside their RRSPs, where dividends get preferential tax treatment. This is a blue-chip equity fund composed mostly of good dividend-paying common stocks like the banks, BCE and the pipelines. The fund's MER of 1.77% could be lowered, now that the fund has approximately $2 billion in assets. Smart Fund 1996, 1998

RISK

How Often Money Was Lost:	19 of 68 Months
	10 of 66 Quarters
	4 of 57 Rolling 12 Months
Worst 3 Months:	-20.29% (1998)
Best 3 Months:	22.32% (1996)

ASSET ALLOCATION

Financial services	33.5%
Bonds	18.7%
Pipelines	9.2%
Utilities	13.7%
Preferreds	4.2%
Other	20.7%

COMPARISON OF FUND TO INDEXES

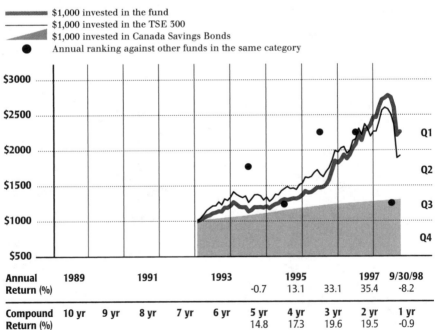

- $1,000 invested in the fund
- $1,000 invested in the TSE 300
- $1,000 invested in Canada Savings Bonds
- Annual ranking against other funds in the same category

Annual Return (%)	1989		1991		1993		1995		1997	9/30/98
						-0.7	13.1	33.1	35.4	-8.2

Compound Return (%)	10 yr	9 yr	8 yr	7 yr	6 yr	5 yr	4 yr	3 yr	2 yr	1 yr
						14.8	17.3	19.6	19.5	-0.9

DYNAMIC EUROPE

Primary Objective:	Growth
Sponsor:	Dundee Mutual Funds
Fund Manager:	Joe Evershed
Style:	Bottom-up, Value
Size (MMs):	$295.956
RRSP:	20%
Management Expense Ratio:	2.50% (Average: 2.35%)

COMMENTS

This is the third best performing fund in the category over five years as well as a first-quartile performer over the same compounded period. Manager Joe Evershed has proven you don't need to reside in Europe to outperform your peer group. He finds some eclectic names that don't appear on most of the conservative large-cap lists. That is why this fund tends to be the most volatile of our Smart Fund European choices. Fund has doubled in the last 12 months as this has been one of the few strong points of Dundee funds over the past couple of years. Smart Fund 1998

RISK

How Often Money Was Lost: ....42 of 107 Months
....34 of 105 Quarters
....27 of 96 Rolling 12 Months
Worst 3 Months:..............................-19.88% (1998)
Best 3 Months: 29.53% (1998)

ASSET ALLOCATION

Sweden 15.4%
Finland 13.0%
UK..6.7%
Switzerland................................6.4%
Spain 5.4%
Other..53.1%

EUROPEAN EQUITY

COMPARISON OF FUND TO INDEXES

- $1,000 invested in the fund
- $1,000 invested in the MSCI Europe ($C)
- $1,000 invested in Canada Savings Bonds
- ● Annual ranking against other funds in the same category

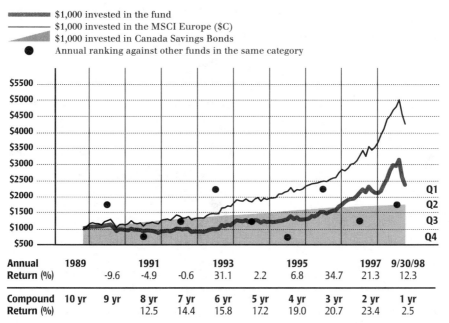

Annual Return (%)	1989		1991		1993		1995		1997	9/30/98
		-9.6	-4.9	-0.6	31.1	2.2	6.8	34.7	21.3	12.3

Compound Return (%)	10 yr	9 yr	8 yr	7 yr	6 yr	5 yr	4 yr	3 yr	2 yr	1 yr
			12.5	14.4	15.8	17.2	19.0	20.7	23.4	2.5

FIDELITY EUROPEAN GROWTH

LOAD

Primary Objective:	Growth
Sponsor:	Fidelity Investments Canada
Fund Manager:	Sally Walden and Thierry Serero
Style:	Bottom-up, Growth
Size (MMs):	$2,047.292
RRSP:	20%
Management Expense Ratio:	2.70% (Average: 2.35%)

COMMENTS

Sally Walden returns with her co-manager Thierry Serero. Mr. Serero is taking on more day-to-day management while Ms. Walden takes on the role of Chief Investment Officer. The fund is managed through Fidelity's London office, with more than 50 analysts to support Walden, typical of the vaunted Fidelity research staff. This is the largest buy-side research team in Europe. A solid fund, with outstanding risk-adjusted returns that put it at the head of the class, that has never returned less than 10% since it opened in 1993. With a six-year CAGR of 18.7%, why buy emerging markets or Asia? As the largest fund in the category, Fidelity should be able to bring down the stiff MER. Smart Fund 1998, 1997, 1996

RISK

How Often Money Was Lost: ......21 of 76 Months
....14 of 74 Quarters
....0 of 65 Rolling 12 Months
Worst 3 Months:................................-13.49% (1998)
Best 3 Months: 18.52% (1998)

ASSET ALLOCATION

France...13.0%
Germany 12.4%
UK 30.3%
Switzerland 11.6%
Italy 6.7%
Other..26.0%

COMPARISON OF FUND TO INDEXES

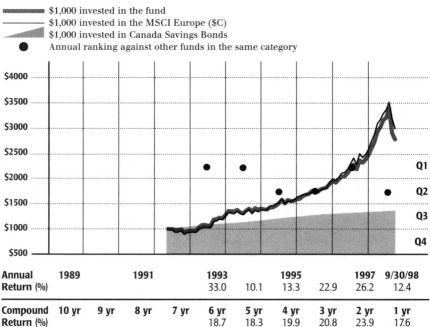

$1,000 invested in the fund
$1,000 invested in the MSCI Europe ($C)
$1,000 invested in Canada Savings Bonds
● Annual ranking against other funds in the same category

Annual Return (%)	1989		1991		1993		1995		1997	9/30/98
					33.0	10.1	13.3	22.9	26.2	12.4

Compound Return (%)	10 yr	9 yr	8 yr	7 yr	6 yr	5 yr	4 yr	3 yr	2 yr	1 yr
					18.7	18.3	19.9	20.8	23.9	17.6

UNIVERSAL EUROPEAN OPPORTUNITIES **LOAD**

Primary Objective:	Growth
Sponsor:	Mackenzie Financial
Fund Manager:	Stephen Peak, Henderson Administration
Style:	Bottom-up, Growth with small caps
Size (MMs):	$810.183
RRSP:	20%
Management Expense Ratio:	2.43% (Average: 2.35%)

COMMENTS

Now in its fourth year as a Smart Fund, it may just be eligible for some rival buyer guides. Stephen Peak managed the fund to the top of the category in both 1995 and 1996. Focusing on small-cap situations in developed Europe and large-caps in emerging Europe, it has suffered as those stocks that soared so much the year before have since given up some of their gains. A recognized authority in European small-cap investing, Peak has more than 20 years experience. This fund has almost doubled to about $900 million since July 1997. Henderson Administration, based in London, has been around since 1934. Smart Fund 1998, 1997, 1996

RISK

How Often Money Was Lost: ....9 of 48 Months
....3 of 46 Quarters
..........................0 of 37 Rolling 12 Months
Worst 3 Months: ....-15.48% (1998)
Best 3 Months: 23.03% (1998)

ASSET ALLOCATION

Germany	13.0%
France	15.0%
UK	29.0%
Western Europe	22.0%
Italy	6.0%
Other	15.0%

COMPARISON OF FUND TO INDEXES

$1,000 invested in the fund
$1,000 invested in the MSCI Europe ($C)
$1,000 invested in Canada Savings Bonds
● Annual ranking against other funds in the same category

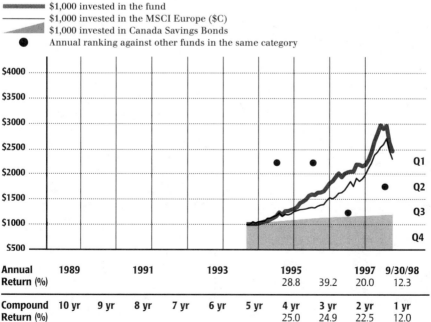

Annual Return (%)	1989		1991		1993		1995		1997	9/30/98
							28.8	39.2	20.0	12.3

Compound Return (%)	10 yr	9 yr	8 yr	7 yr	6 yr	5 yr	4 yr	3 yr	2 yr	1 yr
							25.0	24.9	22.5	12.0

EUROPEAN EQUITY

C.I. EMERGING MARKETS

LOAD

Primary Objective:	Aggressive Growth
Sponsor:	CI Mutual Funds
Fund Manager:	Nandu Narayanan, BEA Associates (since 1/97)
Style:	Top-down
Size (MMs):	$199.123
RRSP:	20%
Management Expense Ratio:	2.74% (Average: 2.83%)

COMMENTS

In January 1997, Nandu Narayanan replaced Emilio Bassini and produced a dramatic turnaround to pull this consistent third-quartile performer into the first quartile for 1997 and for the year-to-date 1998. Remember, that is first quartile on a category that lost an average of 26% for the year ended June 30, 1998. Now is when we look at absolute returns and forget about relative returns. Because it lost just 20% of your money for the last year, ended September 30, 1998, this fund was ranked number two in the Emerging Markets category. Moving to cash and avoiding much of the Asian collapse helped save it from having its NAV completely torpedoed. Now holds many of the telephone utilities around the emerging market countries.

RISK

How Often Money Was Lost: ......28 of 84 Months
....33 of 82 Quarters
.....................................22 of 73 Rolling 12 Months
Worst 3 Months: ....-25.43% (1995)
Best 3 Months: 30.49% (1993)

ASSET ALLOCATION

Mexico 11.3%
India 8.8%
Brazil...6.4%
Russia 5.8%
Cash 37.4%
Other 30.3%

COMPARISON OF FUND TO INDEXES

- $1,000 invested in the fund
- $1,000 invested in the TSE 300
- $1,000 invested in Canada Savings Bonds
- Annual ranking against other funds in the same category

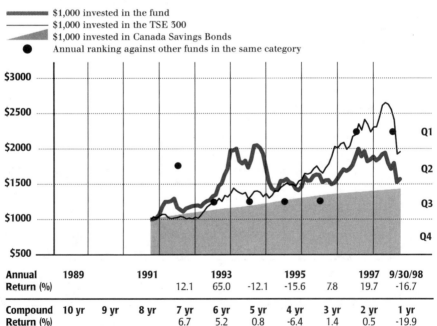

Annual Return (%)	1989		1991		1993		1995		1997	9/30/98
				12.1	65.0	-12.1	-15.6	7.8	19.7	-16.7

Compound Return (%)	10 yr	9 yr	8 yr	7 yr	6 yr	5 yr	4 yr	3 yr	2 yr	1 yr
				6.7	5.2	0.8	-6.4	1.4	0.5	-19.9

SCUDDER EMERGING MARKETS NO LOAD

Primary Objective:	Aggressive Growth
Sponsor:	Scudder Canada Investor Services
Fund Manager:	Joyce Cornell
Style:	Bottom-up
Size (MMs):	$13.899
RRSP:	20%
Management Expense Ratio:	2.40% (Average: 2.83%)

COMMENTS

When Scudder came to Canada we predicted it would make its mark with its international expertise. Manager Joyce Cornell has been well recognized by the U.S. media. This fund is first quartile in a category that has suffered deep losses. Somehow, Ms. Cornell generated returns of 44% in 1996 followed by 10% in 1997. The fund also sports an MER of 2.40%, which is low for the category. It has more exposure to Eastern Europe than the competing Smart Funds in the category. Smart Fund 1998

RISK

How Often Money Was Lost: ......12 of 35 Months

....10 of 33 Quarters

..................................9 of 24 Rolling 12 Months

Worst 3 Months:.............................-16.55% (1998)

Best 3 Months: 24.43% (1996)

ASSET ALLOCATION

Poland...13.0%

Mexico..11.0%

Egypt...11.0%

Brazil..8.0%

Hungary 8.0%

Other...49.0%

COMPARISON OF FUND TO INDEXES

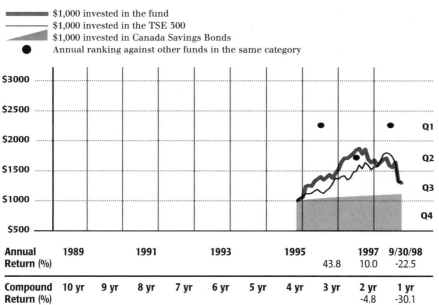

- $1,000 invested in the fund
- $1,000 invested in the TSE 300
- $1,000 invested in Canada Savings Bonds
- ● Annual ranking against other funds in the same category

Annual Return (%)	1989		1991		1993		1995		1997	9/30/98
								43.8	10.0	-22.5

Compound Return (%)	10 yr	9 yr	8 yr	7 yr	6 yr	5 yr	4 yr	3 yr	2 yr	1 yr
									-4.8	-30.1

SPECIAL EQUITY

TEMPLETON EMERGING MARKETS <small>LOAD</small>

Primary Objective: Aggressive Growth
Sponsor: Templeton Management Limited
Fund Manager: Mark Mobius, PhD
Style: Bottom-up
Size (MMs): $611.725
RRSP: 20%
Management Expense Ratio: 3.33% (Average: 2.83%)

COMMENTS
From the guru Mark Mobius, who literally wrote the book on emerging market investing. The 3.33% MER goes a long way to support Dr. Mobius's private plane, which scours the planet looking for emerging market bargains. We are not sure if there are any emerging-market investors still standing after enduring a 44% collapse for the 12 months ended September 30 that brought their CAGR for three years to below treasury bill levels. At least you get country diversification with an emerging markets fund but the ride can be a bumpy one. This fund has lost money in 40% of its months so the ride may not be appropriate for everyone. Templeton Growth may be a more palatable alternative with just a small dose of emerging-markets exposure. Smart Fund 1998, 1997, 1996

RISK

How Often Money Was Lost: ......33 of 83 Months
....31 of 81 Quarters
..............................27 of 72 Rolling 12 Months
Worst 3 Months: ....-28.19% (1998)
Best 3 Months: 21.37% (1993)

ASSET ALLOCATION

Brazil 12.4%
Mexico 10.1%
Turkey..6.7%
Hong Kong....................................6.3%
India 4.0%
Other...60.5%

COMPARISON OF FUND TO INDEXES

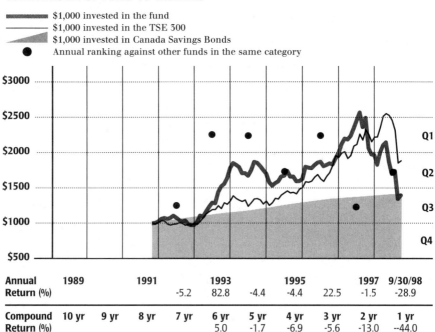

— $1,000 invested in the fund
— $1,000 invested in the TSE 300
— $1,000 invested in Canada Savings Bonds
● Annual ranking against other funds in the same category

Annual Return (%)	1989		1991		1993		1995		1997	9/30/98
			-5.2	82.8	-4.4	-4.4	22.5	-1.5	-28.9

Compound Return (%)	10 yr	9 yr	8 yr	7 yr	6 yr	5 yr	4 yr	3 yr	2 yr	1 yr
					5.0	-1.7	-6.9	-5.6	-13.0	-44.0

AIC ADVANTAGE I OR II

Primary Objective:	Growth
Sponsor:	AIC Limited
Fund Manager:	Jonathan Wellum
Style:	Bottom-up
Size (MMs):	$2,321.221
RRSP:	100%
Management Expense Ratio:	2.31% (Average: 2.93%)

COMMENTS

Jonathan Wellum has had a long-time investment theme that focuses on the business of wealth management. Our advice is to hang on for the long run and ride out the interim dips. This is the number one fund in the Canadian mutual fund industry for the 10 years ended September 30, 1998. Smart Fund (either I or II) 1998, 1997, 1996

RISK

How Often Money Was Lost:....39 of 117 Months
....37 of 115 Quarters
.............................22 of 106 Rolling 12 Months
Worst 3 Months:..............................-25.09% (1998)
Best 3 Months:.................................28.88% (1997)

ASSET ALLOCATION

Financial services....................64.4%
Communications......................9.3%
Consumer products..................8.2%
Gold and metals.......................7.6%
Other..10.5%

COMPARISON OF FUND TO INDEXES

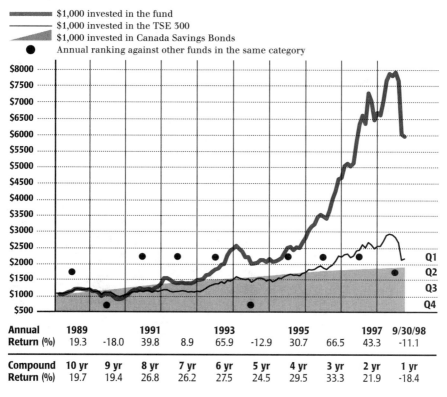

- $1,000 invested in the fund
- $1,000 invested in the TSE 300
- $1,000 invested in Canada Savings Bonds
- ● Annual ranking against other funds in the same category

Annual	1989		1991		1993		1995		1997	9/30/98
Return (%)	19.3	-18.0	39.8	8.9	65.9	-12.9	30.7	66.5	43.3	-11.1

Compound	10 yr	9 yr	8 yr	7 yr	6 yr	5 yr	4 yr	3 yr	2 yr	1 yr
Return (%)	19.7	19.4	26.8	26.2	27.5	24.5	29.5	33.3	21.9	-18.4

SPECIAL EQUITY

AIM GLOBAL HEALTH SCIENCES LOAD

Primary Objective:	Aggressive Growth
Sponsor:	AIM GT Investments
Fund Manager:	John Schroer and Carol Werther, Invesco
Style:	Industry Sector, Bottom-up
Size (MMs):	$339.091
RRSP:	20%
Management Expense Ratio:	2.94% (Average: 2.93%)

COMMENTS

This is the number-two fund in the Canadian industry (behind AIC Advantage) for the five years ended June 30, 1998. But no one seems to notice. It has only about $300 million in it. Not well promoted and poorly supported by the broker/dealer network, it shows the importance of sales and marketing in this industry. The fund's parent has assets over US$1.1 billion and is rated 4-Star by Morningstar. This fund is a good way to participate in the growth of the health care industry. John Schroer has been actively involved since its inception. He has moved heavily into the large blue-chip pharmaceuticals and is rewarded with a performance bonus if the results exceed a recognized benchmark. This has always been our top health care pick. Smart Fund 1998, 1997, 1996

RISK

How Often Money Was Lost: ......23 of 71 Months
....13 of 69 Quarters
..........................2 of 60 Rolling 12 Months
Worst 3 Months: ....-12.66% (1993)
Best 3 Months: 29.77% (1993)

ASSET ALLOCATION

USA 81.1%
Switzerland..................................1.6%
UK..7.9%
Other 9.4%

COMPARISON OF FUND TO INDEXES

$1,000 invested in the fund
$1,000 invested in the TSE 300
$1,000 invested in Canada Savings Bonds
● Annual ranking against other funds in the same category

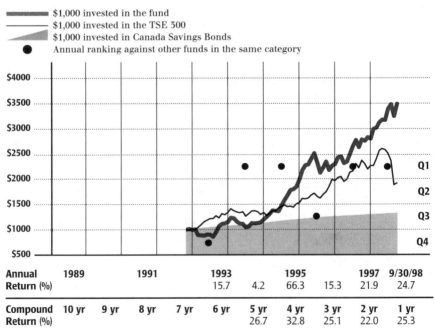

Annual Return (%)	1989		1991		1993		1995		1997	9/30/98
					15.7	4.2	66.3	15.3	21.9	24.7

Compound Return (%)	10 yr	9 yr	8 yr	7 yr	6 yr	5 yr	4 yr	3 yr	2 yr	1 yr
						26.7	32.8	25.1	22.0	25.3

SPECIAL EQUITY

AIM GLOBAL TECHNOLOGY

LOAD

Primary Objective:	Aggressive Growth
Sponsor:	AIM GT Investments
Fund Manager:	Dan Leonard and Gerard Hallaren, Invesco
Style:	Bottom-up
Size (MMs):	$37.064
RRSP:	20%
Management Expense Ratio:	2.94% (Average: 2.93%)

COMMENTS

This is still relatively new for Canada, but is essentially a clone of a top-performing U.S. fund. Manager Dan Leonard has burst out of the gates since its launch with first-quartile performance in 1997 and second so far in 1998. This fund could be bought in combination with AIM's Global Health Sciences fund, to give an investor exposure to the biggest growth areas in North America. These are foreign-content funds, so manage your RRSP accordingly. Contrary to what you might think for a tech fund, Microsoft, Cisco and Dell are not in the top 10 holdings. Smart Fund 1998

RISK

How Often Money Was Lost: ....8 of 22 Months
....6 of 20 Quarters
.........................2 of 11 Rolling 12 Months
Worst 3 Months:..............................-14.86% (1998)
Best 3 Months:..................................25.23% (1997)

ASSET ALLOCATION

Software 38.6%
Hardware..................................20.1%
Cash 18.0%
Communications....................12.8%
Electronics..................................4.4%
Other 6.1%

COMPARISON OF FUND TO INDEXES

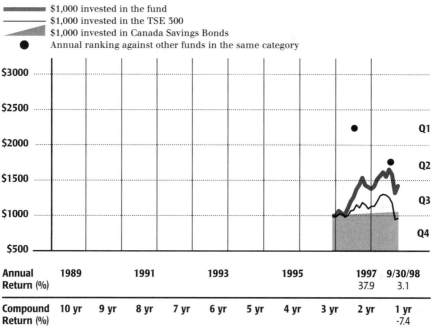

$1,000 invested in the fund
$1,000 invested in the TSE 300
$1,000 invested in Canada Savings Bonds
● Annual ranking against other funds in the same category

Annual Return (%)	1989		1991		1993		1995		1997	9/30/98
									37.9	3.1

Compound Return (%)	10 yr	9 yr	8 yr	7 yr	6 yr	5 yr	4 yr	3 yr	2 yr	1 yr
										-7.4

SPECIAL EQUITY

AIM GT GLOBAL TELECOMMUNICATIONS CLASS LOAD

Primary Objective:	Aggressive Growth
Sponsor:	AIM GT Investments
Fund Manager:	Michael Mahoney
Style:	Bottom-up
Size (MMs):	$363.855
RRSP:	20%
Management Expense Ratio:	2.78% (Average: 2.93%)

COMMENTS

GT Global has lost some managers on previous Smart Funds and has been taken over by AIM, but Michael Maloney remains as one of the largest telecommunications fund managers in the world. He manages this $365 million fund for Canadians, which is a virtual clone of the US$950 billion American version. Although hit with some under-performance in the spring of 1997, this fund and its mandate still seem solid. The Canadian fund has been first quartile in the highly mixed specialty category that includes resource funds. The U.S. version only garners one star from the U.S. rating service Morningstar. When completely integrated into the AIM family you may find you can move across all of these specialty funds in the highest growth sectors in the world: health care, technology and telecommunications. Smart Fund 1998, 1997, 1996

RISK

How Often Money Was Lost:.......16 of 47 Months
....13 of 45 Quarters
....7 of 36 Rolling 12 Months
Worst 3 Months: ....-20.97% (1998)
Best 3 Months:...................................29.94% (1997)

ASSET ALLOCATION

USA 51.8%
Germany 5.3%
UK...3.9%
Finland 4.3%
Italy 4.2%
Other...30.5%

COMPARISON OF FUND TO INDEXES

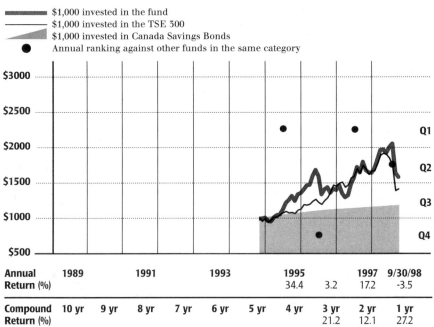

- ▬▬▬ $1,000 invested in the fund
- ─────── $1,000 invested in the TSE 300
- ◥ $1,000 invested in Canada Savings Bonds
- ● Annual ranking against other funds in the same category

Annual Return (%)	1989		1991		1993		1995		1997	9/30/98
							34.4	3.2	17.2	-3.5

Compound Return (%)	10 yr	9 yr	8 yr	7 yr	6 yr	5 yr	4 yr	3 yr	2 yr	1 yr
								21.2	12.1	27.2

SPECIAL EQUITY

ALTAMIRA SCIENCE AND TECHNOLOGY NO LOAD

Primary Objective:	Aggressive Growth
Sponsor:	Altamira Investment Services
Fund Manager:	Ian Ainsworth
Style:	Bottom-up
Size (MMs):	$79.291
RRSP:	20%
Management Expense Ratio:	2.31% (Average: 2.93%)

COMMENTS

Ian Ainsworth has proven up to the task of running a high-tech fund. After leading the Altamira U.S. Larger Companies fund to Smart Fund status he achieves that again with this fund. Hopefully he won't get too stretched with all his duties, as Altamira patches up its portfolio management team. Ainsworth also has responsibility for lead management on the Altamira Equity fund. Investments in Cisco, Microsoft, Intel and AOL have driven returns on this fund to near the absolute top of the specialty category. MER is 2.31%, but then Altamira was never the bargain many people thought it was, despite its no-load status.

RISK

How Often Money Was Lost: ......15 of 37 Months
....9 of 35 Quarters
..........................2 of 26 Rolling 12 Months
Worst 3 Months:..............................-16.03% (1996)
Best 3 Months:...................................26.50% (1997)

ASSET ALLOCATION

Software 29.2%
Communications equipment..19.0%
Semiconductors.........................13.1%
Healthcare 12.5%
Content..8.8%
Other..17.4%

COMPARISON OF FUND TO INDEXES

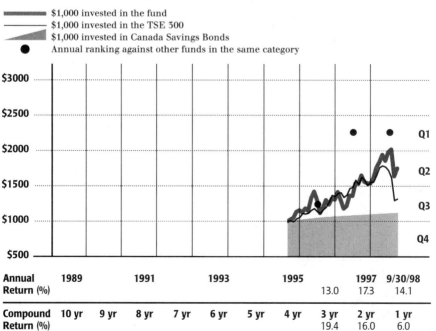

- $1,000 invested in the fund
- $1,000 invested in the TSE 300
- $1,000 invested in Canada Savings Bonds
- Annual ranking against other funds in the same category

Annual Return (%)	1989		1991		1993		1995		1997	9/30/98
								13.0	17.3	14.1

Compound Return (%)	10 yr	9 yr	8 yr	7 yr	6 yr	5 yr	4 yr	3 yr	2 yr	1 yr
								19.4	16.0	6.0

SPECIAL EQUITY

CLARINGTON GLOBAL COMMUNICATIONS LOAD

Primary Objective:	Aggressive Growth
Sponsor:	Clarington Capital Management
Fund Manager:	Oscar Castro, Montgomery Asset Management
Style:	Bottom-up, Growth
Size (MMs):	$36.046
RRSP:	20%
Management Expense Ratio:	2.95%

COMMENTS

Clarington hired former GT Telecom manager Oscar Castro when they contracted Montgomery Asset Management to run their fund. Castro managed GT's fund before Michael Mahoney. Castro, who is often featured in Barron's financial newsweekly, has not disappointed, with a 40% return for the first half of 1998 after a 31% 1997. The sector has been smoking. We don't know where it's going to end up, but we do know that this is the backbone to the ever more omnipresent internet. Smart Fund 1998

RISK

How Often Money Was Lost: ....5 of 21 Months
....5 of 19 Quarters
....0 of 10 Rolling 12 Months
Worst 3 Months: ....-15.13% (1998)
Best 3 Months: 28.95% (1998)

ASSET ALLOCATION

USA 23.6%
Canada...1.9%
Cash 6.2%
Global 68.3%

COMPARISON OF FUND TO INDEXES

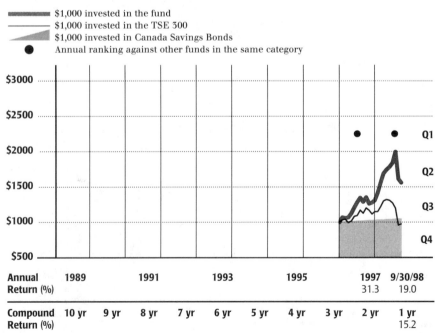

▬▬▬ $1,000 invested in the fund
——— $1,000 invested in the TSE 300
◢ $1,000 invested in Canada Savings Bonds
● Annual ranking against other funds in the same category

Annual Return (%)	1989		1991		1993		1995		1997 31.3	9/30/98 19.0	

Compound Return (%)	10 yr	9 yr	8 yr	7 yr	6 yr	5 yr	4 yr	3 yr	2 yr	1 yr 15.2

SPECIAL EQUITY

DYNAMIC REAL ESTATE EQUITY FUND   LOAD

Primary Objective:	Growth
Sponsor:	Dundee Mutual Funds
Fund Manager:	Anne McLean
Style:	Bottom-up
Size (MMs):	$165.205
RRSP:	20%
Management Expense Ratio:	2.72% (Average: 2.93%)

COMMENTS

Many analysts shied away from real estate after its crash, but Dynamic was prescient in launching this fund and buying real estate equities throughout North America. Lead manager Anne McLean astutely went long on many of the top-performing real estate investment trusts and scored big gains in 1996 and 1997. Fund is number two to AIM Global Health Science in the specialty category for the three-year period ending September 30, 1998. Unlike some of the REITs currently being marketed in Canada, this fund represents an open-end mutual fund redeemable at NAV, but it is also foreign content. As the only real estate fund in our Smart Funds list, it can add income and diversification to a portfolio if you are not overweighted in residential real estate already. Smart Fund 1998, 1997

RISK

How Often Money Was Lost:	11 of 40 Months
	7 of 38 Quarters
	2 of 29 Rolling 12 Months
Worst 3 Months:	-14.15% (1998)
Best 3 Months:	18.94% (1997)

ASSET ALLOCATION

USA	67.4%
Canada	16.9%
Preferreds	6.7%
Cash	5.9%
Foreign	2.0%
Other	1.1%

COMPARISON OF FUND TO INDEXES

▬▬▬ $1,000 invested in the fund
——— $1,000 invested in the TSE 300
▨▨▨ $1,000 invested in Canada Savings Bonds
● Annual ranking against other funds in the same category

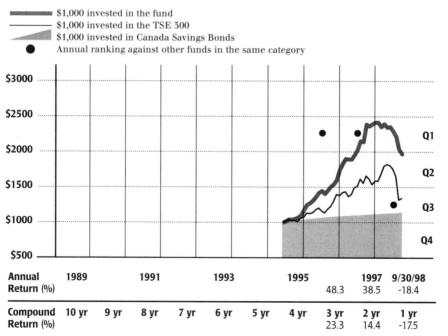

Annual Return (%)	1989		1991		1993		1995		1997	9/30/98
								48.3	38.5	-18.4

Compound Return (%)	10 yr	9 yr	8 yr	7 yr	6 yr	5 yr	4 yr	3 yr	2 yr	1 yr
								23.3	14.4	-17.5

SPECIAL EQUITY

GREEN LINE SCIENCE & TECHNOLOGY NO LOAD

Primary Objective:	Aggressive Growth
Sponsor:	TD Asset Management
Fund Manager:	Charles (Chip) Morris, T.Rowe Price Associates
Style:	Bottom-up, Growth
Size (MMs):	$176.417
RRSP:	20%
Management Expense Ratio:	2.58% (Average: 2.93%)

COMMENTS

We identified this as a Smart Fund in its early days. Manager Charles (Chip) Morris runs one of the largest technology portfolios in the world, the US$3.9 billion T. Rowe Price Science & Technology Fund. You know that T. Rowe Price gets direct access to company managements before most other firms. Technology may be volatile, but it is pervasive in our lives. With a name like "Chip" you wouldn't think Morris would miss out on the chip stocks (semiconductors). He did and has repositioned the fund to capture those and wean out some biotech names. Smart Fund 1998, 1997, 1996

RISK

How Often Money Was Lost: ......23 of 57 Months
....18 of 55 Quarters
....4 of 46 Rolling 12 Months
Worst 3 Months: ....-16.73% (1998)
Best 3 Months: 29.78% (1996)

ASSET ALLOCATION

Technology 88.6%
Information services 3.8%
Cash 2.8%
Other 4.8%

COMPARISON OF FUND TO INDEXES

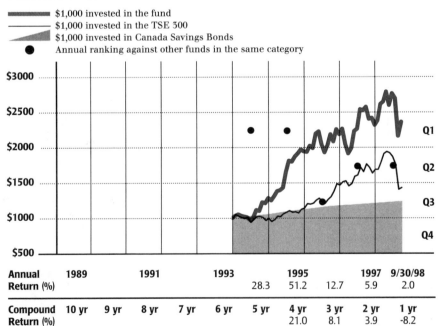

- $1,000 invested in the fund
- $1,000 invested in the TSE 300
- $1,000 invested in Canada Savings Bonds
- ● Annual ranking against other funds in the same category

Annual Return (%)	1989		1991		1993		1995			1997	9/30/98
						28.3	51.2	12.7		5.9	2.0

Compound Return (%)	10 yr	9 yr	8 yr	7 yr	6 yr	5 yr	4 yr	3 yr	2 yr	1 yr
							21.0	8.1	3.9	-8.2

SPECIAL EQUITY

UNIVERSAL WORLD SCIENCE & TECHNOLOGY LOAD

Primary Objective:	Aggressive Growth
Sponsor:	Mackenzie Financial
Fund Manager:	Jim Broadfoot, John Rohr,
	Brian Ashford-Russell
Style:	Bottom-up
Size (MMs):	$201.713
RRSP:	20%
Management Expense Ratio:	2.39% (Average: 2.93%)

COMMENTS

An interesting multi-manager approach to get the best technology ideas from around the world. Jim Broadfoot covers the U.S. small-cap world as manager of former Smart Fund, Universal U.S. Emerging Growth; John Rohr covers large-cap North America as manager of former Smart Fund, Universal Future; and Brian Ashford-Russell covers European names from his offices at Henderson Administration. Launched in September 1996 with an NAV of $5, the fund's NAV at June 30, 1998 was $8.45, for a 69% gain over that period. This one will have more global exposure than Green Line or AIM. There were no U.S. names in the Top 10 as of June 30.

RISK

How Often Money Was Lost: ....8 of 24 Months
....6 of 22 Quarters
....0 of 13 Rolling 12 Months
Worst 3 Months: ....-11.74% (1998)
Best 3 Months:................................24.73% (1997)

ASSET ALLOCATION

Hardware....................................21.0%
Software 14.0%
Services 15.0%
Telecomm 19.0%
Cash 12.0%
Other..19.0%

COMPARISON OF FUND TO INDEXES

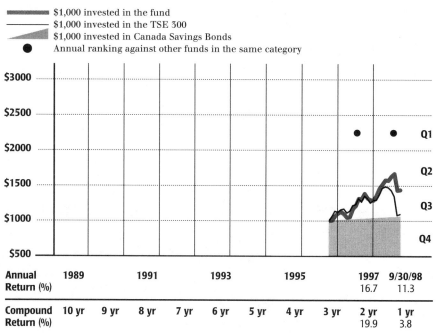

- $1,000 invested in the fund
- $1,000 invested in the TSE 300
- $1,000 invested in Canada Savings Bonds
- ● Annual ranking against other funds in the same category

Annual Return (%)	1989	1991	1993	1995	1997	9/30/98
					16.7	11.3

Compound Return (%)	10 yr	9 yr	8 yr	7 yr	6 yr	5 yr	4 yr	3 yr	2 yr	1 yr
									19.9	3.8

SPECIAL EQUITY

ALTAMIRA BOND

CANADIAN BOND

Primary Objective:	Total Return
Sponsor:	Altamira Investment Services
Fund Manager:	Robert Marcus
Style:	Interest Rate Anticipator
Size (MMs):	$471.363
RRSP:	100%
Management Expense Ratio:	1.30% (Average: 1.61%)

COMMENTS

An aggressive interest-rate anticipator, manager Robert Marcus has managed this to be the number one bond fund over the ten-, five- three-, two, and one- year periods ending June 30, 1998. Fund only invests in AAA credits. Marcus will now take over managing Altamira Income as well. Smart Fund 1998

RISK

How Often Money Was Lost:....36 of 117 Months
....21 of 115 Quarters
....8 of 106 Rolling 12 Months
Worst 3 Months:...............................-10.82% (1994)
Best 3 Months:....................................13.77% (1992)

ASSET ALLOCATION

Short-term 0.8%
Long-term...................................93.7%
Cash 5.5%

COMPARISON OF FUND TO INDEXES

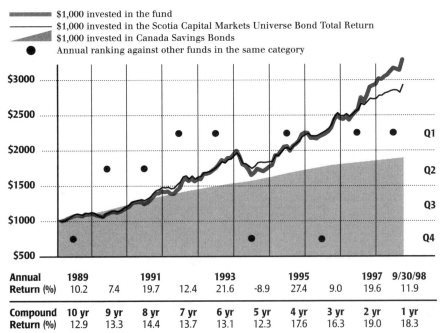

- $1,000 invested in the fund
- $1,000 invested in the Scotia Capital Markets Universe Bond Total Return
- $1,000 invested in Canada Savings Bonds
- Annual ranking against other funds in the same category

Annual Return (%)	1989		1991		1993		1995		1997	9/30/98
	10.2	7.4	19.7	12.4	21.6	-8.9	27.4	9.0	19.6	11.9

Compound Return (%)	10 yr	9 yr	8 yr	7 yr	6 yr	5 yr	4 yr	3 yr	2 yr	1 yr
	12.9	13.3	14.4	13.7	13.1	12.3	17.6	16.3	19.0	18.3

BISSETT CANADIAN BOND

Primary Objective:	Income
Sponsor:	Bissett & Associates
Fund Manager:	Michael Quinn
Style:	Interest Rate Anticipator
Size (MMs):	$202.423
RRSP:	100%
Management Expense Ratio:	0.75% (Average: 1.61%)

COMMENTS

Bissett & Associates proves they are not just an equity house with this top-performing bond fund. This one is no-load, low MER and available through most brokers. Manager Michael Quinn can invest in A-rated bonds and has 30% of fund in corporates. Smart Fund 1998

RISK

How Often Money Was Lost:....33 of 117 Months
....18 of 115 Quarters
..........................5 of 106 Rolling 12 Months
Worst 3 Months:................................-7.34% (1994)
Best 3 Months: 9.82% (1996)

ASSET ALLOCATION

Corporates 38.3%
Provincials..................................23.3%
Canadas.......................................35.9%
Municipals..................................2.5%

COMPARISON OF FUND TO INDEXES

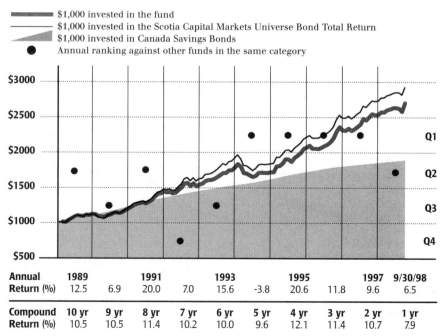

- $1,000 invested in the fund
- $1,000 invested in the Scotia Capital Markets Universe Bond Total Return
- $1,000 invested in Canada Savings Bonds
- Annual ranking against other funds in the same category

Annual Return (%)	1989		1991		1993		1995		1997	9/30/98
	12.5	6.9	20.0	7.0	15.6	-3.8	20.6	11.8	9.6	6.5

Compound Return (%)	10 yr	9 yr	8 yr	7 yr	6 yr	5 yr	4 yr	3 yr	2 yr	1 yr
	10.5	10.5	11.4	10.2	10.0	9.6	12.1	11.4	10.7	7.9

GREEN LINE CANADIAN BOND   NO LOAD

Primary Objective:	Income
Sponsor:	TD Asset Management
Fund Manager:	Paul Gardner and Satish Rai
Style:	Interest Rate Anticipator
Size (MMs):	$972.982
RRSP:	100%
Management Expense Ratio:	0.94% (Average: 1.61%)

COMMENTS

A good fund from one of the top no-load fund companies in the country. Paul Gardner and Satish Rai have been able to find good returns in some corporates. Top-quartile performer with a 0.94 MER, this will be more volatile than some of the others in the category. Smart Fund 1998, 1997

RISK

How Often Money Was Lost: ....29 of 117 Months
....21 of 115 Quarters
....................................10 of 106 Rolling 12 Months
Worst 3 Months: ....-8.84% (1994)
Best 3 Months: 10.84% (1992)

ASSET ALLOCATION

Corporates 67.3%
Provincials 3.9%
Canadas..14.2%
Stripped coupon 12.3%
Other...2.3%

COMPARISON OF FUND TO INDEXES

$1,000 invested in the fund
$1,000 invested in the Scotia Capital Markets Universe Bond Total Return
$1,000 invested in Canada Savings Bonds
● Annual ranking against other funds in the same category

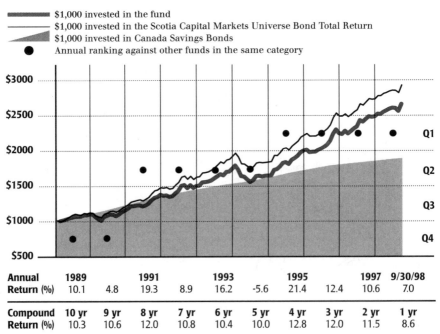

Annual Return (%)	1989		1991		1993		1995		1997	9/30/98
	10.1	4.8	19.3	8.9	16.2	-5.6	21.4	12.4	10.6	7.0

Compound Return (%)	10 yr	9 yr	8 yr	7 yr	6 yr	5 yr	4 yr	3 yr	2 yr	1 yr
	10.3	10.6	12.0	10.8	10.4	10.0	12.8	12.0	11.5	8.6

PH&N BOND

Primary Objective:	Total Return
Sponsor:	Phillips, Hager & North Investment Mgmt
Fund Manager:	Team
Style:	Interest Rate Anticipator
Size (MMs):	$2,061.257
RRSP:	100%
Management Expense Ratio:	0.57% (Average: 1.61%)

COMMENTS

One of the best bond funds in the country: no-load, low MER and consistent performance. Fund has been first or second quartile every year going back to 1989. The 50 basis points MER saving over other funds gives this one a big headstart in the performance game. Smart Fund 1998, 1997, 1996

RISK

How Often Money Was Lost:....31 of 117 Months
....17 of 115 Quarters
.....................................7 of 106 Rolling 12 Months
Worst 3 Months:................................-7.77% (1994)
Best 3 Months: 10.50% (1992)

ASSET ALLOCATION

Corporates 23.0%
Provincials...............................13.2%
Canadas....................................59.9%
Mortgages 1.6%
Cash 2.3%

COMPARISON OF FUND TO INDEXES

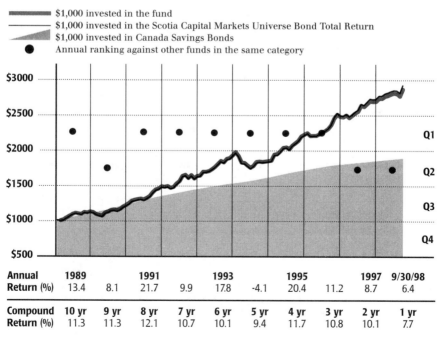

- $1,000 invested in the fund
- $1,000 invested in the Scotia Capital Markets Universe Bond Total Return
- $1,000 invested in Canada Savings Bonds
- Annual ranking against other funds in the same category

Annual Return (%)	1989		1991		1993		1995		1997	9/30/98
	13.4	8.1	21.7	9.9	17.8	-4.1	20.4	11.2	8.7	6.4

Compound Return (%)	10 yr	9 yr	8 yr	7 yr	6 yr	5 yr	4 yr	3 yr	2 yr	1 yr
	11.3	11.3	12.1	10.7	10.1	9.4	11.7	10.8	10.1	7.7

SCEPTRE BOND

NO LOAD

Primary Objective:	Total Return
Sponsor:	Sceptre Investment Counsel
Fund Manager:	Ian Lee, since 3/96
Style:	Interest Rate Anticipator
Size (MMs):	$63.203
RRSP:	100%
Management Expense Ratio:	0.95% (Average: 1.61%)

COMMENTS

A new Smart Fund this year. Ian Lee joined Sceptre in 1996 and turned around this former mediocre performer, pulling it to second quartile in 1996 and first decile since.

RISK

How Often Money Was Lost:....28 of 117 Months
....18 of 115 Quarters
....8 of 106 Rolling 12 Months
Worst 3 Months: ....-6.40% (1994)
Best 3 Months: 10.01% (1996)

ASSET ALLOCATION

Corporates 11.3%
Provincials..................................18.1%
Canadas......................................66.6%
Global bonds.............................2.8%
Other 1.2%

COMPARISON OF FUND TO INDEXES

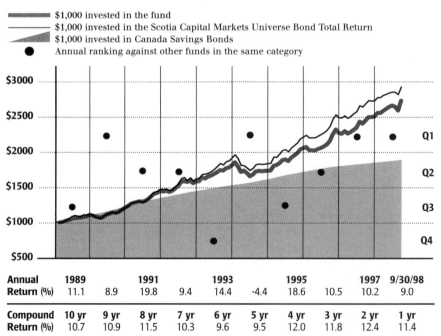

- $1,000 invested in the fund
- $1,000 invested in the Scotia Capital Markets Universe Bond Total Return
- $1,000 invested in Canada Savings Bonds
- Annual ranking against other funds in the same category

Annual Return (%)	1989		1991		1993		1995		1997	9/30/98
	11.1	8.9	19.8	9.4	14.4	-4.4	18.6	10.5	10.2	9.0

Compound Return (%)	10 yr	9 yr	8 yr	7 yr	6 yr	5 yr	4 yr	3 yr	2 yr	1 yr
	10.7	10.9	11.5	10.3	9.6	9.5	12.0	11.8	12.4	11.4

SCUDDER CANADIAN SHORT-TERM BOND NO LOAD

Primary Objective:	Income
Sponsor:	Scudder Canada Investor Services
Fund Manager:	Adam Greshin and Gary Johnson
Style:	Bottom-up
Size (MMs):	$14.300
RRSP:	100%
Management Expense Ratio:	0.85% (Average: 1.61%)

COMMENTS

Many investors are starved for income-generating ideas and with rates so low the alternatives tend to have too much volatility. This is the only short-term Smart Fund this year and makes it because of its top-quartile ranking in the short-term category and because of its 0.85% MER.

RISK

How Often Money Was Lost: ....5 of 35 Months
....3 of 33 Quarters
....0 of 24 Rolling 12 Months
Worst 3 Months: ....-0.66% (1997)
Best 3 Months: 4.93% (1996)

ASSET ALLOCATION

Corporates 57.0%
Provincials 7.0%
Canadas.......................................35.0%
Asset backed...............................1.0%

COMPARISON OF FUND TO INDEXES

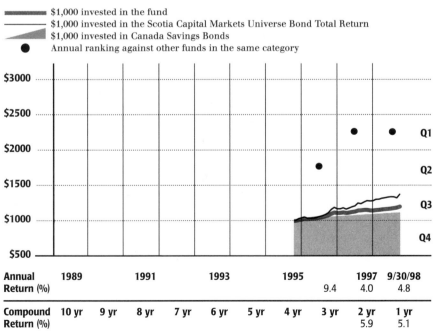

- $1,000 invested in the fund
- $1,000 invested in the Scotia Capital Markets Universe Bond Total Return
- $1,000 invested in Canada Savings Bonds
- Annual ranking against other funds in the same category

Annual Return (%)	1989		1991		1993		1995		1997	9/30/98
								9.4	4.0	4.8

Compound Return (%)	10 yr	9 yr	8 yr	7 yr	6 yr	5 yr	4 yr	3 yr	2 yr	1 yr
									5.9	5.1

TALVEST/HYPERION HIGH YIELD BOND   LOAD

Primary Objective:	Income
Sponsor:	Talvest Fund Management
Fund Manager:	Chris Currie, TAL Investment Counsel
Style:	Bottom-up, Value
Size (MMs):	$98.097
RRSP:	100%
Management Expense Ratio:	2.12% (Average: 1.61%)

COMMENTS

As investors seek yield they are forced to take on more risks. One way to do that is to move from government guaranteed bonds to higher-yielding corporates. This is not for amateurs and we recommend owning corporates through a fund with a professional manager. This is not only a new Smart Fund; it has had this mandate only since 1996. TAL is one of the top fixed-income managers in Canada and with the addition of top high-yield analyst Christopher Currie from Wood Gundy, this should be a good one. MER of 2.12% is as high as an equity fund and needs to be addressed.

RISK

How Often Money Was Lost: ....7 of 23 Months
....2 of 21 Quarters
....0 of 12 Rolling 12 Months
Worst 3 Months: ....-4.85% (1998)
Best 3 Months: 6.62% (1997)

ASSET ALLOCATION

Corporates 38.4%
Foreign pay Canadian 30.8%
Foreign bonds...........................15.2%
Cash 15.6%

COMPARISON OF FUND TO INDEXES

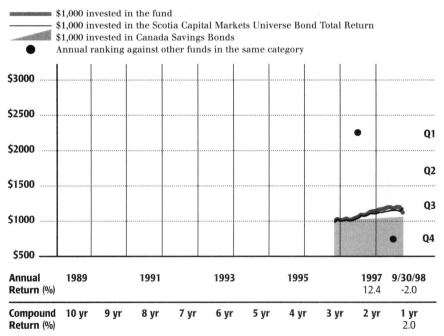

$1,000 invested in the fund
$1,000 invested in the Scotia Capital Markets Universe Bond Total Return
$1,000 invested in Canada Savings Bonds
● Annual ranking against other funds in the same category

	1989		1991		1993		1995		1997	9/30/98
Annual Return (%)									12.4	-2.0

	10 yr	9 yr	8 yr	7 yr	6 yr	5 yr	4 yr	3 yr	2 yr	1 yr
Compound Return (%)										2.0

TRIMARK ADVANTAGE BOND

LOAD

Primary Objective:	Income
Sponsor:	Trimark Investment Management
Fund Manager:	Patrick Farmer
Style:	Bottom-up, Value
Size (MMs):	$761.235
RRSP:	100%
Management Expense Ratio:	1.24% (Average: 1.61%)

COMMENTS

A high-yield fund that invests in corporate as well as government bonds. This solid performer with its low 1.24% MER makes it very competitive. That MER should be the benchmark for others in the category. Note the difference between Talvest/Hyperion and Trimark performance for year-to-date ending June 30, 1998 was 0.90%. Difference in MER is 0.88%. That difference meant Trimark was second quartile while Talvest/Hyperion was fourth. Smart Fund 1998

RISK

How Often Money Was Lost: ....9 of 46 Months
....5 of 44 Quarters
....0 of 35 Rolling 12 Months
Worst 3 Months: ....-2.96% (1998)
Best 3 Months: 9.08% (1996)

ASSET ALLOCATION

Corporates 42.2%
Provincials 2.6%
Canadas.......................................27.2%
Foreign bonds...........................14.2%
Cash 9.9%
Other 3.9%

COMPARISON OF FUND TO INDEXES

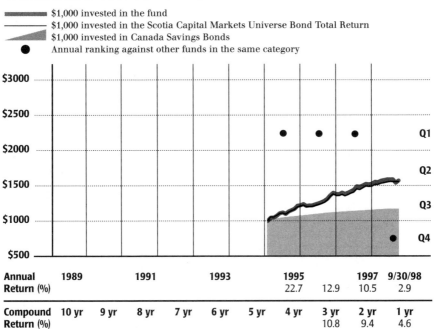

- $1,000 invested in the fund
- $1,000 invested in the Scotia Capital Markets Universe Bond Total Return
- $1,000 invested in Canada Savings Bonds
- ● Annual ranking against other funds in the same category

Annual Return (%)	1989		1991		1993		1995		1997	9/30/98
							22.7	12.9	10.5	2.9

Compound Return (%)	10 yr	9 yr	8 yr	7 yr	6 yr	5 yr	4 yr	3 yr	2 yr	1 yr
								10.8	9.4	4.6

ALTAMIRA HIGH YIELD

NO LOAD

Primary Objective:	Total Return
Sponsor:	Altamira Investor Services
Fund Manager:	Barry Allan
Style:	Bottom-up, Value
Size (MMs):	$13.591
RRSP:	20%
Management Expense Ratio:	1.95% (Average: 2.11%)

COMMENTS

Take the idea of a high-yield fund but open it up to securities from around the world. For the better diversification, investors sacrifice foreign-content room in their RRSP. Still, this may be a good yielding fund outside an RRSP. Altamira decided to drop the descriptive "speculative" in the name, since it was bad for marketing. Smart Fund 1998

RISK

How Often Money Was Lost: ......12 of 37 Months
....5 of 35 Quarters
....1 of 26 Rolling 12 Months
Worst 3 Months: ....-6.27% (1998)
Best 3 Months: 8.83% (1996)

ASSET ALLOCATION

Canada 81.9%
US..13.4%
Korea..2.7%
Cash 2.0%

COMPARISON OF FUND TO INDEXES

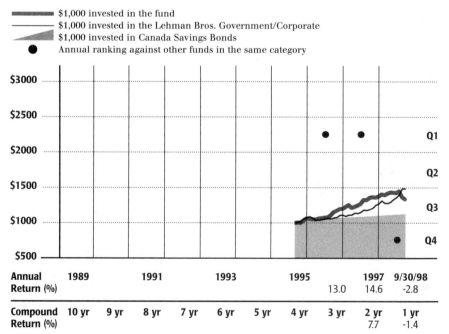

$1,000 invested in the fund
$1,000 invested in the Lehman Bros. Government/Corporate
$1,000 invested in Canada Savings Bonds
● Annual ranking against other funds in the same category

Annual Return (%)	1989		1991		1993		1995		1997	9/30/98
									13.0	14.6 -2.8

Compound Return (%)	10 yr	9 yr	8 yr	7 yr	6 yr	5 yr	4 yr	3 yr	2 yr	1 yr
									7.7	-1.4

GLOBAL BOND

GUARDIAN FOREIGN INCOME A   LOAD

Primary Objective:	Income
Sponsor:	Guardian Mutual Funds
Fund Manager:	Laurence Linklater, Kleinwort Guardian
Style:	Bottom-up
Size (MMs):	$16.514
RRSP:	20%
Management Expense Ratio:	1.68% (Average: 2.11%)

COMMENTS

An RRSP-eligible fund that is a solid, if unspectacular, performer. Small size leaves this one vulnerable to being shut down by Guardian and probably keeps the MER high. Guardian International Income, also managed by Laurence Linklater, was a Smart Fund in 1997. Asset class has been out of favor for some time, but with increased volatility in world markets, some may find comfort in fixed-income products, even with lower yields. Smart Fund 1998

RISK

How Often Money Was Lost:	13 of 49 Months
	5 of 47 Quarters
	0 of 38 Rolling 12 Months
Worst 3 Months:	-1.85% (1996)
Best 3 Months:	10.43% (1998)

ASSET ALLOCATION

USA	64.3%
UK	14.1%
Germany	11.5%
Ecuador	6.3%
Italy	3.8%

COMPARISON OF FUND TO INDEXES

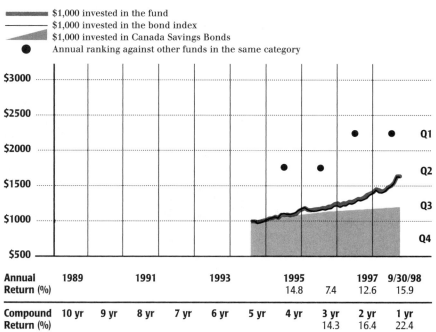

- $1,000 invested in the fund
- $1,000 invested in the bond index
- $1,000 invested in Canada Savings Bonds
- Annual ranking against other funds in the same category

Annual Return (%)	1989		1991		1993		1995		1997	9/30/98
							14.8	7.4	12.6	15.9

Compound Return (%)	10 yr	9 yr	8 yr	7 yr	6 yr	5 yr	4 yr	3 yr	2 yr	1 yr
								14.3	16.4	22.4

ATLAS CANADIAN BALANCED LOAD

Primary Objective:	Growth & Income
Sponsor:	Atlas Asset Management
Fund Manager:	Len Racioppo, Jarilowsky Fraser
Style:	Bottom-up
Size (MMs):	$348.453
RRSP:	100%
Management Expense Ratio:	2.20% (Average: 2.23%)

COMMENTS

Managed by Len Racioppo of Jarislowsky Fraser and sponsored by Merill Lynch Canada's Atlas Group. This is a top-quartile-performing balanced fund that could serve as a solid core holding for many clients. The fund has one of the best risk-return profiles in the class. MER is typical of a load fund at 2.21%. Fund was holding 30% in bonds and large cap domestic names that pay good dividends. Smart Fund 1998

RISK

How Often Money Was Lost:....34 of 109 Months
.....................................25 of 107 Quarters
....8 of 98 Rolling 12 Months
Worst 3 Months:................................-8.30% (1998)
Best 3 Months: 12.16% (1996)

ASSET ALLOCATION

Canadian equities....................30.6%
Corporate bonds 30.4%
US equities...............................18.8%
Cash 9.4%
Canada bonds 5.1%
Other 5.7%

CANADIAN BALANCED

COMPARISON OF FUND TO INDEXES

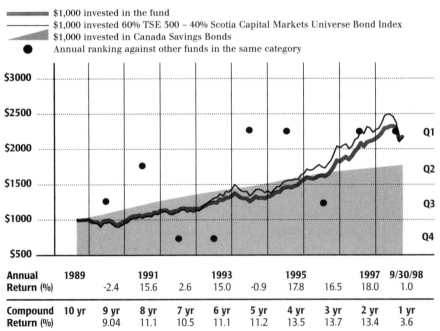

- $1,000 invested in the fund
- $1,000 invested 60% TSE 300 – 40% Scotia Capital Markets Universe Bond Index
- $1,000 invested in Canada Savings Bonds
- ● Annual ranking against other funds in the same category

Annual Return (%)	1989		1991		1993		1995		1997	9/30/98
		-2.4	15.6	2.6	15.0	-0.9	17.8	16.5	18.0	1.0

Compound Return (%)	10 yr	9 yr	8 yr	7 yr	6 yr	5 yr	4 yr	3 yr	2 yr	1 yr
		9.04	11.1	10.5	11.1	11.2	13.5	13.7	13.4	3.6

BISSETT RETIREMENT

NO LOAD

Primary Objective:	Growth & Income
Sponsor:	Bissett & Associates
Fund Manager:	Michael Quinn
Style:	Fund of Funds
Size (MMs):	$197.492
RRSP:	100%
Management Expense Ratio:	0.44% plus MER on the funds (Average: 2.23%)

COMMENTS

This fund of funds has been one of the top-performing balanced funds over the last five years. It has a solid track record of first-quartile and second-quartile performance over each calendar year back to 1992. The fund has a superior risk-reward profile, and manager Michael Quinn decides on the optimum asset mix. The asset mix comes at a cost of 0.44% MER plus expenses in the underlying Bissett funds. The Bissett Canadian Equity, Multi-National Equity and Small Cap Equity Funds are already Smart Funds. With this fund you get it all in one place. Smart Fund 1998

RISK

How Often Money Was Lost: ......26 of 86 Months
....16 of 84 Quarters
....6 of 75 Rolling 12 Months
Worst 3 Months:...............................-12.08% (1998)
Best 3 Months:....................................13.41% (1997)

ASSET ALLOCATION

Other..100.0%

COMPARISON OF FUND TO INDEXES

▭▭▭ $1,000 invested in the fund
──── $1,000 invested 60% TSE 300 – 40% Scotia Capital Markets Universe Bond Index
▨▨▨ $1,000 invested in Canada Savings Bonds
● Annual ranking against other funds in the same category

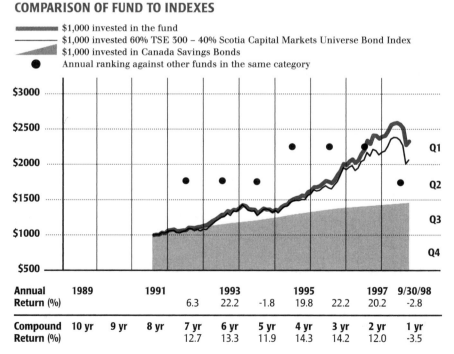

Annual Return (%)	1989		1991		1993		1995		1997	9/30/98
				6.3	22.2	-1.8	19.8	22.2	20.2	-2.8

Compound Return (%)	10 yr	9 yr	8 yr	7 yr	6 yr	5 yr	4 yr	3 yr	2 yr	1 yr
				12.7	13.3	11.9	14.3	14.2	12.0	-3.5

CANADIAN BALANCED

FIDELITY CANADIAN ASSET ALLOCATION LOAD

Primary Objective:	Total Return
Sponsor:	Fidelity Investments Canada
Fund Manager:	Dick Habermann, Alan Radlo, Ford O'Neil
Style:	Top-down
Size (MMs):	$3,140.586
RRSP:	100%
Management Expense Ratio:	2.45% (Average: 2.23%)

COMMENTS

This is a top-decile performing balanced fund over the one-, two- and three-year periods ending June 30. Dick Habermann (see profile on page 35) makes the asset-allocation decision; he does the same on the International Portfolio. The stock picks are left to Alan Radlo, manager of the Canadian Growth Company Fund, and fixed income is managed by Ford O'Neil. This has been a popular fund in the Fidelity group. Its assets have grown from $350 million as of January 1, 1997, to over $3 billion at September 30, 1998. This one comes with higher volatility than most balanced funds but with a standard deviation about 20% lower than most equity funds and still has generated 20+ % returns. Smart Fund 1998

RISK

How Often Money Was Lost: ......13 of 45 Months
....5 of 43 Quarters
....1 of 34 Rolling 12 Months
Worst 3 Months: ....-11.77% (1998)
Best 3 Months:....................................16.51% (1997)

ASSET ALLOCATION

Canadian equities 18.5%
Foreign equities.........................8.2%
Cash 9.8%
Canada bonds...........................33.3%
Other..30.2%

COMPARISON OF FUND TO INDEXES

▬▬▬ $1,000 invested in the fund
──── $1,000 invested 60% TSE 300 – 40% Scotia Capital Markets Universe Bond Index
◢ $1,000 invested in Canada Savings Bonds
● Annual ranking against other funds in the same category

Annual Return (%)	1989		1991		1993		1995		1997	9/30/98
							23.4	22.6	23.4	-1.9

Compound Return (%)	10 yr	9 yr	8 yr	7 yr	6 yr	5 yr	4 yr	3 yr	2 yr	1 yr
								16.2	15.1	-1.5

CANADIAN BALANCED

GLOBAL STRATEGY INCOME PLUS LOAD

Primary Objective:	Growth & Income
Sponsor:	Global Strategy Financial
Fund Manager:	Tony Massie
Style:	Bottom-up
Size (MMs):	$2,075.512
RRSP:	100%
Management Expense Ratio:	2.30% (Average: 2.23%)

COMMENTS

This used to be a little-known Global Strategy offering with steady and good returns. While paying out its 30-cent distribution every quarter, Tony Massie has delivered the performance. It is first quartile across every measurement period ending September 30, 1998, and has an outstanding risk/return profile, making it one of the top balanced-fund choices. Others continue to notice as the fund has increased by over $1.2 billion in the last 12 months. At June 30, fund was holding 21% in cash. Largest holdings were the high dividend-paying banks and utilities. Smart Fund 1998, 1997

RISK

How Often Money Was Lost: ......22 of 77 Months
.....................................13 of 75 Quarters
........................7 of 66 Rolling 12 Months
Worst 3 Months:.............................-13.46% (1998)
Best 3 Months: 13.04% (1996)

ASSET ALLOCATION

Canadian equities....................48.2%
Preferreds.....................................1.7%
Cash 20.6%
Fixed income 29.5%

COMPARISON OF FUND TO INDEXES

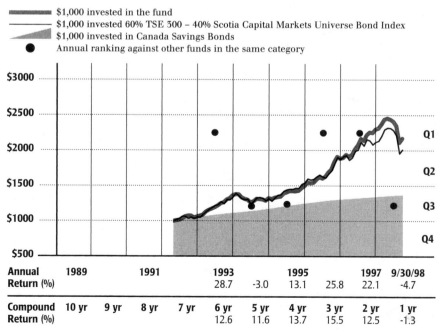

▬▬▬ $1,000 invested in the fund
──── $1,000 invested 60% TSE 300 – 40% Scotia Capital Markets Universe Bond Index
◣ $1,000 invested in Canada Savings Bonds
● Annual ranking against other funds in the same category

Annual Return (%)	1989		1991		1993		1995		1997	9/30/98
					28.7	-3.0	13.1	25.8	22.1	-4.7

Compound Return (%)	10 yr	9 yr	8 yr	7 yr	6 yr	5 yr	4 yr	3 yr	2 yr	1 yr
					12.6	11.6	13.7	15.5	12.5	-1.3

IG SCEPTRE CANADIAN BALANCED   LOAD

Primary Objective:	Growth & Income
Sponsor:	Investors Group
Fund Manager:	Sceptre Investment Counsel
Style:	Bottom-up, Value
Size (MMs):	$298.200
RRSP:	100%
Management Expense Ratio:	2.73% (Average: 2.23%)

COMMENTS

See comments for Sceptre Balanced Growth, which is the parent of this fund. Investors Group has contracted with Sceptre to make this fund available to its large customer base. This is a good choice for those using an Investors Group adviser so all their choices appear on one statement. It will cost you a rich 2.73% MER to get it at Investors; buying direct at Sceptre costs 1.44%. That's 1.29% per year for the advice. With that MER the fund has generated adequate second-quartile performance. Smart Fund 1998

RISK

How Often Money Was Lost: ....9 of 26 Months
....8 of 24 Quarters
......................................2 of 15 Rolling 12 Months
Worst 3 Months:...............................-12.20% (1998)
Best 3 Months:....................................11.72% (1997)

ASSET ALLOCATION

Industrial products..................14.1%
Consumer products..................7.4%
Financial services...................10.7%
Cash 6.6%
Canada bonds..........................43.2%
Other.......................................18.0%

COMPARISON OF FUND TO INDEXES

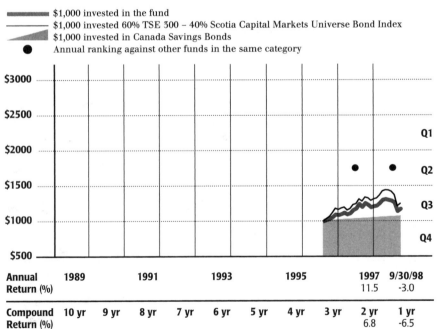

▬▬▬ $1,000 invested in the fund
——— $1,000 invested 60% TSE 300 – 40% Scotia Capital Markets Universe Bond Index
◢ $1,000 invested in Canada Savings Bonds
● Annual ranking against other funds in the same category

Annual Return (%)	1989	1991	1993	1995	1997	9/30/98
					11.5	-3.0

Compound Return (%)	10 yr	9 yr	8 yr	7 yr	6 yr	5 yr	4 yr	3 yr	2 yr	1 yr
									6.8	-6.5

INDUSTRIAL PENSION

LOAD

Primary Objective:	Growth & Income
Sponsor:	Mackenzie Financial
Fund Manager:	Bill Proctor
Style:	Bottom-up, Value
Size (MMs):	$297.571
RRSP:	100%
Management Expense Ratio:	2.33% (Average: 2.23%)

COMMENTS

This is a top-performing balanced fund from the Industrial family of Mackenzie from a family that can give you two other very good balanced funds. Ivy Growth & Income and Universal Canadian Balanced both deserved Smart Fund recognition, but we went with Industrial Pension for its stellar returns. Manager Bill Proctor revitalized this former chronic fourth-quartile performer. In each year since 1992, except 1995, the fund has been a first-quartile performer. This comes with a price, though, as the fund has one of the higher volatilities, as measured by standard deviation, in the balanced class. This one is more equity oriented with the income from the bonds used to pay the fund's expenses. There have been very little distributions for the last three years. Smart Fund 1998

RISK

How Often Money Was Lost:....52 of 117 Months
....46 of 115 Quarters
...............................39 of 106 Rolling 12 Months
Worst 3 Months:.............................-16.06% (1998)
Best 3 Months: 21.73% (1993)

ASSET ALLOCATION

Consumer products.................12.0%
Financial services....................15.0%
Natural resources 11.0%
Fixed income 17.0%
Cash 12.0%
Other..25.0%

COMPARISON OF FUND TO INDEXES

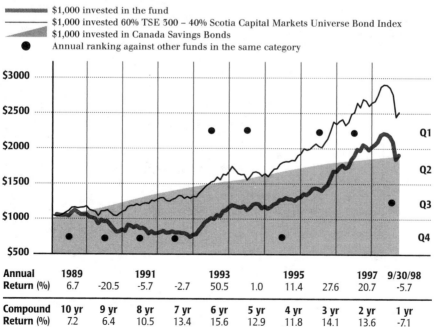

	$1,000 invested in the fund
	$1,000 invested 60% TSE 300 – 40% Scotia Capital Markets Universe Bond Index
	$1,000 invested in Canada Savings Bonds
●	Annual ranking against other funds in the same category

Annual Return (%)	1989		1991		1993		1995		1997	9/30/98
	6.7	-20.5	-5.7	-2.7	50.5	1.0	11.4	27.6	20.7	-5.7

Compound Return (%)	10 yr	9 yr	8 yr	7 yr	6 yr	5 yr	4 yr	3 yr	2 yr	1 yr
	7.2	6.4	10.5	13.4	15.6	12.9	11.8	14.1	13.6	-7.1

CANADIAN BALANCED

LEITH WHEELER CANADIAN BALANCED FUND NO LOAD

Primary Objective:	Growth & Income
Sponsor:	Leith Wheeler Investment Counsel
Fund Manager:	Team
Style:	Bottom-up
Size (MMs):	$178.425
RRSP:	100%
Management Expense Ratio:	1.10% (Average: 2.23%)

COMMENTS

The MER of 1.1% is roughly between the 1.4% of the pure Canadian equity fund and the 0.75% of the fixed income fund. Of the Smart Funds in this category, only PH&N has a lower MER. From 1987 until 1994, this was the only retail-level fund in the Leith Wheeler family. Its 10-year CAGR to June 30th was a first-quartile return of 11.1%. This is a new member to the Smart Fund list and this fund has always had a superior risk/adjusted rate of return. It carries a hefty $50,000 mimimum investment, but the performance is there. In only one year, 1995, of the last seven was the fund below second quartile. Over that same span its worst calendar return was negative 1.7%. You may have difficulty getting this one other than dealing directly with Leith Wheeler.

RISK

How Often Money Was Lost:....41 of 117 Months
....27 of 115 Quarters
.....................................14 of 106 Rolling 12 Months
Worst 3 Months:...............................-12.69% (1998)
Best 3 Months: 11.96% (1996)

ASSET ALLOCATION

Financial services....................12.7%
Consumer products..................9.5%
Industrial products 6.7%
Utilities 5.5%
Oil and gas...................................4.5%
Other..61.1%

COMPARISON OF FUND TO INDEXES

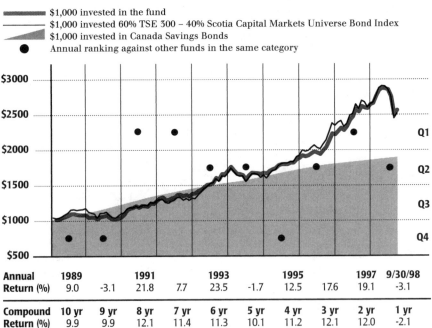

$1,000 invested in the fund
$1,000 invested 60% TSE 300 – 40% Scotia Capital Markets Universe Bond Index
$1,000 invested in Canada Savings Bonds
● Annual ranking against other funds in the same category

Annual	1989		1991		1993		1995		1997	9/30/98
Return (%)	9.0	-3.1	21.8	7.7	23.5	-1.7	12.5	17.6	19.1	-3.1

Compound	10 yr	9 yr	8 yr	7 yr	6 yr	5 yr	4 yr	3 yr	2 yr	1 yr
Return (%)	9.9	9.9	12.1	11.4	11.3	10.1	11.2	12.1	12.0	-2.1

THE 100 SMART FUNDS

PH&N BALANCED FUND

NO LOAD

Primary Objective:	Growth & Income
Sponsor:	Phillips, Hager & North Investment Counsel
Fund Manager:	Team
Style:	Bottom-up, Growth
Size (MMs):	$509.008
RRSP:	100%
Management Expense Ratio:	0.91% (Average: 2.23%)

COMMENTS

For conservative investors, this is as close as it gets to being a one-stop Canadian RRSP holding. It assumes that high-quality stocks are the best way to create long-term wealth; that wealth preservation and income needs can best be met by a balance of stocks and bonds, with periodic adjustment of this mix. Back again on the Smart Funds list and arguably the best of a talented group. Consistently good performance, low volatility, one of the lowest MERs in the category, at 0.91%, and it's managed by one of Canada's top investment management firms. Smart Fund 1998, 1997, 1996

RISK

How Often Money Was Lost: ......26 of 84 Months
....20 of 82 Quarters
....3 of 73 Rolling 12 Months
Worst 3 Months: ....-12.10% (1998)
Best 3 Months: 12.42% (1996)

ASSET ALLOCATION

Canadian equities 37.0%
Foreign equities 8.6%
US equities..................................6.4%
Cash 9.0%
Fixed income 39.0%

COMPARISON OF FUND TO INDEXES

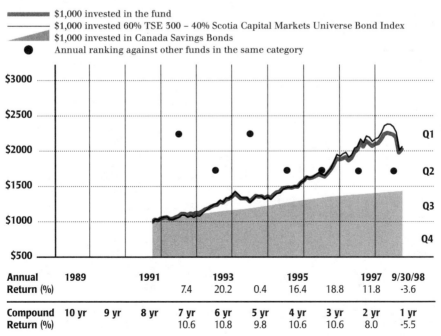

- $1,000 invested in the fund
- $1,000 invested 60% TSE 300 – 40% Scotia Capital Markets Universe Bond Index
- $1,000 invested in Canada Savings Bonds
- ● Annual ranking against other funds in the same category

Annual Return (%)	1989		1991		1993		1995		1997	9/30/98
				7.4	20.2	0.4	16.4	18.8	11.8	-3.6

Compound Return (%)	10 yr	9 yr	8 yr	7 yr	6 yr	5 yr	4 yr	3 yr	2 yr	1 yr
				10.6	10.8	9.8	10.6	10.6	8.0	-5.5

SCEPTRE BALANCED GROWTH

NO LOAD

Primary Objective:	Growth & Income
Sponsor:	Sceptre Investment Counsel
Fund Manager:	Lyle Stein
Style:	Top-down
Size (MMs):	$223.895
RRSP:	100%
Management Expense Ratio:	1.44% (Average: 2.23%)

COMMENTS

Lyle Stein (see profile on page 24) won the 1996 and 1997 mutual fund award for the top balanced fund. He wisely consults with the outstanding Sceptre Canadian equity team for stock ideas. The fund was a top-quartile performer in 1995, 1996, and 1997. It has taken a slight dip so far in 1998 as Mr. Stein turned bearish and went to fixed income. There are no restraints on asset mix, giving Stein the freedom to go with whatever asset class he feels will outperform. Like all the Sceptre funds, this is in the lowest quartile for its MER. Smart Fund 1998, 1997

RISK

How Often Money Was Lost: ....37 of 117 Months
....29 of 115 Quarters
.....................................12 of 106 Rolling 12 Months
Worst 3 Months:...............................-12.35% (1998)
Best 3 Months: 13.72% (1996)

ASSET ALLOCATION

Industrial products....................9.8%
Financial services......................6.2%
Oil and Gas.................................4.2%
Utilities 3.2%
Preferreds...................................2.5%
Other 74.1%

COMPARISON OF FUND TO INDEXES

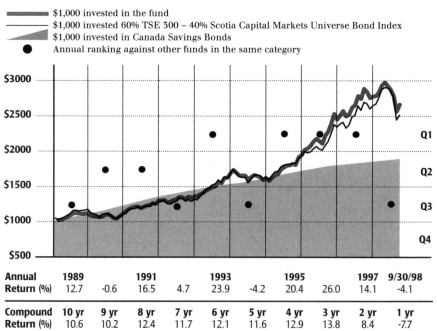

- $1,000 invested in the fund
- $1,000 invested 60% TSE 300 – 40% Scotia Capital Markets Universe Bond Index
- $1,000 invested in Canada Savings Bonds
- Annual ranking against other funds in the same category

Annual Return (%)	1989		1991		1993		1995		1997	9/30/98
	12.7	-0.6	16.5	4.7	23.9	-4.2	20.4	26.0	14.1	-4.1

Compound Return (%)	10 yr	9 yr	8 yr	7 yr	6 yr	5 yr	4 yr	3 yr	2 yr	1 yr
	10.6	10.2	12.4	11.7	12.1	11.6	12.9	13.8	8.4	-7.7

CANADIAN BALANCED

TRIMARK INCOME GROWTH

LOAD

Primary Objective:	Growth & Income
Sponsor:	Trimark Investment Management
Fund Manager:	Vito Maida and Patrick Farmer
Style:	Bottom-up
Size (MMs):	$787.205
RRSP:	100%
Management Expense Ratio:	1.56% (Average: 2.23%)

COMMENTS

This is a common broker's and dealer's choice for a balanced fund. With Patrick Farmer's fixed-income picks, Vito Maida takes the best equity ideas from the rest of the Trimark team. This has traditionally been one of Canada's best balanced funds. From 1991 through 1996 the fund was either first or second quartile. The slump for 1997 and 1998 has the fund almost 500 basis points behind the weighted-average balanced-fund return for the two years ended June 30. We have dropped Trimark Canadian, but with Patrick Farmer's fixed-income picks, this fund deserved at least another year. It has a low MER of 1.56% and is one of the least volatile in the category. Smart Fund 1998, 1997, 1996

RISK

How Often Money Was Lost:....38 of 117 Months
....29 of 115 Quarters
.......................13 of 106 Rolling 12 Months
Worst 3 Months:..............................-13.20% (1998)
Best 3 Months: 12.26% (1991)

ASSET ALLOCATION

Canadian equities....................34.8%
Corporate bonds......................14.1%
US equities...................................12.2%
Foreign equities.........................3.9%
Canada bonds..........................31.2%
Other...3.8%

COMPARISON OF FUND TO INDEXES

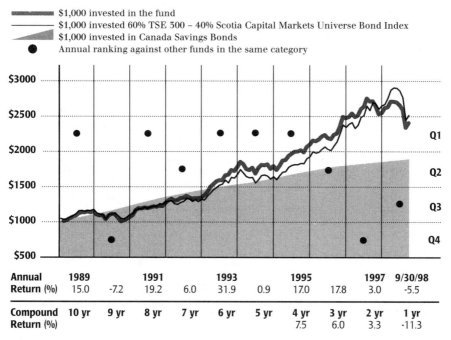

▬▬▬▬ $1,000 invested in the fund
──── $1,000 invested 60% TSE 300 – 40% Scotia Capital Markets Universe Bond Index
▨▨▨▨ $1,000 invested in Canada Savings Bonds
● Annual ranking against other funds in the same category

Annual Return (%)	1989		1991		1993		1995		1997	9/30/98
	15.0	-7.2	19.2	6.0	31.9	0.9	17.0	17.8	3.0	-5.5

Compound Return (%)	10 yr	9 yr	8 yr	7 yr	6 yr	5 yr	4 yr	3 yr	2 yr	1 yr
							7.5	6.0	3.3	-11.3

CANADIAN BALANCED

C.I. INTERNATIONAL BALANCED RSP   LOAD

Primary Objective:	Growth & Income
Sponsor:	CI Mutual Funds
Fund Manager:	Bill Sterling, BEA Associates
Style:	Top-down
Size (MMs):	$261.008
RRSP:	100%
Management Expense Ratio:	2.41% (Average: 2.39%)

COMMENTS

The major strength of this fund is the asset-allocation decisions made by Bill Sterling. The former global strategist for Merrill Lynch, Dr. Sterling led this fund to top-quartile performance. The equity picks are done by Bill Priest, manager of C.I. American and fixed income by Gregg Diliberto. Fund has 53% in equities, mostly large-cap U.S. growth stocks with GE, Microsoft, Exxon, Ford, Coke, and Merck all in the top 10 holdings. Steady second-quartile performer that does not tie up your foreign content and could be considered a core holding in your RRSP. Smart Fund 1998, 1997

RISK

How Often Money Was Lost: ......10 of 46 Months
....6 of 44 Quarters
....0 of 35 Rolling 12 Months
Worst 3 Months: ....-3.89% (1998)
Best 3 Months: 10.36% (1997)

ASSET ALLOCATION

Equities 53.1%
Bonds...32.4%
Cash 14.5%

COMPARISON OF FUND TO INDEXES

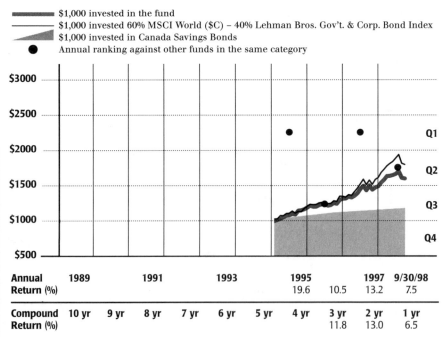

$1,000 invested in the fund
$1,000 invested 60% MSCI World ($C) – 40% Lehman Bros. Gov't. & Corp. Bond Index
$1,000 invested in Canada Savings Bonds
● Annual ranking against other funds in the same category

Annual Return (%)	1989	1991	1993	1995		1997	9/30/98
				19.6	10.5	13.2	7.5

Compound Return (%)	10 yr	9 yr	8 yr	7 yr	6 yr	5 yr	4 yr	3 yr	2 yr	1 yr
								11.8	13.0	6.5

FIDELITY GLOBAL ASSET ALLOCATION LOAD

Primary Objective:	Growth & Income
Sponsor:	Fidelity Investments Canada
Fund Manager:	Dick Habermann
Style:	Top-down
Size (MMs):	$457.735
RRSP:	20%
Management Expense Ratio:	2.67% (Average: 2.39%)

COMMENTS

As mentioned in Smart Fund profile for Fidelity International Portfolio, this may be the conservative way to fill up your foreign content. This asset-allocation fund cuts volatility by utilizing fixed-income securities. Managers Dick Habermann and Bill Eigen determine the asset mix, then use the picks from the equity managers representing the regions. The fund does not sway too far from index country weightings but will move the equity/fixed income mix. This one is new to the Smart Funds list and counts as foreign content in your RRSP. The fund is first quartile across 2 year, 3 year and 5 year compound periods, fuelled by the 40% weighting in the United States.

RISK

How Often Money Was Lost: ......22 of 68 Months
....15 of 66 Quarters
..........................7 of 57 Rolling 12 Months
Worst 3 Months: ....-6.86% (1998)
Best 3 Months: 13.25% (1997)

ASSET ALLOCATION

USA 40.4%
Japan...8.3%
UK..7.2%
France...3.0%
Switzerland.......................................3.0%
Other..38.1%

COMPARISON OF FUND TO INDEXES

▬▬▬▬▬ $1,000 invested in the fund
───── $1,000 invested 60% MSCI World ($C) – 40% Lehman Bros. Gov't. & Corp. Bond Index
◿ $1,000 invested in Canada Savings Bonds
● Annual ranking against other funds in the same category

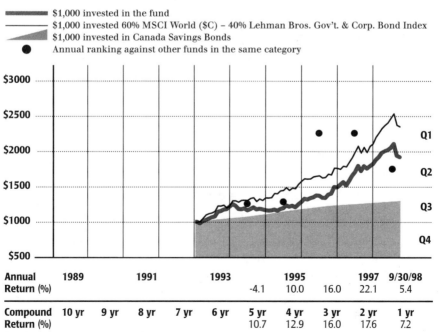

Annual Return (%)	1989		1991		1993		1995		1997	9/30/98
						-4.1	10.0	16.0	22.1	5.4

Compound Return (%)	10 yr	9 yr	8 yr	7 yr	6 yr	5 yr	4 yr	3 yr	2 yr	1 yr
						10.7	12.9	16.0	17.6	7.2

UNIVERSAL WORLD BALANCED RRSP LOAD

Primary Objective:	Growth & Income
Sponsor:	Mackenzie Financial
Fund Manager:	Michael Landry & Barbara Trebbi
Style:	Top-down
Size (MMs):	$245.819
RRSP:	100%
Management Expense Ratio:	2.36% (Average: 2.39%)

COMMENTS

A Smart Fund regular that has recently dipped a bit in performance. Fund dropped to third quartile in 1997 and was fourth quartile for the one year ended June 30, 1998. We like this fund because of its RRSP-friendly structure. By using futures to buy indexes in the major markets, managers Barbara Trebbi and Michael Landry can concentrate on the individual selections in the emerging markets. The 21% weighting in emerging markets will make this more volatile than other funds in the category. This might be just the right amount of emerging-market exposure for investors. Smart Fund 1998, 1997

RISK

How Often Money Was Lost: ......20 of 55 Months
....17 of 53 Quarters
...........................4 of 44 Rolling 12 Months
Worst 3 Months: ....-8.41% (1997)
Best 3 Months: 12.50% (1998)

ASSET ALLOCATION

Global equities..........................49.0%
Government bonds..................23.0%
Emerging markets..................21.0%
Cash 7.0%

COMPARISON OF FUND TO INDEXES

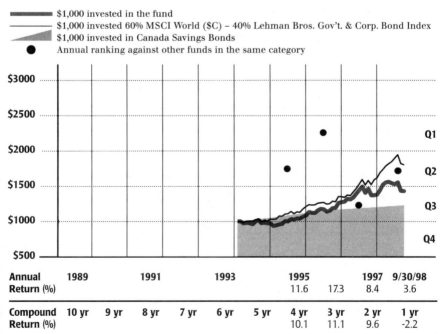

▬▬▬▬ $1,000 invested in the fund
───── $1,000 invested 60% MSCI World ($C) – 40% Lehman Bros. Gov't. & Corp. Bond Index
◢◢◢◢ $1,000 invested in Canada Savings Bonds
● Annual ranking against other funds in the same category

Annual Return (%)	1989	1991	1993	1995		1997	9/30/98
				11.6	17.3	8.4	3.6

Compound Return (%)	10 yr	9 yr	8 yr	7 yr	6 yr	5 yr	4 yr	3 yr	2 yr	1 yr
							10.1	11.1	9.6	-2.2

INTERNATIONAL BALANCED

Index of Smart Funds